QoS & Traffic Management in IP & ATM Networks

David McDysan

McGraw-Hill
New York   San Francisco   Washington, D.C.
Auckland   Bogotá   Caracas   Lisbon   London   Madrid
Mexico City   Milan   Montreal   New Delhi   San Juan
Singapore   Sydney   Tokyo   Toronto

McGraw-Hill

A Division of The McGraw-Hill Companies

Copyright © 2000 by The McGraw-Hill Companies, Inc. All rights reserved.
Printed in the United States of America. Except as permitted under the United
States Copyright Act of 1976, no part of this publication may be reproduced or
distributed in any form or by any means, or stored in a data base or retrieval
system, without the prior written permission of the publisher.

1 2 3 4 5 6 7 8 9 0 AGM/AGM 9 0 4 3 2 1 0 9

ISBN 0-07-134959-6

The sponsoring editor for this book was Steven Elliot, the editing supervisor
was Penny Linskey, and the production supervisor was Claire Stanley. It was
set Vendome ICG and Eras by the author using Microsoft Word, Powerpoint,
Excel, and Lotus Freelance.

Printed and bound by Quebecor/Martinsburg.

Throughout this book, trademarked names are used. Rather than put a trademark symbol after every occurrence of a trademarked name, we use names in
an editorial fashion only, and to the benefit of the trademark owner, with no
intention of infringement of the trademark. Where such designations appear in
this book, they have been printed with initial caps.

This book is printed on recycled, acid-free paper containing a minimum
of 50% recycled de-inked fiber.

To my wife, Debbie and my parents,
Lowell and Martha

CONTENTS

Contents

Contents

Contents

Quality of Service (QoS) and traffic management is becoming an increasingly important subject in the broadband Internet-driven information age. The pioneering work in the development of QoS-aware Asynchronous Transfer Mode (ATM) switches and protocols is the foundation upon which similar capabilities are being developed for an Internet Protocol (IP) based set of applications. Furthermore, the Internet is exploring new approaches to QoS and traffic management to meet the challenges of unprecedented growth and global scale.

Unfortunately, many of the classic works and theoretical results of traffic engineering, queuing theory and other important disciplines remain inaccessible to the web surfer, corporate information worker, network designer, network operator, and communications manager. This book aims to fill the void between high-level, simplistic treatments of the subject, graduate-level texts, and the specialist technical literature. Accordingly, a central theme of the book is old-fashioned common sense.

Traditionally, network managers must enlist a small community of expert traffic engineers and network designers to solve these problems. Although complex problems often require complex solutions, these experts could often do better in explaining their work to others. Toward this end, this book uses real-life analogies to illustrate important concepts in a sincere effort to appeal to a larger number of readers than traditional traffic engineering and queuing theory texts do. The objective of this book is to empower a larger population of network designers, network managers, and end users with an intuitive sense of QoS and traffic management to complement some basic analytical tools.

We are all familiar with the issues involved in QoS and traffic management from our everyday experiences with travel on the highways, trains, and airlines. Different levels of quality are an important way to address shortage of a particular resource or prioritize service, since some customers are willing to pay more in order to receive better service. For example, first class passengers receive preferential treatment and guaranteed reservations, albeit at a higher price. Thus, quality of service has strong policy and economic associations.

Traffic management deals with traffic levels for which a certain QoS applies. One way of avoiding congestion, and the resulting impact on quality, is to apply admission control. For example, there are only a certain number of seats on an airplane or train, or only a maximum number of vehicles can use a highway over a specific time interval. Thus, admitting only those passengers with tickets is an important means of providing the level of quality via a simple traffic control. In the vehicular analogy, signals on the on-ramps to freeways may modulate admitted traffic to optimize traffic flow. As we shall see, direct analogies occur in IP and ATM networks to QoS and traffic management.

This book uses mathematics to quantify QoS parameters and traffic levels. Consistent with the objective of reaching the largest possible audience, we formulate the solution for many problems in spreadsheet format using the Microsoft Excel program. The text identifies trademarked names, like Excel, using initial caps. I will put selected spreadsheets on my home page as pointed to in the author pages on the McGraw-Hill web site, www.mcgraw-hill.com/computing/authors.

Who Should Read This Book

The primary objective of this book is to introduce the theory and practical use of traffic engineering to a broad audience. Beginning users can utilize it as an introduction to traffic engineering and a guide to explore specific subject areas in greater depth. Intermediate users can employ it as an authoritative reference. It also targets the expert who needs to communicate traffic engineering concepts to executives, customers, or colleagues. The book should serve as a reference guide that will assist the engineer or manager in understanding the basic concepts as well as applying the theory to real networking problems. The book targets the hot topics of integrated voice, video and data networking, QoS, and traffic management for IP and ATM networking technologies. Each chapter provides a bibliography for the reader who wishes to further explore certain topics.

How This Book Is Organized

The outline of the book progresses in a logical sequence of parts, stepping the reader through the basic concepts of networking, QOS, traffic, probability theory, queuing theory, congestion control, routing, network design, decision making, and simulation. Each part begins with an introductory chapter that draws analogies with real-life that illustrate important points. The introductory level chapters target a non-technical professional. A beginner could read the first chapter of each part and end up with knowledge of traffic engineering sufficient to understand the standards published on the subject or converse with an expert. These chapters contain only the simplest equations, if they contain any at all. Each successive chapter within each part is more advanced and uses mathematics appropriate to the task.

The second, intermediate level chapter presents formulas in a cookbook style that is easily put to use by the practicing engineer or manager using commonly available computer tools like spreadsheets and macro languages. A technical background is desirable, but not necessary for the intermediate chapters. The book does provide references to other texts and articles so that a reader can obtain the necessary background.

The third and most advanced chapter of each part targets the advanced undergraduate student or the introductory graduate student in the disciplines of mathematics, communications engineering, or computer science. The reader of the advanced chapter in each part should have some background in the particular topic. It provides selected proofs and references for advanced study. A professional could consult these references and extend their capabilities through independent study. The references cite a number of graduate level texts already published in this area.

Each part and chapter begins with a quotation to break up an otherwise dry topic, as well as stimulate the reader to look at traffic engineering problems from a broader perspective, hence honing their intuition. The book is organized into seven Parts, each containing three Chapters. The remainder of this section summarizes the contents of each Part and its constituent Chapters.

PART 1 — Traffic Management in Communication Networks

Part 1 provides some basic background information and introduces the subjects of QoS and traffic management in IP and ATM networks. It describes the basic paradigms and operation of the IP and ATM protocols, emphasizing the traffic management aspects. A reader already familiar with these subjects could skip this part after reviewing the definitions of capacity and traffic parameters in Chapter 3.

1. *Introduction and Overview.* Chapter 1 begins with a brief history of circuit and packet switching as it relates to IP and ATM networking. It includes a high-level introduction and roadmap to the detailed concepts of QoS and traffic management covered in the remainder of the book. It also contains information on how to get the IP and ATM standards referenced in the book.

2. *Review of Circuit- and Packet-Switched Networks*. This chapter provides more in depth background information on circuit switch-

ing, connectionless packet switching used via IP, and connection-oriented packet switching used via ATM and MultiProtocol Label Switching (MPLS).

3.   *Capacity, Throughput, and Service.* Understanding terminology using precise definitions is critical to the study of traffic engineering. Therefore, this chapter defines transmission bandwidth and its relationship to channel capacity. Additionally, it defines the concepts of a bottleneck, throughput, and efficiency. We also define source traffic characteristics like the peak and average rate in general terms. This chapter also precisely defines the means used in IP and ATM networks for measuring and monitoring traffic parameters.

PART 2 — Quality of Service (QoS) and Traffic Control

Part 2 focuses on the subject of QoS and introduces the techniques that IP and ATM networks employ to deliver the required quality for a specific level of traffic. It takes the generic notion of quality and quantifies it in terms of specific measures. Taken together, the first two parts define the basic concepts of traffic and quality applied to specific IP and ATM protocols. This provides the framework used in later parts of the book for computing the QoS delivered via specific systems and network designs in response to a well-defined level of traffic.

4.   *Perception is Reality.* Since human perception is a principal determinant for the required level of quality, this chapter begins by reviewing how our senses react to voice and video communication signals. The coverage includes a description of the terminology employed in IP and ATM networks to request a specific level of QoS.

5.   *Quality of Service (QoS) Defined.* This chapter precisely defines QoS in terms of parameters like loss, delay, availability, and variation in delay specified in IP and ATM standards. It also includes a description of how an end user can request service in terms of a traffic level and an associated QoS.

6.   *Delivering QoS via Traffic Control.* IP routers and ATM switches utilize a range of implementations to deliver differentiated QoS and traffic control. This chapter summarizes these techniques, which include admission control, policing, and shaping. The subject of queuing and scheduling is briefly introduced, but covered in depth in Chapter 10.

PART 3 — The Traffic Phenomenon

Since most offered traffic has at least some random component, Part 3 provides background on the mathematics from probability theory used to compute the quality delivered by a particular design. A reader looking to get an overview could read only Chapter 7. Readers seeking a more in depth understanding of probability theory or statistics should review Chapters 8 and 9.

7. *Randomness in Our Everyday Lives.* Chapter 7 introduces the reader to the concept of randomness through some simple puzzles. It then introduces the concept of stochastic processes commonly used to model traffic phenomena.
8. *Random Traffic Models.* This chapter provides an overview of important results from probability theory used in the analysis of traffic systems. The text summarizes important results and distributions. It identifies the spreadsheet formulas and functions available to compute numerical results. It concludes with an introduction to stochastic processes.
9. *Advanced Traffic Models.* Traditionally, traffic analysis used the relatively simple Markov model summarized in this chapter. This chapter also defines more recently developed methods called self-similar processes that better model the observed characteristics for some traffic types encountered in IP and ATM networks.

PART 4 — Queuing Principles

This part builds upon the foundation of probability theory and random processes established in Part 3 to provide a basic tool kit for analyzing the performance of IP and ATM networks. Called queuing theory, these results describe the statistics of important QoS measures like delay, loss, and availability.

10. *Queuing — A Fancy Name for Waiting in Line.* This chapter defines the basics of all traffic handling systems: arrivals, waiting room, and service discipline. It also describes the role of prioritized and thresholded queues serviced by a scheduling policy employed by routers and switches to deliver differentiated QoS.
11. *Basic Queuing Theory Applied.* A significant body of knowledge exists regarding the performance of queuing systems driven by Markovian traffic. This chapter summarizes the important results as applied to the performance of connection-oriented networks,

buffer design in routers and switches, as well as voice and data integration.

12. *Intermediate Queuing Theory Applied.* The mathematics of queuing system analysis becomes quite complex for non-Markovian traffic models. Chapter 12 surveys this landscape and provides some useful approximations for estimating system performance.

PART 5 — Congestion Detection and Control

Now, after understanding the statistically predictable effect of random traffic on performance, this part addresses the unpredictable phenomenon of congestion. The discussion draws analogies with everyday life and frames the problem structure in terms of the two basic forms of response to congestion: avoidance and reaction. The chapters in the part use this basic structure to analyze the performance of open and closed loop congestion control schemes.

13. *Traffic Jam Up Ahead!* The congestion phenomena we all encounter in our everyday lives are similar in many ways to that experienced in networks. We introduce these concepts, and define the tradeoff between throughput and delay involved in the design of networks. This chapter also describes the effect of congestion on retransmission protocols used in data communication networks.

14. *Open-Loop Congestion Control.* The technique here is to avoid congestion via careful planning and forethought. This includes selective marking of traffic according to conformance with the traffic parameters associated with the flow or connection. The analysis includes performance of Weighted Fair Queuing (WFQ) on a nodal basis and the effective throughput achieved via retransmission protocols with a fixed window size.

15. *Closed-Loop Congestion Control.* When planning isn't possible, or unexpected traffic levels occur, a reactive approach is all that remains. Here, the discipline of control theory tells us much about the basic properties of closed loop congestion control schemes. The chapter applies these techniques to rate- and window-based flow control systems, including a detailed model of TCP/IP performance.

PART 6 — Routing and Network Design

In real networks, traffic and congestion control occur in a complex pattern of interconnected devices serving traffic flows from many users. This part takes the results of the preceding chapters and applies them in a network context. Since extending the result of a single node to an interrelated set of nodes is a complicated problem, we analyze some simple network topologies to expose some general aspects of network design.

16. *Routing Background and Concepts.* This chapter introduces the subject via analogies to transportation systems and some simple network examples. It then describes the link-state routing algorithm and the concept of constrained routing. It concludes with a discussion on the tradeoffs involved in routing algorithm complexity and the efficient utilization of transmission links and switching resources.

17. *Routing Algorithms.* The mathematical description of routing draws upon the disciplines of graph theory, computer science, and operations research. This chapter introduces the terminology from these areas and applies them to generic network design problems.

18. *Performance of Network Routing Designs.* Analyzing the performance of a network of devices is a challenging problem. This chapter summarizes the networks of queues model for computing end-to-end performance for Markovian traffic. It also describes some analytical routing models for symmetric mesh and tree networks.

PART 7 — Putting It All Together

This final part introduces some additional techniques utilized in network design. It also highlights some important practical considerations involved in the design, deployment, and operation of an IP or ATM network. Finally, it concludes with some thoughts and possible future directions of QoS and traffic management in IP and ATM networks.

19. *Traffic Engineering Applied.* Chapter 19 describes some additional networking techniques involved in the design of large networks. It then provides an overview of the network planning and design process, highlighting the role of network design tools.

20. *Designing Real World Networks.* This chapter includes some additional material on network design. This includes the performance of hierarchical network design and the effect of overflow traffic. It also summarizes dynamic routing, and least cost design.

21. *Where to Go From Here.* Here, we introduce the use of event-based simulation tools to model complicated network configurations. This chapter also provides some practical guidelines for formulat-

ing traffic models. It concludes with a brief discussion on the future of QoS and traffic management.

Acknowledgements

A book like this requires a great deal of help and support. First, I would like to acknowledge Steve Elliot of McGraw-Hill who refined the proposal for this book and supported the effort. Secondly, I would like to thank my wife, Debbie, for giving me the time to write this book along with her continual support and encouragement. Finally, I would like to acknowledge the reviewers who carefully read the manuscript, corrected errors, suggested clarifications, and provided additional references. These reviewers were: Professor Thomas Chen of Southern Methodist University, Fatih Alagoz of George Washington University, Roland Smith of Nortel Networks, Byoung-Joon Lee of Cisco Systems, Furrukh Fahim of Fahim Associates, Dr. Cheng Chen of NEC, and Dr. Bharathi Devi, James Liou, and Syeda Sanjana of MCI WorldCom.

This book does not reflect any policy or position of MCI WorldCom. The ideas and concepts expressed herein are those of the author or the cited references.

1

Traffic Management in Communication Networks

"In the following pages I offer nothing more than simple facts, plain arguments, and common sense…"

— Thomas Paine

Traffic. Normally, this word brings to mind unpleasant situations of waiting in long lines and unanticipated delays. In our increasingly busy world, the times and places without traffic become fewer and further between. So, why should the study of something unavoidable be important to you? The answer depends upon your role in a traffic system. As an end user, understanding the traffic phenomenon may mitigate inconvenience. As a switch/router developer, handling traffic effectively is a competitive advantage. As a network designer, balancing between delay encountered by users and the cost of service is important in the optimal engineering of networks in response to offered traffic.

CHAPTER 1

Introduction and Overview

"The man who removes a mountain begins by carrying away small stones."

— Chinese Proverb

Traffic management of communication networks has a long and interesting history. This chapter briefly reviews this history, highlighting the inventions and innovations that drove major paradigm shifts in the way we communicate. Reviewing the evolution of communications networking provides a basic historical foundation for why IP routers and ATM switches work the way they do. The chapter then introduces the subject of traffic management and provides a road map for the remainder of the book. We view traffic in different ways: as an annoying fact, as a pattern, as a measure of usage, or simply the presence of congestion. Each views is valid, but only through a holistic approach can we refine our intuition. This chapter introduces terminology and concepts used throughout the text. Since this book references a number of standards that define how IP routers and ATM switches implement QoS and traffic management, we summarize the major IP and ATM standards bodies and their contact information for obtaining documentation.

A Brief History of Circuits, Packets, and Cells

This section provides a brief overview of the history of circuit, packet, and cell switching. Studying history helps us understand the interplay of societal values, changing economics, and the shift from the industrial to the information age brought on by the large-scale adoption of opto-electronic and software technologies. The remainder of the chapter summarizes specific terminology and concepts referenced later in the text. See References 1 and 2 for more background information.

Origin of the Switched Telephone Network

Connection-oriented circuit switching originated in the public telephone network. Early telephone networks dedicated a physical circuit for an electrical signal to each pair of callers. This type of connectivity made sense when only a few people had telephones. However, when the maze of wires on overhead telephone poles began to block out the sun in urban areas, creative engineers responded with a simple solution. The first step toward switching involved human telephone operators who manually connected parties wishing to communicate using patch cords on a switchboard. Callers identified the called party by telling the operator the name of the person with whom they wished to speak. This design relieved the wiring congestion problem greatly, since now all the wires from each user went back to a central operator station, instead of between every pair of users. However, once the number of users grew beyond what a single operator could handle, multiple operators had to communicate in order to route the call through several manually connected switchboards to the final destination. Demand created the need for a better solution.

Interestingly, the motivation for Almon B. Strowger inventing the first electromechanical circuit switch in 1889 [3] wasn't engineering efficiency, but basic capitalism. As the story goes, he was an undertaker by trade in a moderately sized town that had two undertakers. Unfortunately for Strowger, his competitor's wife was the switchboard operator in that town. As the telephone increased in popularity, when anyone died, their relatives called the telephone operator to request funeral services. Of course, the operator in this town routed the requests to her husband, and not to Strowger. Seeing his business declining, he conceived of the electromechanical telephone switch and the rotary dial telephone so that customers could contact him directly. Therefore, Strowger ended up in an entirely different, but highly successful business. Now, we take for granted the ease of picking up the telephone virtually anywhere in the world and dialing any other person in the world.

Digital Circuit Switching for Voice

In the late 1950s, a need to further increase the efficiency of transmitting voice over the crowded bundles of cables lying beneath the streets of large cities drove the development of a major innovation in multiplexing. This technique made use of emerging solid-state electronics by converting analog voice into digital samples and multiplexing these samples into periodic time slots. Although this technique was relatively expensive, it cost less than replacing existing cables or digging larger tunnels in New York City. Since then, Time Division Multiplexing (TDM) has become the prevalent multiplexing method in all modern telecommunication networks. Digital circuit switches that operated directly on digital voice were first introduced in the late 1960s. We now take for granted the fact that the network converts every voice conversation to digital data, transmits it an arbitrary distance, and then converts the digits back to an audible analog signal. The consequence is that the quality of a voice call carried by digital TDM is now essentially independent of distance. This performance results from digital repeaters that decode and retransmit the digital signal at periodic intervals to achieve extremely accurate data transfer. Data communications is more sensitive to noise and errors than digitized voice, but reaps tremendous benefits from the deployment of TDM infrastructure in public networks. TDM forms the basis of the Narrowband Integrated Services Digital Network (N-ISDN)

The Packet-Switching Alternative

Paul Baran and his research team at the RAND Corporation articulated the concept of packet switching in the early 1960s as a secure, reliable means of transmitting military communications [4]. The challenge was to enable the United States military communications system to survive a nuclear attack. The solution was to segment a longer message into many smaller pieces and then wrap routing and protocol information around each of these pieces, resulting in a string of data called a *packet*. The routing and control information ensured the correct and accurate delivery and eventual reassembly of the original message at the end-user destination. The next step occurred when the Advanced Research Projects Agency (ARPA) of the United States Department of Defense (DoD) implemented packet switching to handle computer communications requirements. The DoD dubbed the resulting network ARPANET. Soon after ARPANET, companies like IBM and DEC developed proprietary packet-based protocols. The Open System Interconnection (OSI) standardization effort attempted to standardize computer communication interfaces and protocols to enable a multi-vendor environment. The ARPANET mandated TCP/IP protocol suite evolved into the Internet, while only the X.25 protocol prospered from the OSI efforts.

Early packet-switching systems targeted terminal-to-host communications. The typical transaction involved the user typing a few lines, or even just a few characters, and then sending a transaction to the host. The host would then return a few lines, or possibly, an entire screen's worth of data. This terminal-host application was very bursty; that is, the peak transmission or reception rate of each terminal was much greater than the average rate. Packet-switching equipment statistically multiplexed many such bursty users onto a single expensive transmission facility.

As the number of computers, applications, and people using computers increased, the need for interconnection increased, creating an accelerating need for bandwidth. Similar to the growth in telephony, it quickly became absurd to have a dedicated circuit to connect every pair of computers that needed to communicate. The industry responded by developing packet-switching and routing protocols to dynamically facilitate the communication between computers on an as needed basis. The tremendous sustained growth of the Internet stands as testimony to the fundamental soundness of this approach.

Connection-Oriented and Connectionless Protocols

Two diametrically opposite paradigms (i.e., a way of doing things) exist for relaying information in networks: connection-oriented and connectionless. As the name implies, a connection-oriented protocol must first establish a path (or connection) between computers before transferring information. Circuit switching, by definition, is connection-oriented. X.25, frame relay, and ATM are examples of connection-oriented packet-switching protocols. At the other extreme, the connectionless paradigm relies on the fields within the information flow itself to dynamically determine the destination. The Internet Protocol (IP) is the prime example of a connectionless packet-switching protocol.

One simple analogy for understanding the difference between a connection-oriented and a connectionless service is that of placing a telephone call compared with sending a telegraph message. To make a connection-oriented voice call, you pick up the telephone and dial the number of the destination. The network makes a connection from your telephone, through one or more switches to the destination switch, and rings the telephone associated with the dialed digits. Once the called party answers, the network keeps the connection active until one of the parties hangs up. If the network can't make the connection, you get a busy signal. Hence, the telephone network consistently delivers high quality for completed calls.

Now here is a connectionless example. Consider the activities involved in sending a telegraph message in the nineteenth century. A person visited the telegraph office and recited a message, giving the destination address as the name, city, and country of the intended recipient. The originating telegraph operator picked a next hop telegraph station, and keyed in the entire message to that telegraph office. Since the originating telegraph operator does not know the status of telegraph lines being up or down except for those lines connected to his own station, he must rely on the other operators to forward the message toward the destination. If a path existed to the destination, then the persistent telegraph operators in this example would likely relay the message to the final destination, eventually, even if some telegraph lines on the most direct path were down. This example is not as dated as it may seem — Internet E-mail systems use basically the same method proven over a century ago by telegraph networks to reliably forward and deliver huge numbers of electronic messages every day.

Economical Local Area Networking

Dr. Robert M. Metcalfe invented Ethernet in the late 1970s at the Xerox Palo Alto Research Center. The design used concepts pioneered in the ALOHA system deployed to implement radio communication in the Hawaiian islands [2]. Most major enterprises embraced Local Area Networks (LANs) in the 1980s, and now even some residences have LANs. Ethernet is the dominant LAN technology today. Network designers then invented bridging to interconnect multiple LANs to provide greater connectivity. Meanwhile, incompatible LAN standards created the need for routers in the environment of diverse interconnected LANs. Some LAN standards also define QoS, which is important since many IP networks operate over LANs.

Cells as Fixed-Length Packets

In the late 1980s the ITU-T realized that the maximum speed of 2 Mbps defined for the Integrated Services Digital Network (ISDN) would not be adequate to transfer video information. Hence, the TDM-based ISDN failed to achieve the goal of a single integrated networking technology supporting voice, data, and video. After considering several TDM and packet-based protocols, the standards body chose a fixed-length cell to support a Broadband ISDN (B-ISDN). It relabeled TDM as Synchronous Transfer Mode (STM) and crowned the new bearer of the broadband era Asynchronous Transfer Mode (ATM). Based upon the state of hardware capabilities as understood at that time, the ITU-T defined ATM as a fixed-length packet, referred to as a *cell*. During most of the 1990s, ATM held the world speed record for the fastest interfaces and largest switching machines. However, with the tremendous growth in popularity of the Internet-driven Web browser application, routers of the twenty-first century in the Internet backbone will greatly surpass the largest, fastest ATM switching machines. ATM, however, has a mature, stable, and tested implementation of QoS and traffic management that serves integrated networks very well, since the ITU-T designed it from the ground up with this goal in mind. Thus, ATM is an important service for many corporate intranets, used widely to carry other data services like frame relay, and provides an excellent access technology for reasons studied later in this chapter. Furthermore, many of the IP-based traffic management and QoS techniques have a basis in, or are enhancements of, ATM-based techniques.

Introduction to QoS and Traffic Management

This section introduces the concepts of Quality of Service (QoS) and traffic management as applied to IP and ATM. We compare and contrast IP and ATM and describe the computer communication networking context that is the focus of this book.

IP and ATM — Different yet Similar

Although IP and ATM networks employ some fundamentally different paradigms — packets versus cells and connectionless versus connection-oriented forwarding being the most evident — the means utilized to manage traffic and deliver QoS are remarkably similar. This is no accident. QoS and traffic management are difficult problems for which network designers, equipment manufacturers, and traffic engineers have only a limited solution set. Furthermore, the need for different levels of capacity and quality is a fundamental aspect of human nature and our capitalistic society.

Thus, studying the similarities between traditional circuit-switched networks and ATM with the problems facing the burgeoning demand for differentiated services in the Internet yields deeper insights. It also applies the time-tested methods of analysis to the complicated issues involved in QoS and traffic management. This book focuses on the management and engineering of traffic in computer communication networks that must deliver a specified level of quality. The remainder of Part 1 introduces the circuit-, packet-, and cell-switched networks currently in use as background information.

Traffic engineering consists of applying mathematical models of source behavior and the services provided by a particular system to deliver a specified quality measure. For example, in a highway system, the sources are vehicles and the rules of the road determine the service discipline, along with other phenomena like the weather, accidents, and policies like car pool and bus lanes. The quality measure here is the amount of delay and congestion encountered by commuters. In a communications network, users place telephone calls, surf the Web, or perform other tasks using computers. As we shall see, the arrival, queuing, and service phenomenon encountered in communications networks are similar in many respects to transportation networks, shopping, and waiting in line for services at banks, post offices, and government agencies.

Many quality measures experienced by communications users are also similar to those encountered in transportation networks. For example, delay, availability of service, and productivity are important measures of quality. Communications networks have some unique QoS attributes as well, such as packet or cell loss and wrongly delivered messages. Part 2 addresses the important topic of QoS.

Traffic engineers frequently employ mathematical models of the source arrival patterns and the network service discipline. Frequently, these models use the concepts of probability and random processes introduced in Part 3. In some well-known special cases, traffic engineers also employ deterministic models for well-behaved arrival processes.

Arrivals and Service in Computer Communication Networks

Typically, arrivals in computer communication networks correspond to discrete measurable events. For example, clicking a button on a Web page is an arrival event that creates a message transmitted by your computer (called the *client*) across the Internet to a server. The response generated by the server is also an arrival event as perceived by the client. The study of the patterns resulting from the composite of many such arrival and service events occurring at devices within a network is called *traffic engineering*.

Figure 1.1 illustrates the basic context of an Internet-based arrival, queuing, and service model studied in this book. On the left-hand side, user Bob surfs the Web from his personal computer (PC). In step 1, Bob's PC generates a request to the router (R1) in his Internet service provider's (ISP) network. Router R1 views this request packet as an arrival, and serves it by determining the best path to take toward the destination. Eventually, the interconnected ISP networks in the Internet deliver the request packet to router R2 that has a connection to the addressed Web server on the right-hand side of the figure. Router R2 services this request packet by transmitting it on the line connected to the server in step 2. The Web server sees this request packet as an arrival. In general, a downstream system views service delivery from an upstream system as an arrival. Note that the Web server may be processing arriving request packets from many clients simultaneously, and hence may take some time before responding to Bob's request. Once the server formulates the response to Bob's request, it transmits it in step 3 back to router R2, which routes the response back towards Bob's ISP. This response looks like an arrival to

Figure 1.1
Basic arrival (request) and service (response) model of the Internet.

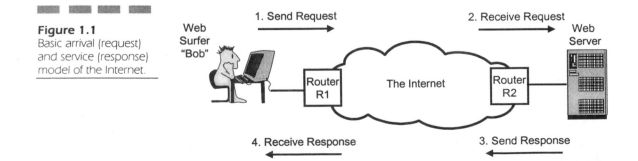

router R2. Note that the return path for the response may be different in the reverse direction in the Internet. After some delay, the interconnected ISP networks deliver the response to router R1, which transmits the response packet to Bob's PC in step 4.

End-to-End Performance — Throughput and Response Time

Note that some delay occurs between step 1 and step 2 of the Web surfer example from the preceding section, because of transmitting the request and delays encountered within the routers in the ISP networks. The processing in the Web server to compute the response also takes some time, along with the return routing path between steps 3 and 4. Frequently, analyses use a graphical technique called a *space-time diagram* to illustrate these delays. Figure 1.2 depicts a space-time diagram for the example described above. The space part of the drawing runs along the top of the figure to the right and left, while the time dimension runs from top to bottom. Starting at the upper left-hand side, the figure depicts Bob at his PC connected to Router R1. The Internet provides a communication path to Router R2 connected to the Web server at the upper right-hand side of the figure. The arrow labeled step 1 at the left-hand side of the figure depicts the amount of time required for Bob's PC to send the request to router R1. On the right-hand side of the figure in step 2, the Internet eventually delivers the request to router R2 after a forward routing delay

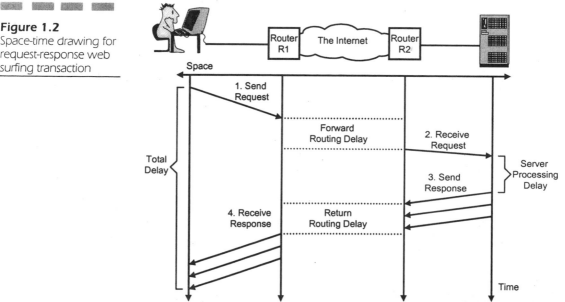

Figure 1.2
Space-time drawing for
request-response web
surfing transaction

as labeled in the figure. Router R2 then transmits the request to the Web server over a high-speed line as indicated in step 2. Note that the slope of the line is shallower than the line corresponding to the request transmitted by Bob's PC because the link speed at the server is much greater than the one at Bob's PC. Hence, transmission of messages to and from the server requires less time when compared with the transfer time of messages to and from Bob's PC.

Continuing with the example, the Web server queues Bob's request if it is busy processing prior requests, eventually computing a response after a server delay, as indicated on the right-hand side of the figure. The server then transmits the response as a series of packets to router R2 in step 3. These packets make their way back across the Internet to router R1 after incurring a return routing delay as indicated in the figure. Finally, Bob's PC begins receiving these response packets in step 4 as indicated in the lower left-hand portion of the figure. As before, router R1 takes longer to transmit these packets to Bob's PC because the connection speed is lower. Finally, after Bob's PC receives the last packet of the response, the transaction is complete. The user, Bob, experienced the total delay as indicated on the left-hand side of the figure. Obviously, this accumulated delay impacts the rate at which Bob can work, since he cannot click on another link until the prior transaction completes. This is why delay is so important in computer communications — it directly impacts end user productivity!

Part 2 studies these issues of performance and QoS, such as response time, application throughput, and loss. It also addresses performance issues that arise involving multimedia traffic when voice and video compete for shared resources in communication network nodes, servers, and end user computers.

IP and ATM Standards Sources

Much of the details regarding the implementation and design consideration for most aspects of IP and ATM networks and services are documented in standards and specifications. This section describes the terminology employed by these groups, as well as the means that a reader can obtain copies of these standards documents.

Internet Engineering Task Force (IETF)

Commensurate with the mandate for global interoperability of the Internet is the need for standards, and lots of them. The United States Defense Advance Research Projects Agency (DARPA) formed the Internet Activities Board (IAB) in 1983. By 1989 the Internet had grown so large that the IAB reorganized, delegating the work of developing specifications for interoperability to an Internet Engineering Task Force (IETF). The initial objective of the IAB/IETF was to define the necessary specifications required for interoperable implementations using the Internet Protocol (IP) suite. IETF members draft documents called Requests For Comments (RFC). These RFCs pass through a draft stage and a proposed standard stage prior to becoming an approved standard. Another possible outcome of an RFC is archival as an experimental RFC. The IETF also publishes informational RFCs. As a housekeeping matter, the IETF archives out-of-date RFCs as historical standards. The archiving of all approved (as well as historical or experimental RFCs) serves as a storehouse of protocol and networking knowledge available to the world — accessible, of course, over the Internet itself.

A number of work groups have produced RFCs or are in the process of creating standards in the areas of QoS and traffic management. This book references specific efforts, but the committee structure of the IETF is ever changing. Therefore, the interested reader should access the search engines and tools available on the Internet to obtain up-to-date information.

The best way to get more information on the IETF draft and approved RFCs describing the Internet Protocol (IP) suite is from the IETF home page located at http://www.ietf.org/home.html. You can also contact them via snail mail or telephone at the secretariat's office as follows:

IETF Secretariat
c/o Corporation for National Research Initiatives
1895 Preston White Drive, Suite 100
Reston, VA 20191-5434, USA
+1 703 620 8990 (voice)
+1 703 758-5913 (fax)

International Telecommunications Union Telecommunications (ITU-T)

The United Nations founded the International Telecommunications Union (ITU) in 1948 to produce telegraphy and telephone technical, operating, and tariff issue recommendations. Formerly known as the Consultative Committee International Telegraph and Telephone (CCITT), the Telecommunications standardization sector, referred to as the ITU-T, produces recommendations on B-ISDN in which ATM is but one component in an overall set of services. The ITU-T also began working on Internet-related standards in the 1990s. For details to obtain further information about the ITU-T contact:

International Telecommunication Union (ITU)
Place des Nations
CH-1211 Geneva 20
Switzerland
Voice: +41 22 730 5111
Fax: +41 22 733 7256
Email:itumail@itu.int

A convenient way to get ITU-T documents is over the Web at http://www.itu.ch. The ITU-T service allows registered subscribers unlimited download of the standards, or purchase of individual documents. The service supports both Microsoft Word and PostScript formats. The ITU-T defines ATM as a component of an overarching vision called Broadband ISDN (B-ISDN). The ITU-T organizes recommendations covering various aspects of B-ISDN in a set of alphabetically identified series. The following series are relevant to ATM (B-ISDN) and certain aspects of the Internet:

- Series E — Telephone network and N-ISDN
- Series F — Non-telephone telecommunication services
- Series G — Transmission systems and media
- Series H — Transmission of non-telephone signals
- Series I — Integrated services digital network
- Series M — Maintenance: international transmission systems, telephone circuits, telegraphy, facsimile and leased circuits
- Series Q — Switching and signalling

The ATM Forum

Four companies founded the ATM Forum in October 1991. The ATM Forum opened membership to the public in January 1992. This book references the traffic management, signaling, and routing specifications generated by the forum. The ATM Forum groups the specifications by the technical subcommittee that generated the document. As of December 1998, these subcommittees were:

- Control Signaling (CS)
- LAN Emulation (LANE) and MultiProtocol Over ATM (MPOA)
- Network Management (NM)
- PHYsical Layer (PHY)
- Residential Broadband (RBB)
- Routing and Addressing (RA)
    - Private Network-Network Interface (PNNI)
    - Broadband InterCarrier Interface (B-ICI)
- Service Aspects and Applications (SAA)
- Testing (TEST)
- Traffic Management (TM)
- Voice Telephony Over ATM (VTOA)
- Wireless ATM (WATM)

The address, phone number, email address, and Web page to obtain information about the ATM Forum are:

The ATM Forum
2570 West El Camino Real, Suite 304
Mountain View, CA 94040-1313
+1 650 949 6700 or +1 415 949 6700 Phone
+1 650 949 6705 or +1 415 949 6705 Fax
info@atmforum.com
http://www.atmforum.com

The ATM Forum has approved over 100 ATM-related specifications to date. All ATM Forum specifications are available online at the ATM Forum Web site in Adobe's Acrobat Portable Document Format (PDF). The Web site includes a list of approved and pending specifications that provides a useful way of tracking the areas in which the ATM Forum is actively working.

Review

This chapter introduced the concepts of Quality of Service and traffic management. Since many concepts and techniques employed in IP and ATM networks to delivery quality at particular traffic levels borrow from prior networking experience, this chapter presented a brief history of communication networking. Finally, since standards and specifications detail the protocols, mechanisms, and objectives utilized by IP and ATM networks in delivering QoS, the chapter summarized how to obtain standards documents referenced in subsequent chapters.

References

[1]   D. McDysan, D. Spohn, *ATM: Theory and Applications, Signature Edition,* McGraw-Hill, 1998.

[2]   A. Tannenbaum, *Computer Communications, Third Edition,* Prentice-Hall, 1996.

[3]   D. Bear, *Principles of Telecommunication — Traffic Engineering,* Peter Petringus, Ltd, 1976.

[4]   P. Baran et al, "On Distributed Communications," RAND Corporation, 1964, www.rand.org/publications/rm/baran.list.html.

CHAPTER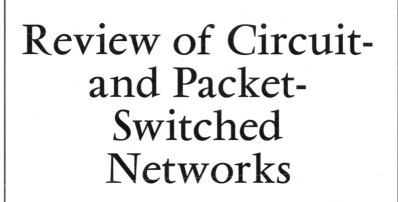

Review of Circuit- and Packet- Switched Networks

"If I have seen farther than others, it is because I have stood on the shoulders of giants."

— Isaac Newton

This chapter provides an overview of the salient characteristics of circuit, packet, and cell switching and multiplexing technologies commonly encountered in private and carrier networks. Specific attributes of these networking technologies constrain the choices available to network designers. Subsequent chapters reference the specific terminology of Time Division Multiplexing (TDM), packet switching, routing, and Asynchronous Transfer Mode (ATM) switching summarized in this chapter. The discussions on queuing theory in Part 4 require that the reader be familiar with the concepts of signaling and statistical multiplexing introduced in this chapter. The text provides a bibliography for reference by the reader interested in more detail.

Circuit Switching

Circuit switching is the oldest digital communication technology. Some concepts carry forward to modern day connection-oriented packet switching and Internet-to-telephony gateway equipment.

Time Division Multiplexing (TDM)

Bell Labs engineers invented TDM in the 1950s to multiplex many voice conversations onto the existing twisted pairs. TDM converts the analog voiceband signals to quantized digital samples prior to transmission as illustrated in Figure 2.1. In 1924, Nyquist derived a theorem proving that the digital samples of an analog signal must be taken at a rate no less than *twice* the bandwidth of that signal to enable accurate reproduction of the original analog signal at the receiver. Thirty years later, telephone engineers put the Nyquist sampling theorem into practice by sampling a standard 4000-Hz bandwidth limited voice channel at 8000 samples per second. Employing 8 (or 7) bits per sample yields the standard 64-kbps (or 56-kbps) digital data stream used in modern digital Time Division Multiplexing (TDM) transmission and switching systems for each direction of a voice channel. Engineers call the digitized coding of each analog voice sample Pulse Code Modulation (PCM). Many networks still transmit voice at 56- or 64-kbps. However, more sophisticated modern digital encoding techniques now enable transmission of a voice channel at speeds as low as 5 kbps (with some loss in quality, of course) when capacity is expensive or scarce.

Figure 2.1
Illustration of a digitized, sampled voiceband signal.

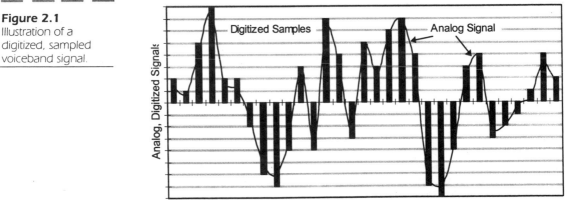

The transmission system then multiplexes 24 such digitized and sampled voice channel (called a Digital Stream 0, or DS0, in North America) onto a single twisted pair using a T1 repeater signal according to a Digital Stream 1 (DS1) signal format. The DS1 transmission rate of 1.544 Mbps derives from multiplying the DS0 rate of 64 kbps by 24 (i.e., 1.536 Mbps), plus an 8-kbps framing and signaling channel. This design decision resulted in an improvement of over 2400 percent in utilization of the scarce twisted pair resource — a tremendous gain in efficiency! International standards adopted a similar multiplexing technique that makes better use of existing twisted pair plant by multiplexing thirty-two 64-kbps channels into a standard E1 format operating at 2.048 Mbps.

The Tyranny of the TDM Hierarchy

The plesiochronous (which means nearly synchronous) digital hierarchy evolved into the North American Digital hierarchy, which gives a specific number to each Digital Stream (DS) format. For example, a DS0 is 64 kbps, a DS1 is 1.544 Mbps, and a DS3 is 44.736 Mbps. Similar hierarchies with different rates evolved in Europe and Japan. Next, standards bodies defined synchronous TDM hierarchies for higher-speed optical signals in a series of standards called the Synchronous Optical Network (SONET) in North America and the Synchronous Digital Hierarchy (SDH) in the rest of the world [1]. The basic rate increment of these SONET and SDH is 51.84 and 155.52 Mbps, respectively. These TDM digital hierarchies impose a high penalty of poor granularity on data communications applications by only supporting a discrete set of fixed rates. Figure 2.2 illustrates the situation for the North American digital hierarchy via a plot of the logarithm base 10 of the bit rate in bps..

At lower speeds, the nx64 kbps granularity exists up to n=24, which is a full DS1. Proprietary multiplexers then extend the granularity up to 8xDS1, or approximately 12 Mbps. The next steps are DS3 at 44.736 Mbps and STS-1 at 51.84 Mbps. After that, the SONET hierarchy goes as OC-3k, where k is an integer that grows by a factor of 4. That is, the levels in the hierarchy are OC-3, OC-12, OC-48, OC-192, and OC-768. In other words, the granularity becomes 155.52 Mbps! Few applications require such course granularity between any points, which means that intermediate equipment must demultiplex out lower-speed TDM levels, drop them off, and then add in and remultiplex other signals to result in the large SONET composites. One of the early ATM proposals [2] emphasized the capability to provide a wide range of speeds as a key advantage of ATM over TDM. Now, similar

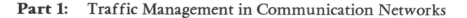

Figure 2.2
Granularity of the
North American TDM
hierarchy.

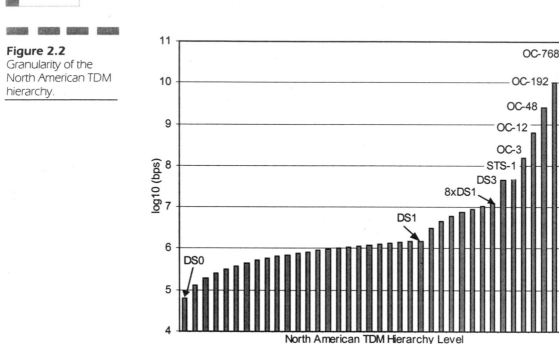

reasoning argues for the wholesale replacement of TDM with either packet or cell switching and routing.

Signaling for Switched Connections

Figure 2.3 shows a space-time diagram illustrating the basic process involved in establishing a circuit-switched connection between two users, A and B. In the example, user A employs a signaling protocol to request a circuit to the called party, B. An example of a signaling protocol is the dialed digits from a telephone set. The network determines a path, propagates the circuit request to the switch connected to user B, and relays the circuit establishment request, for example, ringing the telephone. Telephone networks typically ring the called party within several seconds after the calling party enters the last digit of the telephone number. Telephone engineers refer to this time interval as *post dial delay*. Call setup delay in data communications over the voice network adds an additional 10 to 30 seconds for modem training. While the network alerts the called party, it provides a progress indication to the calling party A, for example, via a ringing tone. If called party B accepts the request, then the network sets up a circuit and dedicates it to the parties until they release the connection. The parties then engage in an information transfer phase, as indicated in the figure. Once the parties complete a higher-layer protocol ex-

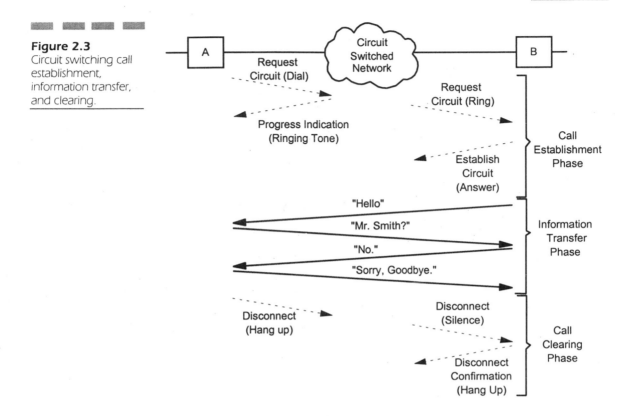

Figure 2.3
Circuit switching call establishment, information transfer, and clearing.

change, for example, the wrong-number scenario indicated in the figure, either party may initiate a disconnect just by hanging up the phone. The network provides an indication to the other party of disconnection, typically silence, and eventually transmits a dial tone or an error signal if the other party doesn't hang up. Normally, the other party confirms disconnection by hanging up, as shown in the example.

Of course, the circuit-switching protocol handles a number of exceptional conditions, such as network blocking, called party busy, call waiting, and many others. Note that if the same two parties hang up and call each other back later, the telephone network establishes another circuit in the same manner, but not necessarily over the same path as before. In this manner, telephone networks share common resources (i.e., circuits and trunk ports) between many users in nonoverlapping time intervals, achieving an economy of scale, since the average telephone call between people lasts only 3 to 5 minutes. More recently, telephone user behavior has changed because dial-up access to the Internet, where the holding time may be on the order of hours instead of minutes. This change in traffic patterns presents a challenge to the engineers designing the local exchange switch and the circuits connected to the Internet service provider.

Traditionally, telephone engineers not only had to plan for trunk and switch capacity, but tone receivers, tone transmitters, announcements, and call processing capacity. The solutions to these telephony problems stimulated the development of the discipline of queuing theory studied in Part 4.

Today, computers "talk" to each other in the same manner using a modem to convert data to signals compatible with the analog access lines connected to the circuit-switched voice network. The word *modem* is a contraction for modulator/demodulator, a process that converts digital data into waveforms for transmission over analog access lines. See References 3 and 4 for more information on low-speed modem communications.

The computer application establishes a point-to-point telephone call whenever data communication is needed, for example, when starting up a Web browser, and leaves the connection up to allow data transmission. The end user disconnects the circuit when either they are finished, or the application automatically disconnects, for example, after a period of inactivity. Since circuit switching is a form of connection-oriented service, the network dedicates the entire circuit bandwidth for the entire call duration. Circuit switching is ideal for applications that require constant bandwidth but can tolerate call establishment and disconnection times on the order of many seconds. For example, most users accept waiting 10 to 30 seconds to connect to an Internet service provider for an hour-long session of Web browsing.

Connectionless Packet Switching

Packet-switched networks have evolved for over 30 years to form the basis of advanced data communications networks today; foremost being the Internet. Packet switching initially provided the network environment needed to handle bursty, terminal-to-host data traffic over the analog telephone network. The emergence of the World Wide Web (WWW) as the predominant user interface to "cyberspace" firmly established IP as the de facto standard for internetworking to the corporate desktop, as well as the home office, and the residential Web browser.

Connectionless Forwarding and Routing

As the name implies, connectionless packet switching never establishes connections of any kind. Instead, network nodes examine the address field in every packet header and forward packets along a path toward the destination by selecting an outgoing link on a hop-by-hop basis. The origin node initiates the forwarding process, with each intermediate node repeating it until the packet reaches the destination node. The destination node then delivers the packet on its local interface to the addressed device.

Typically, the nodes run a distributed routing protocol that consistently determines the next hop forwarding tables to result in optimized, loop-free end-to-end paths. Therefore, unlike connection-oriented protocols, packets do not take a predetermined path through the network. Thus, the connectionless paradigm avoids the overhead of call establishment incurred by connection-oriented protocols. Pretty simple, right?

Yes, and no. The magic in the above simple description is the routing protocol that consistently determines the next hop at the origin and each intermediate node. Part 6 explains more details about different types of routing protocols, but they all meet the goal stated in the previous sentence. In other words, routing protocols determine the contents of the next hop forwarding table such that packets with the same destination address take the same path through the network. A bad routing protocol could create next hop entries that cause endless loops where a packet never arrives at the destination, but instead loops around the network indefinitely. On the other hand, a good routing protocol automatically chooses a path through the network optimized to a specific criterion like minimum cost or delay. Note that if the routing protocol changes the next hop forwarding table during data transfer between end systems (e.g., if a physical circuit fails), then packets may arrive at the destination in a different order than sent by the origin. Some aspects of connectionless services are truly "plug and play," while others require address configuration, subnet mask definitions, and setting of other parameters.

Connectionless services do not guarantee packet delivery; therefore, applications rely on higher-level protocols (e.g., TCP) to perform the end-to-end error detection/correction. Additionally, higher-layer protocols must also perform flow control (e.g., TCP), since connectionless services typically operate on a best effort basis without any notion of bandwidth allocation.

The Internet Protocol (IP) Datagram

In order to practically apply subsequent theoretical results, the reader should keep in mind that routers operate on specific fields within the headers of IP datagrams. Figure 2.4 illustrates the format of the version 4 IP packet [5], [6]. The 4-bit version field specifies the IP protocol version. Each node first checks the version field before processing the datagram. Such use of the version field will be critical in the migration from IP version 4 to IP version 6. Next, the IP Header Length (IP HL) field specifies the datagram header length in units of 32-bit words, the most common length being 5 words, or 20 octets when no options are present. If options are present, then the IP HL field includes the number of words used for the options, for example, a route trace. The 8-bit Type of Service field contains a 3-bit precedence field, plus 3 separate bits specifying other service attributes, and two unused bits. The precedence field ranges from 0 (i.e., normal priority) through 7 (i.e., network control), indicating eight levels of precedence. The three individual bits request low delay, high throughput, and high reliability. Recent IETF standards have reallocated the TOS field to support differentiated services as specified in RFCs 2474 [7] and 2475 [8] as described in Chapter 4.

The Total Length field specifies the total IP datagram length for the header plus the user data. The identification field, flags, and fragment offset fields control fragmentation (or segmentation) and reassembly of IP datagrams. The Time to Live (TTL) field specifies how many seconds the packet can be forwarded in the network before declaring the packet "dead," and hence disposable. Typically, intermediate nodes or routers decrement the TTL field at each hop. When TTL reaches zero, intermediate nodes discard the packet. Therefore, a packet cannot circulate indefinitely through a complex set of networks. The protocol field identifies the higher-level protocol type (e.g., TCP or UDP), that then specifies the format of the data field. The header checksum ensures integrity of the header fields using a

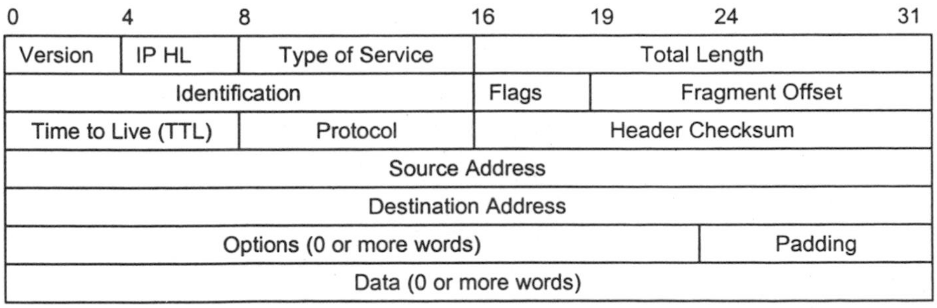

Figure 2.4
IP version 4 (IPv4) datagram format.

0	4	8	16	19	24	31
Version	IP HL	Type of Service	Total Length			
Identification			Flags	Fragment Offset		
Time to Live (TTL)		Protocol	Header Checksum			
Source Address						
Destination Address						
Options (0 or more words)					Padding	
Data (0 or more words)						

simple bitwise-parity check that is easy to implement in software.

The globally unique 32-bit source and destination IP addresses are required fields. Routers must utilize at least the destination address when making a forwarding decision. The destination host uses the source address to return a response to the sender. The Options field can specify security level, source routing, or request a route trace. Two types of source routing option give either a complete list of routers for a complete path, or a list of routers that must be visited in the path. In the route trace, each intermediate router adds its own IP address to the Packet Header Options Field (increasing the IP Header Length Field, of course). The Options field can request that each router add a timestamp as well as its IP address when performing a route trace. The Data field contains higher-layer protocol information or user data.

Since 32-bit addresses were deemed to be insufficient to support continued growth of the Internet, the IETF began defining the next-generation Internet Protocol. An interim protocol designed to support QoS was labeled version 5, and hence the next generation after version 4 was labeled version 6, or IPv6 for short. Figure 2.5 illustrates the version 6 IP packet format [9]. The Version field allows routers to examine the first four bits of the packet header to determine the IP version. Notice how the IPv4 packet header has the same version field in the first four bits so that routers can support both IPv4 and IPv6 simultaneously for migration purposes. The 8-bit Traffic Class field is reserved for experimental purposes. Currently, the diffserv draft standard [8] uses this in the same manner as defined for IPv4. The 20-bit Flow Label field supports protocols like the Resource ReSerVation Protocol (RSVP) to guarantee bandwidth and QoS for streams of packets involved in the same flow.

The Payload Length field indicates the number of bytes following the required 40-byte header. The Next Header field identifies the subsequent header extension field. There are six (optional) header extensions: hop-by-hop options, source routing, fragmentation support, destination options, authentication, and security support. The last extension header field identifies the higher-layer protocol type using the same values as IPv4, typically TCP or UDP. The Hop Limit field determines the maximum number of nodes a packet may traverse. Nodes decrement by 1 the Hop Limit field each time they forward a packet, analogous to the Time to Live (TTL) field in IPv4, discarding the packet if the value ever reaches zero. The source and destination addresses are both 128 bits in IPv6, four times as large as the address fields used in IPv4. Therefore, the required IPv6 header is a constant 40 bytes; however, the optional extension header fields can make the overall header considerably larger.

Figure 2.5
IP version 4 (IPv4)
datagram format.

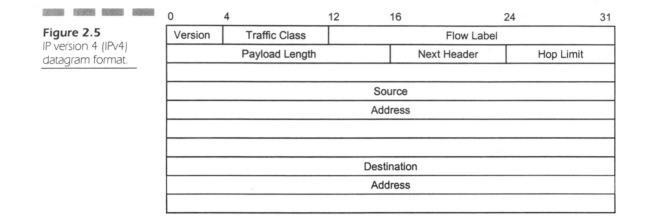

The Language of Routed Internetworks

Let's first review some basic LAN and internetworking terminology of bridging and routing with reference to Figure 2.6, based upon RFC 1932 [10].

A *host* (sometimes called an End System(ES)) delivers and receives IP packets to and from other hosts. A host does not relay packets. Examples of hosts are workstations, personal computers and servers.

A *router* (sometimes called an Intermediate System(IS)) also delivers and receives IP packets, but also relays IP packets between end and intermediate systems. Internet service providers (ISPs) and large enterprises often utilize routers made by companies like Cisco, 3Com, Ascend, Lucent, Nortel, and others.

All members of an *IP subnet* can directly transmit packets to each other. There may be repeaters, hubs, bridges, or switches between the physical interfaces of IP subnet members. Ethernet or Token Ring LANs are examples of an IP subnet. However, multiple Ethernets bridged together may also be a subnet. The assignment of IP addresses and subnet masks determines the specific subnet boundaries.

Bridging makes two or more physically disjoint LAN media appear as a single bridged IP subnet. Bridging implementations occur at the Medium Access Control (MAC) level or via a proxy Address Resolution Protocol (ARP).

A *broadcast subnet* allows any system to transmit the same packet to all other systems in the subnet. An Ethernet LAN is an example of a broadcast subnet.

A *multicast-capable subnet* provides a facility that enables a system to send packets to a subset of the subnet members. For example, an

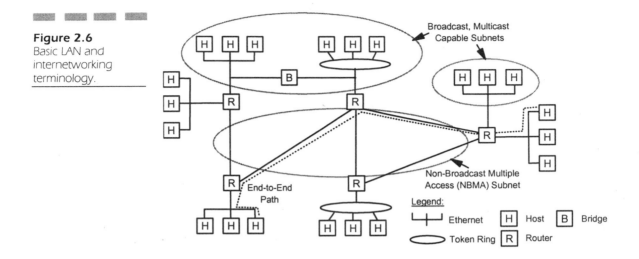

Figure 2.6
*Basic LAN and
internetworking
terminology.*

Ethernet segment or a full mesh of ATM point-to-multipoint connections provides this capability.

A *non-broadcast multiple access (NBMA) subnet* does not support a convenient multi-destination connectionless delivery capability that broadcast and multicast capable subnetworks do. A set of point-to-point ATM connections is an example of an NBMA subnet.

An *internetwork* is a concatenation of networks, often employing different media and lower-level encapsulations, that form an integrated larger network supporting communication between hosts. Figure 2.6 illustrates a relatively small internet when judged in comparison with *the* Internet, which has over 50,000 networks.

The term *network* may refer to a piece of Ethernet cable or to a collection of many devices internetworked across a large geographic area sharing a coordinated addressing scheme.

Vendors of intermediate and end systems strive to implement an efficient process for deciding what to do with a received packet. Possible decisions are local delivery, or forwarding the packet onto another external interface. *IP forwarding* is the process of deciding what to do with a received IP packet. IP forwarding may also require replacement or modification of the media layer encapsulation when transitioning between different LAN media.

IP routing involves the exchange of topology information that enables systems to make IP forwarding decisions that cause packets to advance along an end-to-end path toward a destination. Sometimes routing is also called a *topology distribution protocol.* We cover this important topic in Part 6.

An *end-to-end path* is an arbitrary number of routers and subnets over which two hosts communicate; for example, as illustrated by the dashed line in Figure 2.6. Routers implement this path by the process of IP forwarding at each node as determined by an IP routing algorithm.

An *IP Address Resolution Protocol (ARP)* provides a quasi-static mapping between an IP address and the media address on the local subnet.

Scalability refers to the ability of routing and address resolution protocols to support a large number of subnets, as well as handle the dynamics of a large internetwork. In networks with large numbers of interconnected subnets, routers must exchange large amounts of topology data and store the resultant forwarding information in high-speed memory. Furthermore, as network size increases, so does the likelihood that some network elements are changing state, thus creating the need to update routing topology information. Hence, scalability impacts the required processing power and storage for the implementation of routing protocols within routers.

Anatomy of a Router

Routers implement several interrelated functions, as illustrated in Figure 2.7. Starting on the left-hand side of the figure, routers interface to a variety of LAN or WAN media, encapsulating and converting between link layer protocols as necessary. Thus, routers naturally interconnect Ethernet, Token Ring, FDDI, frame relay, and ATM networks.

The principal function of a router is packet forwarding, often implemented in hardware in high performance machines. The packet-forwarding function contains a lookup table that identifies the physical interface of the next hop toward the destination based upon the high-order bits contained in the received packet's destination address. The connectionless paradigm requires that each network node (e.g., a router) process each packet independently. Common per-packet

Figure 2.7
Functions and interfaces of a router.

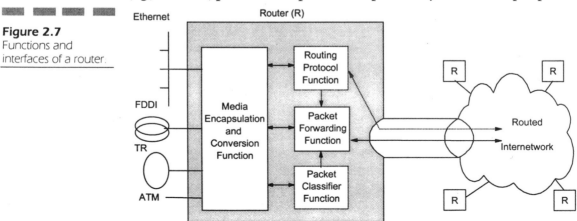

processing functions required in real networks include: classifying packets based upon addresses and other header fields like the diffserv/TOS byte, queuing different packet flows for prioritized service, and data link layer conversions. Older routers implemented this complex processing in software, which limits throughput. Practically, using filtering to implement a firewall can limit router throughput significantly; however, new hardware-based routers avoid these bottlenecks.

Routers employ routing protocols to dynamically obtain knowledge of the location of address prefixes across the entire routed internetwork. The routing protocol engine fills in the next hop forwarding table in the packet-forwarding function. Routing protocols determine the next hop based upon specific criteria, such as least cost, minimum delay, or minimum distance. Thus, the routing algorithm determines the best way to reach the destination address. As studied in Part 6, a commonly used solution to this problem assigns each link in a network a *cost,* and then employs a routing algorithm to find the least-cost routes. This cost may be economic, or may reflect some other information about the link, such as the delay or throughput.

Thus, routing protocols discover network topology changes and flood these throughout the network. Once a router receives the updated topology data, it recovers from link or nodal failures by updating the forwarding tables. Routers employ protocols to continually monitor the state of the links that interconnect routers in a network, or the links with other networks.

Connection-Oriented Packet Switching

This section reviews the basic capabilities and operation of connection-oriented packet switching used by various protocols. Here, the emphasis is on the factors that differ from the connectionless paradigm.

Label Switching

ATM and the IETF's MultiProtocol Label Switching (MPLS) use the technique of label (sometimes also called address) switching. Instead of the packet having the same header at every hop, the label-switching technique potentially changes the label portion of the header at every hop. Label switching operates on a data stream in which the data is organized into packets, each with a header and a payload. The header contains label information used in switching decisions at each node to progress the packet towards the destination on a hop-by-hop basis. The label determines the physical output to which the switch directs the packet, along with any translation of the label.

Figure 2.8 illustrates four interconnected label switches, each with two inputs and two outputs. Packets (either fixed or variable in length) arrive at the inputs as shown on the left-hand side of the figure with labels indicated by letters in the header symbolized by the white square prior to each shaded payload. The figure carries the payload shading through the switching operations from left to right to allow the reader to trace the result of label switching visually. Within each node, the input label indexes into a table using the entries in column In@. The matching entry identifies the label for use on output in the column titled Out@, along with the physical output port on which to send the packet in the column titled Port. For example, switch 1 receives a packet on port 0 with label A and outputs the packet on port 1, using a new label M. Conceptually, each switch functions as a pair of busses that connect to the output port buffers. Each switch queues packets or cells destined for a particular output port, and then transmits them according to a particular priority and scheduling paradigm described in Chapter 10. This buffering reduces the probability of loss when contention occurs for the same output

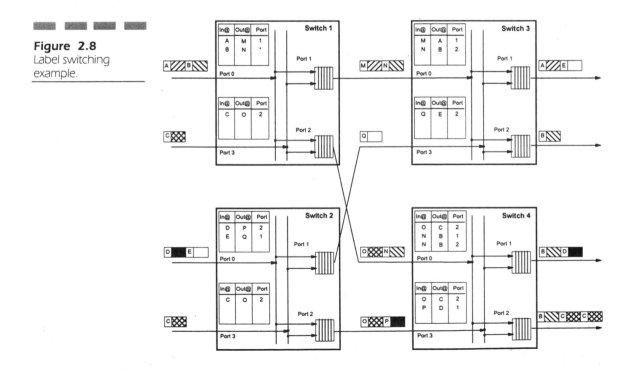

Figure 2.8
Label switching
example.

port. Chapters 11 and 12 present an analysis of the loss probability due to buffer overflow for the principal types of switch architectures used in high-performance routers and ATM switches. At the next switch, the same process repeats until the packets reach the target output on the right-hand side of the figure.

The figure illustrates all possible connection topologies: point-to-point, point-to-multipoint, multipoint-to-point, and multipoint-to-multipoint. The example illustrates these topologies as follows. The packets with labels A and D into port 0 on switch 1, and E into port 0 on switch 2 all form point-to-point connections. The packet labeled B into port 0 on switch 1 forms a point-to-multipoint connection. The packets labeled C on port 3 switch 1 and C on port 3 of switch 2 form a multipoint-to-point connection.

As described in the next section, ATM switches call the label a Virtual Path/Virtual Channel Identifier (VPI/VCI). Currently, label switching operates at link speeds of up to 10 Gbps for packet and ATM cell-switching systems. Of course, label switching and multiplexing is at the heart of high-performance routers and ATM switches [11, 12]. Contemporary router and ATM switch fabric designs scale to total capacities in excess of one trillion bits per second using label switching.

Asynchronous Transfer Mode (ATM) Cell

Figure 2.9 illustrates the format of the 53-byte ATM cell at the User-Network Interface (UNI). The cell header contains a label significant only to the local interface in two parts: an 8-bit Virtual Path Identifier (VPI) and a 16-bit Virtual Channel Identifier (VCI). The cell header also contains a 4-bit Generic Flow Control (GFC), 3-bit Payload Type (PT), and a 1-bit Cell Loss Priority (CLP) indicator. An 8-bit Header Error Check (HEC) field protects the entire header from errors. A fundamental concept of ATM is that switching occurs based upon the VPI/VCI label fields of *each* cell. Switching done on the VPI only is called a Virtual Path Connection (VPC), while switching done on both the VPI/VCI values is called a Virtual Channel Connection (VCC).

The ATM cell at the Network-Node Interface (NNI) is identical to the UNI format with two exceptions. First, there is no Generic Flow Control (GFC) field. Second, the NNI uses the 4 bits used for the GFC at the UNI to increase the VPI field to 12 bits at the NNI, as compared to 8 bits at the UNI.

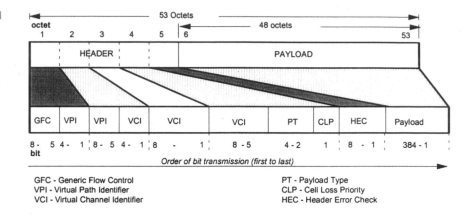

Figure 2.9
ATM cell structure at the User-Network Interface (UNI).

MultiProtocol Label Switching (MPLS) Label

An IETF draft specifies the stand-alone 4-byte MPLS packet *label* as shown in Figure 2.10 [13]. The Point-to-Point protocol (PPP) and Ethernet use this label format. The IETF MPLS working group is also defining other forms of labels; for example, direct use of the ATM VPI/VCI fields. The contents of the label give some insight into the eventual capabilities of the anticipated MPLS standard. The 20-bit label value is the index used in the forwarding table. In early drafts of the MPLS work, the 3-bit experimental field was defined as a Class of Service (COS) field. This function is now handled in the diffserv reuse of the IP header's TOS field. The experimental field can be used to implement other traffic management and QoS functions described in this book, like conformance marking, discard priority indication, or congestion indication. The Stack (S) bit indicates the last label prior to the packet header. The MPLS device only processes the label at the top of the stack (i.e., the outermost label if there is more than one label present). MPLS supports hierarchical networks by prefixing packets with multiple labels, a topic covered in more detail in Chapter 19. Finally, the 8-bit Time to Live (TTL) parameter provides a means for loop detection and removal of old packets.

Figure 2.10
MultiProtocol Label Switching (MPLS) four-byte label.

Four byte MPLS Label			
Label Value	Experimental	Stack (S)	Time To Live (TTL)
20	3	1	8	bits

Benefits and Liabilities of Virtual Connections

The connection-oriented paradigm establishes a path between the origin and destination before transferring any data. The network establishes a connection as a path of one or multiple links through intermediate nodes in a network. Once established, all data travels over the same pre-established path through the network. The fact that data arrives at the destination in the same order as sent by the origin is fundamental to connection-oriented services.

If network management or provisioning actions establish the connection and leave it up indefinitely, then we call the result a Permanent Virtual Connection (PVC). If control signaling dynamically establishes and releases the connection, then we call it a Switched Virtual Connection (SVC).

Virtual connections are familiar to many engineers and network managers from experience with telephony and private-line-based data networks. The connection-oriented paradigm straightforwardly reserves capacity to ensure QoS. It simply tries the available paths to the destination, blocking the attempt only if all routes are busy. Accurately metering usage in terms of the duration of the connection and the amount of data transferred is also straightforward. Finally, performance estimation of the actual QoS delivered and diagnosis of performance issues is easier than in connectionless networks.

Virtual connections also have some liabilities. A principal disadvantage of the connection-oriented paradigm is the complexity and processing expense involved in implementing the PVC and SVC control protocols. In addition, virtual connections reserve capacity even if the parties involved in the call transfer no information. Finally, in order to statistically guarantee QoS, connection-oriented protocols must block new call attempts during periods of overload.

Review

This chapter introduced some basic concepts of TDM networks and circuit switching as background for the connection-oriented ATM switching technique. It then described the connectionless forwarding paradigm employed by the Internet. The material presented included the IP packet headers and the meanings of important fields within them. The coverage then moved on to the concept of label switching employed in ATM and IP networks. The text defined both the ATM cell and MPLS headers.

References

[1]   W. Goralski, *SONET*, McGraw-Hill, 1997.

[2]   J. Turner, "Design of an Integrated Services Packet Network," *IEEE Transactions on Communications*, November 1986.

[3]   G. Held, R. Sarch, *Data Communications*, McGraw-Hill, 1995.

[4]   R. Dayton, *Telecommunications*, McGraw-Hill, 1991.

[5]   J. Postel, *Internet Protocol*, RFC 791, IETF, September 1981.

[6]   F. Baker, *Requirements for IP Version 4 Routers*, RFC 1812, IETF, June 1995.

[7]   K. Nichols, S. Blake, F. Baker, D. Black, *Definition of the Differentiated Services Field (DS Field) in the IPv4 and IPv6 Headers*, RFC 2474, December 1998.

[8]   S. Blake, D. Black, M. Carlson, E. Davies, Z. Wang, W. Weiss, *An Architecture for Differentiated Services*, RFC 2475, December 1998.

[9]   S. Deering, R. Hinden, *Internet Protocol, Version 6 (IPv6) Specification*, IETF, RFC2460 , December 1998.

[10]   R. Cole, D. Shur, C. Villamizar, *IP over ATM: A Framework Document*, RFC 1932, IETF, April 1996.

[11]   P. Newman, "ATM Technology for Corporate Networks," *IEEE Communications Magazine*, April 1992.

[12]   R. Awdeh, H. Mouftah, "Survey of ATM Switch Architectures," *Computer Networks and ISDN Systems*, Number 27, 1995.

[13]   E. Rosen, Y. Rekhter, D. Tappan, D. Farinacci, G. Fedorkow, T. Li, A. Conta, *MPLS Label Stack Encoding*, draft-ietf-mpls-label-encaps-03.txt.

CHAPTER 3

Capacity, Throughput, and Traffic Levels

"Give me a lever long enough, and a fulcrum strong enough, and single-handed I can move the world."

— Archimedes

How can end users and network designers quantify and agree on the level of traffic support required? The answer takes the form of a contract between the user and the network regarding capacity. This chapter summarizes commonly used terminology and methods used to define the capacity and throughput of IP routers and ATM switches. First, the chapter defines communication channel bandwidth and transmission capacity. Next, we introduce the concepts of bottlenecks and throughput. The treatment then details the efficiency of packet- and cell-based switching.

The text then moves on to define measures frequently employed in quantifying traffic levels. These include parameters like the peak rate, average rate, and the burst duration. Finally, this chapter describes the means to accurately measure these traffic parameters. Specifically, we cover the IETF's token bucket, the ATM leaky bucket, and the way in which they interoperate.

Bandwidth, Capacity, Bottlenecks, Throughput, and Efficiency

This section defines the basic terminology and concepts involved in communication networks. First, we describe how the spectral bandwidth and modulation scheme used on a transmission link determines the link capacity. Along an end-to-end path, the smallest link capacity determines the bottleneck, and hence the end-to-end path capacity. Next, the operation of the protocol in conjunction with the bottleneck determine the actual throughput available to the end user. Finally, the manner in which the switch or router encapsulates information determines link-level efficiency.

Bandwidth and Link Capacity

Some books and articles erroneously equate the term *bandwidth* with the capacity of a transmission link. Strictly speaking, this is not accurate. Let's see why this is so. The simplest signal is a pulse of electromagnetic energy, for example, a laser transmitting over an optical fiber. The presence of light represents a binary 1, while the absence of light represents a binary 0. Figure 3.1a shows the time domain representation of such a on/off pulsed signal mapping the input sequence of ones and zeros into either a transmitted pulse or the absence of a pulse, respectively, once every T seconds. The *capacity* of this transmission link is R=1/T bits per second. Communication engineers define the waveform transmitted every T seconds as a *baud*. Since each waveform (i.e., either a pulse or nothing) transmitted on the channel in our simple example conveys exactly one bit, the baud rate of this system is also R. In some systems, the bit rate is much greater than the baud rate. For example, modern analog modems transmit over 8 bits per baud interval to achieve rates greater than 32 kbps over a standard 4 kHz telephone line [1]. Note that the baud rate of the transmission link is always less than or equal to the bit rate.

The power spectral density, or frequency spectrum for short, is the Fourier transform in the frequency domain of a random time domain signal [2, 3, 4]. Communications engineers define frequencies in a measure defined in terms of the number of complete sinusoidal cycles of an electromagnetic wave in a 1-s interval. The unit of Hertz (abbreviated Hz) corresponds to one sinusoidal cycle per second. Common alternating current (AC) power systems in the United States operate at 60 Hz. Although some texts and publications use the term *bandwidth* to refer to the bit rate (i.e., capacity) of a transmission link, note that communication engineers use the term *bandwidth* to refer to the *frequency passband* of a particular signal.

Figure 3.1b illustrates the frequency spectrum for the binary on/off signal used on fiber optic transmission links. Binary on/off keying does not make efficient use of the available frequency passband. As indicated on the figure, the bandwidth of the central spectral lobe is four times the source bit rate R=1/T. Furthermore, at frequencies equal to three times the source bit rate, the energy is still over 5 percent (-13 dB) below the peak signal power level. For a particular absolute signal-to-noise ratio, x, the SNR in decibels is computed as SNR=10 log(x). For example, x=2 corresponds to roughly 3 dB, x=4 corresponds to approximately 6 dB, x=10 corresponds to 10 dB, and so on. The frequency *sidelobes* from one signal's spectrum can interfere with signals in adjacent frequency bands. Hence, shrewd designers use more spectrally contained signals in band-limited circumstances.

However, on optical fiber systems available spectrum is frequently less of a concern, since each fiber has over 50 trillion Hertz (THz) of available bandwidth. Furthermore, on/off keying is the cheapest means to pulse a laser or light-emitting diode (LED) in an optical communications system. In addition, Dense Wavelength Division

Figure 3.1
Binary on/off signal trace and frequency spectrum.

a. Binary On/Off Keying (OOK) Time Domain Signal

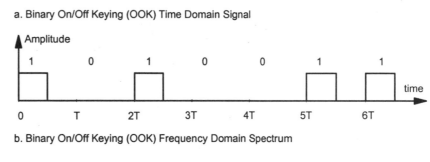

b. Binary On/Off Keying (OOK) Frequency Domain Spectrum

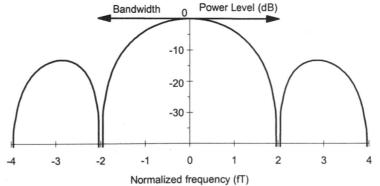

Multiplexing (WDM) promises to deliver significant increases in capacity over long-haul fiber networks [5]. On the other hand, radio frequency spectrum is a limited resource, and hence wireless networks employ more bandwidth-efficient transmission schemes.

Bottlenecks and Path Capacity

An end-to-end path is made of a series of nodes connected by links, as shown in Figure 3.2. A common convention is to designate the pipes connecting the hosts to the switch/router nodes as *access links* and the pipes interconnecting switch/router nodes as *trunk links*, as indicated in the figure. The figure indicates the relative capacity of each link by the size of the pipe. In this case, the link with the smallest capacity is the bottleneck, as indicated in the figure.

Note that a number of resource types may be the bottleneck in a communication network, for example:

- Transmission link capacity
- Router packet forwarding rate
- Specialized resource (e.g., tone receiver) availability
- Call processor rate
- Buffer capacity

Generally, for an end-to-end path, the smallest link bottleneck determines the path capacity for a particular resource type.

Path Capacity and Throughput

Although related, capacity and throughput are not the same. *Capacity* is the maximum rate at which the communication network can transfer data. *Throughput* is a measure of how much data the network actually delivers between end applications. Throughput is always less than or equal to capacity. As described in Chapter 15, the interaction of the closed-loop flow control implemented in IP's Transmission

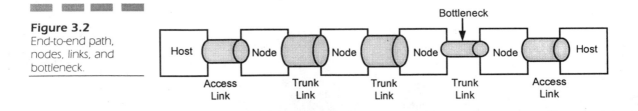

Figure 3.2
End-to-end path, nodes, links, and bottleneck.

Control Protocol (TCP) can have a significant impact on throughput.

In physical layer, or circuit-based, networks, capacity is usually defined in bits per second (bps). On the other hand, packet- or cell-based networks define capacity defined in units of packets or cells per second instead. Inevitably, packet-based information transfer reduces overall efficiency since a portion of the transmitted data is the header field, as examined in the next section. Furthermore, some implementations have a bottleneck that limits the maximum sustainable transfer rate to a value less than the transmission capacity of the physical transmission link.

Link-Level Efficiency

If the router or switch can transmit at the link rate, then a precise calculation of the link capacity in units of packets or cells per second requires knowledge of the histogram of the packet size distribution. On the other hand, if only the average packet size is available, then we can only estimate the maximum throughput. We compare two cases in the following efficiency analysis:

- Transfer of connectionless data (e.g., IP)
- Connectionless versus connection-oriented transfer of circuit data (e.g., digitized voice)

Efficiency for the Transport of Packet Data

A major criticism leveled against ATM is its inefficient carriage of variable-length packets when compared with the efficiency of a frame-based protocol like High Level Data Link Control (HDLC). A frame-based protocol uses variable-length packets with an overhead of H bytes per packet. Typical values of H used when transporting IP over HDLC ranges from 7 to 13 bytes [1]. HDLC employs a stuffing procedure that increases the line bit rate by a fraction S for nonsynchronous links. HDLC stuffs a zero bit for any sequence of five consecutive ones in the data stream to avoid replicating the six ones in a flag ('01111110'). For random bit patterns, each bit is a one or a zero half the time. Hence, the likelihood of encountering five consecutive ones is one out of 32, or a value of S of approximately 3.1 percent. IP over synchronous links as defined in RFC 1619 [6] uses byte stuffing for the flag character, which results in a value of S of approximately 1 percent (i.e., 1/128) [7].

Therefore, the protocol efficiency for a frame-based protocol using HDLC framing is:

$$\text{HDLC\_Efficiency}(P,S,H) \; = \; \frac{P}{(1+S)\;(P+H)} \tag{3-1}$$

where   P is the packet size expressed in bytes,
          H is the per-packet overhead in bytes,
          S is the bit-stuffing factor.

The majority of ATM networks transporting packet data employ ATM Adaptation Layer 5 (AAL5) [8]. The AAL5 protocol adds 8 bytes of overhead per packet. Additionally, RFC 1483 [9] defines additional 8 bytes of overhead if an ATM Virtual Channel Connection (VCC) carries more than one protocol. Therefore, the per-packet protocol overhead H for AAL5 is either 8 or 16 bytes. Furthermore, AAL5 must generate an integer number of cells for each packet. Each ATM cell has 5 bytes of header overhead for each 48 bytes of payload. Combining these factors results in the following formula for AAL5 link-level efficiency:

$$\text{AAL5\_Efficiency}(P,H) \; = \; \frac{P}{53} \; \left\lceil \frac{P+H}{48} \right\rceil^{-1} \tag{3-2}$$

where $\lceil x \rceil$ is the smallest integer $\geq$x (called the CEILING function in Microsoft Excel),
          P is the packet size expressed in bytes,
          H is the per-packet overhead in bytes.

Thus, if all packets have the same length, we can use Equations (3-1) and (3-2) to compare the link-level efficiency of HDLC with that of an AAL5-based protocol for transporting packet data. Figure 3.3 illustrates the result of such a calculation using S=3.1% and H=7 for an HDLC-based protocol and H=8 bytes for an AAL5-based protocol for a representative range of packet sizes. The saw-toothed-shaped plot for AAL5 results from the roundup to an integer number of cells for each packet. The choice of a 48-byte payload is just right for a typical 40-byte TCP/IP packet only if the 8 bytes of RFC 1483 encapsulation are not used. If multiple protocols are multiplexed over a single AAL5 VCC, then the additional RFC 1483 overhead reduces efficiency markedly, as shown in the figure.

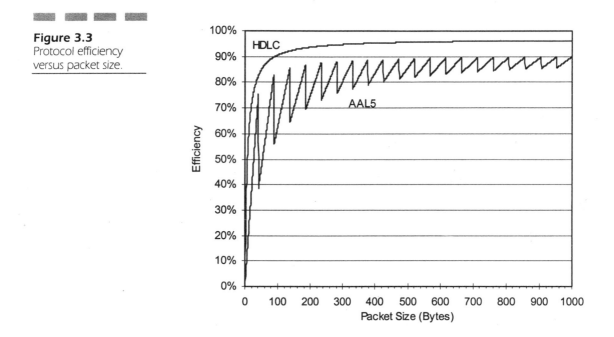

Figure 3.3
Protocol efficiency
versus packet size.

The preceding analysis assumed that each packet had the same size. Real traffic, however, has packets of different sizes, as reported in recent studies of IP network traffic [10]. The average efficiency is then a function of weighting the efficiency of each packet length by the relative frequency or each packet size (i.e., the probability Pr[P]) determined from the histogram of observed packets sizes as follows:

$$\text{Efficiency} \quad = \quad \sum_{P=1}^{\text{Max}} \text{Pr[P]} \quad \text{Efficiency(P)}$$

where the Efficiency(P) represents the formula for protocol P; for example, Equation (3-1) for HDLC and Equation (3-2) for AAL5.

Figure 3.4 shows a spreadsheet calculation implementing the result of this calculation for a representative, but shortened, histogram of IP packet sizes. Note that in many networks approximately 40 to 50 percent of the packets are TCP/IP acknowledgment packets that are exactly 40 bytes long. The majority of packets are less than or equal to the maximum Ethernet frame size of 1500 bytes. Very few packets have lengths greater than 1500 bytes. The actual efficiency is sensitive to the packet size distribution; however, the difference between HDLC and AAL5 networks typically ranges between 10 and 20 percent for typical packet size distributions.

Figure 3.4
Efficiency computed
from relative
frequency of IP packet
sizes.

	A	B	C	D	E
1		S	3.1%		
2		H	7	8	
3					
4	P (Bytes)	Pr[P]	HDLC_Efficiency	AAL5_Efficiency	
5	40	50%	82.5%	75.5%	
6	44	10%	83.7%	41.5%	
7	552	15%	95.8%	86.8%	
8	576	10%	95.8%	83.6%	
9	1500	15%	96.5%	88.4%	
10	=A9/(A9+C$2)/(1+C$1)			=A8/53/CEILING((A8+D$2)/48,1)	
11					
12	Overall Efficiency		88%	77%	
13					
14	=SUMPRODUCT(B5:B9,C5:C9)			=SUMPRODUCT(B5:B9,D5:D9)	

Efficiency for the Transport of Circuit Data

This section compares the link-level efficiency of packetized voice over IP and ATM [1]. The fundamental difference between this case and the case involving transport of IP packet data is that since ATM is connection-oriented, it need not include the IP header in every packet. Furthermore, since ATM supports QoS, it need not transmit a timestamp and sequence number in every packet as IP does in the RTP header, because the receiver can recover timing from the arriving, in-order sequence of cells. ATM defines two methods for supporting voice: AAL1 and AAL2. The analysis considers cells partially filled to 20 octets for direct comparison with IP and frame relay, as well as completely filled cells. Voice over IP and voice over frame relay support a range of coding techniques; hence, the packet sizes differ markedly for these techniques. Of course, silence suppression applies in a comparable manner to all of these approaches. The PPP protocol allows voice over IP to compress the IP and User Datagram Protocol (UDP) headers on an access line to 6 bytes, as indicated in the table. Indeed, without this header compression, IP Telephony loses much of its attractive attributes on access lines. Note that the sequence number and timestamp information conveyed by Real Time Protocol (RTP) comprise approximately one-half of the overhead. However, the routers in the Internet backbone and the destination gateway require the complete larger header size for packet forwarding and voice conversion at the destination. Table 3.1 shows the overhead (in bytes) incurred by each approach, the packet size, and the resulting efficiency.

In conclusion, ATM looks attractive for transporting voice on access lines from an efficiency point of view, while IP with PPP header

TABLE 3.1

Voice over packet and
cell efficiency analysis.

Overhead	Voice over AAL1	Voice over AAL2	Voice over IP Access	Voice over IP Backbone
AAL	1-2	3-4		
ATM	5	5		
IP			6	40
UDP				8
RTP			12	12
HDLC			6-8	6-8
FR				
Total Overhead	6-7	8-9	24-26	66-68
Packet Size	20-47	20-44	20-50	20-50
Efficiency	38%-89%	38%-85%	37%-59%	23%-41%
Voice Bit Rate (kbps)	6-32	6-32	6-32	6-32

compression provides acceptable efficiency on dial-up lines or lower-speed access circuits. However, as noted in Chapter 5, on lower-speed links, long data frames impose problems in achieving QoS.

Source Traffic Characteristics

There are two basic philosophies for characterizing source traffic parameters: deterministic and random. These approaches often embody a tradeoff between accuracy and simplicity.

Deterministic models use specific parameters in conjunction with a specific function that determines whether a particular arrival pattern conforms to a traffic specification. The IP token bucket and ATM leaky bucket precisely define the worst-case arrival pattern of a sequence of packets or cells, respectively. Thus, the deterministic traffic model clearly bounds the source characteristics in a measurable, repeatable, and unambiguous way. Unfortunately, accurately characterizing a source and formulating these parameters can be rather complicated.

The other philosophy for modeling source behavior utilizes random (also called probabilistic or stochastic) models for traffic parameters. Usually, random model parameters correspond to measurable long-term averages. However, a random model also describes the statistics of a source's short-term behavior. While these statistical methods are not standardized, they are useful approximations. These methods are useful in analysis when employing a simple statistical model, as shown in Parts 3 and 4. This section now defines some traffic parameters commonly used to describe the behavior of voice, video, and data sources in IP and ATM networks.

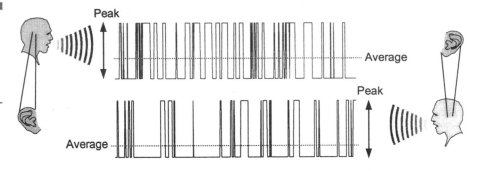

Figure 3.5
Example of peak and
average rates
resulting from a two-
way voice
conversation.

Peak and Average Rate

A source may send at a peak rate, limited by transmission speed of the physical link or other mechanisms, such as traffic shaping or processor speed. Typically, we express the rate in bits/second for physical transmission links, packets/second for frame-based protocols like IP, or cells/second for ATM networks. Usually, the peak rate is equivalent to a short-term measurement corresponding to a small number of packets or cells. A longer-term average corresponds to the average rate.

Figure 3.5 shows an example of a voice conversation that gives an illustration of how peak and average rates capture the essence of actual communication network traffic. Often, when talking on the telephone one party speaks while the other listens. There are, however, instances when we interrupt each other, or make brief comments while the other person speaks as a part of normal interactive conversation. The two traces in the figure depict the transmission of speech in each direction at a peak rate when one person is talking and the other is listening over the duration of a short telephone call. Typically, the peak rate on TDM-based digital telephone systems is 64 kbps, as described in Chapter 2. The figure shows the average transmission rate over the duration of the call as a horizontal line. In this example, the person in the upper part of the figure talked approximately twice as much as the one in the lower part of the figure.

Burstiness and Source Activity Probability

Burstiness is another measure of source traffic. Traffic engineers call a source that sends traffic at markedly different rates at different times bursty, while a source that always sends at the same rate is nonbursty. A simple measure of burstiness is the ratio of peak-to-average rate of traffic over a specific sampling period, as specified by the following equation:

$$\text{Burstiness} = \frac{\text{Peak Rate}}{\text{Average Rate}}$$

This simple measure captures only a portion of the source's traffic characteristics. For example, the traffic from two sources could have the same peak-to-average ratio, but have quite different characteristics in terms of the time scale of the traffic bursts. We will analyze other definitions of burstiness later in this book, beginning with the burst duration as described in the next section.

The *source activity probability* is a measure of how frequently the source sends, defined by the following formula:

$$\text{Source Activity Probability} = \frac{1}{\text{Burstiness}} = \frac{\text{Average Rate}}{\text{Peak Rate}}$$

For example, if a source has a peak rate of 10 Mbps and an average rate of 500 kbps; then the traffic source has a burstiness factor of 20. Alternatively, the source activity probability is only 5%. Typically, Local Area Network (LAN) users exhibit burstiness on the order of 10 to 100, or more. In other words, they use the LAN at the peak rate less than 10% of the time. Usually, burstiness approaches unity if the source aggregates the outputs from many individual users. Such is often the case in Wide Area Network (WAN) backbone networks. For example, a router connecting a medium-to-large enterprise to the Internet aggregates the traffic flowing to and from many individual workstations. In these situations, the burstiness often approaches 1 during the busiest hours of the workday. On the other hand, the burstiness of a dial-up connection for an individual Internet user can vary widely depending upon the application. If the user is downloading a large file, then the burstiness in the network-to-user direction approaches 1; that is, the activity is continuous. Note that a casual Web surfer may generate traffic that has a burstiness factor of 10 or more!

Burst Duration

Generally, the data stream generated by many sources has a statistically predictable on-off pattern. The intervals of time that a source can generate data are a result of many factors. For example, a person can only speak for so long before he or she must take a breath. Many computer communication protocols have a maximum window, which limits the amount of data that can be sent without acknowledgement. Sometimes, the network may limit the maximum duration of a burst to ensure that it can deliver the desired service quality.

Continuing the above example, note that the specification of a source with a peak rate of 10 Mbps and an average rate of 500 kbps is incomplete. For example, a source that sends a 500,000-bit burst once a second has the same average rate as a source that sends 500-bit bursts 1,000 times a second. Thus, a complete traffic specification must also quantify the burst duration in addition to the peak and average rates.

Statistical Multiplexing

Traffic engineers call the action of combining the outputs from many variable-rate sources into one data stream *statistical multiplexing*. Figure 3.6 illustrates example plots of the activity of a number of sources: bulk data, interactive data, video, and voice. Each has a peak and average rate and burst duration as defined earlier in this section. The trace at the bottom of the figure shows the resulting aggregate bit rate resulting from adding the output of the various sources. Note how the statistically multiplexed data stream only reaches the peak rate a small fraction of the time. This is the basis for networks providing statistical guarantees on QoS. Namely, when aggregating

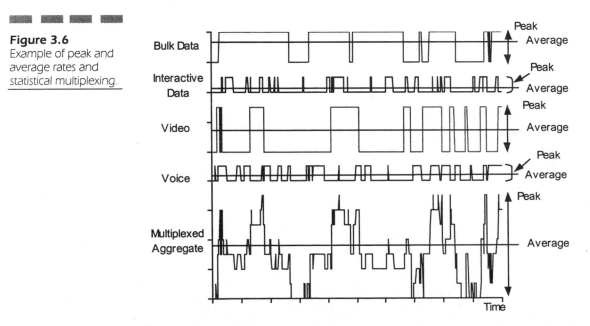

Figure 3.6
Example of peak and average rates and statistical multiplexing.

enough traffic the probability of arriving traffic exceeding allocated resources can be statistically predicted with high confidence. Chapter 12 covers this effect and the topic of statistical multiplexing in detail.

Measuring and Monitoring Traffic Parameters

Recall the old adage about how different people describe a glass containing a fluid volume equal to 50 percent of its capacity. Some say that the glass is half full, while others say that it is half empty. An analogous situation exists between the deterministic methods defined for IP and ATM when specifying and measuring traffic parameters. Fortunately, although these are different points of view, we can reconcile them to an objective viewpoint similar to that of observing the level of fluid in a glass.

In the Internet, a bucket collects tokens that control the average transmission rate and burst duration. The network periodically adds tokens to the bucket(s) corresponding to each flow at a rate determined by the traffic parameters. If a token bucket is full, nothing adverse happens — it simply means that the source hasn't transmitted any data in a while and has a full set of token permissions to transmit once it becomes active again. On the other hand, in ATM, arriving cells fill a logical set of buckets, which leak at a rate as specified by the traffic parameters. If an arriving cell would overflow any of the buckets, then the network considers the cell noncompliant to the traffic parameters. Confused? Let's examine each of these methods in more detail via some examples and then map their measurement methods and conformance determination back to the generic traffic parameters of peak rate, average rate, and burst duration described in the previous section.

IP's Token Bucket Algorithm

The Internet's Resource reSerVation Protocol (RSVP) [11, 12, 13] uses the token bucket algorithm to describe traffic parameters corresponding to a specific flow of IP packets. Two parameters completely specify the token bucket: an average rate r and a bucket depth b. RFC 2215 [13] defines the token-controlled average rate r as the number of bytes of IP datagrams per second permitted by the token bucket. The maximum value of r can be 40 terabytes per second. RFC 2215 defines the bucket depth b in units of bytes with values ranging from 1 byte to 250 gigabytes. The RFCs intentionally specify a large range for these parameters to support capacities achievable in future network.

Figure 3.7 depicts the basic operation of the token bucket algorithm [14, 15]. Conceptually, a device measures the conformance of a sequence of packet arrivals using the token bucket that contains up to b bytes worth of tokens. The device adds tokens to the bucket at a rate of r bytes per second, as shown in the figure. An arriving packet conforms to the token bucket traffic specification if the level of the tokens in the bucket equals or exceeds the packet length. Specifically, when a packet arrives, the device checks the current level of tokens in the bucket X against the length L of the arriving packet. If X≤L, then the packet conforms to the token bucket traffic specification; otherwise, the packet is nonconforming. Normally, conforming packets remove the number of tokens (i.e., bytes) equal to their length. Nonconforming packets do not remove any tokens. Typically, a network guarantees QoS for only conforming packets because resources are allocated based upon the traffic parameters.

The basic effect of the token bucket parameters r and b is that the amount of data sent D(T) over any interval of time T obeys the rule:

$$D(T) \le rT+b \qquad\qquad (3\text{-}3)$$

Since Equation (3-3) limits the maximum amount of data that can arrive over an interval T via a linear function, some experts dub the resulting deterministic process a Linearly Bounded Arrival Process (LBAP) [16]. The above rule also means that the actual average rate A(T) over a time interval T is actually somewhat greater than r, namely:

$$A(T) = D(T)/T = r+b/T \qquad\qquad (3\text{-}4)$$

Note from Equation (3-4) that as T→∞ the actual rate A(T) approaches the desired rate r asymptotically.

The full RSVP traffic specification starts with the token bucket specification and adds three additional parameters: a *minimum-policed unit* m, a *maximum packet size* M, and a *peak rate* p. The packet size parameters, m and M, include the application data and all protocol headers at or above the IP level (e.g., IP, TCP, UDP, RTP, etc.). They exclude the link-level header size.

The minimum-policed unit requires that the device remove at least m token bytes for each conforming packet. The parameter m also allows the device to compute the peak packet-processing rate as b/m. It also bounds the link-level efficiency by H/(H+m) for a link-level header of H bytes.

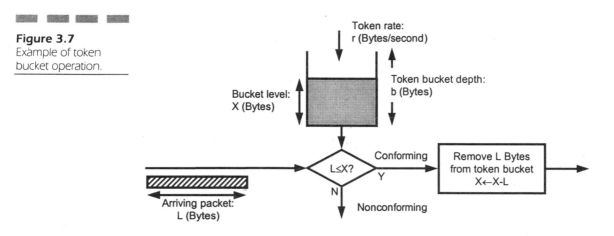

Figure 3.7
Example of token
bucket operation.

The maximum packet size M determines the largest permissible size of a conforming packet. In other words, any arriving packet with a length greater than M bytes is nonconforming. Of course, the inequality M≥m must hold.

The measure for the peak traffic rate p is also bytes of IP datagrams per second, with the same range and encoding as the token bucket parameter r. When the peak rate equals the link rate, a node may immediately forward packets that conform to the token bucket parameters. For peak rate values less than the link rate, a leaky bucket shaper following the token bucket conformance checking ensures that the transmitted data D(T) over any interval of time T satisfies the following inequality:

$$D(T) \leq Min[pT+M, rT+b] \tag{3-5}$$

Figure 3.8 depicts the block diagram model for a token bucket with parameters r and b operating in conjunction with a peak rate shaper with parameters p and M. The shaping buffer must be of size b bytes to admit a burst of packets conforming to the token bucket. The

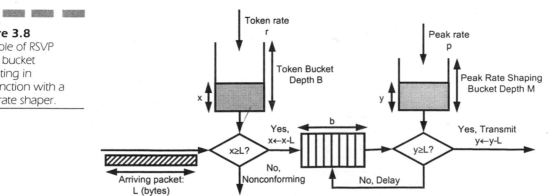

Figure 3.8
Example of RSVP
token bucket
operating in
conjunction with a
peak rate shaper.

peak rate shaper only operates on packets conforming to the token bucket parameters.

The next example illustrates a worst-case example of how the peak rate shaper affects the scheduling of packet transmission with reference to Figure 3.9. Starting on the left-hand side at t=0, the peak rate shaper bucket contains M tokens. A conforming packet of maximum length M arrives from the token bucket, followed shortly thereafter by the arrival of another conforming packet of length L. The peak rate shaper transmits the maximum-length packet at the line rate R, which requires M/R seconds. The peak rate shaper must now wait until the token bucket contains enough tokens to begin transmitting the packet of length L. Since the shaper bucket fills at the peak rate p, the required level is L minus the number of tokens that will arrive during transmission of the L byte packet, as indicated in the figure.

The peak rate shaper delays the transmission of the next packet of length L in order to satisfy Equation (3-5). This means that pT+M=L+M, which implies that T=L/p, the time required to transmit a packet at the peak rate. Noting that T=W+L/R as well, results in the solution that the shaper may have to wait up to W seconds before transmitting the next packet of length L as follows:

$$ W \; = \; \frac{L}{p} \; - \; \frac{L}{R} $$

Shaping implies that some arriving packets must wait in order to comply with traffic parameters specified by the peak and average rate and the maximum burst duration.

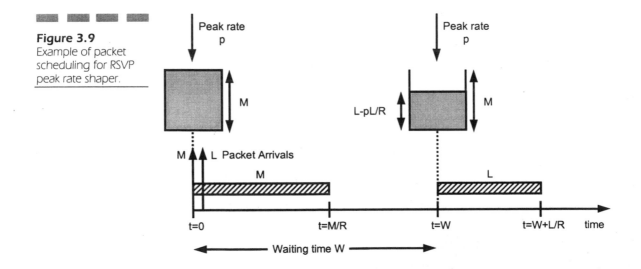

Figure 3.9
Example of packet scheduling for RSVP peak rate shaper.

ATM Traffic Parameters

The ATM traffic contract is an agreement between a user and a network, where the network guarantees a specified QoS — *if and only if* the user's cell flow conforms to a negotiated set of traffic parameters. The ATM traffic descriptor employs the following traffic contract parameters [17] to capture intrinsic source traffic characteristics:

- A mandatory Peak Cell Rate (PCR) in cells/second in conjunction with a CDV Tolerance (CDVT) in seconds
- An optional Sustainable Cell Rate (SCR) in cells/second (always less than or equal to PCR) in conjunction with a Maximum Burst Size (MBS) in cells

Figure 3.10 illustrates these traffic contract parameters in greater detail for a worst-case, bursty traffic scenario:

- Peak Cell Rate (PCR) = 1/T in units of cells/second, where T is the minimum intercell spacing in seconds (i.e., the time interval from the first bit of one cell to the first bit of the next cell).
- Cell Delay Variation Tolerance (CDVT) = τ in seconds. Normally,

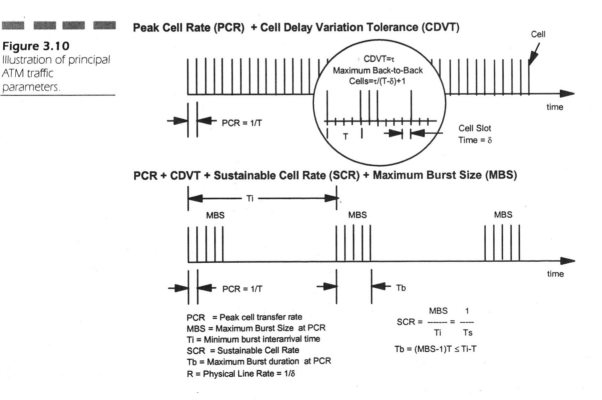

Figure 3.10
Illustration of principal ATM traffic parameters.

the network specifies this traffic parameter as a function of the line rate as defined in ITU-T Recommendation I.371 [18]. The number of cells that can be sent back-to-back at the physical interface rate $R=\delta^{-1}$ is $\tau/(T-\delta)+1$.

■ Sustainable Cell Rate (SCR) $=1/T_s$ is the rate that a bursty, on-off traffic source can send. The worst case is a source sending MBS cells at the peak rate for the burst duration T_b, as depicted in Figure 3.10.

■ Maximum Burst Size (MBS) is the maximum number of consecutive cells that a source can send at the peak rate. A Burst Tolerance (BT) parameter, formally called τ_s (in units of seconds), defines MBS in conjunction with the PCR and SCR cell rate parameters.

The MBS in units of cells is defined in terms of the burst tolerance τ_s and the inverse of SCR T_s as follows [17]:

$$\text{MBS} \equiv \left\lfloor 1 + \frac{\tau_s}{T_s - T} \right\rfloor$$

where $\lfloor x \rfloor$ is the integer part of x.

ATM standards specify use of the *leaky bucket* algorithm to determine conformance of an arriving cell stream to the above traffic parameters in an action called *Usage Parameter Control* (UPC). Standards also refer to this technique as *policing*. A leaky bucket algorithm in the network checks conformance of a cell flow from the user by conceptually pouring a cup of fluid for each cell into two buckets. One bucket has a depth proportional to CDVT leaking at a rate corresponding to the PCR, while the second has a depth defined by MBS leaking at a rate corresponding to the SCR. If the addition of any cup of cell fluid would cause a bucket to overflow, then the cell arrival is *nonconforming*, and its fluid is not added to the bucket. The next section formally defines the leaky bucket algorithm.

An increasing amount of ATM user equipment and switches also implement traffic shaping according to the above parameters. Traffic shaping ensures that the cell stream generated by an ATM device for a particular connection conforms to the traffic contract so that the network doesn't discard violating cells. Traffic shaping implementations operate at either the peak rate only, or at the combined peak and sustainable rates subject to a maximum burst size. Shaping is also useful when interconnecting networks to ensure that traffic exiting one network conforms to the traffic contract with the next network down the line.

ATM's Leaky Bucket Algorithm

The leaky bucket algorithm precisely defines the meaning of conformance to a set of traffic parameters. The leaky bucket analogy refers to a bucket with a hole in the bottom that causes it to "leak" at a certain rate corresponding to a traffic parameter (e.g., PCR or SCR). The "depth" of the bucket corresponds to a tolerance parameter (e.g., CDVT or BT). Each cell arrival creates a "cup" of fluid flow "poured" into one or more buckets for use in conformance checking. In the leaky bucket analogy, the cells do not actually flow through the bucket; only the check for conformance to the traffic contract does. Note that one implementation of traffic shaping is to actually have the cells flow through the bucket.

The ATM Forum specified a formal algorithm as a reference model in the UNI 3.1 specification in 1994 [19]. Figure 3.11 illustrates the two equivalent interpretations of the ATM Forum and the ITU-T Recommendation I.371 [18] Generic Cell Rate Algorithm (GCRA): the virtual scheduling algorithm and the leaky bucket algorithm. Each of these algorithms utilizes the two traffic parameters that define either the peak rate or the sustainable rate and the associated tolerance parameters: an Increment (I) and a Limit (L), both expressed in units of time. As stated in the standards, these representations are equivalent. The virtual scheduling representation appeals to time-sequence-oriented people, while the leaky bucket method appeals to the mathematical and accounting types among us.

Figure 3.11
Virtual Scheduling and Leaky Bucket Algorithms for ATM's Generic Cell Rate Algorithm (GCRA).

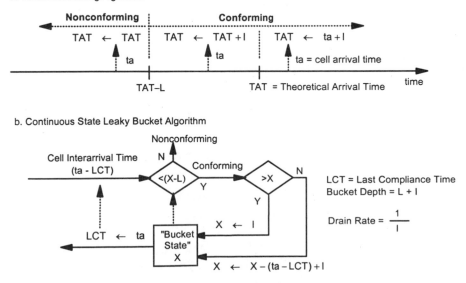

Figure 3.11a illustrates the virtual scheduling algorithm which utilizes the concept of a Theoretical Arrival Time (TAT) for the next conforming cell. If a cell arrives more than the tolerance limit, L, earlier than the TAT, then it is nonconforming, as shown in the figure. Cells arriving within the tolerance limit are conforming, and update the TAT for the next cell by the increment, I, as indicated in the figure. Cells arriving after the TAT make the tolerance available to subsequent cells, while cells arriving within the tolerance interval reduce the tolerance available to subsequent cells.

The flowchart in Figure 3.11b shows the detailed workings of the leaky bucket algorithm. Here, the GCRA parameters have the interpretation that the bucket depth is L+I and the bucket drain rate is 1/I. The leaky bucket algorithm uses the concepts of a Last Compliance Time (LCT) variable to hold the arrival time of the last conforming cell, as well as a bucket fill state variable X. The algorithm compares the difference between a cell arrival time and LCT to the bucket state minus the tolerance limit (i.e., X-L) to determine if the cell arrival would overflow the bucket. If overflow would occur, then the cell is deemed nonconforming. Otherwise, the flowchart checks to see if the bucket completely drained since the LCT before updating the bucket state variable X accordingly. The algorithm then substitutes for the current values of the LCT and bucket state X in preparation for processing the next cell arrival.

The ATM Forum TM 4.0 specification uses the GCRA(I,L) rule to formally define the conformance checks for the peak and sustainable rate conformance checks as follows:))

- Peak Rate: GCRA(T, τ), where PCR=1/T and CDVT=τ
- Sustainable Rate: GCAR(T_s, τ_s), where SCR=1/T_s and BT=τ_s

The reader interested in more details on the formal GCRA algorithm should download the ATM Forum's TM 4.0 specification [17] from www.atmforum.com or consult normative Annex A of ITU-T Recommendation I.371 [18].

Token and Leaky Bucket Interworking

So, if the IETF's token bucket and ATM's leaky bucket algorithms are simply different ways of expressing a deterministic description of a traffic flow, can they interoperate? The answer is yes, they can, as defined in IETF RFC 2381 [20]. This specification defines the mapping of the various parameters and the procedures to invoke them. Table 3.2 illustrates the mapping of the signaling protocols, algorithms, and pa-

TABLE 3.2

Parameters and
protocol interworking
between IP's RSVP
and ATM.

Parameter/ Protocol	IP	ATM
Signaling Protocol	RSVP	SVC (Q.2931)
Traffic Parameters	Token Bucket	Leaky Bucket
	peak (p), rate (r), bucket (b)	PCR, SCR, MBS
	Maximum packet size (M)	
	Minimum policed unit (m)	
QoS Parameters	Delay	CLR, CTD, CDV
		Loss, Delay, Jitter
Service Classes	Best Effort	UBR
	Controlled Load	nrt-VBR, ABR
	Guaranteed Service	CBR, rt-VBR
Conformance	Treat excess as best effort	Mark excess using CLP

rameters. As seen from the table, most parameters have a one-to-one correspondence. The next part covers the topics of QoS parameters, service classes, and conformance checking against the traffic parameters.

Review

This chapter precisely defined some basic terminology involved in planning and designing switches, routers, and networks. Recapping some highlights, transmission networks utilize bandwidth to deliver a specific link capacity to interconnect switches and routers. In an end-to-end path involving several nodes, one particular resource is frequently the bottleneck, usually limiting the end-to-end capacity to that of the link with the lowest capacity. Furthermore, other factors like interaction with the higher-layer protocols and packet overhead limit the efficiency and overall throughput of communication. Next, the text introduced the concept of traffic parameters like the peak and average rates and burst duration. Finally, we summarized, compared and contrasted the means to measure traffic parameters adopted for IP and ATM. In particular, the text analyzed the token bucket algorithm adopted by the IETF and the leaky bucket algorithm chosen by the ITU-T and the ATM Forum.

References

[1] D. McDysan, D. Spohn, *ATM — Theory and Application, Signature Edition,* McGraw-Hill, 1998.

[2] A. Papoulis, *Probability, Random Variables and Stochastic Processes,* McGraw-Hill, 1965.

[3]   G. Held, R. Sarch, *Data Communications,* McGraw-Hill, 1995.

[4]   I. Korn, *Digital Communications,* Van Nostrand Reinhold, 1985.

[5]   J. Ryan, "WDM: North American Deployment Trends," *IEEE Communications Magazine,* February 1998.

[6]   W. Simpson, *PPP over SONET/SDH,* RFC 1619, IETF, May 1994.

[7]   J. Manchester, J. Anderson, B. Doshi, S. Dravida, "IP over SONET," *IEEE Communications Magazine,* May 1998.

[8]   ITU-T, *B-ISDN ATM Adaptation Layer (AAL) Specification,* Recommendation I.363, March 1993.

[9]   J. Heinanen, *RFC 1483: Multiprotocol Encapsulation over ATM Adaptation Layer 5,* IETF, July 1993.

[10]   K. Thompson, G. Miller, R. Wilder, "Wide-Area Internet Traffic Patterns and Characteristics," *IEEE Network,* November/December 1997.

[11]   J. Wroclawski. *Specification of the Controlled-Load Network Element Service,* RFC 2211, IETF, September 1997.

[12]   S. Shenker, C. Partridge, R Guerin. *Specification of Guaranteed Quality of Service,* RFC 2212, IETF, September 1997.

[13]   S. Shenker., J. Wroclawski, *General Characterization Parameters for Integrated Service Network Elements,* RFC 2215, IETF, September 1997.

[14]   C. Partridge, *Gigabit Networking,* Addison-Wesley, 1994.

[15]   W. Stallings, *High-Speed Networks — TCP/IP and ATM Design Principles,* Prentice-Hall, 1998.

[16]   S. Keshav, *An Engineering Approach to Computer Networking,* Addison-Wesley, 1997.

[17]   ATM Forum, *ATM Forum Traffic Management Specification, Version 4.0,* af-tm-0056.000, April 1996.

[18]   ITU-T, *Traffic Control and Congestion Control in B-ISDN,* Recommendation I.371, 1996.

[19]   ATM Forum, *User-Network Interface Signaling Specification, Version 3.1,* af-uni-0010.002, September 1994.

[20]   M. Garrett, M. Borden, *Interoperation of Controlled-Load Service and Guaranteed Service with ATM,* RFC 2381, IETF, August 1998.

Quality of Service (QoS) and Traffic Control

"When you can measure what you are talking about and express it in numbers, you know something about it."

— Lord Kelvin

This part defines the criteria for which the traffic engineer is inevitably responsible for and by which the end user assesses value — Quality of Service (QoS). Chapter 4 begins by examining the end user perspective on performance, in particular, how the human nervous system and psyche place well-defined bounds on acceptable delay and loss. Chapter 5 moves from the subjective notion of perceived quality into objectively defined and measurable parameters. It compares and contrasts the definitions of QoS used in networks of the past, focusing on the recent refinements defined for IP and ATM networks. Finally, Chapter 6 introduces the principal means that IP routers and ATM switches employ to process QoS requests and traffic contracts for end user applications.

CHAPTER **4**

Perception Is Reality

"Concepts without intuitions are empty; intuitions without concepts are blind."

— Immanuel Kant

Largely, the nuances of our senses affect the perceived quality of communication. Furthermore, the means that communication engineers employ to reduce the required transmission capacity impacts the sensitivity of audio, video, or data quality to performance impairments such as loss, errors, and delay encountered in real networks. ATM was the first networking technology designed with QoS in mind from the outset; however, as studied in Chapter 5, the concept of QoS in ATM is rather complex. Therefore, the ATM Forum defined the simpler notion of service categories tailored to broad classes of applications. Although ATM was first, during the latter half of the 1990s designers have busily been defining ways to add QoS capabilities to the Internet Protocol (IP). The chapter summarizes the state of the art in adding QoS to IP networks by introducing the concepts involved in Integrated Services, the Resource reSerVation Protocol (RSVP), and differentiated services.

Perception and Quality

What does QoS in IP and ATM networks mean to you? In the business world, it determines whether you can have a normal voice conversation, whether a videoconference is productive, or if a multimedia application actually improves productivity for your staff. At home, it determines whether the savings offered by an inexpensive voice service are worthwhile, or if you complain about the quality of a video-on-demand movie. Around the world, discriminating businesses and residential users demand higher quality than the one-size-fits-all best effort service offered by the initial Internet design. Literally, what you see (and what you hear) is what you get. This section looks at how our perceptions operating in concert with audio and video coding algorithms respond in the face of degradations encountered in IP and ATM networks.

How We See and Hear Affects Quality

Telephone engineers know the performance requirements for voice based upon forty years of experience with digital telephony. Newer applications do not have such a historical basis; however, we do know something about their performance requirements. Largely, how our ears hear and our eyes see determines the acceptable quality when operating in conjunction with communication protocols used to encode audio and video signals. Let's explore these QoS drivers in more detail, starting with a review of the relevant aspects of human auditory and visual senses.

The blink of an eye is approximately one-fiftieth of a second, or 20 ms. When video display devices play back frames at a rates of between 25 and 30 frames per second using the image persistence provided by display systems like the cathode ray tube, the human eye-brain perceives continuous motion. When loss or errors disrupt a few frames in succession, the human eye-brain detects a discontinuity, which is subjectively objectionable.

The human ear-brain combination is less sensitive to short dropouts in received speech, being able to accept loss rates ranging from 0.5 percent to 10 percent [1] depending upon the type of voice coding employed. This level of loss may cause an infrequent clicking noise, or loss of a syllable. More severe levels of loss can result in the loss of words or even phrases. Although few relationships or business transactions have ended because of low voice quality, a poor communication channel can only make a tense conversation worse. If the price is low enough, however, some users may accept reduced performance to achieve cost savings. For example, voice over IP sometimes does not work at all; however, in some areas of the world it is still essentially free. Although, once this economic disparity normalizes, a voice service must have acceptable quality to be competitive.

The human ear is only sensitive to frequencies between approximately 100 Hz and 10 kHz. As studied in Chapter 2, voice signals occupy the frequency band below 4 kHz. Music and other sounds occupy the higher frequencies. The ear-brain combination is sensitive to delay in several scenarios. A common impairment encountered in telephony occurs when a speaker receives an echo of his or her own voice. Indeed, for a round-trip delay of greater than 50 ms, standards require echo cancellation [2].

One-way communication like video broadcast (e.g., television) or an audio signal (e.g., radio) can accept relatively long absolute delays. However, delay impedes two-way, interactive communication if the round-trip latency exceeds 300 ms. For example, conducting a voice conversation over a satellite link illustrates the problem with long delays, since the listener can't tell if the speaker has stopped or merely paused, and simultaneous conversation frequently occurs.

Combined video and audio is very sensitive to differential delays. Human perception is highly attuned to the correct correlation of audio and video, as is readily apparent when the speech is out of synch with lip movement, as occurs in some foreign language dubbed films.

How Protocols Affect Our Perception

Protocols determine other aspects of QoS. Many audio and video protocols tolerate errors in the received information to a certain degree; however, most data protocols cannot handle errors. Modern voice and video coding algorithms often mask small numbers of bit errors. However, loss of an entire frame may result in loss of a slice of a picture or an audible degradation.

Most audio and video protocols are sensitive to delay variation. Delay variation is a QoS parameter that measures the clumping or dispersion that occurs when multiplexing packets or cells from multiple sources in an end system, switch, or router. The resulting effect accumulates after traversing multiple routers or switches. Streaming audio and video protocols employ a limited playback buffer to account for delay variation. If too little or too much data arrives while the application is playing back the audio or video, then the application either starves for data or overflows the playback buffer.

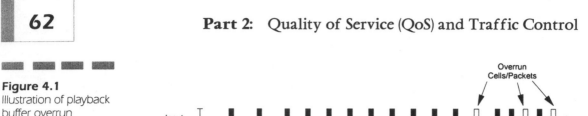

Figure 4.1
Illustration of playback buffer overrun scenario.

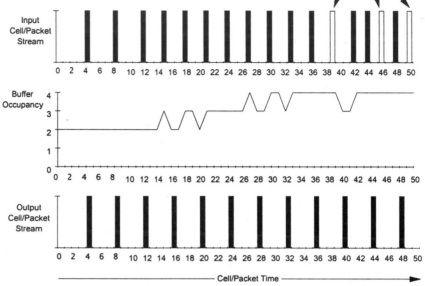

The playback buffer ensures that underrun or overrun events occur infrequently in response to the clumping and dispersion of packets or cells that accrues across a network. In our examples, the nominal cell or packet spacing is four unit intervals, and the playback buffer has space for four cells or packets. In our example, the playback buffer begins operation at a centered position (i.e., holding two cells or packets).

In the overrun scenario depicted in Figure 4.1, cells or packets arrive too closely clumped together, until finally a cell or packet arrives and there is no space in the playback buffer; thus cells or packets are lost. This is a serious event for a video coded signal because an entire sequence or frame may be lost due to the loss.

In the underrun scenario shown in Figure 4.2, cells or packets arrive too widely dispersed in time, such that when the time arrives for the application to remove the next cell or packet from the playback buffer, the buffer is empty. This too has a negative consequence on a video application because the underrun will disrupt continuity of motion or even create the need to resynchronize.

Most audio or video applications also require an accurate clock with which to remove data from the playback buffer and present the signal to the end user. Audio is sensitive to the playback clock, since the human ear perceives variation in the playback rate as a change in pitch, which can affect speaker recognition. In interactive video ap-

Figure 4.2
Illustration of playback
buffer underrun
scenario.

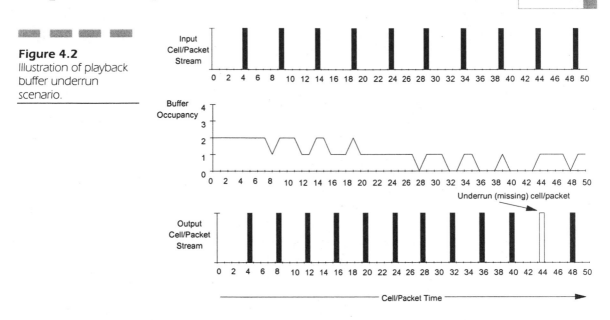

plications, variations in delay greater than 20 to 40 ms cause perceivable jerkiness.

For example, the advanced audio-video coding standard, MPEG-2, relies on an ATM network providing a low-level of cell delay variation to recover the Program Clock Reference (PCR) to control the playback buffer. The Internet employs a Real Time Protocol (RTP) to timestamp information for playback by the end application [3].

Most video coding schemes rely on the fact that after a scene change, the transmitter need only send the difference between subsequent images and the initial image of video sequence. Specifically, in MPEG-2, an intra-coded picture (I-picture) specifies the "bootstrap" image for a subsequent series of Predictive-coded pictures (P-pictures) that use information from previous I- or P-pictures, or Bidirectionally-predicted pictures (B-pictures) that use information from previous or subsequent pictures [4]. The reason for doing predictive coding is that the size of P-pictures ranges is typically 30-50 percent of an I-picture, while a B-picture is often only half the size of a P-picture. Of course, the actual sizes depend upon the video source. However, if the network loses the beginning of an I-picture, then an entire video scene may be disrupted. As studied in the next section, MPEG-2 defines the means to prioritize critical information essential to reproduction of the basic image over that of finer-grained detail information.

Video coding is also sensitive to errors and loss, since the error may cause the loss of some or all of the content in an I-picture. In order to protect against loss of such critical information, video coding often employs error correction techniques [5]. For example, the MPEG-2 video-coding standard requires a bit error rate of 10^{-11} to deliver broadcast-quality video [4].

Many data protocols respond to delay and loss through retransmission strategies to provide guaranteed delivery. One example is the Transmission Control Protocol (TCP), widely used to flow-control the transfer of World Wide Web text, image, sound, and video files. Data applications are sensitive to loss because they respond by retransmitting information. Consequently, a user perceives increased delay, since retransmission extends the time required to deliver a large file containing a video or audio image. Since many packet-switched data networks exhibit significant delay variation (especially over congested portions of the Internet), applications usually insert a substantial delay before starting playback.

Data communications protocols are extremely sensitive to errors and loss. An undetected error can have severe consequences if it is part of a downloaded program. Loss of a packet or cell frequently requires retransmission, which decreases throughput and increases response time, as studied in Part 5. On the other hand, many data communication protocols are less sensitive to delay variation, unless the delay varies by a large fraction of a second, which causes a retransmission time-out resulting in inconsistent response time and decreased productivity. Consistent response time (or the lack thereof) affects how users perceive data service quality.

The ideal for interactive applications is latency approaching that of the speed of light in fiber. A practical model is that of performance comparable to a locally attached disk drive or CD-ROM, which has an access time ranging from 10 to 100 ms. In other words, the goal of high-performance networking is to make the remote resource or application appear as if it were locally attached to the user's workstation.

Physics and Perceived Quality

The speed of light places a fundamental limit on the delay of any communication network or computing device. Since the propagation of light in optical fiber is approximately 5 μs/km [6], communication over hundreds of kilometers creates delays in the millisecond range, which may be noticeable, as described earlier. Other components in a wide area TDM network also create delay. A useful rule of thumb is that the propagation velocity of any electromagnetic signal in optical fiber with electronic repeaters and amplifiers is approximately 1 ms per 100 miles. At distances over several hundred miles, human sensory mechanisms detect propagation delay. As we shall see, high-performance, data-oriented applications increasingly encountered in IP and ATM networks are also sensitive to delay.

The Inequality of QoS

Philosophically, the use of resource reservation for guaranteeing quality creates inequality [7, 8]. In other words, user requests admitted by the network get the QoS and capacity they require, while users who pay less, or are latecomers, do not. A similar situation occurs when the network employs simple priority schemes to serve some users preferentially over others.

The Value of Quality

The following set of questions and answers illustrates the fundamental inequality of QoS and reserved capacity. When you connect to a Web site, are you willing to experience only part of its potential audio, visual, video, and interactive capabilities? Possibly; it depends on the content. How does your response change if the quality was so poor that you had to go back and visit that site later? Sure, everybody does that today. What is your answer if you had to pay for each individual visit? — for example, as you do when you watch a movie, receive educational training, or receive consultation? No, of course not, most people would answer.

A number of researchers and network providers have broached the subject of quantifying the value of quality by defining pricing or charging based upon the level of QoS that the network delivers [9]. These efforts attempt to balance the value perceived by the user against the cost required by the network provider to deliver a specific level of quality. An important dimension of any charging policy is that of reserving resources (e.g., capacity) versus the amount of resources actually consumed by the user (e.g., packets or cells actually delivered by the network). Typically, real-time services require resource reservation based charging, while networks may charge for non-real-time services at a flat rate on an actual usage basis. Furthermore, services with more stringent QoS requirements are generally more expensive to provide. Historically, providing a high-quality service sets the benchmark for all services to follow. Users tolerate reduced quality only if the price is substantially less.

Blocking versus Reduction of Quality

An alternative to a blocking system is to offer graceful degradation in case of overflows via adaptive voice and video coding [7]. However, most voice and video coders have an avalanche performance curve in response to increasing loss and delay variation: they degrade gracefully until a certain point where they become unusable. In essence, however, the network could factor in the allowable degradation as part of the admission control process. Alternatively, the network or server could offer varying grades of service at different prices. Some video codec designs use loss priority to distinguish between the essential information for image replication and the non-essential details. During congested conditions, the network discards only the detailed information, hence the video and audio is still usable. When the network is not congested, then the user receives higher quality. Frame relay and ATM support this concept of user-specified priority via the Discard Eligible (DE) and Cell Loss Priority (CLP) bits in their header fields, respectively. The current approach in the IETF's differentiated service working groups allow, but do not require, a similar selective discard concept.

Figure 4.3 gives an example of how hierarchical, prioritized video coding makes use of selective ATM cell discard congestion avoidance. The MPEG-2 standard defines the protocol specifics to implement this technique [4]. Hierarchical video coding identifies the critical information required to construct the major parts of the video image sequence as the higher-priority CLP=0 marked cells, while encoding the remaining, detailed minor change information as a separate stream of lower-priority CLP=1 marked cells. Thus, when a scene change occurs, the video codec generates CLP=0 cells at an increased rate for periods

Figure 4.3
Illustration of
hierarchical video
coding.

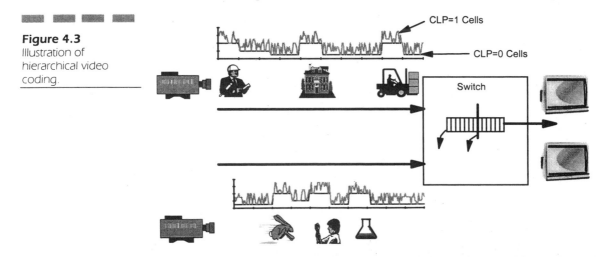

indicated by the slowly varying dark, solid line in the figure. The video application sends the detail and minor adjustments within the scene as CLP=1 cells, as shown by the lighter jagged line in the figure. When a switch multiplexes several such video sources together and utilizes selective cell discard with different thresholds for CLP=0 and CLP=1 cells, as shown in Figure 4.3, this scheme ensures that the critical scene change information gets through, even if the method loses some detail during transient intervals of congestion. Chapter 14 examines the performance of selective discard in detail.

Quality in the Connection-Oriented and Connectionless Paradigms

The fundamental difference between the connection-oriented and connectionless paradigms has significant consequences regarding QoS. For example, the concept of QoS per connection has no meaning in a connectionless protocol like IP. Instead, some Internet protocols adopt the notion of QoS to a flow of packets. As studied in Chapter 6, the premier protocol for reserving capacity and delivering QoS in the Internet is the Resource reSerVation Protocol (RSVP). RSVP transfers reservation requests between devices, requiring each device to either accept or reject each request. Therefore, it exhibits some aspects of a connection-oriented service.

A more recent approach in the Internet relies on the notion of differentiated service priorities using long-term traffic engineering statistics or traffic contracts for Virtual Private Network (VPN) customers. Thus, MPLS label-switched paths begin to look like the guaranteed-capacity VPN solutions offered by QoS-enabled frame relay and ATM PVC networks.

We will describe a number of instances where the connection-oriented and connectionless paradigms take related approaches when reserving capacity and delivering different levels of quality. Of course, due to the fundamental differences in these paradigms, some significant differences exist as well.

ATM Service Categories and QoS

As described in the next chapter, ATM precisely defines the concept of QoS, but unfortunately, in a rather complicated manner. Therefore, in order to make the usage of QoS clearer to end users for specific applications, the ATM Forum defined a range of service categories employing simple acronyms relating to the bit rate and an implicit quality specification. Since we use these terms repeatedly, this section explains each in lay terms using the definitions of ATM traffic parameters defined in Chapter 3. Each service category definition includes terms that define the traffic contract parameters and QoS characteristics. The ATM Forum Traffic Management 4.0 specification [10] (commonly abbreviated TM 4.0) defines the following ATM-layer service categories:

- CBR   Constant Bit Rate
- rt-VBR   Real-time Variable Bit Rate
- nrt-VBR   Non-real-time Variable Bit Rate
- UBR   Unspecified Bit Rate
- ABR   Available Bit Rate

The ATM Forum defines attributes, application characteristics, and networking design guidelines for each of these service categories [11] as summarized below.

- The CBR service category supports real-time applications requiring a fixed amount of capacity defined by the PCR. CBR supports tightly constrained variations in delay. Example applications are voice, constant-bit-rate video, and Circuit Emulation Service (CES). Normally, networks must allocate the peak rate to these types of sources.
- The rt-VBR service category supports time-sensitive applications, which also require constrained delay and delay variation requirements, but which transmit at a time varying rate constrained to a PCR and an "average" rate defined by the SCR and MBS. The three parameters PCR, SCR, and MBS define a traffic contract in terms of the worst-case source traffic pattern for which the network guarantees a specified QoS. Examples of such bursty, delay-variation-sensitive sources are voice and variable-bit-rate video. A network may be able to statistically multiplex these types of traffic sources together.
- The nrt-VBR service category supports applications that have no constraints on delay and delay variation, but which still have variable-rate, bursty traffic characteristics. This class of applications expects a low Cell Loss Ratio (CLR). The traffic contract is the same as that for rt-VBR. Applications include packet data transfers, terminal sessions, and file transfers. Networks may statistically multiplex these VBR sources effectively.

▓ The ABR service category works in cooperation with sources that can change their transmission rate in response to rate-based network feedback used in the context of closed-loop flow control further defined in Part 5. The aim of ABR service is to dynamically provide access to capacity currently not in use by other service categories to users who can adjust their transmission rate in response to feedback. In exchange for this cooperation by the user, the network provides a service with very low loss. Applications specify a maximum transmit-rate (PCR) and the minimum required rate, called the Minimum Cell Rate (MCR). ABR service does not provide bounded delay variation; hence real-time applications are not good candidates for ABR. Example applications for ABR are LAN interconnection, high-performance file transfers, database archival, non-time-sensitive traffic, and web browsing.

▓ The ATM Forum also calls the UBR service category a "best-effort" service, which requires neither tightly constrained delay nor delay variation. In fact, UBR provides no specific quality of service or guaranteed throughput whatsoever. This traffic is therefore "at risk" since the network provides no performance guarantees for UBR traffic. The Internet and local area networks are examples of this type of "best effort" delivery performance. Example applications are LAN emulation, IP over ATM, and non-mission-critical traffic.

Table 4.1 summarizes the attributes of these ATM-layer service categories from the ATM Forum's Traffic 4.0 specification. Each ATM service category uses one or more of the traffic contract parameters defined in the previous section. ABR uses these parameters, and more. Furthermore, most service categories require guarantees on loss, delay variation, or transfer rate. The one exception is UBR which, being a best-effort service, requires no guarantees whatsoever. Finally, only ABR utilizes feedback control, as described in Chapter 13.

Table 4.2 summarizes the above discussion and shows the suitability of the ATM service categories for a number of commonly encountered applications [11]. In general, CBR service applies best to applications that currently require the dedicated capacity and minimal delay variation that TDM networking provides. The nrt-VBR service category best serves traditional loss-sensitive packet-switched data applications, such as frame relay, IP, and LAN traffic. The ATM Forum specified the rt-VBR service category for transport of variable-bit-rate video. The ABR service category serves LAN and WAN data transport effectively via its sophisticated flow control mechanism. Finally, al-

TABLE 4.1

ATM Forum service category attributes, QoS guarantees, and usage of feedback.

| Service Category | Traffic Descriptor | Guarantees | | | Feedback Control |
		Loss (CLR)	Delay Variance (CDV)	Reserved Capacity	
CBR	PCR	Yes	Yes	Yes	No
rt-VBR	PCR, SCR, MBS	Yes	Yes	Yes	No
nrt-VBR	PCR ,SCR, MBS	Yes	No	Yes	No
ABR	PCR, MCR, ...	Yes	No	Yes	Yes
UBR	PCR	No	No	No	No

TABLE 4.2

Suitability of ATM Forum service categories to various applications.

Applications	CBR	rt-VBR	nrt-VBR	ABR	UBR
Critical data	Good	Fair	Best	Fair	No
LAN interconnect	Fair	Fair	Good	Best	Good
WAN data transport	Fair	Fair	Good	Best	Good
Circuit emulation	Best	Good	No	No	No
Telephony	Best	Good	No	No	No
Videoconferencing	Best	Good	Fair	Fair	Poor
Compressed audio	Fair	Best	Good	Good	Poor
Video distribution	Best	Good	Fair	No	No
Interactive multimedia	Best	Best	Good	Good	Poor

though UBR may not be the best for any application, it may well be the least expensive.

IP's QoS-Oriented Services

This section describes the terminology defined in the *Integrated Services* architecture for IP networks. The Resource reSerVation Protocol (RSVP) uses the token bucket defined in Chapter 3 to describe a data flow's traffic parameters. The network need only provide a certain level of quality for the packets in a flow that conform to these traffic parameters. The Integrated Service and RSVP-related RFCs define two levels of service, called *Controlled Load* and *Guaranteed Quality of Service*. Finally, recent work in the IETF has focused on defining scalable QoS capabilities for the Internet backbone using differentiated services.

Best-Effort Service

Traditionally, the Internet offered only a single QoS, best effort, with available capacity, delay, and loss characteristics dependent on instantaneous load and the state of the network. Network designers controlled QoS via provisioning routers, links, and routing parameters based upon historical traffic patterns. When the only Internet users were researchers, universities, and government agencies, best-effort performance was adequate. This was true because much of the communication was non-real-time, for example, E-mail and file transfer. Interestingly, the use of a limited multicast backbone called MBONE to broadcast portions of IETF meetings over the best effort Internet of the early 1990s was a principal driver for adding QoS awareness to IP [12]. During intervals of congestion, video and audio applications may not work when provided best-effort service.

Controlled-Load Service

IETF RFC 2211 [13] defines the controlled-load service which applies to the portion of a flow that conforms to the token bucket Traffic Specification (Tspec) as defined in Chapter 3. RFC 2211 defines the end-to-end behavior observed by an application for a series of network elements providing controlled-load service in terms of the behavior visible to applications receiving best-effort service "under unloaded conditions" from the same series of network elements. Although this definition may seem somewhat vague, it is not. As shown in Part 4, the discipline of queuing theory defines this notion rather precisely in terms of the likelihood of packet delivery and the statistics regarding the delay incurred. Specifically, RFC 2211 states that "a very high percentage of transmitted packets will be successfully delivered by the network." RFC 2211 also states that "the transit delay experienced by a very high percentage of the delivered packets will not greatly exceed the minimum transmit delay."

Controlled-load service requires that each network element provide the QoS to conforming flows even if some flows do not conform to the Tspec. This means that simply serving all controlled-load flows with a shared set of resources (e.g., a buffer) is insufficient, unless the network element prevents nonconforming flows from starving conforming flows of the necessary resources. Furthermore, the specification requires that the network attempt to forward nonconforming packets on a best-effort basis. RFC 2211 states that the network element may either degrade the performance of all packets in a nonconforming flow, or only those packets that exceed the Tspec parameters.

Guaranteed Quality of Service (QoS)

IETF RFC 2212 [14] states that Guaranteed QoS applies to only the portion of a flow that conforms to the token bucket Traffic Specification (Tspec) defined in Chapter 3 and a desired service (Rspec) parameter.

The Rspec defines the actual service rate R delivered by the network and some additional terms that precisely bound the actual delay delivered to the flow. Chapter 5 details the Rspec parameter and its role in defining QoS.

Interestingly, the Guaranteed QoS protocol bounds the maximum delay encountered by an individual flow by exchanging information in RSVP messages. Chapter 5 summarizes the process of how IP network elements exchange information to compute the maximum end-to-end delay. Note that the maximum end-to-end delay will not change as long as the IP routing path remains constant. Guaranteed QoS does not control minimum or average delay. As noted earlier in this chapter, applications like video and audio playback require bounded delay variation, which Guaranteed QoS supports.

In a manner similar to controlled load service, Guaranteed QoS should strive to treat packets that fail to conform to the Tspec on a best-effort basis. Since network elements must provide a precisely defined transfer rate in order to meet the delay specification, RFC 2212 defines policing and shaping requirements in terms of the Tspec and the delay parameters as detailed in Chapter 5.

Differentiated Services (diffserv)

The IETF has specified an approach for the differentiated services in the Internet called *diffserv*. It aims to provide services differentiated on performance utilizing weighted priority queuing and quasi-statically configured routing [15, 16]. In diffserv, the performance (i.e., QoS) measures to which differentiated service applies, are responsiveness and availability. Diffserv requires that edge routers classify traffic flows into a member from a set of categories based upon the TCP/IP header fields in what is called a *microflow*. The diffserv utilizes a standard 3-bit field within the IPv4 or IPv6 header to indicate the result of this classification.

Figure 4.4 illustrates the diffserv field defined in RFC 2474 [16]. This one-byte header is present in the IPv4 or IPv6 packet header as summarized in Chapter 2. Because the diffserv is present in every IP

Figure 4.4
Internet Protocol differentiated services (diffserv) field.

0	1	2	3	4	5	6	7
Differentiated Services Code Point (DSCP)						Currently Unused	

Pool	DSCP Codepoints	Assignment Policy
1	XXXXX0	Standards Action
2	XXXX11	Experimental/ Local Usage
3	XXXX01	Experimental/ Local Usage/Future Standards Action

packet header, each node can provide differentiated services on a per-hop basis. What is necessary is a standard interpretation of what these per-hop behaviors are. RFC 2474 requires that implementations must match the entire 6-bit Differentiated Services Code Point (DSCP) when determining the packet handling mechanism necessary to provide a Per Hop Behavior (PHB). These PHBs are the building blocks from which an end-to-end service can be constructed. As indicated in the figure, specific bit patterns within the DSCP field are the subject of standardization, experimental usage, or local usage by an Internet service provider. We analyze possible uses of the Experimental and Local Usage fields in terms of selective discard in Chapter 14 or congestion indication in Chapter 15.

RFC 2474 assigns DSCP codepoints of the form 'XXX000' from Pool 1 to a class selector codepoint. These codepoints provide backward compatibility to the IP Precedence field. A packet with a class selector codepoint having a higher numerical value should experience a higher probability of timely forwarding when compared with a packet having a class selector codepoint of a lower numerical value. Furthermore, an RFC 2474-compliant implementation must implement at least independently forwarded classes of traffic.

Currently, diffserv is unidirectional, allowing a user to specify performance separately in each direction. The envisioned services include the concepts of a Traffic Conditioning Agreement (TCA) and a Service Level Agreement (SLA). The traffic and performance specifications may vary not only by direction, but also by geographic region and time of day. The parameters may be qualitative or quantitative. An example of a qualitative service is simple prioritization. An example of quantitative service uses traffic parameters analogous to those defined for RSVP, namely the peak and average rates along with a burst size. Quantitative performance parameters are also analogous to RSVP and include latency and packet loss.

The network must provision its routing and PHBs in response to the contracted traffic levels and historical traffic patterns. Currently, the diffserv approach primarily considers long-term allocation and does not address the issue of dynamic reservation. Examples of PHBs include an assured forwarding group that specifies selective drop priorities and adaptive congestion avoidance [17] and an expedited forwarding behavior [18] that uses class-based queuing. We analyze these techniques in Parts 4 and 5. The diffserv documents refer to well-established tools and procedures for how to perform the provisioning function. We cover these topics in Parts 6 and 7.

An example of a basic service is one with two priorities: Expedited Forwarding and Default Handling. Initially, single ISPs can employ this basic capability to implement high-performance Web hosting,

Virtual Private Networks (VPNs), and high-priority Web site access. Of course, the ISP would bill for the expedited forwarding service at a rate higher than that for the default best-effort service. As ISPs form service-level agreements between themselves, then experts predict that differentiated service will spread across the Internet.

Review

This chapter introduced the topic of QoS by first summarizing how the human sensory mechanisms affect perceived quality. The text then described how communication engineers take advantage of limitations in our sight and hearing to reduce the required transmission capacity. Although these shortcuts dramatically reduce the required transmission capacity, they also create additional sensitivity to the quality delivered by the underlying network. In particular, loss, errors, variations in delay, and even the absolute value of delay can have an adverse impact on the perceived quality of a communication service.

The chapter then introduced the concept of service categories employed in ATM to combine the notions of QoS, source traffic characteristics, and feedback control into groupings that target the major application classes currently in use. Finally, the text concluded by describing the QoS capabilities defined for the Internet. These included the Controlled Load and Guaranteed QoS capabilities defined in the Integrated Services suite for IP networks, as well as the differentiated services functions.

References

[1]   T. Kostas, M. Borella, I. Sidhu, G. Schister, J. Grabiec, J. Mahler, "Real-Time Voice over Packet Switched Networks," *IEEE Network*, Jan/Feb 1998.

[2]   ITU-T, Control of Talker Echo, *Recommendation G.131*, August 1996.

[3]   H. Schulzrinne, S. Casner, R. Frederick, V. Jacobson, *RTP: A Transport Protocol for Real-Time Applications*, RFC 1889, IETF, January, 1996.

[4]   M. Orezessek, P. Sommer, *ATM & MPEG-2 — Integrating Digital Video into Broadband Networks*, Prentice Hall, 1998.

[5]   E. Biersack, "Performance Evaluation of Forward Error Correction in an ATM Environment," IEEE JSAC, May 1993.

[6]   S. Personick, *Fiber Optics — Technology and Applications*, Plenum, 1985.

[7]   V. Antonov, "ATM: Another Technological Mirage," Pluris Inc., http://www.pluris.com/ip_vs_atm/, 1996.

[8]   C. Lewis, "QoS: Creating Inequality In An Equal World," Network Computing On Line, http://techweb.cmp.com/nc/809/809ws2.html, May 1996.

[9]   D. Ferrari, L. Delgrossi, "Charging for QoS," Sixth International Workshop on QoS, 1998.

[10]   ATM Forum, *ATM Forum Traffic Management Specification, Version 4.0*, af-tm-0056.000, April 1996.

[11]   L. Lambarelli, *ATM Service Categories: The Benefits to the User*, http://www.atmforum.com/atmforum/service_categories.html.

[12]   R. Braden, D. Clark, S. Shenker, *Integrated Services in the Internet Architecture: an Overview*, RFC 1633, IETF, June 1994.

[13]   J. Wroclawski, *Specification of the Controlled-Load Network Element Service*, RFC 2211, IETF, September 1997.

[14]   S. Shenker, C. Partridge, R Guerin, *Specification of Guaranteed Quality of Service*, RFC 2212, IETF, September 1997.

[15]   S. Blake, D. Black, M. Carlson, E. Davies, Z. Wang, W. Weiss, *Architecture for Differentiated Services*, RFC 2475, IETF, December 1998.

[16]   K. Nichols, S. Blake, F. Baker, D. Black, *Definition of the Differentiated Services Field (DS Field) for the IPv4 and IPv6 Headers*, RFC 2474, IETF, December 1998.

[17]   F. Baker , J. Heinanen , W. Weiss , J. Wroclawski, *Assured Forwarding PHB Group*, RFC 2597, IETF, June 1999.

[18]   V. Jacobson , K. Nichols , K. Poduri, *An Expedited Forwarding PHB*, RFC 2598, IETF, June 1999.

CHAPTER 5

Quality of Service (QoS) Defined

"The best is the enemy of the good."

— Voltaire

What is Quality of Service (QoS)? Many definitions exist in the press, and the concept continues to evolve in the Internet standards. Since ATM precisely defines QoS, we begin with this definition. In ATM terminology, QoS is the performance observed by an end user. The principal QoS parameters are delay, delay variation, and loss. As studied in the previous chapter, applications operate well only within certain performance limits. The basic proposition in ATM is that a network guarantees to provide a specified QoS for a traffic level that conforms to a precisely specified set of parameters. Together, these conditions form a traffic contract between the user and network. We define the basic QoS parameters involving errors, loss, and delay through precise definitions complemented by practical examples. Finally, this chapter describes the means by which ATM and IP networks allow end users or network administrators to request QoS. ATM uses a signaling protocol similar to that used in telephone networks on a per-connection basis, while IP uses a Resource reSerVation Protocol (RSVP) to convey reservation requests and responses.

Quality of Service (QoS)

This section defines a generic framework for QoS. This includes a reference model, a review of how network characteristics affect QoS parameters, and a summary of the QoS required by various classes of applications.

Reference Model

Standards define QoS on an end-to-end basis — the perspective most relevant to an end user. An end-to-end QoS reference model usually contains one or more intervening networks, each potentially with multiple nodes, as depicted in Figure 5.1. Each of these intervening networks may introduce delay, loss, or errors due to multiplexing, switching, or transmission, thereby impacting QoS. Furthermore, statistical variations in the offered traffic may result in loss due to buffer overflow on links connecting congested network nodes. Of course, a network can also implement shaping between nodes or between networks to minimize the accumulation of variations in delay and loss. In principle, the user should not need to know about the intervening networks and their characteristics, as long as the network delivers the end-to-end QoS for conforming traffic.

As described later in this chapter, ITU-T Recommendation I.356 takes the approach of defining a worst-case concatenation of networks and devices for specifying the QoS. Therefore, as long as connections across networks stay within these bounds, users experience a consistent level of QoS.

Figure 5.1
End-to-end QoS
reference model.

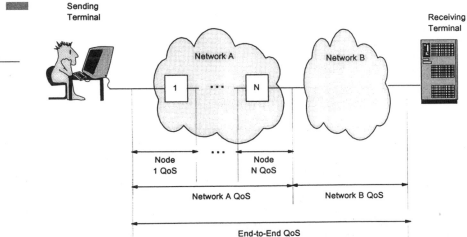

Impact of Network Characteristics on Quality of Service Parameters

Table 5.1 lists major causes of QoS impairments introduced by the characteristics of IP and ATM networks [1]. Note that the offered traffic load and functions performed by the switch primarily determine the delay, variation in delay, and loss parameters. The principal QoS parameters affected by IP routers and ATM switches are delay, variation in delay, and loss due to buffer overflow. Bit and burst errors create random errors in delivered packets and cells, but also may create misinsertion events when several errors corrupt a header so that a packet or cell erroneously appears valid. Of course, the more switching nodes a cell traverses, the more the quality degrades. All QoS parameters accrue in approximately a linear fashion except for delay variation, which grows at a rate no less than the square root of the number of nodes traversed, as described in Chapter 18.

Application-Level QoS

Selecting precise values of QoS parameters like loss, delay, and delay variation is not an easy task. As discussed in Chapter 4, part of the difficulty arises from the subjective nature of perceived quality. A commonly employed approach groups applications with similar QoS requirements into broad generic classes and then specifies the QoS parameters for these classes. Figure 5.2 [2, 3, 4] illustrates several examples of application-level QoS requirements for the loss and delay variation parameters. As described in Chapter 4, these are the principal parameters of interest to the majority of applications. The other major distinction is that a real-time application requires latency

TABLE 5.1

Mapping of network characteristics to QoS parameters.

Characteristic	Delay	Delay Variation	Loss	Random Errors	Misinsertion
Propagation delay	✓				
Switch/router queuing architecture	✓	✓	✓		
Switch/router link rate	✓	✓			
Packet size	✓	✓	✓		
Switch/router buffer capacity	✓	✓	✓		
Switch/router resource allocation	✓	✓	✓		
Variations in traffic load	✓	✓	✓		✓
Switch/router and link failures		✓			
Bit and burst errors			✓	✓	✓
Number of switches/routers traversed	✓	✓	✓	✓	✓

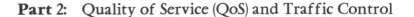

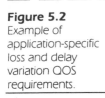

Figure 5.2
Example of
application-specific
loss and delay
variation QOS
requirements.

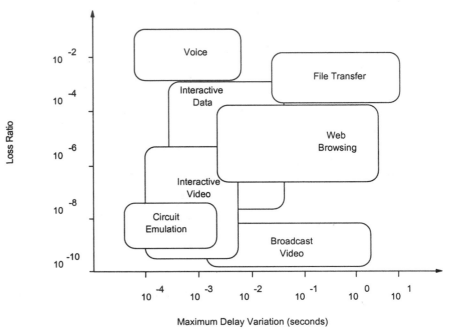

bounded by the propagation speed of light over the transmission medium. The bubbles in this chart show a set of ranges that the indicated applications may be able to use. As described later in this chapter, ATM protocols allow applications to specify QoS in two ways: through the generic service categories (e.g., CBR, nrt-VBR) described in Chapter 4, or through explicit enumeration of the QoS parameters in signaling messages. In addition, as described later, RSVP defines a means to request and confirm specific bounds on delay variation for the Guaranteed QoS Integrated Service. The current Internet standards assume that loss is always low for applications given preferred levels of quality. Indeed, RFC 1633 [5] characterizes applications as either real time (e.g., voice), predictive (e.g., broadcast video), or elastic (e.g., file transfer), based upon the ability to handle variations in delay.

Delay Variation and Link Speed

A major source of delay variation occurs when one packet arrives to a buffer serving a link and encounters several other packets that are either already in service or are of higher priority than the arriving packet. For example, a packet-switching node with a link speed R and a maximum packet length M introduces at least the following delay variation:

$$\text{Min[Delay Variation]} \ = \ \frac{M}{R}$$

As studied in subsequent chapters, waiting for other packets to complete service causes even more variation due to queuing delays. Figure 5.3 illustrates the minimum delay variation defined by the above formula for IP router and ATM switch nodes as a function of link speed R. The maximum packet size for ATM is M=53×8=424 bits. Our example assumes that M=1,500×8=12,000 bits for IP packets. Of course, IP networks can achieve lower delay variation by decreasing the maximum packet size M, but only at the expense of increased processing and reduced efficiency via fragmenting longer packets into a sequence of shorter segments. Since absolute delay is the QoS parameter important to the application, the large packet sizes supported by packet-based switch/routers can be a QoS limit in networks with lower-speed links. The figure shows the approximate levels where major QoS impacts occur. For example, interaction is difficult for delays greater than 100 ms, while the need for echo cancellation occurs when the delay exceeds a few tens of milliseconds. The additional delay above propagation delay deliverable via TDM networks is on the order of 1 ms. As seen from this figure, IP cannot use large packets over low-speed modems and still support truly interactive applications. The situation improves for DS1 or xDSL line rates to the point where IP could avoid echo cancellation (if we only considered store and forward delay), and ATM performance exceeds that of jitter absorption in TDM networks. As the speed increases above DS3 rates, IP store and forward minimum delay variation becomes less than TDM's jitter absorption delay. Keep in mind that this is the absolute

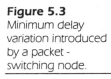

Figure 5.3
Minimum delay
variation introduced
by a packet -
switching node.

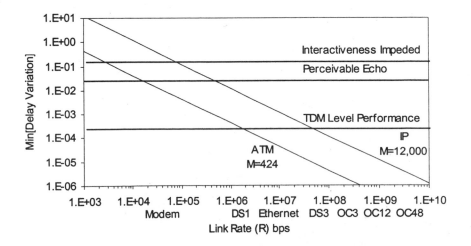

best case for delay variation — it only involves a source and destination connected via a single link and only two traffic sources that contend for that link. As studied in Chapter 18, the end-to-end delay traversing a number of nodes shared by other traffic streams can introduce substantially greater levels of delay variation than those considered in this simple example.

ATM QoS Parameters

The ATM Forum's UNI 4.0 Traffic Management Specification [1] defines specific Quality of Service (QoS) performance parameters for cells conforming to the parameters of the traffic contract.

Definitions and Terminology

Table 5.2 lists the ATM layer QoS parameters defined in ATM standards along with the commonly used acronyms. The last column provides an indication of whether the ATM Forum's protocols define a means for the user to dynamically negotiate the QoS parameter with a network. Non-negotiated parameters are implicitly defined in the switch implementation via network management configuration.

Cell Transfer Delay, Delay Variation, and Loss Ratio

The principal ATM QoS parameters are the Cell Transfer Delay (CTD), Cell Delay Variation (CDV), and Cell Loss Ratio (CLR). Propagation delay dominates the fixed-delay component of CTD, while queuing behavior contributes to delay variations in heavily loaded networks. The effects of queue service strategy and buffer sizes dominate loss and delay variation performance in congested networks. Chapter 11 shows that a large single, shared buffer achieves

TABLE 5.2

ATM's QoS parameter terminology.

QoS Acronym	QoS Parameter Name	Negotiated?
peak-to-peak CDV	Cell Delay Variation	Yes
maxCTD	maximum CTD	Yes
CLR	Cell Loss Ratio	Yes
CER	Cell Error Ratio	No
SECBR	Severely Errored Cell Block Ratio	No
CMR	Cell Misinsertion Rate	No

lower loss, but greater average delay and delay variation. As studied in Chapter 10, multiple buffers offer more flexibility in the tradeoff between delay variation and loss. The Cell Loss Ratio (CLR) is simply the ratio of lost cells to total transmitted cells. Transmission link error characteristics largely determine the CER, SECBR, and CMR QoS parameters. See ITU-T Recommendations I.356 [6] and I.610 [7] or Reference 8 for more details on ATM QoS parameters.

Various components within ATM devices contribute to the statistics of delay within ATM network as illustrated in Figure 5.4 [6]. In general, fixed and variable delays occur on the sending and receiving sides of the end terminal, in intermediate ATM switches, as well as on the transmission links connecting ATM switches.

The detailed delay components indicated in Figure 5.4 are:

- T1 Coding and Decoding Delay:
    - T11   Coding delay
    - T12   Decoding delay
- T2   Segmentation and Reassembly Delay:
    - T21   Sending-side AAL segmentation delay
    - T22   Receiving-side AAL reassembly/smoothing delay
- T3   Cell Transfer Delay (End-to-End):
    - T31 Inter-ATM node transmission propagation delay
    - T32 Total ATM node processing delay

The principal statistical fluctuations in delay occur due to the random component of queuing embodied in the T32 variable. Other terms contribute to a fixed delay, such as the terminal coding/decoding delays T11 and T12, along with the propagation delay T31. Part 4 covers the effects of random cell arrivals, queuing, and switching techniques on the loss and delay parameters. The interaction of the sources of random and fixed delay depicted in Figure 5.4 result in a probabilistic representation of the likelihood that a particular cell experiences a specific delay.

Mathematicians call such a plot a *probability density function*, as illustrated in Figure 5.5. The x-axis represents particular values of delay t, which occur with a probability f(t) specified on the y-axis. The interpretation of such a probability density function is that delay oc-

Figure 5.4
Sources of delay in
an ATM network.

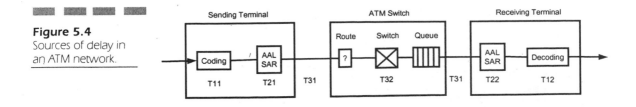

curs between the values of t and t+Δt, with probability f(t)Δt as shown in the figure. Chapter 8 precisely defines the concept of a probability density. Of course, no cells arrive sooner than the fixed-delay component, but cells arriving after the peak-to-peak Cell Delay Variation (peak-to-peak CDV) interval are considered late. The device may discard cells received later than this interval. Therefore, the Cell Loss Ratio (CLR) QoS parameter bounds this area under the probability density curve, as indicated in the right-hand side of the figure. Note that transmission errors may also cause cell loss. The maximum Cell Transfer Delay (maxCTD) is the sum of the fixed delay and peak-to-peak CDV delay components as indicated at the bottom of the figure.

ATM standards currently define Cell Delay Variation (CDV) as a measure of cell clumping and dispersion. Cell clumping is of concern because if too many cells arrive too closely together, then cell buffers may overflow. Cell dispersion occurs if the network creates too great of a gap between cells, in which case the playback buffer would underrun. Chapter 4 gave examples of how playback buffer overflow and underrun affect applications. CDV occurs either at a single point as measured against the nominal intercell spacing, or as the variability in the pattern measured between an entry point and an exit point. ITU-T Recommendation I.356 [6] and the ATM Forum UNI specifications 3.1 [9] and 4.0 [1] cover details on computing CDV and its interpretation.

An upper bound on the peak-to-peak CDV at a single queuing point is the buffer size available to the particular QoS class or connection. This bound results by observing the fact that the worst-case (i.e., peak-to-peak) variation in delay occurs between the buffer-empty and buffer-full conditions. The worst-case end-to-end CDV is the aggrega-

Figure 5.5
Cell Transfer Delay
probability density
model.

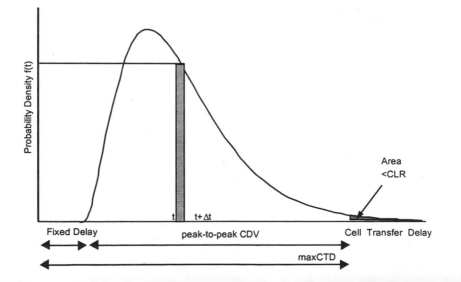

tion of the individual bounds across a network. As shown in Chapter 18, tighter bounds on CDV result if the network performs admission control in conjunction with traffic control.

Dynamic and Predefined QoS in ATM Networks

ATM allows applications to specify QoS in two ways. First, a PVC or SVC may request one of the generic service categories (i.e., CBR, rt-VBR, nrt-VBR, UBR, or ABR) as defined in Chapter 4. The second method applies only to the UNI 4.0 version of SVCs that allows the application to explicitly enumerate QoS parameters in the SETUP message, as summarized in Table 5.1.

The static preallocation method builds upon a technique traditionally used in the engineering of voice and connection-oriented data communication networks. The first step involves defining a hypothetical reference connection, such as that depicted in Figure 5.1. Typically, the reference connection specifies the number of nodes traversed, the characteristics of these nodes, and parameters that define the links that connect the nodes. Specifically, ITU-T Recommendation I.356 [6] defines QoS objectives for a reference configuration spanning multiple ATM networks operated by different carriers. The reference configuration considers networks spanning distances of up to 27,500 km that have a propagation delay of approximately 170 ms. The reference configurations traversing up to five networks contain up to 25 switches interconnected via links with capacity of 155 Mbps or higher.

Table 5.3 shows the provisional numerical values cited in ITU-T Recommendation I.356 for three QoS classes. The ITU-T may change these objectives to better, or worse, values based upon actual operational experience. QoS class 1 meets the stringent requirements of CBR traffic, while tolerant QoS class 2 addresses applications that do not differentiate between CLP=0 and CLP=1 loss. The bi-level QoS class 3 targets applications that expect guaranteed performance on

TABLE 5.3

Recommendation I.356 QoS class performance objectives.

QoS Parameter	Notes	QoS Class 1	QoS Class 2	QoS Class 3
CTD	Mean value	400 ms	Unspecified	Unspecified
CDV	10^{-8} quantile	3 ms	Unspecified	Unspecified
CLR (0+1)	Applies to CLP=0+1	3×10^{-7}	10^{-5}	Unspecified
CLR(0)	Applies to CLP=0	N/A	Unspecified	10^{-5}
CER	Upper Bound	4×10^{-6}	4×10^{-6}	4×10^{-6}
CMR	Upper Bound	Once per day	Once per day	Once per day
SECBR	Upper Bound	10^{-4}	10^{-4}	10^{-4}

CLP=0 cells, but don't expect guarantees on CLP=1 cells — for example, the two-level variable bit rate video coding scheme used by MPEG2 as summarized in Chapter 4 is a typical application for QoS class 3 that uses the CLP bit to tag lower priority cells. Recommendation I.356 also defines an unspecified class similar to the ATM Forum's definition of UBR.

IP QoS Parameters

IETF RFC 2216 [5] defines QOS as "the nature of the packet delivery service provided, as described by parameters such as achieved bandwidth, packet delay, and packet loss rates." As the precise definition of QoS evolves in the Internet, it leaves some room for interpretation and further definition [10]. The IETF Integrated Services focus primarily on bounding absolute packet delay as the principal QoS parameter [5, 11], as detailed below. More recent standards activity in the IETF differentiated services working group extends the definition of QoS to include availability and loss.

Table 5.4 lists the IP QoS parameters defined for the Controlled Load and Guaranteed QoS Integrated Services introduced in Chapter 4 summarized from RFCs 2211 and 2212, respectively. Contrary to the ATM preallocation method, there is no reference configuration. In addition, an application cannot dynamically request specific QoS parameter values. In fact, as seen from the table, the specifications for Controlled Load are just guidelines. As we shall see, when operating in conjunction with TCP's closed-loop flow control, this often results in acceptable performance for elastic traffic. The Guaranteed QoS capability takes a different tact towards delivering bandwidth and quality, as summarized in the table. As detailed in the next section, the guaranteed service defines parameters and a mechanism to report back to the receiver the maximum delay variation that packets will

TABLE 5.4

IP's Integrated Services QoS parameter terminology and definitions.

QoS Parameter	Controlled Load	Guaranteed QoS
Maximum delay variation	Not specified	Automatically measured using Adspec
Packet loss rate	Little or no congestion loss, should be error-limited	Sufficient buffer required for zero congestion loss
Minimum delay	High percentage of packets do not exceed minimum delay	Not specified
Average delay	Little or no queuing delay over timeframes greater than round trip delay	Not specified

experience while traversing the end-to-end path. Furthermore, the specification precisely defines the required buffering such that network elements can guarantee zero queuing loss. Thus, Guaranteed QoS dynamically takes into account the actual path and reports an upper bound on the delay variation. A real-time application can then employ this maximum delay variation bound to set its playback point to avoid the buffer underrun case. The application can use the maximum buffer calculation to avoid overrun.

Approaches for Requesting and Specifying QoS

While both RSVP and ATM are both signaling protocols, they employ different approaches to support communication of traffic and QoS parameters. First, RSVP employs receiver-initiated reservations, while ATM employs sender-initiated signaling. Second, RSVP signals independently for each direction of a flow, while an ATM sender may signal through the downstream network the traffic and QoS requirements for both directions of a full-duplex connection. Finally, ATM signaling provides a reliable means to inform the requestor of the status of the attempt, while RSVP cannot reliably confirm a successful attempt. Let's look into the details of each.

ATM's Connection-Oriented Signaling

The ATM Forum UNI 4.0 signaling specification [12] and ITU-T Recommendation Q.2931 [13] define the message formats and procedures for ATM signaling protocols. These standards define the valid sequence of messages exchanged between a user and the network, the rules for verifying consistency of the parameters, and the actions taken to establish and release ATM layer connections. A significant portion of signaling standards and specifications handle error cases, invalid messages, inconsistent parameters, and a number of other unlikely situations. These are important functions, since the signaling protocol must be highly reliable to support user applications. This section presents an example of signaling procedures for the establishment of a point-to-point connection with reference to Figure 5.6. See References 3 and 8 for examples of releasing point-to-point connections and point-to-multipoint connections. This example employs: a calling party (a client) on the left, an ATM network shown as

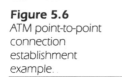

Figure 5.6
ATM point-to-point connection establishment example.

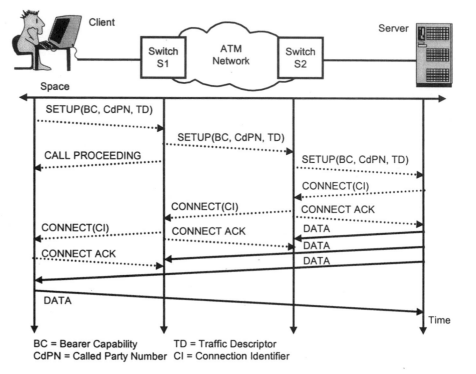

BC = Bearer Capability   TD = Traffic Descriptor
CdPN = Called Party Number   CI = Connection Identifier

switches S1 and S2 connected via a cloud in the middle, and a called party (a server) on the right. Time runs from top to bottom in the example.

Starting from the upper left-hand side of Figure 5.6, the calling party initiates the call attempt using a SETUP message containing Information Elements (IEs) defining the Called Party Number (CdPN), the desired Bearer Capability (BC), and the Traffic Descriptor (TD). ATM signaling allows the call originator to establish the traffic and QoS parameters in both the forward and backward directions simultaneously. The ATM Forum UNI 4.0 signaling specification defines how the ATM service categories are defined in terms of the BC and TD IEs. The network responds to the caller's SETUP message with a CALL PROCEEDING message, as shown in the figure. The network routes the call attempt across any intermediate switches using the SETUP message, reserving the required capacity and other resources based upon the BC and TD IEs. Eventually, the network routes the call to switch S2, which outputs a SETUP message on the physical interface corresponding to the Called Party Number, as shown on the right-hand side of the figure. The called user answers the call via the CONNECT message, indicating the locally assigned VPI/VCI label values in the Connection Identifier (CI). The network propagates the CONNECT message back to the originator as rapidly as possible in order to minimize call setup time. The users and network switches confirm receipt of the CONNECT message using the CONNECT ACKNOWLEDGE message as shown in the figure.

The ATM call setup procedures specify "clipping allowed" for the establishment of the data communication path. This means that a switch or end user need not establish a connection until after receiving the CONNECT message in the backwards direction. In our example, we assume that the switch or user does not make the connection until receiving (or transmitting) the CONNECT ACK message. The figure illustrates clipping by showing the point where DATA cells (shown by the solid line) sent by the called party propagate back towards the calling party in relation to the CONNECT and CONNECT ACK messages. Specifically, the first DATA cells only reach switch S2, and stop there, since S2 has not established the connection yet. The next sequence of DATA cells arrive at switch S1, but are discarded there, since S1 has not yet received the CONNECT ACK message from the calling party. The third (and subsequent) DATA cells now flow between the calling and called parties since the end-to-end connection is now established. The historical reason for implementing clipping is to prevent clever users from reducing carrier revenues. Clipping prevents the scenario where a caller sends the SETUP message, immediately followed by a short burst of data. If the network established the connection in the forward direction in response to the SETUP message, then the called party could quickly respond to the data burst and then issue a RELEASE message (not shown in the figure). Thus, data transfer occurred without ever answering the call, and hence, before usage charging could begin. Consequently, the carrier would receive no revenue because the called party rejected the call attempt. However, the clever user would have completed a short request-response transaction for no cost. By not establishing the communication path until the called party answers the call with a CONNECT message, the carrier ensures that the call can be billed.

IP's Resource reSerVation Protocol (RSVP)

The series of Internet RFCs numbered 2205 to 2216 define how Integrated Services utilize the RSVP protocol to reserve resources and guarantee QoS over the best-effort IP infrastructure. The RSVP designers chose to implement an overlay and not modify the fundamental connectionless forwarding paradigm of IP. Hence, the Integrated Services requirements that routers maintain flow state as well as implement an explicit setup mechanism [5] make the resulting service appear more connection-oriented to the end application.

The IETF standards define operation of RSVP over unicast (i.e., unidirectional) and multicast connections. For brevity, we cover only the unicast case in the example depicted in Figure 5.7. Contrary to ATM, RSVP employs receiver-initiated, unidirectional reservation. However, the transmitter must first inform the potential receiver(s) about its Sender Template (ST), Tspec, and optional Adspec using the Path message as shown starting in the upper right-hand portion of the figure. The ST field carries the IP address of the sender, the protocol type field of the IP header, and optionally, the TCP/UDP port number. This sender template effectively defines a filter such that intermediate devices can identify the flow from this particular sender, and allocate reserved resources to it. Intermediate routers also use the Path message to establish the path over which other RSVP messages will take by communicating the previous hop IP address. This design allows RSVP to operate over network elements that do not implement the RSVP protocol. If these intervening networks are not congested, then the RSVP protocol may still deliver the desired QoS. The Path message contains a field that indicates traversal of any non-RSVP networks for diagnostic purposes

After receiving the Path message, the receiver (i.e., client) responds with a Resv message, as shown on the left-hand side of Figure 5.7. The

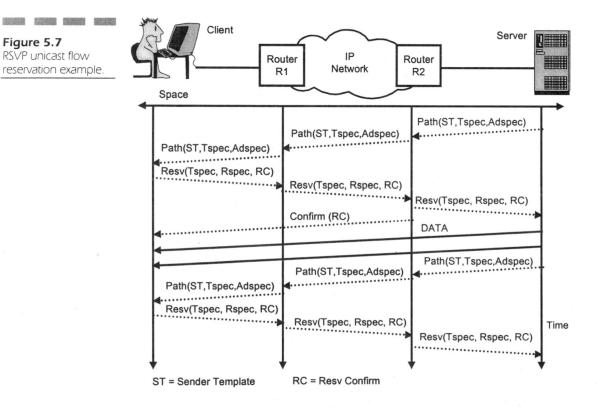

Figure 5.7
RSVP unicast flow reservation example.

Resv message contains a Tspec derived from the Path message. The Guaranteed QoS also employs a Reserve specification (Rspec). Finally, the Resv message may optionally contain a Resv Confirm (RC) object, as shown in the example. The router that performs a merging of Resv messages responds to the confirmation message. In the unicast case, this is a true confirmation of the reservation, as shown in the figure. In the multicast case, the confirmation message only reflects the reservation status up to the router that merged the receiver's Resv message with other Resv messages. RSVP indicates failure to grant a reservation through a Resv Error message. However, either of these messages may be lost due to errors or congestion. Hence, the client must periodically retry the reservation to keep it active. Generally, once an IP network element grants a reservation, the capacity and QoS are available unless a link or node failure occurs. However, if the user does not periodically refresh the reservation, the network element will time out the request and free up the resources. The IETF is working on enhanced RSVP signaling procedures that would be hard-state like ATM and telephony to avoid the need for periodic refresh.

The sender may transmit data at any time; however, the resources and QoS guarantees will only be in place after the Resv message has propagated back to the sender, as shown in the figure. RSVP does not require reliable delivery of these messages. Instead, the protocol periodically requires a receiver to refresh its reservation and the sender to advertise its traffic parameters, as indicated at the bottom of Figure 5.7. Experts call this soft-state reservation versus the hard-state reservation of connection-oriented networks like ATM. Currently, the default refresh interval is 30 seconds [14]. Thus, if a message is lost, the periodic refresh keeps the reservation active, since a router does not delete a reservation until several time-out intervals elapse.

Dynamically Advertising Delay in RSVP

Recall from Chapter 3 that the RSVP token bucket defines a Traffic specification (Tspec) in terms of an average rate r, a bucket depth b, a peak rate p, and a maximum packet size M. The Reserve specification (Rspec) is an additional parameter in an RSVP message that specifies a rate R and a slack term S, where R is greater than or equal to r and S is nonnegative. The units of the rate R are bytes of IP datagrams per second, while the slack term S has units of microseconds. The RSVP protocol can use the optional Advertisement specification (Adspec) field in the Path message to indicate to the receiver a bound on the delay delivered by the network for the specified flow as defined in RFC 2212 [11]. The Adspec field contains parameters Ctot and Dtot (described further below) used in computing the following end-to-end delay bound τ as follows:

$$
\tau = \begin{cases} \dfrac{(b - M)(p - R)}{R(p - r)} + \dfrac{M + Ctot}{R} + Dtot & , r \leq R < p \\[4mm] \dfrac{M + Ctot}{R} + Dtot & , r \leq p \leq R \end{cases} \tag{5-1}
$$

As seen from the above equation, making the Rspec rate R larger than the Tspec rate r reduces the delay τ. If the Rspec rate R is less than the flow's peak rate p, then the network elements along the path must implement peak rate shaping, which increases the delay τ as seen from the above equation. Note that if p=R, the two expressions in Equation (5-1) are equivalent. As studied in Chapters 11 and 18, Weighted Fair Queuing (WFQ) provides a means to achieve the delay bounds required by the RSVP specifications.

The RSVP Adspec characterizes the implementation of guaranteed QoS by network element i by two error terms, Ci and Di, which represent deviation from an ideal fluid model. The error term Ci has units of bytes, while the error term Di has units of microseconds. The terms Ctot and Dtot are the sum of the Ci and Di error terms, respectively, along the network elements in the end-to-end path.

The Ci error terms are rate-dependent; that is, they are divided by the Rspec rate R as seen from Equation (5-1). The manner in which the network element implements shaping affects the Ci term. For example, in a packet-switching network element, Ci would be greater than or equal to the maximum packet size M. In a cell-switching network element, Ci would be greater than or equal to 53 bytes.

The error term Di is rate-independent, which represents the worst-case, non-rate-based delay variation that the network element can introduce. Typically, this term includes the effects of the link rate L as follows. For a packet-switching network element, the Di term is the path Maximum Transfer Unit (MTU) size divided by the link rate. For a cell-switching network element, the Di term is at least 53 bytes divided by the link rate.

The Adspec parameter in the Path message also contains two partial sums of the error terms since the last shaping point called Csum and Dsum. RFC 2212 requires that a network element derive the required buffer space B to ensure no queuing loss from the aforementioned parameters according to the following formula:

$$
B = \frac{(b - M)(p - X)}{(p - r)} + X\left(\frac{Csum}{R} + Dsum\right)
$$

$$\text{where } X = \begin{cases} r & \dfrac{b-M}{p-r} < \dfrac{Csum}{R} + Dsum \quad \text{and} \quad p > R \\ R & \text{otherwise} \end{cases}$$

Comparison of ATM with RSVP

Each of these approaches has advantages and disadvantages. An important difference revolves around the fact that the ATM "hard-state" approach enables networks to guarantee QoS and reserve bandwidth by denying connection attempts if admitting the additional traffic would degrade the quality for the existing connections. The ATM network then attempts another route, blocking the service request only if all routes are full. On the contrary, the "soft-state" approach cannot perform this function easily, since the order of the reservation packets arriving at routers along the path may differ. Furthermore, RSVP signaling provides no means to reliably confirm a user request. This effect means that not all of the routers along the path may reserve capacity for the same flows consistently. Thus, ATM provides a more predictable network, an important consideration when supporting voice, video, and performance-sensitive data traffic.

This brings us back to the requirement for end-to-end ubiquitous handling of QoS. RSVP requires that the receiver periodically refresh reservation requests. Also, the network may deny a refresh request, or simply stop providing the reserved capacity and QoS during the middle of a flow under certain conditions. ATM avoids this issue since each node along the end-to-end path explicitly verifies through admission control that the requested QoS can be met at the specified traffic level in both directions. In other words, in IP, reservations and routing operate independently, while in ATM, they operate concurrently during the connection establishment interval.

Note that a connection-oriented service may also disconnect during the middle of a session, for example, due to a network failure. The user can redial the connection, of course, but may find the network busy during the redial attempt. Because of the arguments summarized above, most experts concede that the RSVP model better supports the native IP interface present in many applications. However, ATM achieves efficient connection establishment and resource allocation in backbone networks, which is an acknowledged weakness of RSVP [15]. A pivotal issue with both approaches is scalability in the backbone, since each protocol effectively operates on a per flow basis.

When millions of flows share a large trunk, processing of each flow is simply not practical. As stated in the RSVP RFC, some form of aggregation is essential to building a scalable network. ATM uses virtual paths to address this issue. We shall see how aggregating many flows improves efficiency and simplifies traffic engineering.

Regarding QoS guarantees, ATM is ahead of any IP-based approach. Although years in the making, RSVP still has a number of problems and is only an experimental protocol as defined by the IETF. ATM has been out for since 1995, while IETF-defined RSVP rolled out in full production form in 1999. QoS and reserved bandwidth is an area where ATM is the incumbent over IP [16]. However, most experts believe that IP will eventually emulate or improve on ATM's traffic management and QoS capabilities.

Review

First, the chapter defined a generic reference model for QoS and described how IP and ATM network characteristics impact quality. We also gave examples of application-specific quality requirements. Next, the text summarized the older and precisely defined terminology used in ATM for QoS and the specific values for these parameters defined in the ITU-T standards. We then summarized the QoS parameters for the Internet's Integrated Services: Controlled Load and Guaranteed QoS. The coverage then moved on to a description of the protocols ATM and IP users employ to signal requests for QoS at specific capacity levels. We summarized the technique that RSVP's Guaranteed QoS protocol employs to report back a bound on end-to-end delay and the buffering required to achieve zero congestion loss. Finally, the chapter concluded by comparing RSVP with ATM.

References

[1]   ATM Forum, *ATM Forum Traffic Management Specification, Version 4.0*, af-tm-0056.000, April 1996.
[2]   G. Woodruff, R. Kositpaiboon, "Multimedia Traffic Management Principles for Guaranteed ATM Network Performance," *IEEE JSAC*, April 1990.
[3]   R. Onvural, R. Cherakuri, *Signaling in ATM Networks*, Artech, 1997.
[4]   Z. Dziong, *ATM Network Resource Management*, McGraw-Hill, 1997.

[5] R. Braden, D. Clark, S. Shenker, *Integrated Services in the Internet Architecture: an Overview,* RFC 1633, IETF, June 1994.

[6] ITU-T, *B-ISDN ATM Layer Cell Transfer Performance,* Recommendation I.356, October 1996.

[7] ITU-T, *B-ISDN Operation And Maintenance Principles and Functions,* Recommendation I.610, November 1995.

[8] D. McDysan, D. Spohn, *ATM — Theory and Application, Signature Edition,* McGraw-Hill, 1998.

[9] ATM Forum, *User-Network Interface Signaling Specification, Version 3.1,* af-uni-0010.002, September 1994.

[10] P. Ferguson, G. Huston, *Quality of Service — Delivering QoS on the Internet and in Corporate Networks,* Wiley, 1998.

[11] S. Shenker, C. Partridge, R Guerin. *Specification of Guaranteed Quality of Service,* RFC 2212, IETF, September 1997.

[12] ATM Forum, *User-Network Interface Signaling Specification, Version 4.0,* af-sig-0061.000, July 1996.

[13] ITU-T, *Broadband Integrated Services Digital Network (B-ISDN) — Digital Subscriber Signalling System No. 2 (DSS 2) — User-Network Interface (UNI) Layer 3 Specification for Basic Call/Connection Control,* Recommendation Q.2931, February 1995.

[14] R. Braden, Ed., L. Zhang, S. Berson, S. Herzog, S. Jamin, *Resource ReSerVation Protocol (RSVP) -- Version 1 Functional Specification,* RFC 2205, IETF, September 1997.

[15] A. Mankin, Ed., F. Baker, B. Braden, S. Bradner, M. O'Dell, A. Romanow, A. Weinrib, L. Zhang, *Resource ReSerVation Protocol (RSVP) -- Version 1 Applicability Statement Some Guidelines on Deployment,* RFC 2208, September 1997.

[16] M. Cooney, "Can ATM Save the Internet?," *Network World; Framingham,* May 20, 1996.

CHAPTER **6**

Delivering QoS via Traffic Control

""It is not because things are difficult that we do not dare, it is because we do not dare that they are difficult."

– Seneca

Now that we've defined how quality affects our perception, quantified what QoS means, and how users can request different levels of quality and capacity: how do real routers and switches deliver QoS? What tools do network nodes have at their disposal? This chapter introduces basic building blocks used by IP routers and ATM switches to deliver the requested QoS at the required traffic levels. One means involves admitting only those flows that the network can support, and then policing these flows. IP and ATM define similar means for nodes to police traffic flows and selectively process packets or cells based upon the traffic contract. Shaping and weighted prioritized queuing are other commonly employed options. Scheduling and queue management are other important techniques introduced in this chapter. Chapter 10 covers these topics in depth.

Generic Router/Switch QoS Architecture

IP routers and ATM switches employ similar techniques to deliver QoS [1, 2, 3]. As illustrated in Figure 6.1, a router or switch is a collection of ports interconnected by a switching fabric. The fabric may be as simple as a bus or a complex matrix of switching elements capable of supporting aggregate capacities of trillions of bits per second and more. The fabric connects a number of ports, which the figure splits into an output and an input side. First, beginning on the input side of each port, a classifier function determines the QoS and traffic control profile required by each flow or connection that the queuing and service scheduling functions will employ. Next, an optional policing function ensures conformance of the IP flow or ATM connection to the traffic parameters. The switch fabric itself may also perform queuing and scheduling prior to delivering packets or cells to the destination output port.

At the output port, a classifier function determines whether to invoke an optional reshaping function. The classifier also controls the queuing and service scheduling provided to each packet or cell on the output side. Together, the functions on the input side, within the fabric and the output side ensure that each IP or ATM network node delivers the required performance necessary to achieve the end-to-end QoS for a flow or connection. The next section describes concept of admission control, which considers the end-to-end QoS requirements and the nodal components.

Figure 6.1
Generic block diagram of router/switch QoS functions.

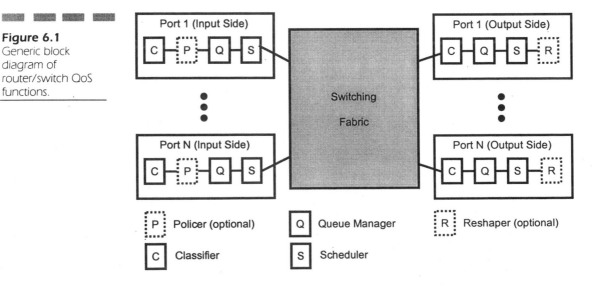

Admission Control

Admission control ultimately decides whether to admit or reject the request to add a new flow or connection based upon whether the newcomer would violate delivering on QoS for the existing flows or connections.

Admission Control and Scheduling

This section describes an important means that connection-oriented protocols employ to deliver QoS. ATM, RSVP, MPLS, and diffserv all effectively operate in a connection-oriented paradigm, and therefore they have similar admission control policies. Admission control involves each node checking every request against available capacity and current QoS capabilities. The node admits the request only if it can provide the requested QoS after adding the traffic corresponding to the existing connections.

One commonly encountered technique for implementing admission control is that of schedulable regions [4, 5]. Admission control reserves scheduling resources to ensure QoS for each connection. In simple admission control systems, each connection, or flow, can be assigned to a class with other connections or flows that have the same (or at least similar) QoS and traffic parameters. Figure 6.2 illustrates a simple example for a switch or router serving only two traffic classes. Class 1 has 25 percent of the capacity requirement of class 2. The shaded area indicates the schedulable region for combinations of class

Figure 6.2
Simple example of a schedulable region.

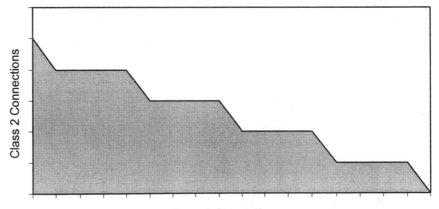

Class 1 Connections

1 and class 2 connections or flows. If a connection request would cause the combination of class 1 and 2 traffic to fall outside of the schedulable region, then admission control should deny the request, since allowing it could degrade the QoS of the already admitted connections.

A problem with the schedulable region approach is complexity. Since the traffic classes are a function of QoS and traffic parameters, the number of classes is potentially quite large. Therefore, precomputing and storing the schedulable region for all of the possible combinations of QoS and traffic parameters is not implemented in real-world switches or routers. Indeed, as studied in Chapter 12, approximating the schedulable region via a simpler algorithm is an important practical design consideration.

ATM Connection Admission Control (CAC)

Connection Admission Control (CAC) is a function commonly implemented by software in ATM switches that determines whether to admit or reject connection requests. A connection request includes traffic parameters, along with either the ATM service category, requested QoS class, or the user specified QoS parameters. As described in Chapter 5, ATM switches use CAC to determine whether admitting the connection request at Permanent Virtual Connection (PVC) provisioning time or Switched Virtual Connection (SVC) call origination time would violate the QoS already guaranteed to active connections. In other words, CAC admits the request only if the network can still guarantee QoS for all existing connections after accepting the request. Frequently, each node performs CAC for SVCs and Soft Permanent Virtual Connections (SPVCs) in a distributed manner for performance reasons. A centralized system may perform CAC for PVCs. For accepted requests, CAC determines policing and shaping parameters, routing decisions, and resource allocation. Resources allocated include trunk capacity, buffer space, and internal switch resources like VPI/VCI lookup table ranges.

CAC must be simple and rapid to achieve high SVC call establishment rates. On the other hand, CAC must be accurate to achieve maximum utilization while still guaranteeing QoS. CAC complexity is related to the traffic descriptor, the switch queuing architecture, and the statistical traffic model.

The simplest CAC algorithm is peak rate allocation, where the ATM switch simply keeps a running total of the peak rate of all admitted connections. Peak rate allocation CAC denies a connection request if adding the peak rate of the candidate connection to the counter indicating capacity already allocated exceeds the trunk capacity. It adds the peak rate of admitted requests to the running counter, and decrements the peak rate of released connections from the running counter.

Figure 6.3 illustrates peak rate allocation. Starting in the upper left-hand corner, the ATM device's CAC logic receives a request with a peak cell rate R. The trunk capacity is P, of which a certain portion A is already assigned according to peak rate allocation. If the request R exceeds the available capacity (P-A), then CAC denies the request; otherwise, CAC accepts the connection request, incrementing the allocated capacity by R. Actually, the admission threshold may be somewhat less than (P-A) due to the slack implied by the compliant connection definition, the CDV tolerance parameter, and the buffer size available for a certain cell loss and delay QoS objective.

Observe that if a network sets the Usage Parameter Control (UPC) (i.e., policing) action to discard cells in excess of the peak rate, and the switches allocate all trunk capacity and buffer resources for the peak rate, then congestion simply cannot occur. The worst that can happen is that arrivals of various streams will randomly clump at highly utilized ATM network nodes, creating some Cell Delay Variation (CDV). A modest amount of buffering keeps the probability of loss quite small in most applications of peak rate allocation, as analyzed in Chapter 12. Extending this design to reserve enough capacity to handle likely network failure scenarios is straightforward.

Although this approach avoids congestion completely, the resulting utilization of the network may be quite low if the average rate is much less than the peak rate, making this a potentially expensive proposition. Note that loose resource allocation policies can make

Figure 6.3
Illustration of Peak
Rate Connection
Admission Control.

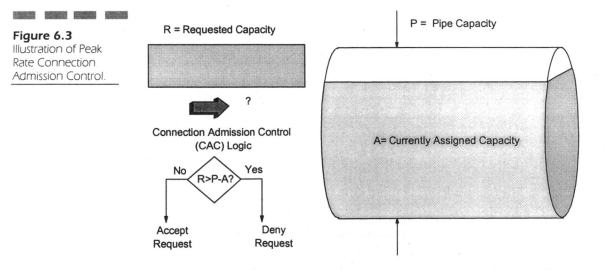

sense in a local area where transmission and ports are relatively inexpensive. The literature refers to the practice of consistently allocating more resource than required as "overengineering." In other words, the network designer allocates more than enough capacity to the problem at every potential bottleneck point. As stated before, this approach always works — if you can afford it.

In general, a network uses the peak cell rate, sustainable cell rate, and maximum burst size for the two types of CLP flows (0 and 1) as defined in the traffic contract to allocate the buffer, trunk, and switch resources. Peak rate allocation ensures that even if all sources send the worst-case, conforming cell streams, the network still achieves the specified Quality of Service (QoS). Similar CAC algorithms using the SCR and MBS parameters also achieve lossless multiplexing. CAC implementations may also permit a certain amount of resource oversubscription in order to achieve statistical multiplex gain. CAC algorithms may also use a concept called *equivalent capacity* in an admission algorithm based upon a combination of the PCR, SCR and MBS as described in Chapter 12 when used in conjunction with Weighted Fair Queuing (WFQ). Networks that oversubscribe certain service categories usually employ some form of congestion avoidance or recovery procedures.

IP's Resource reSerVation Protocol (RSVP)

There is an old saying that "when everything is high priority, there is no priority." Analogously, RSVP over IP only delivers QoS if the underlying layer 2 network delivers QoS. The most straightforward way to assure QoS in the underlying layer 2 network is to ensure that it isn't congested. In the LAN, Switched Ethernet often fills the bill by allocating a dedicated 10- or 100-Mbps segment to each server or client host. In wide area networks subject to congestion, ATM is the only current layer 2 wide area network that delivers QoS. Therefore, many experts believe that ATM and RSVP together are the most viable near-term approach for supporting QoS-aware IP-based applications.

As described in Chapter 5, receiver applications in IP hosts utilize RSVP to indicate to upstream nodes their traffic requirements. RSVP is not a routing protocol, but like routing protocols it operates in the background, not in the data forwarding path shown by the solid arrow and shaded boxes in Figure 6.4.

A *packet classifier* in each RSVP-capable device utilizes the filter specification to determine the QoS class of incoming data packets, and then selects the route. Each node also utilizes a *packet scheduler*, em-

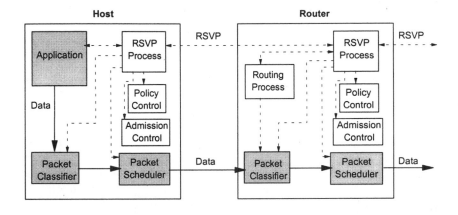

Figure 6.4
Illustration of RSVP functions in hosts and routers.

ploying methods such as packet-level traffic shaping, priority queuing, and weighted fair queuing to achieve the requested QoS.

The admission control function, resident in RSVP-aware nodes along the path between the destination and the source, interprets the flow specification in RSVP control packets and determines whether the node has sufficient resources to support the requested traffic flows. The node may also perform policy control, for example, to ascertain that the requester has the right to make such reservations. If either the admission or policy control process checks fail, the RSVP process in the node returns an error message to the requesting application. If the node does not accept a request, it must take some action on the offending flow, such as discarding the packets or treating them at a lower priority. Thus, every intermediate node must be capable of prioritized service and selective discard. If a layer 2 network interconnects layer 3 devices (e.g., routers), then it too must be QoS-aware. This is an important point, as many IP networks span multiple link layer types and intermediate networks, making a ubiquitous, end-to-end implementation of RSVP unlikely. One device or link layer in the midst of an end-to-end RSVP flow may invalidate any traffic or quality level guarantees.

Traffic Parameter Control — Policing and Shaping

Both IP and ATM network elements perform policing and shaping functions. The policing function checks to see whether incoming traffic conforms to a specific traffic contract. On the other hand, the shaping function delays outgoing packets or cells to ensure conformance to a traffic contract. Properly shaped traffic never fails a policing check when both functions employ the same traffic contract.

Generic Placement of Policing and Shaping Functions

Normally, the first network node performs policing; that is, the network node polices end users as shown by the solid boxes in Figure 6.5. Optionally, one network may police the traffic received from another. When operating in this role, the downstream network must account for accumulated impairments, unless the previous network performs shaping. Frequently, end users shape their traffic outputs to ensure conformance by the policing function at the first network node.

ATM's Usage Parameter Control (UPC)

ATM networks employ Usage Parameter Control (UPC) and Network Parameter Control (NPC) to check conformance of cell flows from a user, or another network, against negotiated traffic parameters, respectively. Another commonly used name for UPC/NPC is *policing* [6]. This is a good analogy, because UPC and NPC perform a role similar to the police in society. Police enforce the law, ensuring fair treatment for all people. The ATM UPC and NPC algorithms enforce traffic contracts between a user and the network or between networks, respectively. Connection Admission Control (CAC) determines which requests to admit and fairly allocates capacity and buffering resources among the users. Without UPC/NPC and CAC, unfair situations where a single user greedily usurps resources can occur. Most of the functions and discussion in the following sections apply equally to UPC and NPC, with any differences identified explicitly.

Standards do not specify the precise implementation of UPC and NPC functions. Instead, they bound the performance of any UPC/NPC implementation in relation to a Generic Cell Rate Algo-

Figure 6.5
Generic placement
of policing and
shaping functions.

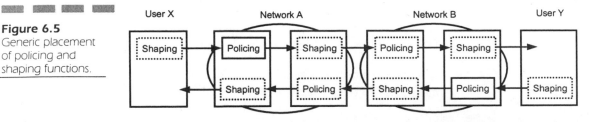

rithm (GCRA), which is essentially a fancy name for the leaky bucket algorithm as defined in Chapter 3. Indeed, the compliant connection definition part of the traffic contract identifies how much nonconforming traffic a network will still provide a QoS guarantee. A UPC should not take a policing action (i.e., tag or discard) more than the fraction of cells which do not conform to the leaky bucket rule. In other words, the UPC cannot be too tight and disproportionately police user cell flows.

Note that the UPC may police different cells than a leaky bucket algorithm does. This may occur due to inevitable differences in initialization, the latitude defined for a compliant connection, or the fact that the UPC implementation of a particular device is not the leaky bucket algorithm.

Leaky Bucket UPC/NPC. The example of Figure 6.6 has an input cell stream shown at the top of the drawing. The nominal interarrival time is four cell times, which is the bucket increment I, and the bucket depth L is equivalent to six cell times. Four gremlins "Dump," "Tag," "Discard," and "Monitor," illustrate the range of UPC actions in this example.

Cell arrivals occur along the horizontal axis at the top of Figure 6.6, with the "Dump" gremlin pouring the fluid from nonconforming

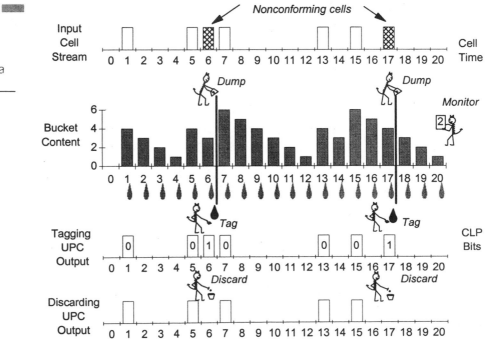

Figure 6.6
Example of ATM's Usage Parameter Control (UPC) via a leaky bucket.

cells (indicated by cross-hatching in the figure) past the leaky buckets. The other gremlins "Tag," "Discard," and "Monitor," all operate in conjunction with "Dump's" identification of a nonconforming cell. "Tag" sets the CLP bit to 1 (regardless of its input value) and lets the cell pass through, with its position unchanged. "Discard" simply deletes the cell. "Monitor" keeps track of the number of nonconforming cells on his notepad. There is a fourth possible UPC action in the standard, namely, do nothing, which corresponds to all of the gremlins being out to lunch in this example.

Guaranteed Frame Rate (GFR).   In 1999, the ATM Forum specified another service category targeted to provide specified QoS to higher-layer protocols using ATM Adaptation Layer 5 (AAL5). What distinguishes this category from the other cell-based categories is that the service either accepts entire frames, or else rejects entire frames at every queuing point.

The Guaranteed Frame Rate (GFR) service targets users who either cannot specify ATM traffic parameters (e.g., PCR, SCR, MBS), or cannot comply with the implied source behavior. Many existing user devices (e.g., routers, hosts, and servers) fall into this category. Currently, these users access ATM networks via UBR connections, which provide no QoS guarantees. Therefore, many users with legacy devices have little incentive to migrate to ATM technology.

The GFR service aims to provide ATM performance and service guarantees in support of such non-real-time applications. The GFR service requires that the user data cells employ AAL5 to segment frames into cells. It provides the user with a Minimum Cell Rate (MCR) guarantee under the assumption of a given Maximum Frame Size (MFS) and a given Maximum Burst Size (MBS) in the traffic contract. Both parameters have units of cells. GFR provides a minimum service rate (determined by MCR) during intervals of network congestion, while the user may be able to send at a higher rate during uncongested intervals.

If the user sends frames with less than MBS cells in a burst, which is also less than the MBS, then the network should deliver the associated frames with minimal loss. GFR allows a user to send traffic exceeding MCR and the associated MBS; however, the network provides no performance guarantees for this excess traffic. Furthermore, the network should service excess traffic using available resources fairly across all GFR users in proportion to the traffic contract. Additionally, the user may mark cells for entire frames as lower priority using the CLP bit. The MCR traffic parameter applies only to unmarked frames. Similar to VBR services, the network may tag cells in unmarked frames only if the user requests the tagging option, either via signaling (for SVCs) or via subscription (for PVCs). Currently, the GFR service only applies to virtual channel connections, since AAL5 delineates frames at this level.

Traffic Shaping

For a user to derive maximum benefit from the guaranteed QoS from ATM, then the device connecting to the network should ensure that the cells sent to the network conform with the parameters in the traffic contract. Standards call the method to achieve this goal *traffic shaping*. In other words, the user equipment processes the source cell stream such that the resultant output toward the network conforms to the traffic parameters according to the leaky bucket algorithm. Although standards make traffic shaping optional, the network need not guarantee QoS performance for nonconforming cells. Therefore, a user wanting guaranteed QoS must shape traffic to ensure conformance to the traffic parameters in the contract. A network may employ shaping when transferring a cell flow to another network in order to meet the conditions of a network-to-network traffic contract, or in order to ensure that the receiving user application operates in an acceptable way.

Figure 6.7 gives an example of traffic shaping using buffering and a

Figure 6.7
Traffic shaping
example.

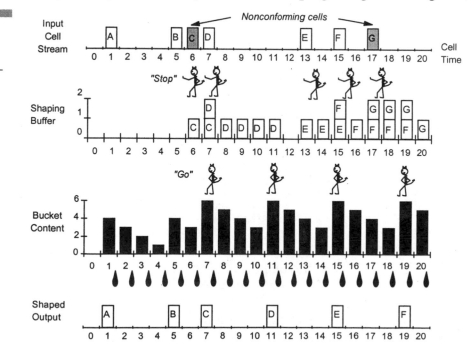

leaky bucket algorithm to transform a nonconforming cell flow into a conforming cell flow by delaying the transmission of nonconforming cells. This example uses the same notation for cell arrivals over time along the horizontal axis, the same nominal interarrival time of 4 cell times and the same leaky bucket depth of 6 as the previous example. We're pleased to introduce two new gremlins: "Stop" and "Go," to illustrate the buffering and scheduling operation of this shaper.

The gremlin "Stop" replaces "Dump" in the nonconforming example. "Stop" commands the ATM hardware genie to buffer the cell if its fluid flow would cause bucket overflow, and "Go" allows a cell transmission as soon as the bucket drains far enough to admit the oldest cell delayed by "Stop." When "Stop" and "Go" are out of synch, then cells build up in the shaping buffer as shown in Figure 6.7. The figure illustrates operation of the shaper by labeling cells A through G, with the nonconforming cells indicated by shading. Cell arrivals A and B are conforming, and leave the bucket in a state such that arrival C at cell time 6 is nonconforming, and hence, "Stop" stores cell C in the shaping buffer. Cell D arrives immediately after C, so the gremlin "Stop" also buffers D. In the same cell time the bucket empties enough so that "Stop's" partner "Go" transmits cell C and adds its flow to the bucket. At cell time 11, "Go" sends cell D and fills the bucket. At cell time 13, the arrival of cell E would cause the bucket to overflow; hence "Stop" buffers it. Cells F and G are similarly buffered by "Stop" and transmitted at the earliest conforming time by "Go" as illustrated in the figure. For the reader wishing to continue the example, cell G would be transmitted at cell time 23 (not shown). Note that the output cell flow from this process is conforming, as can be checked from the conformance test of the leaky bucket defined in Chapter 3. The leaky bucket shaper smoothes the input stream and will not drop any cells unless its buffer overflows. The size of the shaping buffer determines the amount of CDV introduced by the ATM device.

Policing and Shaping in RSVP

The Guaranteed QoS Integrated Service employs both policing and shaping. As in ATM, policing compares arriving traffic against a Tspec. Shaping, actually called reshaping in RFC 2212 [7], attempts to restore the possibly distorted shape of a downstream traffic pattern to the original Tspec. Note that traffic that violates the Tspec over an extended period will overflow the reshaping buffer. Policing is only done at the ingress point of the network to ensure conformance to the token bucket parameters. Nonconforming packets are treated as best effort instead of tagging them as a lower priority, as occurs in

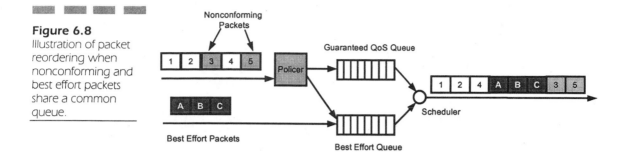

Figure 6.8
Illustration of packet reordering when nonconforming and best effort packets share a common queue.

ATM, although RFC 2212 recommends that marking of nonconforming packets be employed when an Internet RFC defines the means to do so. This action creates the potential for out of sequence packet delivery, as illustrated in the simple example of Figure 6.8. Some TCP receivers handle out of order packet delivery efficiently, while others do not. On the other hand, some applications, for example, voice and video, do not perform well with out of order packets. RFC 2212 recognizes this problem and suggests that implementations consider use of a separate queue for nonconforming and best-effort packets to avoid this misordering problem.

Since RSVP focuses on support for multicast applications, RFC 2212 details reshaping requirements for branch and merge points. As shown in Figure 6.9, RSVP performs reshaping at all heterogeneous source branch points and at all source merge points. The upper right-hand part of the figure illustrates a heterogeneous source branch point. Such a point occurs where the multicast tree branches to multiple distinct paths which have different Tspec reservations, indicated as $r_{1 \rightarrow P}$ for paths P=A and P=B. As shown in the figure, the branch point need only reshape the traffic bound for links with a Tspec less

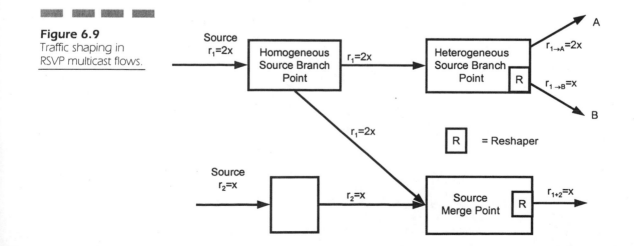

Figure 6.9
Traffic shaping in RSVP multicast flows.

than the reservation for the link immediately upstream from the branch point. The lower right-hand side of the figure illustrates a source merge point, where the distribution tree from two or more different sources share the same reservation. In this case, the reshaper must use the smaller of the Tspec reservations from the upstream links.

At merge or branch points where the input rate is greater than the shaped output rate, reshaping will likely cause a large queue to form if traffic arrives at the higher rate for a significant interval. This would cause both substantial delays, as well as force the router to treat some packets as nonconforming.

Figure 6.10 illustrates the function implemented by a reshaper. Building upon the concepts introduced in Chapter 5, a reshaper combines two buffers with a token bucket and peak rate regulator as indicated in the figure. The combination of buffers and regulators delays packets until transmission is in conformance with both the token bucket and peak rate parameters. The logic that compares the number of tokens in the bucket with the length of the first packet in the buffer achieves this objective.

The amount of buffer B required to reshape any conforming traffic flow back to its original token bucket parameters without loss is:

$$B = b + Csum + Dsum \times r$$

where Csum and Dsum are the sums of the parameters Ci and Di error terms (see Chapter 5), since the last reshaping point. If no reshaping occurs on the path, then Csum=Ctot and Dsum=Dtot.

The buffer for the peak rate regulator is still b bytes to support the maximum length burst allowed by the token bucket regulator. Note that any arriving packets that find a token bucket reshaping buffer full are nonconforming. This means that a reshaper is effectively a

Figure 6.10
Traffic shaping via buffering in conjunction with a token bucket and peak rate regulator.

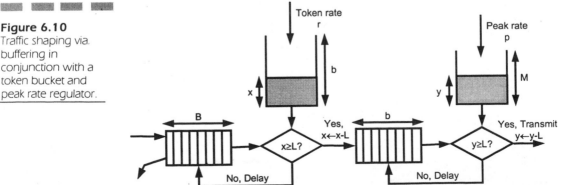

policer as well. Note that the reshaping buffer B does not affect the guaranteed delay bound since the Csum and Dsum terms are part of the Ctot and Dtot error terms in the end-to-end delay bound defined in Chapter 5.

Review

This chapter described the principal means that IP router and ATM switching devices employ to deliver QoS. First, each node must admit a connection or flow request. A simple form of admission control operates on only the peak rate; however, low utilization results if the average rate is substantially less than the peak rate. Second, the user must ensure that the traffic level transmitted by the connection or flow falls within the traffic parameters associated with the accepted request. Typically, at the entry point to a network, the first router or switch usually performs policing to determine the conformance of a particular flow or connection to the negotiated traffic parameters. After this initial policing action, intermediate network elements may reshape the packets or cells for a particular flow or connection such that it complies with the traffic parameters.

References

[1] S. Blake, D. Black, M. Carlson, E. Davies, Z. Wang, W. Weiss, *Architecture for Differentiated Services*, RFC 2475, IETF, December 1998.

[2] ITU-T, *Traffic Control and Congestion Control in B-ISDN*, Recommendation I.371, 1996.

[3] R. Braden, D. Clark, S. Shenker, *Integrated Services in the Internet Architecture: An Overview*, RFC 1633, IETF, June 1994.

[4] S. Keshav, *An Engineering Approach to Computer Networking*, Addison-Wesley, 1998.

[5] J. Hyman, A. Lazar, G Pacifici, "Real-Time Scheduling with Quality of Service Constraints," *IEEE JSAC*, September 1991.

[6] E. Rathgeb, "Modeling and Performance Comparison of Policing Mechanisms for ATM Networks," *IEEE JSAC*, April 1991.

[7] S. Shenker, C. Partridge, and R Guerin. *Specification of Guaranteed Quality of Service*, RFC 2212, IETF, September 1997.

PART

The Traffic Phenomenon

"Common sense is the best distributed item in the world, since everyone thinks he is well supplied with it."

— Rene Descartes

Many traffic systems have analogs to everyday situations. Chapter 7 introduces the reader to the concept of randomness through some simple puzzles. It then introduces the concept of random processes. Chapter 8 defines the basic mathematical models commonly used in the traffic engineering of communication networks. These include popular probability distributions and densities, along with random processes defined via mathematical formulas specified by measurable parameters. We emphasize a pragmatic, cookbook approach using spreadsheet calculations throughout. Chapter 9 delves into more-advanced topics. This includes derivations of key concepts to give further insight to the curious, as well as less commonly used probability and random process models employed by experts to model special networking situations.

CHAPTER 7

Randomness in Our Everyday Lives

"The calamity that comes is never the one we had prepared ourselves for."

— Mark Twain

This chapter introduces the notion of probability and random events through some simple puzzles. The concept of randomness is the foundation for traffic engineering to achieve a specific Quality of Service level. Since probability theory arose in the seventeenth century as a means to predict the likelihood in games of chance, the examples and illustration are rich with coin flipping, rolling dice, and drawing cards at random. This foundation of probability theory in the pastime of gambling has served traffic engineers well for nearly a century. However, recent measurements of data and video traffic indicate that matters can actually be worse than predicted by the classical models. This chapter concludes with an introduction to the self-similar traffic models that capture the characteristics of modern IP and ATM traffic in real-world networks. These modern models describe the sustained intervals of congestion experienced in large enterprise networks and on the Internet.

Introduction to Probability

One of the primary goals of this book is to give the reader the background, methodology, and experience necessary to achieve an improved intuitive understanding of randomness in real-world traffic systems. Probability theory is the foundation upon which queuing theory is built. Unfortunately, all too often our intuition regarding the behavior of systems involving probabilities is incorrect, as the following simple examples illustrate. We suggest that you take out a pencil and paper and jot down the answers to the following puzzles and then compare your responses to the solutions given later in this section.

A Few Probability Puzzles

First, consider the simple example of a friend with three cards: an ace, a king, and a queen, as shown in Figure 7.1a [1]. After a random shuffle and deal, he asks you to pick the card that you believe is the ace in step b. You select the middle card as shown in the figure. Clearly, the chances of you picking the ace is 1/3. He then peeks at the other two cards. Since there is only one ace among the three cards, one of the other two cards must be a face card. Your friend then turns over a face card as illustrated in step c. Now, what is the probability that our finger is on the ace?

The second example is called the gambler's fallacy [2]. Two friends use different strategies in picking numbers for the lottery. Tim always selects the same set of numbers, while Tom selects a different set

Figure 7.1
Illustration of card
selection example.

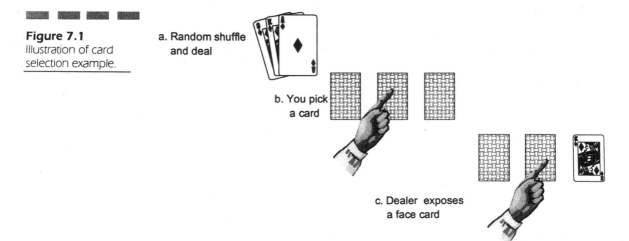

a. Random shuffle
   and deal

b. You pick
   a card

c. Dealer exposes
   a face card

of numbers each time they play the lottery. Tim believes that the odds improve for him winning in each successive lottery drawing because he always selects the same numbers. Tom counters that since the lottery is a random drawing, selecting the same set of numbers each time has no advantage. Who is right? Why?

The third puzzle illustrates another facet of the gambler's fallacy involving two co-workers. Tina and Tammy engage in a coin flipping game to see who pays for lunch. They flip a coin to determine who pays for the next lunch: if a head shows, then Tammy pays; otherwise, if a tail shows, then Tina pays. This goes on for a month, until for 5 days in a row, every time that Tina flipped a coin, it came up heads and Tammy paid for lunch. Distraught at this apparently nonrandom run of bad luck, Tammy accuses Tina of cheating by using an unfair coin. Was Tammy justified in this accusation?

Our fourth problem involves Carl the commuter, who rides the bus to and from his office. Since Carl works in a downtown, congested urban area, the buses arrive randomly at the stop. On average, a bus arrives once every 20 minutes. Furthermore, Carl gets off work at a random time, and hence arrives at the bus stop at a random point in time. What is the average amount of time that Carl must wait for the next bus to arrive?

Our fifth and final puzzle involves Stephanie, who begins riding the subway to and from a new job. Stephanie has a choice of two subway routes between her home and place of work, which take an equal amount of time. The subway train lines each depart at 20-minute intervals. Like Carl, Stephanie arrives randomly at the subway station. However, in this case the subway trains arrive and depart on a strict, deterministic schedule every 20 minutes. After commuting to her new job for a few weeks, Stephanie notes that she is taking the blue route 75% of the time and the yellow route only 25% of the time. How can this be so?

Answers to the Probability Puzzles

Okay, have you recorded your answers to the five puzzles in the previous section? If not, go back and jot down your initial intuitive responses to each of the problems. A good way to sharpen your intuition is to learn from mistakes. Don't feel bad if you get any of the problems wrong. For example, consider the case where Marilyn vos Savant published a version of the first puzzle involving three doors and a car behind one of them in *Parade* magazine in 1990. She received angry letters from many mathematicians who debated the correct solution that we now present [1].

We describe the solution to the card selection problem with reference to Figure 7.2, which depicts the 6 possible outcomes resulting from a random deal of an ace, king, and queen of diamonds. Many people answer that the probability is now 1/2 that the selected card is an ace, since there are only two unexposed cards left. This is incorrect. To see why this is so, observe that only 2 out of these 6 possible outcomes have the ace as the middle card, as shown by the dashed circles in the first two rows of the figure. Hence, the probability that the middle card is an ace is independent of the face card exposed. That is, the probability is still only 1/3.

What is interesting is how the dealer's exposure of a face card changes the probability that the unselected face-down card is an ace. There are four possible outcomes where the unexposed, unselected card is the ace as shown by the solid circles in the last four rows of Figure 7.2. Thus, the probability that the unexposed, unselected card is the ace is 4/6=2/3. If your friend offers you the choice of changing the selection at this point in the game — do it! You'll seldom see better odds in a game of chance. This simple example illustrates two basic tenets of probability theory detailed in Chapter 8, namely the notion of *experimental outcomes*, and the grouping of such outcomes

Figure 7.2
Solution to card
selection probability
puzzle.

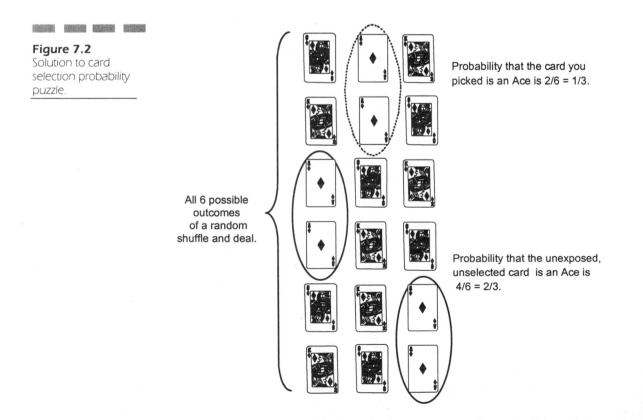

All 6 possible
outcomes
of a random
shuffle and deal.

Probability that the card you
picked is an Ace is 2/6 = 1/3.

Probability that the unexposed,
unselected card is an Ace is
4/6 = 2/3.

into sets.

Now, we present the answer to the second problem. Assume that the lottery involves the player selecting 5 different numbers, each from the range 0 to 99. A publicized random drawing selects five numbers at random, in sequence. Each subsequent random drawing repeats the same procedure. As studied in Chapter 8, there are over 9 billion possible outcomes (or permutations) to such a random selection of 5 items from a set of 100 elements. The chance of any one particular sequence of numbers occurring is no more likely than any other sequence. Thus, Tom was right. The odds that the random selection equals a particular number are always the same for a fair lottery drawing. This concept of *independent trials* greatly simplifies the task of modeling.

Now, for the third problem involving Tammy and Tina flipping a coin to determine who pays for lunch. Most people believe that randomness implies disorder in the sequence of events. However, if you perform an experiment by flipping a coin and adding +1 if heads shows and -1 if tails shows to a sum and plot the result, you'll generate traces like those shown in Figure 7.3. What frequently happens in such a sequence of repeated trials are relatively long runs of heads and tails. In fact, as shown in Chapter 8, the probability that 5 heads (or tails) come up in a row at least once after 25 trials (i.e., 5 working weeks) is 62.5%. Therefore, Tammy was not justified in accusing Tina

Figure 7.3
Results from a
sequence of
random coin flips.

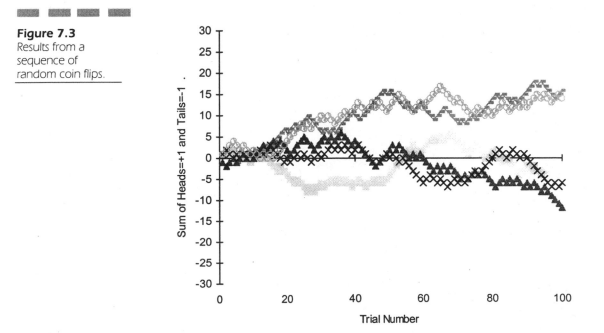

of cheating: she was just unlucky, since the probability that Tina would have had to pay for 5 lunches in a row is also 62.5%. This probability is constructed using the same technique of articulating all of the possible outcomes, and grouping the outcomes with 5 heads (or tails) in a row of 25 successive coin flips as was done in the card selection example.

Note that the absolute number of lunches usually diverges the longer they continue this process. For example, Tina could end up having paid hundreds of dollars more for lunches than Tammy over a 6-month interval. Figure 7.3 illustrates the concept of the how long-term absolute count from the mean is a phenomenon observed in a random walk, as studied in Chapter 9. The net effect is that, at times, random processes appear to be quite orderly. We see this counterintuitive phenomenon in many traffic patterns.

On the other hand, we expect that the long-term average of the fraction of times that a fair coin toss results in heads for the same sequence of random coin flips as shown in Figure 7.3 should converge to a value of 0.5. Statisticians call the ratio of the number of heads (or tails, it doesn't matter) to the total number of trials the *sample mean*, a concept studied in Chapter 21. Figure 7.4 illustrates the trend for the sample mean to regress to the actual probability.

The fourth puzzle involved Carl randomly catching a bus having random departure times occurring on average once every 20 minutes.

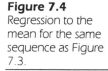

Figure 7.4
Regression to the mean for the same sequence as Figure 7.3.

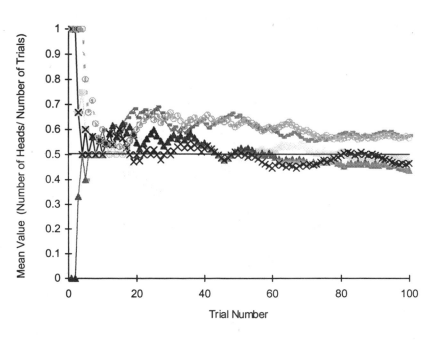

Most people answer that Carl must wait 10 minutes on average to catch the next bus. In fact, the answer is that Carl must wait 20 minutes on average. The formal explanation for this counterintuitive effect is the *paradox of residual life*. The heuristic explanation is that Carl is more likely to arrive during an interval where the waiting time for the next bus is longer.

The fifth problem illustrates an important characteristic of deterministic service when compared with random service times. The explanation of Stephanie's unequal usage of one subway route comes from the fact that the subway train arrivals occur deterministically at an interval of 20 minutes, but are phased in a particular way. The train that she uses 75% of the time arrives at 20-minute intervals starting at the hour, while the train that she uses 25% of the time arrives at 20-minute intervals starting at 5 minutes after the hour. Since Stephanie arrives at a random time at the subway station, she is three times more likely to catch the train leaving at 20-minute intervals starting on the hour than the one leaving at 20-minute intervals starting at five minutes after the hour. Interestingly, her average waiting time is only 6 minutes and 15 seconds. This occurs because she waits an average of 2.5 minutes 25% of the time when she catches the train at five minutes after the hour. Combining this with an average wait of 7.5 minutes 75% of the time when she catches the train departing on the hour, resulting in the counter-intuitive result of approximately a 6-minute waiting time. If one of the subway train lines is closed, then her average wait for the next train would increase to 10 minutes, as expected. An important lesson here is that deterministic service time reduces the average waiting time. To many users, time is very important, hence whether the service policy is random or deterministic often has a noticeable effect, as shown by this simple example.

Deterministic versus Probabilistic Modeling Philosophy

Taking a random, or probabilistic, view of phenomena like shuffling cards, flipping a coin, or rolling dice is often a simplifying point of view. These models ignore the possibility that a cardsharp may shuffle cards unfairly, an unscrupulous player may employ an unfair coin with two heads, or a hustler might use loaded dice weighted to make certain numbers come up more frequently. Furthermore, if we tracked the actual shuffling of the cards, the flipping of a fair coin, or the physical trajectory of the thrown dice accurately enough, we could predict the outcome with certainty. However, the level of effort required to turn these games of chance into scientific experiments is usually too expensive.

Sometimes, however, unexpected events can occur. Take for example the incident in medieval times where King Olaf of Norway and a Swedish king agreed that the highest roll of a pair of dice would decide who would take sole possession of a disputed island [3]. After rolling a pair of sixes, the Swedish king was confident of winning the wager, or at worst of having a tie. However, King Olaf (later revered as a saint) rolled the dice next. The first die showed a six, but the second die cracked in half; one half showed six dots and the other showed one. Hence, Olaf's roll of thirteen bested the Swedish king's double sixes, and he took possession of the island without dispute.

As studied in Chapter 21, ensuring a truly random outcome in a man-made experiment is difficult, even with modern computers. Interestingly, natural systems exhibit truly random phenomena, as studied in subsequent chapters. Einstein found the probabilistic modeling of Quantum mechanics applied to explain experimental data in subatomic physics philosophically distasteful. He expressed this in the popular quote: "God does not play dice with the universe." His belief that the observation of randomness was simply due to the fact that our observational capabilities were insufficient. Einstein's supposition has not been disproved; however, no experimental evidence supports it either. Although Einstein abhorred the notion of randomness used in the quantum mechanical model of physics, it nonetheless describes the phenomenon occurring at the microscopic level better than any other model. The famous Heisenberg Uncertainty Principle defines a fundamental limit on what we can measure. Loosely stated, it says that we can never measure both the position and velocity of any particle with 100 percent accuracy. However, for engineering purposes we often get close enough.

Traffic engineers regularly play dice with their customers, service policies, and networks when they adopt a probabilistic model of user behavior. The alternative is deterministic modeling. Unfortunately, deterministic modeling tends to underestimate the required level of service if traffic patterns exhibit any randomness at all, and hence users may be dissatisfied with such solutions. In some cases, a deterministic model explains certain phenomena better than a random model. For example, the last puzzle, involving Stephanie's unequal selection of a particular train route despite, is best explained using a deterministic model. Choosing the appropriate model is an essential component in solving a particular traffic-engineering problem.

Introduction to Random Processes

This section introduces the basic concepts of random arrivals using a simple dice rolling analogy. Subsequent chapters extend these concepts to the common mathematical models employed in traffic engineering.

Rolling the Dice

Interestingly, rolling a set of fair dice and counting the appearance of a certain number as an arrival is a good model for many events encountered in networks. Probability theory defines the act of rolling a set of fair dice as an independent trial. For example, if the trial consists of rolling one die, we count the occurrence of a six as an arrival in the following example. Since there are six possible outcomes for rolling the single die, an arrival will occur on average once every six trials. We can construct other such trials by using more than one die, or using dice that have more than six sides. We call this sequence of trials a discrete random process, and study its properties in the next two chapters.

Figure 7.5 illustrates the results of such a discrete random process involving the roll of a single die with an arrival indicated by a spike on the graph whenever a six turns up. Note how some intervals occur where the arrival rate is more frequent than once every six trials, while during other intervals, gaps much longer than six trials occur without any arrivals at all. This variability of random arrivals occurs frequently in the study of traffic phenomena. As we shall see, a clumping of outcomes that occurs in rolling dice or flipping a coin also occurs in many real-world traffic systems and communications networks. The traffic patterns resulting from independent events are called *Poisson processes*. This is a good model for many games of chance and human-initiated traffic. However, Poisson processes do not model all types of traffic. In particular, if the underlying events are not independent, but correlated in some way, then the Poisson model

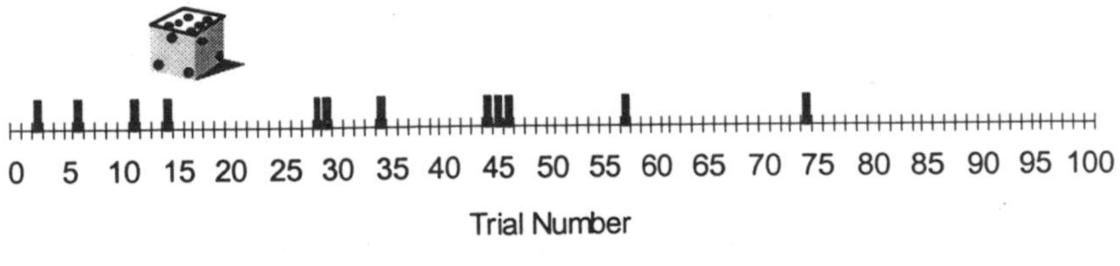

Figure 7.5
Example arrival process
— occurrences of sixes
when rolling a fair die.

0   5   10 15 20 25 30 35 40 45 50 55 60 65 70 75 80 85 90 95 100

Trial Number

can yield overly optimistic predictions.

Hopefully, this example helps explain the old adage, "when it rains, it pours," when referring to runs of good (or bad) luck. Nothing mysterious is going on; this is simply the nature of random arrivals. This may explain part of the fascination some people have with gambling. In games of chance runs of good fortune, as well as bad luck, occur on a regular basis.

Self-Similarity — An Introduction

A relatively recent traffic model has its roots in the modeling of physical phenomena. In the late 1970s, Benoit Mandelbrot and his colleagues coined the term *self-similarity* to describe phenomena where a particular characteristic is similar at different dimensions — either space or time. An example of self-similar models in the spatial dimension is that of using smaller aircraft models for wind tunnel experiments. The behavior of the smaller model is similar to that of the life-size airplane, and much cheaper to experiment with. Self-similarity occurs in a number of geometric, natural phenomena as articulated by Mandelbort [4]. Commonly, this type of property is also called *fractal*. The application of fractal analysis is broad; for example, even financial analysts use it [5].

In random processes, self-similarity occurs in the dimension of time instead of space. As studied in Chapter 9, this has significant consequences on the statistics of offered traffic. A parameter used to characterize the degree of self-similarity is named after H. E. Hurst, a hyrdrologist [6] who studied the Nile and other rivers to determine requirements on the design of water supply reservoirs. Hurst studied the water levels of the Nile recorded over 800 years to design a reservoir that never overflowed, nor ran dry. Key to this model was a measure of the variability of the water level of the river feeding the reservoir. Hurst observed that while some rivers had relatively small fluctuations, the Nile exhibited wide ranges of fluctuations over multiple time scales. Although we might expect the long-term average of a river level to average out, this was not the case for the Nile. The empirical data showed that long periods of drought were followed by years of flooding. Chapter 21 summarizes one method for measuring the Hurst parameter H, called the *variance-time plot*.

Continuing the theme of gambling analogies used throughout the history of probability theory, consider the game of Blackjack or Twenty-one. The object is to draw a set of cards totaling as close as possible to, but not exceeding 21. In this game, face cards have a value of 10 and an ace has a value of 1 or 11 at the player's choice. Long ago, gambling casinos realized that shrewd players could count the cards already played and hence increase their odds of winning by knowing the likelihood that certain card values were more or less likely. For example, if the remaining cards in the deck have a larger fraction of 10's than in a completely new deck, then the player's odds of being dealt two cards with a total value of 20 or 21 (i.e., a Blackjack comprised of a face card or a 10 along with an ace) become larger. This is an example of correlation in a random process. In other words, correlation means that knowledge of the past history of a random process, like dealing cards in Blackjack, increases our knowledge of the future, statistically at least. Of course, in response to card counters, most casinos shuffle together many decks of cards in Blackjack games to make the process behave more randomly.

Examples of Poisson and Self-Similar Processes

As the old adage goes, a picture is worth a thousand words. This is certainly true for the analysis of self-similar traffic patterns as reported in many papers in the literature; for example, see References 6 and 7. The presentation of this type of comparison began when researchers analyzed traces of LAN traffic data collected by Bellcore in the early 1990s. The measurements recorded the number of packets received in very small time intervals. Researchers aggregated the number of packets received over increasingly larger time intervals and observed a surprising result. Instead of the traffic patterns smoothing out as the averaging intervals increased, the traces showed similarity of the traffic patterns across time scales ranging from milliseconds to many minutes. Only when the time scales reached hours or weeks did this self-similar pattern abate due to daily and weekly characteristics of the LAN user community.

Figure 7.6 shows what has become a classic method to illustrate the difference between self-similar and the traditional uncorrelated Poisson arrival model. The figure plots simulated traffic traces for Poisson and self-similar traffic using techniques detailed in Chapter 9 across time scales ranging from 10 milliseconds to 1 second. Each of the plots depicts the simulated number of packets received in an interval determined by the time scale. The three plots on the left-hand side of the figure were generated by a Poisson traffic model described in Chapter 8, while the three plots on the right-hand side were generated by the Fractional Brownian Motion (FBM) traffic model described in Chapter 9. Observe how the Poisson-generated plots on the left-hand side of the figure are very bursty at a time scale of 10 milli-seconds — that is, the number of packets received varies significantly from time instant to time instant. As the time scale increment increases for the Poisson process to 100 ms up to 1 s, the burstiness decreases, as seen from the increasingly smoother simulated traffic traces. This smoothing out of traffic due to averaging over increasingly larger time intervals represents the classical intuition developed over a century of telephone traffic engineering.

The right-hand side of Figure 7.6 illustrates the results of a simulated self-similar traffic trace using an FBM process with a Hurst parameter H=0.8, a value typically observed for data traffic. Some video traffic also exhibits self-similar tendencies. Similar to the Poisson process, the self-similar traffic is very bursty at a time scale of 10 ms. However, contrary to the Poisson traffic traces, the burstiness of the self-similar traffic traces persists as the time scale increases from 10 ms up to 1 s. In other words, the traffic pattern traces exhibit a similar

Figure 7.6

Examples of Poisson and self-similar traffic patterns over a range of time scales.

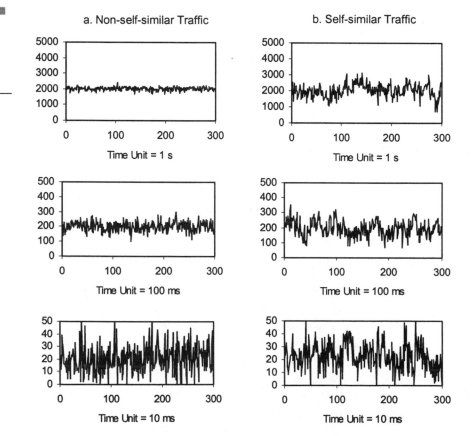

jagged appearance across a broad range of time scales, in sharp contrast to the Poisson traces. We detail the mathematics of self-similar traffic in Chapter 9 as a prelude to an analysis of the impact on IP and ATM networks in Part 4.

Review

This chapter introduced the notion of randomness, and illustrated how our intuition may fail us at times even in relatively simple situations. Understanding the means for solving these problems starts the reader on the path to understanding one of the fundamental principles of traffic engineering — probability theory. We saw that randomness does not equate to disorder, and in fact, random processes generate periods of apparent order. This effect underlies the unpredictability of many traffic systems in real-world situations.

This chapter concluded with an introduction to the concept of self-similar random processes that model some types of data and video traffic. Through a simple example, we showed that self-similar traffic exhibits behavior that presents a greater challenge to IP and ATM networks concerned with delivering specific levels of quality.

References

[1] M. Gardner, "A Quarter-Century of Recreational Mathematics," *Scientific American*, August 1998.

[2] J. Paulos, *Inummeracy*, Vintage, 1988.

[3] I. Ekeland, *The Broken Dice and Other Mathematical Tales of Chance*, The University of Chicago Press, 1993.

[4] B. Mandelbrot, *The Fractal Geometry of Nature*, W.H. Freeman, 1982.

[5] B. Mandelbrot, "A Multifractal Walk Down Wall Street," Scientific American, February 1999.

[6] W. Stallings, *High-Speed Networks — TCP/IP and ATM Design Principles*, Prentice-Hall, 1998.

[7] W. Leland, M. Taqqu, W. Willinger, D. Wilson, "On the Self-Similar Nature of Ethernet Traffic (extended version)," IEEE/ACM Transactions on Networking, February 1994.

CHAPTER **8**

Random Traffic
Models

"Chance favors only the prepared mind."

— Louis Pasteur

For as long as traffic has existed, people have devised ways of describing it in the hopes of achieving greater understanding to economically balance provisioning of resources to achieve a desired level of quality. Random models are an essential component of traffic engineering, best applied to populations of many users arriving to a traffic system. First, we introduce some basic definitions from probability theory. The text then uses networking examples of discrete- and continuous-time random arrival processes to define pivotal concepts used in queuing theory and traffic engineering analysis. This includes the concepts of probability distributions, the average (or mean) value, and the variance (or dispersion) about the mean. As we shall see, the network design problem under consideration and the relative ease of solution often drive the choice of a particular probability model. This chapter concludes with an introduction to the important practical problem involving sequences of random variables. Called *stochastic processes*, these mathematical models provide the foundation for queuing theory studied in Part 4.

Probability Theory

As much as anything, probability theory provides a style, or a way of thinking, when employed in problem solving. Much of this book is about helping the reader develop and refine this technique and apply it to communication network design. Although several models and approaches to probability have been defined [1], this text uses an approach consistent with observed performance in real networks.

Set Theory and the Definition of Probability

Probability theory began in the seventeenth century as a means to calculate the odds in games of chance. We will refer to applicable work by people like Chevalier de Méré, Blaise Pascal, and the Bernoulli brothers when introducing concepts conceived in this time. In addition, the more contemporary notion of sets, or groupings, of experimental outcomes is central to the theory of probability. Georg Cantor founded set theory in the latter part of the nineteenth century [2]. The notation is somewhat cumbersome, but allows theorists to replace imprecise language with compact mathematical formulations. Set theory forms the basis of theoretical probability and many other branches of mathematics. This section defines a minimum set of definitions and terminology, and then the next section applies them to the communication-networking problem.

A formal introduction to probability begins with a few definitions and a small set of assumptions, called *axioms*. Most of the important results in probability theory can be derived from these axioms. Formally, a finite set is a list of elements, for example, the notation:

$$\mathbb{S} \equiv \{\, a_1,\, a_2,\, ...,\, a_n \},$$

indicates that the set $\mathbb{S}$ contains elements a_1, a_2, through a_n. The symbol $\varnothing \equiv \{\}$ denotes the *empty set*. That is, the empty set is the set with no elements. Set theory denotes that an element a is part of a set $\mathcal{A}$ by the notation $a \in \mathcal{A}$.

The definitions from set theory of the union and intersection of sets are also fundamental to probability. Denoted by the symbol $\cup$, the union of two sets includes members from each set. For example, the union of the set $\mathcal{A} = \{0, 1, 2\}$ with set $\mathcal{B} = \{2, 3, 4\}$ is:

$$\mathcal{A} \cup \mathcal{B} = \{0, 1, 2, 3, 4\}$$

Denoted by the symbol $\cap$, or also by simply writing the labels for two sets adjacent to each other, the intersection of two sets is the elements that the two sets have in common. The intersection of the sets $\mathcal{A}$ and $\mathcal{B}$ used in the previous example is the following:

$$\mathcal{A} \cap \mathcal{B} = \mathcal{A}\mathcal{B} = \{2\}$$

The three axioms of probability define the probability of an event $\mathcal{A} \in \mathcal{S}$ via the notation $\Pr(\mathcal{A})$ as follows:

I. $\Pr(\mathcal{A}) \geq 0$
II. $\Pr(\mathcal{S}) = 1$ (8-1)
III. If $\mathcal{A} \cap \mathcal{B} = \varnothing$, then $\Pr(\mathcal{A} \cup \mathcal{B}) = \Pr(\mathcal{A}) + \Pr(\mathcal{B})$

A similar set of axioms defines the concept of probability for infinite sets [3]. In words, the first two axioms say the following: probability is a non-zero measure of the likelihood of an event $\mathcal{A}$ drawn from the set of all possible events $\mathcal{S}$. The set $\mathcal{S}$ is also called the certain event. The third axiom states that the probability measure of non-overlapping events is additive.

Frequently, texts employ the visual aid of a *Venn diagram* to illustrate these concepts. For example, consider the case where during a time interval T; 0, 1, 2, and so on up to infinity arrivals can occur. Let A_k be the event where k arrivals occur during the interval T, as shown by dots in Figure 8.1. Define the set $\mathcal{B}$ as the event where one or more arrivals occur in the interval T. Define the set $\mathcal{A}$ as the event that exactly 0 arrivals occur in the interval T. The certain event set $\mathcal{S}$ denoted by a box in the figure contains all possible arrival events. The figure shows sets $\mathcal{A}$ and $\mathcal{B}$ as circled grouping of dots. Observe that $\mathcal{A} \cap \mathcal{B} = \varnothing$ because the points in the set do not overlap. Hence, from the axioms of Equation (8-1), $\Pr(\mathcal{A}) + \Pr(\mathcal{B}) = 1$. Expressed in plain English, the probability of no arrivals plus the probability of one or more arrivals is 100 percent.

The earliest book on probability, written by the sixteenth century mathematician Gerolamo Cardano, was published in 1663, over 87 years after the author's death. This early work defined probability [2] as "the number of favorable outcomes divided by the number of pos-

Figure 8.1
Illustration of probability mapping to a set of arrival events.

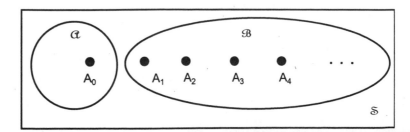

sible outcomes." This is essentially the definition employed in the modern theory. A familiar example of a set with two outcomes is the result of a fair coin toss: that is, the elements are heads and tails. A generalization commonly used as an introduction to probability theory involves balls drawn from an urn [4]. The balls may be of different colors, or numbered. The random drawing of a ball from the urn constitutes an experimental trial by selecting one element from the set (i.e., picking a ball from the urn). This relatively simple definition models a broad range of practical problems in probability.

Consider a simple example with M balls in an urn where m balls are black, and therefore M-m balls are white. The symbol $\mathcal{S}$ denotes the set of all balls. If one draws a ball randomly from the urn, there are m possible outcomes where the ball is black and M-m outcomes where the ball is white. We place the selected ball back in the urn after each trial. After repeating this experiment many times, we expect to draw a black ball with likelihood m/M, and a white ball with likelihood (M-m)/M. Probability theory defines the collection of all possible outcomes in an experiment as a sample space and subsets as events. For example, denote the m elements from the set (i.e., the black balls) as event $\mathcal{E}$. Therefore, the probability that the event $\mathcal{E}$ occurs is:

$$\Pr[\mathcal{E}] \equiv \frac{m}{M}$$

The complement of event $\mathcal{E}$ (i.e., a white ball is drawn) is denoted by writing the symbol for the event with a bar over the top, as follows: $\overline{\mathcal{E}}$. Formally, the sets $\mathcal{E}$ and $\overline{\mathcal{E}}$ are *mutually exclusive*, or disjoint, since $\mathcal{E} \cap \overline{\mathcal{E}} = \varnothing$. In other words, the sets $\mathcal{E}$ and $\overline{\mathcal{E}}$ contain no common elements. The *theorem of total probability* states that the sum of the probabilities for a set of mutually exclusive events covering the sample space is unity. For the above example, $\Pr(\mathcal{E}) + \Pr(\overline{\mathcal{E}}) = 1$. In general, if the set of all possible event outcomes, $\mathcal{E}$, is arranged into n mutually exclusive and exhaustive subsets, $\{E_1, E_2, ..., E_n\}$, then the theorem of total probability is expressed as:

$$\sum_{k=1}^{n} \Pr[E_k] = 1$$

An important notion is that of *statistical independence*. Probability theory states that two events $\mathcal{A}$ and $\mathcal{B}$ as statistically independent if and only if the following is true:

$$\Pr[\mathcal{A}\mathcal{B}] = \Pr[\mathcal{A}]\Pr[\mathcal{B}]$$

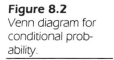

Figure 8.2
Venn diagram for conditional probability.

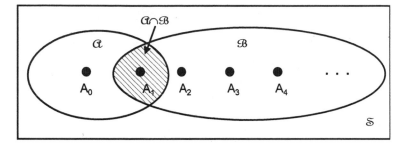

The set of events depicted in Figure 8.1 are mutually exclusive since the circles in the Venn diagram do not overlap. Another definition is that of the *conditional probability* of an event A given that the event B has already occurred, denoted as follows:

$$Pr[\mathcal{A}|\mathcal{B}] \; \equiv \; \frac{Pr[\mathcal{A}\mathcal{B}]}{Pr[\mathcal{B}]} \tag{8-2}$$

Figure 8.2 illustrates the Venn diagram for conditional probability for the events A_k denoting the occurrence k arrivals occurs during an interval. In this example, set $\mathcal{A}$ denotes either 0 or 1 arrivals, while set $\mathcal{B}$ denotes 1 or more arrivals. Observe that the circles denoting these sets overlap since they both contain the event A_1, the occurrence of a single arrival. Using Equation (8-2) yields the following result. The probability of $\mathcal{A}$ (0 or 1 arrivals) given $\mathcal{B}$ (one or more arrivals) is equal to the probability of $\mathcal{A} \cap \mathcal{B}$ (exactly one arrival) divided by the probability of $\mathcal{B}$ (one or more arrivals).

An important result used in queuing is called *Baye's Theorem*, which allows solution of one conditional probability in terms of another as follows:

$$Pr[\mathcal{A}|\mathcal{B}] \; \equiv \; \frac{Pr[\mathcal{B}|\mathcal{A}]Pr[\mathcal{A}]}{Pr[\mathcal{B}]} \tag{8-3}$$

We've thrown quite a few formulas at you, but we needed to define some basics. Don't worry, we'll use all of these over the course of the next several chapters. The next section begins applying some of these definitions to the Web access problem introduced in Chapter 1.

Probability Theory and Communications

The following description applies the definitions of probability to arrivals in a communication network with reference to Figure 8.3. Consider the case where n=4 Web surfers randomly generate requests to a router or Web server during short time intervals, say, one second. This figure uses the same space-time notation introduced in Chapter 1, where the space dimension runs from right to left and time runs from top to bottom. The horizontal dashed lines mark off the time intervals in discrete increments. Note how the Web surfers may generate one or more requests during the same interval. The column of numbers on the right-hand side of the figure counts the total number of requests k arriving during the corresponding interval. During each time interval, the probability that a Web surfer generates a request event is p=1/4. Usually, the requests don't all arrive within the same interval. In fact, they may arrive in a number of different orders and result in the same number of cumulative requests in an interval. We study the number of possible orders in which k events out of n possible outcomes can occur in the next section.

Permutations and Combinations

Another important notion in probability theory concerns independently repeating the same experiment on a set of n distinct elements.

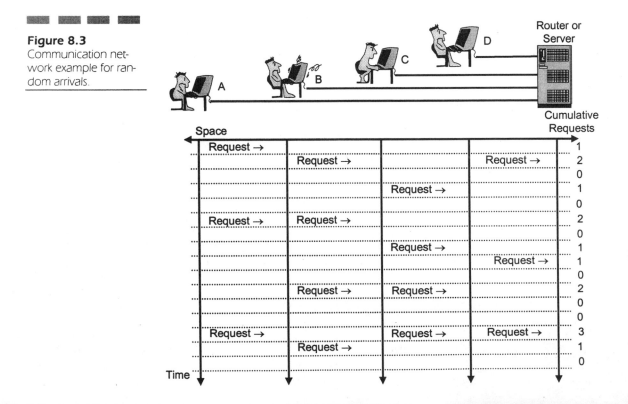

Figure 8.3
Communication network example for random arrivals.

If the experiment of drawing balls from an urn is repeated k times, and we replace the ball in the urn after each draw, then the number of possible outcomes is simply n^k. This occurs because each subsequent trial is independent of any previous trial because there are always n balls in the urn.

Scenarios that are more interesting result when drawing n numbered balls from an urn without replacement. In this case, the order of the draw is important. Calculation of the number of possible outcomes is straightforward. There are n possible draws for the first ball, leaving (n-1) possibilities for the second draw, and so on until there is only one possibility for drawing the last ball. Thus, the number of permutations of n distinct elements from a set drawn without replacement is the product of the integers ranging from n through 1. Since this product frequently occurs in the study of probability, mathematicians define this product as *n factorial* (abbreviated as n!) as follows:

$$n! \equiv n \times (n-1) \times \cdots \times 1 \qquad (8\text{-}4)$$

The convention is that $0! \equiv 1$. Applying this formula to the Web surfer example, the number n! determines the number of orderings that all of the Web surfers could generate requests. Specifically, Table 8.1 shows all of the $4!=4\times3\times2\times1=24$ permutations of the order that the four Web surfers A, B, C, and D depicted in Figure 8.3 could generate.

Since the value of n! grows rapidly as n increases, it is difficult to compute using the definition of Equation (8-4) even for moderate values of n. *Stirling's approximation* gives an easier to compute formulation for n! applicable for larger values on n as follows:

$$n! \approx n^n \times e^{-n} \sqrt{2\pi n} \qquad (8\text{-}5)$$

Another commonly encountered experiment involves drawing only k elements out of the n elements in the set without replacement when order is important. Using the same reasoning as above, the number of outcomes is the product of the integers ranging from n through (n-k-1). This result determines the number of orderings in our network example if only k out of the n Web surfers generate a

TABLE 8.1				
	ABCD	BACD	CABD	DABC
	ABDC	BADC	CADB	DACB
The 4!=16	ACBD	BCAD	CBAD	DBAC
permutations of 4	ACDB	BCDA	CBDA	DBCA
elements: A,B,C,D.	ADBC	BDAC	CDAB	DCAB
	ADCB	BDCA	CDBA	DCBA

request during a specific interval. Probability theory defines the number of possible outcomes in this case as the number of *permutations* of k elements selected from the set of n elements without replacement as follows:

$$^{n}P_{k} \equiv \frac{n!}{(n-k)!} \tag{8-6}$$

The Microsoft Excel function PERMUT(n,k) computes the value of $^{n}P_{k}$. Applying this formula to the Web surfer example, the formula for $^{n}P_{k}$ determines the number of orderings when k out of the n=4 Web surfers generate requests. Table 8.1 shows the permutations all k=4 Web surfers depicted in Figure 8.3: A, B, C, and D for the formula $^{4}P_{4}$. Table 8.2 list the permutations for $^{4}P_{3}$, $^{4}P_{2}$, $^{4}P_{1}$, and $^{4}P_{0}$ for the same set of Web surfers.

Another commonly encountered result is calculation of the number of outcomes resulting from drawing k elements from a set of n distinct elements where the order is of no importance. In this case, there are k! permutations of k things taken at a time, order important, which have the same elements. Hence, the number of *combinations* of k elements selected from a set of n distinct elements is the corresponding number of permutations, order important given by Equation (8-6), divided by k!. The notation for the number of combinations of n things taken k at a time where order is not important is:

$$\binom{n}{k} \equiv \frac{n!}{(n-k)! \ \ k!} \tag{8-7}$$

This formula determines the number of ways that k out of n Web surfers can generate requests during a one-second interval, without regard to order. Communications network design frequently takes this point of view, since the router or server is not specifically concerned with the precise arrival order of the requests. Table 8.3 depicts these combinations for n=4 for all possible values of k. The table lists each possible set of elements (order not important) separated by commas for each combination. The Microsoft Excel function

TABLE 8.2 The permutations of 4 elements (A,B,C,D) taken 3, 2, 1, and 0 at a time.	$^{4}P_{3}=24$				$^{4}P_{2}=12$		$^{4}P_{1}=4$	$^{4}P_{0}=1$
	ABC	BAC	CAB	DAB	AB	CA	A	∅
	ABD	BAD	CAD	DAC	AC	CB	B	
	ACB	BCA	CBA	DBA	AD	CD	C	
	ACD	BCD	CBD	DBC	BA	DA	D	
	ADB	BDA	CDA	DCA	BC	DB		
	ADC	BDC	CDB	DCB	BD	DC		

TABLE 8.3

Combinations of k = 4, 3, 2, 1, and 0 things taken from a n=4 element set.

$\binom{4}{4} = 1$	$\binom{4}{3} = 4$	$\binom{4}{2} = 6$	$\binom{4}{1} = 4$	$\binom{4}{0} = 1$
A, B, C, D	A, B, C	A, B	A	∅
	A, B, D	A, C	B	
	B, C, D	A, D	C	
	C, D, A	B, C	D	
		B, D		
		C, D		

COMBIN(n,k) returns the value of Equation (8-7).

A handy computational technique is to employ the recursive definition of the number of combinations of n things taken k at a time where order is of no importance as follows:

$$\binom{n}{k} = \frac{n-k+1}{k} \times \binom{n}{k-1} \tag{8-8}$$

Note that $\binom{n}{0} = 1$ by definition.

Bernoulli Trials and the Binomial Distribution

This section uses the definition of combinations and randomly occurring arrivals to define some basic elements of random processes. During each one second interval, each of the n Web surfers independently either generates an arrival request with probability p, or doesn't generate any request with probability (1-p). Therefore, the probability that k requests arrive from Web surfers (and hence (n-k) do not generate requests) in a specific order is:

$$\Pr[k \text{ arrivals} \mid \text{specific combination}] = p^k (1-p)^{n-k} \tag{8-9}$$

Equation (8-7) gives the number combinations of k requests drawn from the population of n Web surfers. Hence, from the theorem of total probability, the product of Equations (8-7) and (8-9) gives the probability of k requests arriving from n Web surfers in a particular time slot as follows:

$$B(n,k,p) = \binom{n}{k} \ p^k \ (1-p)^{n-k} \qquad (8\text{-}10)$$

The result of n independent trials in an experiment where the probability of an event is p is called a *Bernoulli trial*. The probability that k events occur (and hence n-k don't occur) as a result of n repeated Bernoulli trials as defined by Equation (8-10) is called the *binomial probability density*. Microsoft Excel computes b(n,k,p) via the BINOMDIST(k, n, p, FALSE) function.

Random Variables

A random variable is a mapping from the outcome of an experimental trial to a number. Loosely defined, a probability density is essentially the probability that a random variable takes on a certain value. Random variables may be either discrete, or continuous. Probability theory defines both discrete and continuous random variables. We deal largely with discrete random variables; however, in some cases continuous random variables yield a good approximation and simpler results for some problems.

Probability Densities, and Distributions

The first, and often most difficult, step in defining a problem is assigning events from a set to numerical values. In many queuing theory problems, this is relatively straightforward: we assign a 1 to an arrival, and a 0 to the absence of an arrival. In the case of Bernoulli trials covered above, we assign the random variable x probabilities as follows:

$Pr[x=1$ for an arrival in a time slot$] = p$
$Pr[x=0$ for no arrival in a time slot$] = 1\text{-}p$

The discrete *probability density function* (or pdf for short) of the random variable x is defined as the mapping where a specific instance of the random variable x_i takes on a value x with a specific probability corresponding to an event E_i as follows:

$$f_x(x) \quad \equiv Pr[\text{Event } E_i \text{ mapped to random variable } x_i = x]$$
$$\equiv Pr[x_i = x] \equiv p_i$$

This book uses the notation $\Pr[x_i=x]$ and p_i interchangeably to denote the pdf that a discrete random variable takes on the ith value corresponding mapped to the ith event. The binomial distribution function, $b(n,k,p)$ of Equation (8-10) is an example of a discrete pdf. When using the continuous parameter notation in $f_x(x)$ for a pdf with discrete steps, this text utilizes the Dirac delta function to ensure continuous differentiability and integration when performing manipulation using standard Riemann calculus [5].

Another commonly used measure in probability is that of the cumulative distribution function (cdf), also called the probability distribution function. This measures the probability that a random variable x is less than or equal to some value x, namely:

$$F_x(x) \equiv \Pr[X \le x] = \sum_{x_i \le x} \Pr[x_i = x] \tag{8-11}$$

In traffic and communications engineering, we are commonly interested in the probability that a random variable exceeds a certain value. This viewpoint models the probability that an arrival creates a buffer overflow, or the probability that a switch blocks the admission of an arrival to the network. Commonly, theorists call this measure the *tail* of the distribution, also called the *survivor function*, which has probability:

$$\Pr[x > x] \equiv Q(x) = 1 - F_x(x) = \sum_{x_i > x} \Pr[x_i = x]$$

Analogous definitions exist for continuous random variables. See Reference 3 for a detailed derivation of how to extend the above discrete definitions to continuous variables with sets containing an infinite number of elements. The next section looks at an example of a commonly encountered continuous random variable, the normal or Gaussian distribution.

Mean and Variance

Some important characteristics used to specify random variable distributions are the average, or mean value, and the deviation about the mean, called moments. The name used for second-order moment is variance. The mean value is the expected value of a random value x as follows:

$$E[\mathbf{x}] \; \equiv \; \overline{X} \; \equiv \; \sum_{\text{All } i} x_i \; f_\mathbf{x}(x_i) \tag{8-12}$$

The notation $E[X]$ for expectation and $\overline{X}$ are equivalent, denoting the mean value of the random variable $\mathbf{x}$. The nth central moment is the expected value of the random variable minus the mean value raised to the nth power as defined by the following formula:

$$E[(\mathbf{x} - \overline{X})^n] \; \equiv \; \sum_{\text{All } i}(x_i - \overline{X})^n \; f_\mathbf{x}(x_i)$$

The most commonly used higher order central moment is the *variance*, usually denoted by the Greek letter sigma as follows:

$$\sigma_\mathbf{x}^2 \; \equiv \; E[(X - \overline{X})^2] \; = \; E[X^2] \; - \; \overline{X}^2$$

A closed related measure is the *standard deviation*, which is simply the square root of the variance. In other words, the standard deviation of a random variable X is:

$$\sigma_\mathbf{x} \; \equiv \; \sqrt{E[(X - \overline{X})^2]}$$

The next section examines how these concepts of mean and variance apply to the normal distribution.

Important Properties of Two Random Variables

The preceding concepts extend to two or more random variables. For example, the joint probability density of two random variables $\mathbf{x}$ and $\mathbf{y}$ is defined as $f_{\mathbf{xy}}(x,y)$. In traffic engineering, we frequently consider the statistics of two random variables derived as samples at different points in time from the same random process. A measure of the relationship between two random variables is the *correlation*, defined as follows:

$$E[\mathbf{xy}] \; = \; \sum_x \sum_y xy \; f_{\mathbf{x,y}}(x,y)$$

If two random variables, $\mathbf{x}$ and $\mathbf{y}$, are *independent*, then the joint probability density has the following property:

$$f_{xy}(x,y) = f_x(x) \ f_y(y)$$

The correlation of two independent random variables then reduces to the following:

$$E[xy] = \sum_x \sum_y xy \ f_x(x) \ f_y(y)$$
$$= E[x] \ E[y]$$

Independent random variables are *uncorrelated.*; however, uncorrelated random variables are not necessarily independent.

Limit Theorems In Probability

Often our interest is only in the tail of the distribution. Hence, if a reasonably accurate, easier to calculate approximation exists, we can opt to use the approximation instead of a exact formulation involving complex calculation. Furthermore, use of an approximation may afford deeper insights into the trends and tradeoffs involved in a particular instance of a traffic engineering problem.

Central-Limit Theorem

The central-limit theorem states that a random variable formed as the sum of n independent, identically distributed random variables converges on the normal density as n becomes large. Specifically, given n independent random variables x_1, x_2, ..., x_n with identical pdf having finite mean μ and variance σ^2, then the random variable x is formed as the sum of these inputs, namely:

$$x = \frac{1}{n}\sum_{i=1}^{n} x_i$$

The random variable x is called the sample mean, and tends toward the normal density given by the following formula:

$$f_x(x) \cong \frac{1}{\sqrt{2\pi} \ \sigma} \ e^{\frac{-(x-\mu)^2}{2\sigma^2}} \tag{8-13}$$

where the mean and variance of x are:

$$\mu = \frac{1}{n}\sum_{i=1}^{n} E[x_i] \quad , \quad \sigma^2 = \frac{1}{n}\sum_{i=1}^{n} \sigma_i^2$$

As n tends to infinity, the approximation in Equation (8-13) becomes an equality for an extremely general set of conditions [6]. This text uses the symbol $\cong$ to denote this asymptotic behavior. If you have a relatively large number of independent observations of some apparently random phenomenon (usually at least several dozen) then a normal distribution is frequently a good approximation.

The Normal, or Gaussian Distribution

A frequently encountered continuous random variable is the Gaussian, or normal, distribution. It models a number of physical phenomena and statistics encountered in communications engineering, sociological, and business processes. Its pdf is given by the following formula with a mean value $E[x]=\mu$ and standard deviation σ:

$$f_x(x) \equiv \frac{1}{\sqrt{2\pi}\,\sigma}\, e^{\frac{-(x-\mu)^2}{2\sigma^2}}$$

The deMoivre-Laplace and Central-limit theorems states that the above formula is a good approximation to the binomial distribution when $E[X]=np$ is a large number in the $\sigma^2=np(1-p)$ region about the mean [3]. Figure 8.4 compares the probability densities of the discrete binomial and continuous normal random variables for an example where n=100 and p=0.2 to illustrate this point. Note how the discrete binomial density has values only at the discrete integer points k, while the continuous normal density has values at all points along the real number axis x. The distributions have essentially the same shape, and for relatively large mean values, the normal distribution is a good approximation to the binomial distribution.

The normal approximation is helpful in analyzing relative performance, since many published tables, spreadsheets, and mathematical programming give the value of the probability area under the tail of the normal distribution. The cumulative area under the tail of the normal density, defined as $Q(\alpha)$ below, is a good approximation to tail of the binomial distribution.

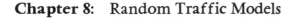

Figure 8.4
Normal approximation
to binomial density.

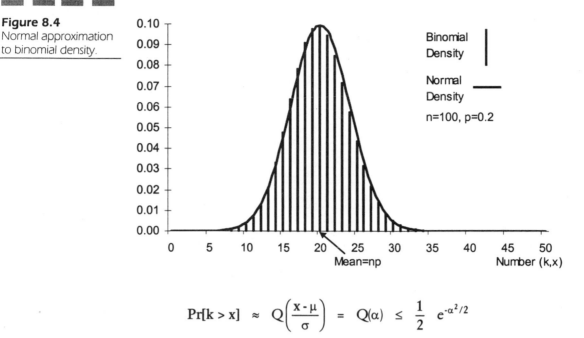

$$\Pr[k > x] \;\approx\; Q\!\left(\frac{x-\mu}{\sigma}\right) \;=\; Q(\alpha) \;\leq\; \frac{1}{2}\;e^{-\alpha^2/2}$$

where $Q(\alpha) \;\equiv\; \dfrac{1}{\sqrt{2\pi}} \displaystyle\int_{\alpha}^{\infty} e^{-x^2/2}\;dx$

This text uses this approximation in several contexts to estimate loss probability, statistical multiplexing gain, and delay variation in subsequent chapters. Microsoft Excel implements the commonly used function $Q((x-\mu)/\sigma)$ as 1-NORMDIST(x,μ,σ,TRUE) for a normal random variable with mean μ and standard deviation σ. Note that the above approximation for $Q(\alpha)$, yields a closed form expression for $\varepsilon \approx \Pr[k>x]$:

$$\alpha \;\approx\; \sqrt{-2\;\ln(\varepsilon)\;-\;2\ell n(2\pi)}$$

Note that Microsoft Excel implements the function to determine α more precisely as $\alpha= -$NORMINV($\varepsilon,0,1$). The above approximation overestimates the required capacity; therefore, use the accurate formula if your software provides it.

Chernoff Bound a Distribution's Tail

Often we are interested in only the probability mass contained under the tail of the pdf. This is the probability that the random variable **y** exceeds some value Y. For some distributions, the expression for this

TABLE 8.4

Chernoff bound for
important probability
densities in traffic
engineering.

Pdf Name	Mean	Variance	Chernoff Bound on $\Pr[y \geq Y]$
Binomial	Np	$np(1-p)$	$\left[\dfrac{Np}{Y}\right]^{Y} \left[\dfrac{Np(1-p)}{Np-Yp}\right]^{N-Y}$
Normal, or Gaussian	μ	σ^2	$e^{-\dfrac{(Y-\mu)^2}{2\sigma^2}}$
Poisson	λT	λT	$\left[\dfrac{Y}{\lambda T}\right]^{-Y} e^{Y-\lambda T}$
Geometric	$\dfrac{1}{p}$	$\dfrac{1-p}{p^2}$	$\dfrac{(Y+1)^{Y+1}}{Y^Y}\ p\ (1-p)^{Y-1}$

exceedance probability is cumbersome. Analysts often employ an exponentially tight bound which has a simpler formula as determined by the solution to the Chernoff bound as follows [5]:

$$\Pr[y \geq Y] \leq e^{-\nu Y}\ E[e^{\nu y}] \tag{8-14}$$

To compute the Chernoff bound for a specific pdf, first compute the right-hand side of Equation (8-14). Since the bound is valid for all values of ν, differentiate the right-hand side with respect to ν and solve for the value of ν that minimizes the bound. This yields the following formula:

$$Y = \frac{E[y e^{\nu y}]}{E[e^{\nu y}]} \tag{8-15}$$

Solving for the value of Y from Equation (8-15) and substituting into Equation (8-14) yields the Chernoff bound. Table 8.4 gives the result of this calculation applied to the pdf's described in this chapter which do not have a neat closed form formula for the area underneath the tail of a probability density function.

Stochastic Processes

The word *stochastic* comes from the Greek *stochaszethai,* which means, "to guess at." This section introduces the concept of stochastic processes by looking at a set of n Web surfers connected to a router or server from a different point of view. This leads to a definition of the commonly encountered Poisson and geometric distributions used widely in the area of traffic engineering. There are four types of sto-

TABLE 8.5

The four types of stochastic processes.

		STATE	
		Discrete	**Continuous**
T I M E	**Discrete**	Markov Chain Example: repeated coin flips	Imbedded Markov Chain Example: Daily Dow Jones Average
	Continuous	Continuous-Time Markov Chain Example: population growth	Diffusion Process Example: Room temperature

chastic processes determined by whether the state and time parameters are either discrete or continuous, as indicated in Table 8.5. The table gives examples of each type of stochastic process. We study primarily systems with discrete state, and either a discrete or continuous time variable in this book. Chapter 11 covers continuous time Markov processes applied to queuing theory.

Random Poisson Arrivals in Time

Consider the case of a number of Web surfers attached to a router or server in the Internet introduced earlier in this chapter, but now remove the notion of discrete time increments. Now, arrivals for various end users occur at unique instants in time, since we now divide

Figure 8.5

Example of random arrivals in an Internet application.

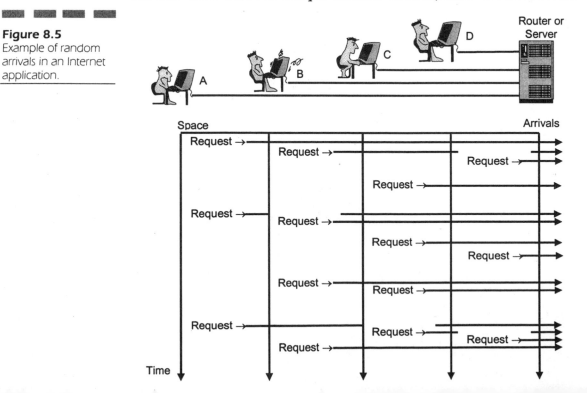

time into infinitesimally small intervals. Figure 8.5 depicts the sequence of requests generated by the four Web surfers shown in Figure 8.3, using the fine-grained time intervals that guarantee non-overlapping arrivals.

The Poisson arrival model results from the assumption that each of the n users generates requests at an average rate of λ arrivals every T/n seconds. Therefore, the probability that an arrival occurs from a particular user within a T second interval is λT/n. Therefore, the probability density for the random variable **k** is the probability that k arrivals occur within a T second interval from the population of n sources. The solution results from substituting p=λT/n into the binomial probability density of Equation (8-10) as follows:

$$f_{\mathbf{k}}(n,k) = \binom{n}{k} \left(\frac{\lambda T}{n}\right)^k \left(1 - \frac{\lambda T}{n}\right)^{n-k}$$

Taking the limit as the number of sources n approaches infinity results in the famous *Poisson density* for the probability that k arrivals occur within a T second interval as follows:

$$f_{\mathbf{k}}(k) \equiv \lim_{n\to\infty} f_{\mathbf{k}}(n,k) = \frac{(\lambda T)^k}{k!} e^{-\lambda T} \qquad (8\text{-}16)$$

Interestingly, Siméon Denis Poisson developed these statistical models based upon his experience regarding the outcome of lawsuits, criminal trials, and the likelihood of soldiers dying after being kicked by their horses [4]. Like many random events (most not quite so litigous nor so morbid), Poisson arrivals occur such that for each increment of time (T), no matter how large or small, the probability of arrival is independent of any previous history. These events may be individual telephone calls, Web sessions, file transfers, packets, streams of packets, file transfers, ATM cells, or other phenomenon, like link or node failures. Note that the mean and variance of a Poisson distributed random variable are both λT. For values of λT>>1, say 5 to 10 or more, the normal distribution is a good approximation to the Poisson distribution. The Microsoft Excel function POISSON(k,λT,FALSE) returns the numerical value of Equation (8-16).

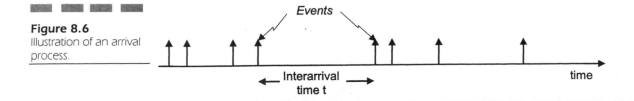

Figure 8.6
Illustration of an arrival process.

Poisson Interarrival Time Distribution

Another important property of random arrivals is the elapsed interval of time t between arrival event, as shown in Figure 8.6. We call the elapsed time between two events the *interarrival time*. Let's begin our analysis by considering a discrete time system where an arrival occurs with probability p every discrete time interval Δt. The probability that **m** intervals elapse between arrivals is equivalent to rolling a single die m times until a certain value (e.g., a six) shows when p=1/6. Thus, for a six to show, m-1 rolls other than a six must have turned up first. Hence, the probability of m-1 unsuccessful trials (i.e., not a six or an arrival) followed by an arrival is given by the *geometric probability density* as follows:

$$g_m(m) \equiv p \ (1-p)^{m-1}$$

Nicolas Bernoulli solved this problem in 1708 for the special case where p=1/6 for the roll of a single die [4]. Using Equation (8-12), we compute the solution for the mean value of the geometric distribution as follows:

$$E[m] \equiv \sum_{m=0}^{\infty} m \ p \ (1-p)^{m-1} = -p \ \frac{\partial}{\partial p} \sum_{m=0}^{\infty}(1-p)^m$$

$$= -p \ \frac{\partial}{\partial p} \ \frac{1}{1-(1-p)} = \frac{-p}{-p^2} = \frac{1}{p}$$

where we recognized that the infinite sum $\sum_{m=0}^{\infty} x^m = \dfrac{1}{1-x}$ for x<1

since by long division the value of 1/(1-x) is determined as follows:

$$
\begin{array}{r}
1 \ + \ x \ + \ x^2 \ + \ x^3 \ + \ \cdots \\
1-x \ \overline{\big)\ 1 } \\
\underline{1 \ - \ x } \\
x \\
\underline{x \ - \ x^2 } \\
x^2 \\
\underline{x^2 \ - \ x^3 } \\
x^3 \\
\underline{x^3 \ - \ x^4}
\end{array}
$$

Many proofs of properties of discrete random variables involve manipulation of sums such as that in the above example. Using long division with symbols instead of numbers as illustrated above is a simple way to confirm the solution for a particular sum. Of course, any good text on probability or queuing theory, such as Reference 1, 3, 5, or 7 contains proofs of these properties as well.

The geometric distribution is, of course, the probability that the interarrival time is less than or equal to x time intervals. This is simply one minus the probability that all m trials had no arrivals (sixes) as follows:

$$G_m(m) = 1 - (1-p)^m \tag{8-17}$$

Now, assume that Poisson arrivals occur during each infinitesimal time interval Δt. From Equation (8-16), the probability that no arrivals occur in a time interval Δt is simply:

$$\Pr[\text{no arrivals in } \Delta t] = 1-p = e^{-\lambda \Delta t}$$

Substituting this result into Equation (8-17), yields the cumulative distribution function that $t=m\Delta t$ seconds elapse between Poisson arrivals as follows:

$$A(t = m\Delta t) = 1 - e^{-\lambda m \Delta t} \tag{8-18}$$

The interarrival time probability density function, a(t), is computed from basic calculus as follows:

$$
\begin{aligned}
a(t) &\equiv \lim_{\Delta t \to 0} \frac{G((m+1)\Delta t) - G(m\Delta t)}{\Delta t} \\
&= \lim_{\Delta t \to 0} \frac{e^{-\lambda t}\left[1 - e^{-\lambda \Delta t}\right]}{\Delta t} \\
&= \lambda\, e^{-\lambda t}
\end{aligned}
\tag{8-19}
$$

The above calculation uses the fact that $e^{-x} \approx 1-x$ for $x \ll 1$ and noting that m approaches infinity as Δt approaches zero to result in a finite value of $t=m\Delta t$. Equation (8-19) is the *negative exponential* probability density associated with Poisson arrivals. Microsoft Excel implements the pdf a(t) in the function EXPONDIST(t,λ, FALSE), while the function call EXPONDIST(t,λ,TRUE) returns the cdf A(t).

This negative exponential interarrival time density greatly simplifies the study of basic queuing systems. Note that the average and standard deviation of a negative exponentially distributed interarrival time is $1/\lambda$.

Memoryless Property of Poisson Arrivals

Queuing theorists call Poisson arrivals a *memoryless process*, because the probability that the interarrival time is t seconds is independent of the *memory* of how much time has already expired. To understand this important result, we apply the definition of conditional probability from Baye's Theorem given in Equation (8-3) to the probability density for a negative exponentially distributed interarrival time as follows:

$$a(t|t > t_0) \ = \ \frac{a(t)}{1 \ - \ A(t_0)} \ = \ \lambda e^{-\lambda(t-t_0)} \ = \ a(t - t_0) \qquad (8\text{-}20)$$

The above result notes that the probability that $t > t_0$ is unity and uses the interarrival distribution A(t) given in Equation (8-18). Figure 8.7 illustrates the memoryless property of Equation (8-20) by plotting the densities a(t) and a(t-t$_0$). Note how the densities have the same shape, only shifted in time by t$_0$ seconds. Also observe that the tail of any negative exponential always has the same shape as shown in the figure. The negative exponential is the only continuous density function with this property [5]. This fact greatly simplifies the analysis of random processes, since no history, or memory, affects the outcome

Figure 8.7
Memoryless property of the negative exponential density.

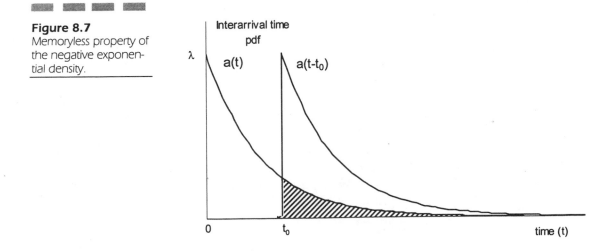

of the next arrival time. The literature calls these *Markov processes*, named after the work published by the famous Russian mathematician in the early twentieth century.

Merge and Split of Poisson Processes

Another important property of Poisson processes is that the merging of two or more independent Poisson processes results in another Poisson process with arrival rate equal to the sum of the arrival rates of the individual inputs [8]. For example, the result of merging two Poisson processes with arrival rates of λ_1 and λ_2 is a Poisson process with arrival rate $\lambda = \lambda_1 + \lambda_2$.

Furthermore, if we randomly split arrivals from a single Poisson process into two or more streams, the resulting processes still have all of the Poisson properties. For example, assume that a single Poisson process with arrival rate λ is split into stream 1 with probability p_1 and into stream 2 with probability p_2, where $p_1 + p_2 = 1$. Stream 1 is then a Poisson process with arrival rate $p_1\lambda$ and stream 2 is a Poisson process with arrival rate $p_2\lambda$.

When analyzing a network of queues in Part 6, we will use this result to model the operating of routing and distribution in networks. The fact that the above properties of merging and splitting preserve the desirable Poisson nature of the random traffic model using only the average rates greatly simplifies the complex task of modeling large networks.

Review

This chapter introduced the reader to the foundations of probability theory and applied it to the modeling of events in computer communication networks. It included many formulas and basic concepts of probability. It also focused primarily on how to compute and apply the results to the traffic engineering of computer communication networks. We then introduced the concept of random (or stochastic) processes as an introduction to Chapter 9. This included the discrete geometric and the continuous negative exponential distributions.

Table 8.6 lists these important probability densities, their mean and variance, the equation for the probability density function (pdf), and the corresponding Microsoft Excel function. Note that replacing

TABLE 8.6

Important probability densities in traffic engineering.

Name	Mean	Variance	Equation for pdf	Microsoft Excel Function
Binomial	np	$np(1-p)$	$\binom{n}{k} p^k (1-p)^{n-k}$	BINOMDIST(k, n, p, FALSE)
Normal, or Gaussian	μ	σ^2	$\dfrac{1}{\sqrt{2\pi}\,\sigma} e^{\frac{-(x-\mu)^2}{2\sigma^2}}$	NORMDIST(x,μ,σ,FALSE)
Poisson	λT	λT	$\dfrac{(\lambda T)^k}{k!} e^{-\lambda T}$	POISSON(k,λT,FALSE)
Geometric	$\dfrac{1}{p}$	$\dfrac{1-p}{p^2}$	$p\,(1-p)^{m-1}$	p*(1-p)^(m-1)
Negative Exponential	$\dfrac{1}{\lambda}$	$\dfrac{1}{\lambda}$	$\lambda\,e^{-\lambda t}$	EXPONDIST(t,λ, FALSE)

FALSE in the Microsoft Excel functions returns the cumulative distribution function as defined in Equation (8-11) instead of the pdf.

References

[1] R. Hamming, *The Art of Probability for Scientists and Engineers*, Addison-Wesley, 1991.

[2] J. Gullberg, *Mathematics, From the Birth of Numbers*, Norton, 1997.

[3] A. Papoulis, *Probability, Random Variables and Stochastic Processes*, McGraw-Hill, 1965.

[4] W. Weaver, *Lady Luck — The Theory of Probability*, Dover Press, 1963.

[5] L. Kleinrock, *Queuing Systems Volume I: Theory*, Wiley, 1975.

[6] A. Papoulis, *Probability, Random Variables and Stochastic Processes, Third Edition*, McGraw-Hill, 1991.

[7] D. Gross, C. Harris, *Fundamentals of Queuing Theory*, Wiley, 1985.

[8] L. Kleinrock, R. Gail, *Queuing Systems — Problems and Solutions*, Wiley, 1996.

CHAPTER 9

Advanced Traffic Models

"A mathematical theory is not to be considered complete until you have made it so clear that you can explain it to the first man whom you meet on the street."

— David Hilbert

Inevitably, experts rely on mathematical formulations of problems in the analysis of traffic behavior in communication networks. The material in this chapter is a prerequisite for the coverage of queuing theory in Part 4., beginning with an analysis of the commonly used models involving discrete and continuous time Markov chains with discrete states. Since the analysis of random processes is quite complex, sophisticated analytical tools summarize critical characteristics of these traffic models. We cover some important tools used in the analysis of random processes, in particular the correlation and power spectrum functions. The coverage then continues with an introduction to the concept of Brownian motion and random walks. Widely used in other scientific disciplines, extensions of this technique are also commonly used to model self-similar traffic. Finally, the chapter concludes with a thorough review of important properties involved in the use of self-similar traffic models applied to communications network traffic engineering.

Commonly Used Markov Models

This section builds upon the foundations established in the previous chapter, and sets the stage for the analysis of queuing systems in the next part.

Discrete-Time Markov Chains

The definition of a discrete-time Markov chain consists of a set of states and probabilities of transitioning between them at discrete instants in time. The Markov property requires that the transition probabilities are a function of only the current state [1]. The transitions need not occur at regular time intervals, just at specific instants in time. As an example, consider the system depicted in Figure 9.1, which is a simple model of bursty traffic sources. It depicts a two-state process with states labeled 0 and 1, where state 0 models the idle periods and state 1 models the active periods. The labels of the form p_{ij} on the arcs connecting the states in the figure identify the probability that the system transitions to state j given state i initially at a discrete instant in time. That is, $p_{ij} \equiv \Pr[\text{state } j \mid \text{state } i]$. Specifically, in the example, p_{00} defines the probability that the system remains in state 0 at a transition instant, while p_{01} defines the probability that the system transitions to state 1 from state 0. Obviously, from the theorem of total probability observe that $p_{00} + p_{01} = 1$. Similar remarks apply to the two possible transitions originating from state 1.

The state probability vector $\underline{\pi}(n)$ defines the probability of the system at step n as follows:

$$\underline{\pi}(n) \equiv \; <\pi_0(n) \; , \; \pi_1(n)>$$

where $\pi_k(n)$ is the probability that the system is in state k at step n. The vector $\underline{\pi}(0)$ defines the initial condition of the system. The solution for $\underline{\pi}(n)$ is by writing down the equations for $\pi_k(n)$ in matrix form as follows:

$$\underline{\pi}(n) \equiv \underline{\pi}(0) \; P^n \tag{9-1}$$

Figure 9.1
Two-state discrete Markov chain state-transition diagram.

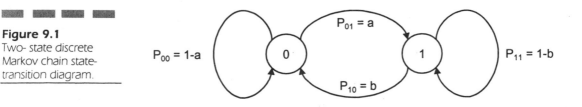

with transition probability matrix $P \equiv \begin{bmatrix} P_{00} & P_{01} \\ P_{10} & P_{11} \end{bmatrix} = \begin{bmatrix} 1-a & a \\ b & 1-b \end{bmatrix}$.

The steady state solution occurs as n approaches infinity, which is denoted by $\underline{\pi}$. In the steady state, the probability after yet another transition as defined by the transition probability matrix remains unchanged. Hence, the steady state probability $\underline{\pi}$ for the system is the solution to the following equation:

$$\underline{\pi} \equiv \underline{\pi} \; P \qquad \qquad (9\text{-}2)$$

Writing out matrix Equation (9-2) into two separate linear equations illustrates how we use the definitions of conditional and total probability to set up the steady state solution as follows:

$$\begin{aligned} \pi_0 &= \pi_0 \, p_{00} + \pi_1 \, p_{10} = \pi_0(1\text{-}a) + \pi_1 \, b \\ \pi_1 &= \pi_1 \, p_{11} + \pi_0 \, p_{01} = \pi_1(1\text{-}b) + \pi_0 \, a \end{aligned} \qquad (9\text{-}3)$$

These equations are *linearly dependent,* since by simple algebraic manipulation they both simplify to the same equation, namely $\pi_1 \, b = \pi_0 \, a$. In general, a discrete Markov chain with N states results in only N-1 linearly independent equations. The application of standard matrix techniques for solving a system of linearly independent equations to Equation (9-2) yields the following result:

$$\underline{\pi} \; [I - P] = \underline{0} \qquad \qquad (9\text{-}4)$$

where I is the *identity matrix* comprised of all zeroes except for ones on the diagonal. In order to remove the linearly dependent equation, we substitute the result from the theorem of total probability, namely $\pi_1 + \pi_0 = 1$, for the second formula in Equation (9-3). Substituting this linearly independent equation into Equation (9-4) yields the following formula:

$$\underline{\pi} \; [(I-P)\Lambda_1 + U] = \underline{\pi} \; Q = \langle 0, \; 1 \rangle \qquad (9\text{-}5)$$

where Λ_k is a matrix with the first k elements of the diagonal set equal to 1, and U is a matrix with ones in the last column. Writing out the above matrix equation as two one-dimensional equations clarifies the meaning of Equation (9-5) as substituting ones in the last column of the matrix Q as follows:

$$\begin{aligned} \pi_0 \, a + \pi_1 &= 0 \\ -\pi_1 \, b + \pi_0 &= 1 \end{aligned}$$

That is, Equation (9-5) is expanded and solved as follows:

$$< \pi_0, \ \pi_1 > \ = \ < 0, \ 1 > Q^{-1} \ = \ < 0, \ 1 > \begin{bmatrix} a & 1 \\ -b & 1 \end{bmatrix}^{-1} \tag{9-6}$$

Applying basic matrix algebra, the solution to this equation is:

$$< \pi_0, \ \pi_1 > \ = \ < \frac{b}{a+b}, \ \frac{a}{a+b} >$$

Note that Equation (9-6) gives a general numerical solution technique for any discrete Markov chain using Microsoft Excel as follows. First, enter the N×N matrix for (I-P) as a Microsoft Excel array named A. Next, define an array in a single row with N columns with 0 in the first N-1 cells followed by a 1 and name this x. Finally, enter the following array formula in a single row of cells with N columns.

$$MMULT(x,MINVERSE(Q))$$

Note that to enter an array formula in Microsoft Excel you must press Ctrl+Shift+Enter instead of Enter after typing in the formula (or using the function wizard dialog box). Figure 9.2 illustrates this calculation in a Microsoft Excel spreadsheet for the two-state discrete Markov chain solution of Equation (9-6).

The technique of discrete time Markov chains applies to arbitrary state diagrams connected in a variety of ways subject to a few conditions. If some states are unreachable from others, then the solution fails because this chain is reducible to two or more separate chains. We are concerned only with *irreducible Markov chains* in this text. Furthermore, for these models to have a probabilistic meaning, the sum of all probabilities leaving a state must sum to unity.

The systems under study may be of the form of a birth-death chain with transitions between adjacent states only, a tree structure,

Figure 9.2
Spreadsheet solution for two-state discrete time Markov chain.

	A	B	C	D	E	F
1						
2	Q	0.2	1		a	0.2
3		-0.4	1		b	0.4
4						
5	x	0	1			
6						
7	π	0.666667	0.33333	MMULT(x,MINVERSE(Q))		

`or arbitrary connectivity. Note that if any state transitions back to it-self with probability 1, then the system converges to that state and remains there, resulting in the degenerate case of an absorbing chain.

Note that the number of transitions spent in any state is geometri-cally distributed. That is, if 1-p is the probability of remaining in a particular state, then the probability that the system remains in the same state is:

$$\Pr[k] \ = \ p \ \ (1-p)^{k-1}$$

As described in Chapter 8, the average number of transitions spent in the state is $E[k]$, which has the value of p^{-1}. We now use this fact to construct and solve a discrete time Markov model for a Web surfer's behavior. This model assumes that transitions occur once a second. Therefore, the amount of time spent in a particular state is the mean of the geometric distribution described above. Our model has three states as shown in Figure 9.3: an idle, or logged off state (0), a state where the user is thinking (1), and a state where the Web surfer waits for a response from the server. Note that the transition probabilities leaving a state always sum to unity. In this example, we assume that transitions occur at regular intervals.

When in the "idle" state, the user logs on with a probability α, and remains idle with probability 1-α. Hence, the average amount of time spent between Web sessions in the idle state is α^{-1} seconds. Once logged on, the user transitions between the "think" and "wait" states until logging off from the "think" state with probability δ. While in the "think" state, the Web surfer either generates a request with prob-ability β, logs off with probability δ, or remains in the "think" state with probability 1-β-δ. Thus, the average amount of time spent in the "think" state is $(\beta+\delta)^{-1}$. Next, in response to the user's request, the net-work and the server complete service with probability γ while in the "wait" state. Therefore, the average amount of time spent in the "wait" state is γ^{-1}. The list below summarizes the above formulations for the

Figure 9.3
Web surfer discrete
Markov chain model.

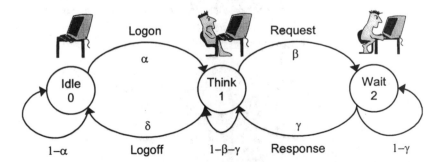

average amount of time between state transitions and the average number of transactions per session:

Average time in the "idle" state: $\quad \overline{I} = \alpha^{-1}$
Average "wait" time: $\quad \overline{W} = \gamma^{-1}$
Average "think" time: $\quad \overline{T} = (\beta+\delta)^{-1}$

Notice that we have three equations in four unknowns. In order to solve the problem we need a fourth equation. We get this by solving for the steady state probability that the user is in the "idle" state (π_0), in the "think" state (π_1), or in the "wait" state (π_2) using the matrix solution technique described above. After some algebraic manipulation (left as an exercise for the reader) we obtain the following result:

$$< \pi_0, \; \pi_1, \; \pi_2 > \; = \; \frac{<\overline{I}, \; (\overline{N}+1)\overline{T}, \; \overline{N}\;\overline{W}>}{\overline{I}+(\overline{N}+1)\overline{T}+\overline{N}\;\overline{W}} \tag{9-7}$$

where $\overline{N} = \dfrac{\beta}{\delta}$.

We give a physical interpretation to the solution of Equation (9-7) and the variable $\overline{N}$ with reference to Figure 9.4. Looking at the user activity over time; there is an idle interval of average duration $\overline{I}$ followed by a session comprised of an interval of think time lasting an average of $\overline{T}$ seconds. On average, the user generates $\overline{N}$ requests per session, each of which incurs a waiting time $\overline{W}$, as shown in the figure. At the end of the session, the user enters another think time, and decides to log off. Hence, there are $\overline{N}+1$ intervals of think time in a session — one paired with each request and a final one where the user finally decides to end the session. Comparing this reasoning and the figure gives an intuitive explanation for Equation (9-7). It isn't intuitively obvious what the probability is that the user remains in the "think" state.

Of course, you can solve this problem numerically using the Microsoft Excel spreadsheet technique described previously. For more complicated systems, the algebraic manipulation becomes quite tedious and complex. The spreadsheet calculation allows you to check your algebra for specific numeric parameters.

Techniques exist to solve for the transient probability of the system after the nth iteration given an initial condition $\pi(0)$. The calculation

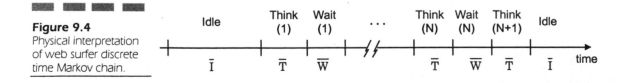

Figure 9.4
Physical interpretation of web surfer discrete time Markov chain.

is tedious and involves calculating the eigenvalues and eigenvectors of a matrix, frequently employing transform techniques [1, 2].

Continuous Time Markov Chains

Now, consider a system with multiple users connected to a router or accessing a server. As seen in Chapter 8, a better model for this type of system is one where events occur at fine-grained instants in time. As the time increment approaches zero, the limiting approximation is that of continuous time. However, we must now utilize the mathematics of differential calculus instead of simple multiplication of probabilities employed in the analysis of discrete-time Markov chains to arrive at a solution.

Since the solution of continuous-time Markov chains is an essential concept in this text, this section provides a brief derivation of the important results. See References 1, 2, or 3 for further details. The treatment begins with the consideration of a system with a number of potential states indicated as j=0, 1, 2, ..., n. First, we define the probability that the system is in state j at time t+Δt, given that it was in state i at time t using the following notation:

$$p_{ij}(t, t + \Delta t) \equiv q_{ij} \Delta t$$

The parameter q_{ij} is the probability that the system transitions from state i to state j in the infinitesimal interval Δt, as shown in Figure 9.5. We refer to the value q_{ij} as the *state transition rate*. The literature frequently refers to the general case where these transition rates take on different values depending upon the current state of the system as a Markov Modulated Poisson Process (MMPP) [4]. Note that the Markov property where the system behavior depends only upon the previous instant in time remains; hence, the above result holds for all values of time t.

Now, define the system state by random variable x(t)=j with the following probability density:

$$\pi_j(t) \equiv \Pr[x(t) = j]$$

We can now write down the probability that the system is in state j at any point in time t from the state-transition-rate diagram of Figure 9.5 as follows:

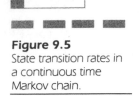

Figure 9.5
State transition rates in
a continuous time
Markov chain.

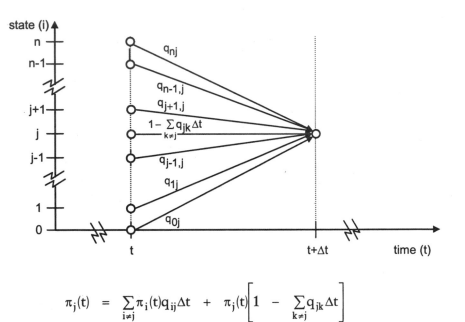

$$\pi_j(t) = \sum_{i\neq j}\pi_i(t)q_{ij}\Delta t + \pi_j(t)\left[1 - \sum_{k\neq j}q_{jk}\Delta t\right]$$

The first term in the above equation is the probability that the system is in some state other than j and transitions to state j in the interval Δt. The second term is the probability that the system remains in state j during the interval Δt. Rearranging terms, dividing both sides of this equation by Δt, and taking the limit as $\Delta t \to 0$ results in the following differential equation:

$$\frac{\partial \pi_j(t)}{\partial t} = \sum_{i\neq j}\pi_i q_{ij} + \pi_j \sum_{k\neq j}q_{jk}$$

Observe that we can express the above equation for all values of j in matrix form as follows:

$$\frac{\partial \underline{\pi}(t)}{\partial t} = \underline{\pi}(t)Q \tag{9-8}$$

where $\underline{\pi}(t) \equiv <\pi_0(t), \pi_1(t), \pi_2(t), ..., \pi_n(t)>$, and

$$Q \equiv \begin{bmatrix} -\sum_{j\neq 0}q_{0j} & q_{01} & \cdots & q_{0n} \\ q_{10} & -\sum_{j\neq 1}q_{1j} & \cdots & q_{1n} \\ \vdots & \vdots & \vdots & \vdots \\ q_{n0} & q_{n1} & \cdots & -\sum_{j\neq n}q_{nj} \end{bmatrix}$$

We call the matrix Q the *infinitesimal generator matrix.* Note that each row of Q sums to 0. The solution to Equation (9-8), easily verified by substitution, is as follows:

$$\underline{\pi}(t) = e^{Qt} = I + \sum_{k=1}^{\infty} \frac{Q^k t^k}{k!} \tag{9-9}$$

Frequently, we are interested in the steady-state, or the long-run, performance of the system under the following conditions:

$$\frac{\partial \underline{\pi}(t)}{\partial t} = \underline{0} \quad \text{and} \quad \lim_{t \to \infty} \underline{\pi}(t) = \underline{\pi}$$

Thus, the steady-state solution to Equation (9-8) is the following matrix equation:

$$\underline{\pi}Q = \underline{0} \tag{9-10}$$

Note the similarity in form of the above equation to the analogous solution for a general discrete-time Markov chain in Equation (9-4). Some differences between the continuous time and discrete-time Markov solutions are important to keep in mind. First, in the discrete-time case, the matrix P contains the state-transition probabilities, while in the continuous-time case, the entries in the matrix Q are the state-transition-rates. That is, we must multiply the elements of Q by Δt to yield a probabilistic interpretation.

The consequence of this similarity is that the same analytical and numerical techniques described in the previous section are applicable to the solution of continuous-time Markov chains. Note that only n of the equations of the infinitesimal generator matrix Q are linearly independent. Hence a solution requires invocation of the theorem of total probability for the (n+1)th equation. The continuous-time Markov chain model occurs in a number of commonly encountered problems.

Once we have a set of differential difference equations of the form given by Equation (9-10), one of several techniques yield elegant closed form solutions for specific systems. The next section and Part 4 give several examples of these solution techniques. Of course, the same numerical techniques in Excel spreadsheets described earlier are applicable to the solution of birth-death continuous-time Markov chains.

A Simple Example — System Availability

This section describes the use of a continuous time Markov chain to compute the availability of a system such as a component, a switch or router, or even the connectivity provided by an entire network. Figure 9.6 illustrates a two-state continuous Markov chain used in the analysis of availability (and other traffic engineering phenomena covered in the next Part as well). State 0 corresponds to the system being unavailable, and state 1 corresponds to the system being available. The figure indicates state transition rates next to the arcs connecting the states. By convention, state-transition-rate diagrams for continuous-time Markov chains omit the drawing of self-loops back to the same state.

Availability is the probability that the system is in state 1. Using the technique described above, the equations for the long-run steady-state probabilities for the system are:

$$\lambda\pi_0 \ - \ \mu\pi_1 \ = \ 0$$
$$\pi_0 \ + \ \pi_1 \ = \ 1$$

Substituting the equality $\pi_0=\mu\pi_1/\lambda$ from the first equation into the second yields the solution for the probability that the system is in state 1 (e.g., available) as follows:

$$\pi_1 \ = \ \frac{\lambda}{\lambda \ + \ \mu} \tag{9-11}$$

Usually, engineers employ the conventions of Mean Time Between Failure (MTBF) and Mean Time To Repair (MTTR) when computing availability, as indicated in Figure 9.6. Hence, $\lambda=1/$MTTR has the interpretation of the repair rate and $\mu=1/$MTBF is the failure rate when modeling availability. Substituting these definitions into Equation (9-11) yields the commonly encountered expression for the availability of a system:

Figure 9.6
Two-state continuous Markov chain state-rate transition diagram.

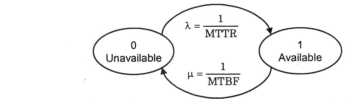

Figure 9.7
Illustration of serial and
parallel system
availability models.

a. Serial Systems

b. Parallel Systems

$$\text{Availability } A = \pi_1 = \frac{\text{MTBF}}{\text{MTBF} + \text{MTTR}} \qquad (9\text{-}12)$$

System availability is often expressed as the number of "nines" in the value A. For example, a system with availability A=0.999 (or 99.9 percent) has "three nines" of availability. For the Markov model, the probability density of the failure and repair intervals has a negative exponential distribution. Interestingly, Equation (9-12) holds even if the failure and repair processes are not Markovian [5].

A system may have multiple units operating either serially, or in parallel, as illustrated in Figure 9.7. When two units X and Y operate serially, as shown in Figure 9.7a, the overall system is available only if both X and Y are available. If X and Y operate independently, then from the basic definitions of probability in Chapter 8, the probability of these two mutually exclusive events is simply the product of the constituent events. If the availability of both units X and Y is A, then the overall system availability for X and Y operating in series is A^2. The unavailability of a serial system with two identical units is $U = 1 - A^2$. In general, the availability for N identical units operating in series is A^N. Thus, as N increases, the overall availability decreases for a serial system.

On the other hand, a parallel system requires that only one of two independent units (X and Y) be operational in order for the overall system to be available, as illustrated in Figure 9.7b. Here, the overall system is unavailable with probability U only if both units are unavailable, which occurs with probability $(1-A)^2$. Therefore, the availability with two identical units operating in parallel is:

$$\text{Availability(Parallel)} = 1 - (1 - A)^2 \qquad (9\text{-}13)$$

Reliability engineers refer to the parallel configuration of Figure 9.7b as one-for-one operation, usually abbreviated as 1:1. In other words, units X and Y act as backups for each other. For units with high availability, (i.e., A is close to 1) let A=1-z. This means that z≈0. Now the expressions for system unavailability for systems operating with two identical units in the serial and parallel configurations are:

$$\text{Unavailability(Serial)} \approx 2z$$

$$\text{Unavailability(Paralllel)} = z^2$$

Observe from this equation how the parallel system markedly decreases unavailability, and hence increases availability. For further details on the application of probability theory and stochastic processes to the analysis of availability and reliability, see Reference 6.

Properties of Continuous Random Processes

Applied statisticians frequently utilize sophisticated mathematical techniques to assist in the analysis of random processes. This section gives the definitions for autocorrelation, covariance, and power spectra, along with several motivating examples.

Statistics of Continuous Random Variables

When the value of the random variable as well as time become continuous, the random process x(t) has a probability distribution with relative frequency interpretation as follows [7]:

$$F(x,t) \equiv \Pr[x(t) \le x] \cong \frac{n_t(x)}{n}$$

where $n_t(x)$ is the number of trials performed where the value of the random process is less than or equal to x at time t, and n is the total number of trials performed overall.

The joint probability distribution function of x(t) at two instants in time, denoted as t_1 and t_2, is as follows:

$$F(x_1, x_2; t_1, t_2) \cong \Pr[x(t_1) \le x_1, x(t_2) \le x_2]$$

An important class of random processes has statistics that only depend upon the time interval between observations. That is, the probability distribution function reduces to the following for all values of time t:

$$F(x_1, x_2; \tau) \cong \Pr[x(t) \le x_1, x(t+\tau) \le x_2]$$

Statisticians call such processes *stationary* in the strict sense. The probability density function $f(x_1, x_2, \tau)$ of the random process $x(t)$ is the derivative of the distribution function taken with respect to the value x. We deal primarily with stationary process models in this book. In other words, the statistics of a stationary process are invariant to a shift of the time origin [7].

Expectation, Autocorrelation, and Autocovariance

A stationary, real-valued random process $x(t)$ has mean value [7]:

$$\eta(t) \;=\; E[x(t)] \;\equiv\; \int_{-\infty}^{\infty} x \; f(x;t) \; dx$$

The *autocorrelation* function $R(t_1, t_2)$ is the expected value of the product of the values of the random process at two instants in time:

$$R(t_1, t_2) \equiv E[x(t_1)x(t_2)] = \int_{-\infty}^{\infty}\int_{-\infty}^{\infty} x_1 x_2 \; f(x_1, x_2; t_1, t_2) \; dx_1 dx_2 \qquad (9\text{-}14)$$

For a discrete random variable, finite sums replace the integrals in the above equation. A closely related property of a random process is *the autocovariance* function, which subtracts out the mean value as follows:

$$\begin{aligned}
C(t_1, t_2) \;&\equiv\; E[\{x(t_1) - \eta(t_1)\}\{x(t_2) - \eta(t_2)\}] \\
&=\; R(t_1, t_2) \;-\; \eta(t_1)\eta(t_2)
\end{aligned}$$

Note that the value of the autocovariance function at $t_1 = t_2 = t$ is equal to the variance of $x(t)$, namely: $C(t,t) = \sigma_x^2$.

The random process $x(t)$ is *wide sense stationary* if it has constant mean η and its autocorrelation depends upon only the time interval $\tau = t1 - t2$ as follows:

$$R(\tau) \;\equiv\; E[x(t+\tau)x(t)] \;=\; \int_{-\infty}^{\infty}\int_{-\infty}^{\infty} x_1 x_2 \; f(x_1, x_2; \tau) \; dx_1 dx_2$$

The autocovariance function C(τ) for a stationary random process is given by the following formula:

$$C(\tau) \;\equiv\; E[\{x(t+\tau)-\eta\}\{x(t)-\eta\}] \;=\; R(\tau) \;-\; \eta^2$$

Note that the value of the autocovariance function at τ=0 is equal to the variance of x(t), namely: $C(0) = \sigma_x^2$. Finally, the *correlation coefficient* is the normalized autocovariance as follows:

$$r(\tau) \;\equiv\; \frac{C(\tau)}{\sigma^2}$$

Power Spectra

Statisticians use techniques from communications engineering involving Fourier transforms to represent properties of stationary random processes. Called the *power spectrum* (or spectral density), S(ω) is the Fourier Transform of the autocorrelation R(τ) as defined in the following formula:

$$S(\omega) \;\equiv\; \int_{-\infty}^{\infty} R(\tau)\; e^{-j\omega\tau}\; d\tau \tag{9-15}$$

where $j \equiv \sqrt{-1}$, and ω≡2πf for a frequency of f Hz (See Chapter 3). Equation (9-15) uses integration with the complex exponential $e^{-j\omega\tau} \equiv \cos(\omega\tau) - j\sin(\omega\tau)$ to map the characteristics of the autocorrelation function in the time domain into frequency components. Let's look at a few examples to better understand the relationship between autocorrelation and power spectra.

First, consider a zero-mean process x(t) that is completely random from instant to instant. The autocorrelation function takes on the form of R(τ)=δ(τ), where δ(τ) is the Dirac delta function defined as follows:

$$\delta(\tau) \;\equiv\; \begin{cases} 1 & \tau = 0 \\ 0 & \text{otherwise} \end{cases}$$

Substituting R(τ)=δ(τ) into Equation (9-15) yields a power spectral density of S(ω)=1. Frequently, engineers call this process *white noise* because the power spectrum is equal for all "colors" (i.e., values of ω) of the frequency spectrum.

Next, we analyze a process that is not random. Instead, the process takes on a single deterministic value for all values of time. From Equation (9-14), the autocorrelation function is $R(\tau)=1$. The corresponding power spectrum is $S(\omega)=2\pi\delta(\omega)$. This type of signal is commonly referred to as Direct Current (DC).

The Poisson process introduced in Chapter 8 traditionally employed for modeling voice and data processes has autocorrelation function derived as follows [8,9]. Let $x(t)$ be a Poisson process. For an interval of time T, form the following Poisson increment process, which has the interpretation of the average arrival rate over the interval T as follows:

$$y(t) = \frac{x(t+T) - x(t)}{T}$$

This Poisson increment process has the following probability density function:

$$\Pr\left[y(t) = \frac{k}{T}\right] = \frac{(\lambda T)^k}{k!} e^{-\lambda T} \tag{9-16}$$

Clearly, the expected value is $E[y(t)]=\lambda$. In addition, the process has *independent increments*, since the probability density of $y(t)$ is independent of the choice of time t, as seen from Equation (9-16). In other words, the term "independent increments" implies that the statistics of the stochastic process is independent for all non-overlapping time intervals. Employing Equation (9-16), the autocorrelation function defined in Equation (9-14) for the Poisson increment process $y(t)$ is given by the following formula:

$$R(t_1, t_2) = \begin{cases} \lambda^2 & |t_1 - t_2| \geq T \\ \lambda^2 + \dfrac{\lambda}{T} - \dfrac{\lambda|t_1 - t_2|}{T^2} & |t_1 - t_2| < T \end{cases}$$

Note that $y(t)$ is wide sense stationary since its mean is constant and the autocorrelation function depends only upon $\tau=t_1-t_2$. Thus, the power spectrum is meaningful and takes on the following value:

$$S(\omega) = 2\pi\lambda^2\delta(\omega) + \lambda \operatorname{sinc}^2(\omega T / 2) \tag{9-17}$$

where $\sin c(x) \equiv \dfrac{\sin(x)}{x}$.

Figure 9.8 plots the autocorrelation functions and the corresponding power spectral density for the above examples. From the white noise example, note that an uncorrelated process has a broad spectrum. On the other hand, a highly correlated process like a constant valued DC signal has a narrow spectrum. In general, a sinusoidal signal has a spectrum that has a single frequency. Finally, a Poisson increment process combines the constant valued autocorrelation function of a DC signal corresponding to the mean arrival rate along with a triangular function. The resulting power spectrum is the superposition of the spectra corresponding to the components of the autocorrelation function as indicated in Equation (9-17). This is a delta function with magnitude $2\pi\lambda^2$ at $\omega=0$ along with the $\text{sinc}^2(\omega T/2)$ function as shown in the plot in the lower right-hand corner of the figure. Note that the majority of the power in the spectrum resides in the frequency passband (i.e., bandwidth) defined by the inverse of the duration of the period of positive correlation equal to 2T.

In addition to providing an intuitively appealing interpretation of the properties of random processes, power spectra are a useful practical tool for studying real-world random processes and modeling them. Indeed, a technique developed by San-Qi Li allows characterization of any random process based upon spectral measurements of an actual traffic process [10]. If you have real traffic measurements at a fine time granularity, then this technique would allow development of a good simulation model. These techniques accurately model the corre-

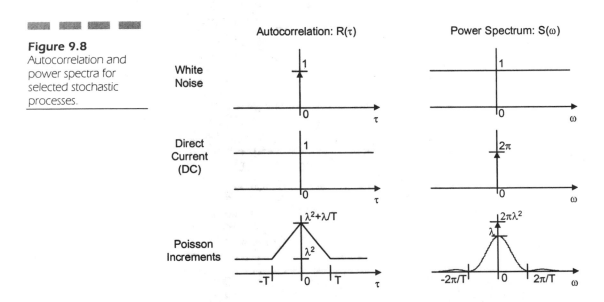

Figure 9.8
Autocorrelation and power spectra for selected stochastic processes.

lation properties experienced in traffic with self-similar properties. The next section introduces the classical models of physical processes and physical phenomena and concludes with a review of the important attributes of self-similar processes.

Random Walks, Brownian Motion, and Self-Similar Processes

This section describes important techniques used in modeling communication link performance in IP and ATM networks for specific types of commonly encountered traffic. Typically, analyses employ these processes to study the probability that IP or ATM traffic overflows a buffer.

Generalized Random Walk

The example given in Chapter 7 of flipping a fair coin and either increment or decrement a counter by ±1 based upon whether heads or tails appeared, respectively, is a specific discrete-state, discrete-time random walk process. A general random walk process results if we increment or decrement a counter $x(i\Delta)$ by a step function $f(i,\Delta)$ every Δ seconds. A number of interesting random processes result from different forms of the step function. The value of the counter after n iterations (i.e., after $n\Delta$ seconds) is the sum of the n coin flip outcomes ($\phi_i=\pm1$) multiplied by the step-size function $f(i,\Delta)$, namely:

$$x(n\Delta) \;=\; \sum_{i=1}^{n}\phi_i \;\; f(i,\Delta)$$

Recall from Chapter 8 that for large values of n, the Demoivre-Laplace theorem states that the probability density of the number of coin flips that are heads k is asymptotically normal within a few standard deviations about the mean. The value of the random walk is therefore x=2k-n, which takes on the values ranging from -n through +n. Thus, we need only compute the mean and variance of $x(n\Delta)$ as follows to completely specify the probability density of x at the nth step of the random walk:

$$E[x(n\Delta)] = 0$$

$$Var[x(n\Delta)] = E[x^2(n\Delta)] - E[x(n\Delta)]^2 = \sum_{i=1}^{n} f^2(i, \Delta)$$

When the number of sources n becomes large, and the behavior of the sources are homogeneous, then the law of large numbers applies and the probability distribution tends toward normal or Gaussian. When the mean and variance are equal, then the normal and Poisson distribution have similar shapes. For example, people placing telephone calls exhibit similar behavior (at least before the era of the World Wide Web) and when considered over large populations, a Poisson model is quite good. On the other hand, if the source behavior is heterogeneous, as occurs in some IP and ATM networks, then the aggregated statistics may follow quite different distributions, as we shall see.

Brownian Motion and the Wiener Process

In the late nineteenth century, the botanist Robert Brown observed random frenetic motion of minute pollen grains under a microscope. In the early twentieth century, Albert Einstein showed that a random walk where the forces acted randomly to move the particles a distance proportional to the square root of time explained Brown's observations. Consequently, the process commonly used in a variety of sciences to model the motion of microscopic particles due to random collisions in a liquid or a gas is called *Brownian motion*. This process results if we assume that the function $f(i,\Delta) = \sqrt{\lambda\Delta}$ and take the limit as the time increment Δ approaches zero to yield the process [7]:

$$w(t) = \lim_{\Delta \to 0} x(n\Delta)$$

where $t = n\Delta$. Since $x(n\Delta)$ is normal, calculating the mean and variance completely determines the statistics of the process w, also called the Wiener process, as follows:

$$E[w(t)] = \lim_{\Delta \to 0} E[x(n\Delta)] = 0$$

$$Var[w(t)] = E[w^2(t)] - E[w(t)]^2 = \lim_{\Delta \to 0} \sum_{i=1}^{n} \lambda\Delta = \lim_{\Delta \to 0} \lambda n\Delta = \lambda t$$

The autocorrelation function for the process w results from straightforward calculation [7, 9] with the following result:

$$R(t_1, t_2) = \lambda \ \min(t_1, t_2) \tag{9-18}$$

Note that this process is not wide sense stationary, since the auto-correlation does not depend upon the difference between two instants in time. A Brownian motion process may also have a constant drift rate, which the above summary did not include in the interest of brevity. The plots illustrating a non-self-similar process at the end of Chapter 7 employed a Brownian motion process. This process has independent increments, which means that we need only generate independent normal random variables with the appropriate mean and variance at each instant in time to simulate Brownian motion. When the mean value equals the variance (λ) Brownian motion closely approximates a Poisson counting process. See References 7 and 11 for more details, examples, and derivations of the properties of Brownian motion and the Wiener process.

Self-Similar Traffic

Okay, all this modeling seems rather complex. Are there models for processes that exhibit higher degrees of uncertainty? The answer is, unfortunately, yes. Research based upon actual LAN traffic measurements in the early 1990s [12, 13] indicates that traditional Markovian traffic models may be overly optimistic in some situations. These exist for non-flow controlled traffic on Ethernet LANs [14], Web traffic [15, 16], and ATM-encoded variable bit rate video [17]. These papers report that the LAN traffic measured on some local area networks, Web transactions, and encoded video signals are *self-similar*, which means that the traffic has similar properties over a broad range of observation time scales. This stands in sharp contrast to the Poisson and Markovian models, where the traffic tends to become smoother and more predictable when considering increasingly longer time averages. However, as studied in Part 5, neither self-similar nor Poisson traffic models capture the behavior of the closed-loop flow control widely utilized in TCP/IP end systems.

We examine the Fractional Brownian Motion (FBM) process [13, 14] as an extension of the generalized random walk introduced earlier in this section. The FBM process uses a different function for the increment at each coin flip as follows:

$$f(i, \Delta) \;=\; (\lambda\Delta)^H \quad (2i)^{H-0.5}$$

where $0.5 \leq H < 1$ is the Hurst parameter. Note that for $H = 0.5$, Brownian motion results as described above. The FBM process still has a normal density with zero mean. However, the variance takes on a different value given by the following formula.

$$Var[w(t)] = E[w^2(t)] - E[w(t)]^2$$

$$= \lim_{\Delta \to 0} \sum_{i=1}^{n} (\lambda\Delta)^{2H} (2i)^{2H-1} = \lim_{\Delta \to 0} (\lambda n\Delta)^{2H} = (\lambda t)^{2H}$$

Note that the above formula is only valid for the evolution of an FBM process after t seconds have elapsed given an initial condition that $w(0)=0$. In order to compute statistics for intermediate points in time, we need to understand the correlation properties of the process. The autocorrelation of the FBM process is [9, 14]:

$$R(t_1, t_2) \;=\; \frac{\lambda^{2H}}{2}\left(t_1{}^{2H} + t_2{}^{2H} - |t_1 - t_2|^{2H}\right)$$

Thus, the FBM process is also not wide sense stationary, since it depends on more than just the difference in time instants. Note that the autocorrelation of FBM exactly equals the autocorrelation function for Brownian motion given in Equation (9-18) when $H=0.5$. Furthermore, the FBM process does not have independent increments. This gives rise to the phenomenon of long-range dependence in self-similar processes discussed in the next section.

While Brownian motion is independent from instant to instant, an FBM process is not for $0.5 < H < 1$. Therefore, generating a simulated sequence of an FBM process is more involved. The technique used to generate the self-similar traffic traces at the end of Chapter 7 employed the Random Displacement Method (RDM) [18, 19]. The RDM procedure that generates a simulated sequence of $N=2^M+1$ samples of the arrivals $y(k)$ for an FBM with mean μ and variance λ for a time increment Δ is as follows:

1. Set the points $x(0)=0$ and $X(N)=\eta 2^{MH}$, where η is a zero-mean, unit-variance normal random variable.
2. Iterate and linearly interpolate between each pair of points, beginning with the endpoints defined in step 1, successively halving each interval.

3. Add a zero-mean, unit-variance normal random variable η scaled by the value $2^{(M-i)H}\sqrt{1-2^{2H-2}}$ to the result of 2 to yield x(i).
4. Repeat steps 2 and 3 until all N points for x(i) are generated.
5. Beginning with i=1, set y(i) equal to x(i)-x(i-1) multiplied by λ^H plus $\mu\Delta$ for i ranging from 1 to N.

A number of other techniques exist to generate simulated FBM traffic and other models of self-similar traffic. See References 16, 20, 21, and 22 for alternative approaches.

Important Properties of Self-Similar Processes

This section defines the discrete-valued case and then presents some additional important properties of generic self-similar processes.

Discrete-Valued Self-Similar Processes

Many papers in the literature [13, 16] model and analyze a sequence of discrete samples x_i of a series sampled at discrete instants in time. This corresponds well to measurements taken from LANs, the Internet, ATM switches, and video devices. The analysis then defines the m-aggregated time series $\mathbf{x}^{(m)} \equiv \left\{\mathbf{x}_k^{(m)}, k = 0, 1, 2, ...\right\}$, where

$$\mathbf{x}_k^{(m)} \equiv \frac{1}{m} \sum_{i=km-(m-1)}^{km} x_i$$

is the sum of the original time series over adjacent blocks of m samples.

This is the technique employed for generating the traces at the end of Chapter 7. Specifically, $\mathbf{x}^{(1)}$ is equivalent to the original set of simulated points for 10-ms intervals, $\mathbf{x}^{(10)}$ is the sequence of samples for 100-ms intervals, and $\mathbf{x}^{(100)}$ is the sequence of 1-s intervals.

The literature uses the following notation for the correlation coefficient [22, 23] (beware that it is called the autocorrelation function in some papers [9,22]) for an m-aggregated discrete-time series $\mathbf{x}_n^{(m)}$:

$$r^{(m)}(k) \equiv \frac{E[(x_{n+k}^{(m)} - \mu)(x_n^{(m)} - \mu)]}{Var[x_n^{(m)}]} \qquad (9\text{-}19)$$

where $\mu \equiv E[x_n^{(m)}]$.

Signatures of Self-Similarity

A continuous-time process $x(t)$ is self-similar in the strict sense if for any $0.5 \leq H < 1$ the process $a^{-H}x(at)$ has the same statistical properties as $x(t)$ [14, 9]. The process $x(t)$ is second-order self-similar if the mean and autocovariance obey the following relationships:

$$
\begin{aligned}
a^H E[x(t)] &= E[x(at)] \\
a^{2H} Var[x(t)] &= Var[x(at)] \\
a^{2H} C_x(t,s) &= C_x(at,as)
\end{aligned}
$$

A discrete-time process x is self-similar in the strict sense if the process $mx_k^{(m)}$ is statistically identical to the process $m^H x_k$ for all values of m [22]. Generally, we concern ourselves with processes that are (asymptotically) second-order self-similar [13, 22, 23], which requires that only the following relationships hold:

$$
\begin{aligned}
E[x_k] &= E[x_k^{(m)}] \\
m^{-\beta} Var[x_k] &= Var[x_k^{(m)}] \\
r(k) &= r^{(m)}(k), \text{ as } m \to \infty
\end{aligned}
$$

where $\beta \equiv 2(1-H)$. When we cover the application of theory to real-world networks in Chapter 21, the text summarizes procedures for estimating the Hurst parameter H in self-similar processes.

Short- and Long-Range Dependence

An important difference between self-similar processes and other random processes is how correlation depends (or more precisely, decays) for relative ranges of time [9, 13, 22]. A process is *short-range dependent* if the correlation coefficient $r(k)$ decays at least as fast as exponentially, namely:

$$r(k) \cong \alpha^{|k|} \quad \text{as } k \to \infty, \quad 0 < \alpha < 1$$

An alternative definition for short-range dependent processes is that $\sum_k r(k) < \infty$. If a process is not short-range dependent, then it is *long-range dependent*. When a process is long-range dependent, then the correlation coefficient $r(k)$ decays hyperbolically as defined by the following formula:

$$r(k) \cong |k|^{-\beta} \quad \text{as } k \to \infty, \quad 0 < \beta < 1$$

Long-range dependence is one of the most important properties of self-similar processes. It mathematically captures the reason that clustering of busy and idle periods occurs in observations of real-world self-similar traffic processes across a wide range of time scales.

Since the correlation coefficient $r^{(m)}(k)$ for discrete-time series self-similar processes depends upon k only, and not the specific time series as defined in Equation (9-19), the process $x_k^{(m)}$ is wide sense stationary. Therefore, the power spectral density applied to the autocovariance function is meaningful. The long-range dependence property manifests itself as follows:

$$S(\omega) \cong |\omega|^{-\gamma} \quad \text{as } \omega \to \infty, \quad 0 < \gamma < 1$$

where $S_x(\omega) \equiv \sum_{k=0}^{\infty} \sigma^2 r(k) \ e^{-j2k\omega}$, and $\gamma = 1 - \beta = 2H - 1$.

Since $\omega \equiv 2\pi f$, the above equation states that the power spectrum is of the form $1/f$ in the region as $f \to 0$, which as seen from Figure 9.8 means that the time domain signal has a nearly DC, or constant, value [24]. This is yet another explanation for the long-range, slowly varying aspects of the traces of a self-similar process shown at the end of Chapter 7 and reported in various measurements.

Heavy-Tailed Probability Densities

Measurements of Internet traffic indicate that although the arrivals resulting from interactive sessions are Poisson distributed, the duration of these sessions have a probability distribution where very long sessions are likely [15]. Researchers call these probability densities "heavy-tailed" because the likelihood of a large value is much higher than the negative exponential distribution studied in Chapter 8. Initially called "packet-trains" [25] to describe the occurrence of a long string of packets generated in response to a request, subsequent studies have shown that files retrieved via WWW sessions tend to follow a heavy tailed distribution. In general, a distribution is heavy-tailed if the following condition holds:

$$\Pr[X \geq x] \; \cong \; x^{-\alpha} \quad \text{as } x \to \infty, \; \alpha \geq 0.$$

Theorists have employed the Pareto distribution to model heavy-tailed phenomena in social sciences, computer utilization, and traffic phenomena [15]. The Pareto probability density has the following form [9, 15, 16]:

$$f(x) \; \equiv \; \frac{\alpha}{\varepsilon} \left(\frac{\varepsilon}{x}\right)^{\alpha+1}, \quad x > \varepsilon, \; \alpha > 0$$

The two parameters of the Pareto distribution have the following meaning: ε determines the minimum value, while α determines the mean and variance. If $\alpha \leq 2$, then x has infinite variance, and if $\alpha \leq 1$, then x also has infinite mean. For the case $\alpha > 1$, a Pareto distributed random variable x has mean value:

$$E[x] \; \equiv \; \frac{\alpha}{\alpha - 1} \varepsilon$$

For example, Reference 15 chose $\varepsilon = 1$ and $\alpha = 0.95$ as a good model for observed Telnet traffic. Reference 16 found that $\alpha = 1.21$ was a good fit for the distribution of Web data transfer durations and $\alpha \approx 1$ was a good fit for FTP data. Choices of the parameters ε and α in these ranges result in a probability distribution markedly different than the negative exponential density introduced in Chapter 8 with equivalent mean value (for $\alpha > 1$).

Figure 9.9 plots the values of the probability that x exceeds a threshold T (i.e., $\Pr[x > T]$) for several values of α for the Pareto and negative exponential distributions normalized to have the same mean using the following formula:

$$\Pr[x > T] \; = \; \begin{cases} \left(\dfrac{\varepsilon}{T}\right)^{\alpha} & \text{Pareto} \\[2ex] e^{-\left(\frac{\alpha-1}{\alpha}\right)T} & \text{Negative Exponential} \end{cases}$$

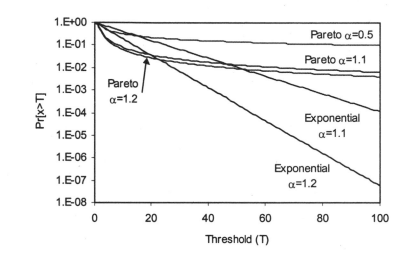

Figure 9.9
Comparison of
negative exponential
and Pareto probability
densities.

The parameter ε=1 for all Pareto curves in Figure 9.9. The difference between the shapes of the Pareto and negative exponential curves is striking. As clearly seen from the figure, packet interarrival times or burst durations obeying the Pareto model will either be much more widely spaced or clumped than a Poisson model (i.e., negative exponential), respectively. Chapter 12 explores the effect of this difference in modeling assumptions in greater depth when considering buffer sizing requirements in IP routers and ATM switches.

The use of heavy-tailed distributions is useful in simulation models since it determines the interval until the next simulated event. However, the fact that the distribution of inter-event times is heavy-tailed does not necessarily mean that the process is self-similar. For example, although the Pareto distribution has a heavy tail, it is, strictly speaking, not a self-similar process [15].

Review

We covered a number of formulas and mathematical techniques in this section. The chapter defined the techniques of matrix manipulations and the semi-graphical stochastic balance technique for birth-death Markov chains for the solution of systems of linear equations encountered in queuing systems studied in Chapter 11. Examples analyzing the performance of a request-response system and system availability illustrated these techniques. The text then defined important properties of random processes in terms of the autocorrelation function and the notion of stationarity for which the power spectral density is a powerful tool.

We then moved on to cover the topics of random walks, Brownian motion, and self-similar processes. The text described the techniques used to generate the simulated traffic traces presented at the end of Chapter 7. Finally, the chapter concluded with an overview of other important properties of self-similar processes encountered in some LAN, Internet, ATM, and video applications as background to subsequent discussion. Specifically, Chapter 12 examines the application of self-similar processes to IP router and ATM switch buffer sizing, while Chapter 21 summarizes how a network operator or user can determine if traffic is self-similar or not based upon actual measurements. Readers seeking further details should consult the references cited in the relevant subject areas.

References

[1]   L. Kleinrock, *Queuing Systems Volume I: Theory*, Wiley, 1975.

[2]   N. Hock, *Queuing Modeling Fundamentals*, Wiley, 1996.

[3]   D. Gross, C. Harris, *Fundamentals of Queuing Theory*, Wiley, 1985.

[4]   M. Schwarz, *Broadband Integrated Networks*, Prentice-Hall, 1996.

[5]   E. Parzen , *Stochastic Processes*, Holden-Day, 1962.

[6]   I. Ushakov, *Reliability Engineering*, Wiley, 1994.

[7]   A. Papoulis, *Probability, Random Variables and Stochastic Processes, Third Edition*, McGraw-Hill, 1991.

[8]   A. Papoulis, *Probability, Random Variables and Stochastic Processes*, McGraw-Hill, 1965.

[9]   W. Stallings, *High-Speed Networks — TCP/IP and ATM Design Principles*, Prentice-Hall, 1998.

[10]   H. Che, S. Q. Li, "Fast Algorithms for Measurement-Based Traffic Modeling," IEEE Journal on Selected Areas in Communications}, Vol. 16, June 1998.

[11]   E. Suhir, *Applied Probability for Engineers and Scientists*, McGraw-Hill, 1997.

[12]   H. Fowler, W. Leland, "Local Area Network Traffic Characteristics, with Implications for Broadband Network Congestion Management," *IEEE JSAC*, September 1991.

[13]   W. Leland, M. Taqqu, W. Willinger, D. Wilson, "On the Self-Similar Nature of Ethernet Traffic (extended version)," IEEE/ACM Transactions on Networking, February 1994.

[14]   I. Norros, "On the Use of Fractional Brownian Motion in the Theory of Ethernet Traffic (Extended Version)," *IEEE JSAC*, August 1995.

[15]   V. Paxson, S. Floyd, "Wide Area Traffic: The Failure of Poisson Modeling," IEEE/ACM Transactions on Networking, June 1995.

[16]   Crovella, A. Bestavros, "Explaining World Wide Web Traffic Self-Similarity," Technical Report TR-95-015, 1995, http://www.cs.bu.edu/fac/crovella/paper-archive/self-sim/paper.html.

[17]   M. Garrett, W. Willnger, "Analysis, Modeling, and Generation of Self-Similar VBR Video Traffic," Proceedings SIGCOMM '94, August 1994.

[18]   J. Beran, *Statistics for Long-Memory Processes,* Chapman & Hall, 1994.

[19]   P. Karlsson, D. Bouillant, "Traffic Models," http://buggy.itm.hk-r.se/ttn410/models/.

[20]   L. Decreusefond, A.S. Üstünel, "Fractional Brownian Motion: Theory and Applications," Proceedings of the ESAIM, http://www.emath.fr/Maths/Proc/Vol.5/index.html.

[21]   B. Ryu, "Fractal Network Traffic: From Understanding to Implications," Ph.D. Thesis, Columbia University, 1996, http://www.wins.hrl.com/people/ryu/.

[22]   H. Michiel, K. Laevens, "Teletraffic Engineering in a Broad-Band Era," Proceedings of the IEEE, December 1997.

[23]   B. Tsybakov, N. Georganas, "On Self-Similar Traffic in ATM Queues: Definitions, Overflow Probability Bound, and Cell Delay Distribution," IEEE/ACM Transactions on Networking, June 1997.

[24]   B. Mandelbrot, *Multifractals and 1/f Noise*, Springer, 1998.

[25]   R. Jain, S. Routhier, "Packet trains — Measurements and a New Model for Computer Network Traffic," IEEE JSAC, September 1986.

4

Queuing Principles

"How can it be that mathematics, being after all a product of human thought independent of experience, is so admirably adapted to the objects of reality?"

— Albert Einstein

A fundamental traffic engineering issue involves selection of appropriate capacity for the links connecting routers or switches to yield the desired QoS. Part 4 puts together the three components of queuing theory to analyze the relationships between performance and link capacity, random arrivals, and queue service policy. Because queuing is simply a fancy name for waiting in line, Chapter 10 puts together real-world arrival processes with commonly encountered queuing policies. And since in this modern world we all spend so much time waiting in line, we have a wealth of practical experience on which to hone our intuition. Chapter 11 formalizes these notions by introducing the basic concepts defined in queuing theory. Finally, Chapter 12 moves further into more-advanced topics in queuing theory applied to IP and ATM networks.

10

Queuing — A Fancy Name for Waiting in Line

"Each problem that I solved became a rule which served afterwards to solve other problems. "

- Rene Descartes

This chapter shows how the basic queuing model encountered in everyday activities applies to IP and ATM networks. As we shall see, queuing theory provides deep insight into the performance of communication networks. First, we define the basic components of a queueing system: arrivals, a waiting room, and a service policy illustrated by a simple example. Next, the text introduces the variations in service policy that affect QoS, namely: reservations, limited waiting room, and priority.

We then introduce some basic concepts of queuing systems in general, followed by application to IP and ATM communication networks in particular. These include Little's result that describes how the number in queue is proportional to the product of the waiting time and the arrival rate. The chapter summarizes important queue service algorithms used in real IP and ATM switches like priority queuing and Weighted Fair Queuing (WFQ).

Queuing Systems

This section introduces the terminology and concepts employed in the analysis of traffic systems using queuing theory. Next, we apply the dice-rolling arrival process from Chapter 7 with a deterministic service policy to illustrate the queuing phenomenon. The section then summarizes the range of service policies analyzed in the remainder of Part 4.

The Generic Queuing System Model

Figure 10.1 illustrates the commonly used queuing terminology employed in this book. Starting on the left-hand side, a population of users decide to request service in a random fashion. As users *arrive* at a system they seek *service*. If the system is busy when a new arrival occurs, then the system may provide waiting room, or a *queue*, for those arrivals that the system cannot immediately serve, as shown in the middle of the figure. The system serves users according to some policy, for example, First Come First Served (FCFS) or in a prioritized manner. Users then depart the system once service is complete. Examples of such queuing systems surround us. Arriving at a post office, bank, or a store and having to wait in line for a service is a common occurrence in modern day life. We feel fortunate to arrive and not have to wait in line. Governments, bank officers, and storeowners seek to provide the minimum service while keeping the waiting line to a reasonable length. In addition, encountering congestion in transportation networks is also an altogether too familiar phenomenon for many of us, especially during rush hours. Transportation engineers trade off providing greater service (e.g., more lanes on the highway) against providing more waiting room (e.g., wider entrance ramps and frontage roads) to minimize overall cost. Many of these systems have direct analogs to problems in the realm of traffic engineering for communication networks. However, beware, some commonly encountered queuing situations do not apply to communications net-

Figure 10.1
A basic traffic system: arrivals, waiting room, and service.

| User Population | Arriving Users | Waiting Room, or Queue | Service Policy | Departing Users |

works. Throughout this text, we endeavor to give examples that apply to communications networks, and point out those that don't. This chapter introduces the subject of traffic modeling by describing a few simple arrival processes.

As we shall see, the system comprised of a single random arrival stream, a single waiting area, and a single server is the best understood. Examples are a store, bank, or post office with a single clerk. The behavior of a single communication link is often analogous to the behavior of these types of everyday queuing systems. However, many stores, banks, and post offices have multiple clerks. What is the communication network analogy here? Why do many of these commonplace systems have a single queue (i.e., waiting line) for the multiple servers? What is the advantage of such an arrangement over that of a separate line for each server? We answer these questions later in the next chapter.

Random Processes and Queuing Systems

Let's begin by extending the dice roll example from Chapter 7 to understand the impact of combining a deterministic service policy and a waiting area in response to random arrivals in a queuing system. A dice-rolling random process creates an arrival to the queue for each roll of a six that occurs on a fair die as shown in Figure 10.2a. A simple deterministic service policy removes this entry after five successive dice rolls. This has the effect of measuring how clumped the arrivals are, since a six should come up on the dice on average only once every six trials. Figure 10.2b plots the resulting number of entries in the queue. Note how clumps of arrivals cause the queue to build up,

Figure 10.2
Example queuing process — arrivals generated by occurences of sixes when rolling a fair die served once every five rolls and the resulting number in queue.

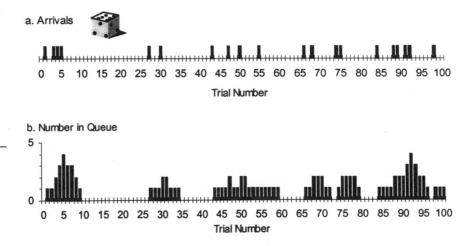

while long gaps of no arrivals allow the queue to empty.

As studied in this part, this basic analogy of random processes and dice rolling captures the essential behavior of a number of traffic phenomena encountered in real networks rather well. The chapters in this part put together random arrivals, the service discipline, and waiting room and apply it using queuing theory to the problem of traffic engineering IP and ATM networks to deliver a desired level of quality.

Resource Reservation and Service Policies

An important concept in IP and ATM networks is the allocation of resources and the determination of the service policy required to deliver a specified QoS. We encounter examples of resource reservation and service policies in many aspects of travel. Airlines, hotels, and car rental agencies all use reservation systems. There are two aspects of a reservations system: booking the reservation and honoring the reservation. Booking a reservation begins with a user inquiring about reserving a seat on an airplane, a room in a hotel, or a rental car. The agent consults a scheduling system to determine if the resource (i.e., the seat, room, or car) is available at the requested dates and times. Typically, many agents simultaneously access a shared scheduling system. Once the customer decides on the date, time, and other features of the requested service, the agent then books the reservation.

A scheduling system then implements a specific service policy for honoring the reservation according to the parameters of the booking. The scheduler may track bookings using a fully occupied or peak allocation policy. Alternatively, the scheduler may overbook reservations if experience indicates that a predictable fraction of customers do not claim their reservations at the requested date and time.

Typically, hotels book reserved rooms on a guaranteed basis. They then offer unreserved rooms on a first come, first served basis. Hotels often employ a billing policy where they bill the customer for the room even if the traveler never arrives. This policy guarantees revenue in the event that the traveler does not arrive and the hotel had to turn away other paying arrivals. At the opposite extreme, airlines typically overbook popular flights since a relatively predictable portion of travelers arrive earlier or later than the scheduled flight time.

These scheduling and service systems handle exceptional events in different ways. Usually, hotels can do the best job of honoring reservations if they implement guaranteed late arrival billing and enforce the checkout times of guests. This is an example of a *non-blocking* queuing system.

Unfortunately, some hotel chains give precedence to guests already staying in the hotel, allowing them to stay longer and hence potentially violating the reservations of guests arriving later. Even if a hotel enforces the checkout date, a depletion of resources, for example, a fire or broken plumbing in one or more rooms, may place the hotel in the situation of being unable to honor future reservations. This is an example of a *blocking* queuing system. An example of blocking occurs when you receive a busy signal after attempting to place a telephone call. All real-world switches and routers have some degree of blocking, although often the likelihood of blocking is so small that we call it *virtually non-blocking*.

Analogous reservation and scheduling problems occur in communications networks. For example, a television broadcast network may arrange a reserved time slot for broadcasting the World Cup soccer championship at a specified date and time. A network provider that denied service to such a broadcast because of extensions of prior commitments will likely lose the business of such a customer.

An alternative scheduling policy occurs when the system provides a waiting area for customers that cannot immediately be served. Car rental agencies often implement this type of policy. The return date and time of a rental car is more difficult to predict than requesting that a guest vacate a hotel room at the previously agreed upon date and time. Therefore, car rental companies sometimes find themselves without rental cars when renters fail to return vehicles on time. Hence, they typically provide some waiting room. The resources are also more susceptible to depletion since the car may be involved in an accident or break down. The scheduling system may also transfer resources (cars) from nearby agencies to meet unanticipated demands. We call this type of service a queuing system with *waiting room*. Airlines also provide waiting room to speed up the boarding process and increase throughput.

Airlines are an example of the other extreme in terms of service scheduling. Typically, airlines overbook flights, since travelers do not always use their reservations. When more travelers arrive than can fit on the airplane, the airline motivates some users to take a later flight by compensating them with vouchers offering discounted or free travel on subsequent dates. This is an example of *preemptive queuing*. An example of preemption occurs in ATM networks when a cell from a high-priority connection (e.g., voice) preempts transmission of a long string of cells that makes up a data packet.

Finally, many systems provide prioritized levels of service when honoring the reservation. For example, airlines often have a queue with dedicated agents for first-class passengers separate from the coach class queue and agents, as shown in Figure 10.3. Other service

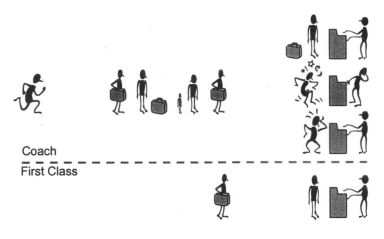

Figure 10.3
Example of a prioritized queuing system with weighted service.

disciplines include agents for passengers needing to purchase tickets separate from those only needing to check baggage. A similar situation exists in stores with express checkout lines. The separate queues implement priority, and the separate servers implement weighted service. Note that when no first-class passengers are in queue, a first-class agent can serve a coach passenger. This provides greater system throughput, but does increase the waiting time of first-class passengers who arrive and must wait for the first-class agent to finish with the coach passenger. This type of service policy aims to provide better service to the higher-priority (and presumably higher-paying) customers. An analogous notion of weighted, prioritized queuing is central to delivering QoS in IP and ATM.

Using the relevant mathematics studied in Part 3, the remainder of Part 4 studies the implications of these various service policies on the blocking probability and waiting time performance observed in communication networks.

Queuing System Properties

This section draws some analogies with common experience to illustrate basic concepts of queuing systems.

Traffic Flows, Stability, and Loading

The flow of traffic depends upon many factors, such as the season, day of week, time of day, and special events. In order to make analysis tractable, queuing theory usually simplifies the problem by assuming that the traffic flow is constant (or steady) over the interval of time under study. This model accounts for variations over time by analyzing performance over each time interval independently of the others, using the result from the prior interval as the starting point for the next interval. We call such a process *doubly stochastic*, since not only does traffic vary within a time interval, but the statistics of the traffic process also vary over time.

Any queuing system has a capacity determined by the characteristics of the service policy. For example, a roadway can only carry a certain number of vehicles per hour, a clerk takes a few minutes to service each customer, or an airplane makes a certain number of flights each day. Intuitively, if the average arrival rate exceeds the average service rate, then the waiting line will grow without bound. We call such a system unstable. Hence, a basic principle for queuing system *stability* is that the average arrival rate must be strictly less than the average service rate over the long run.

In a deterministic system like a beer bottling plant, a conveyor belt moves empty bottles (i.e., generates regularly spaced arrivals) for the machine that fills the bottles and caps them (i.e., serves each arrival in a fixed amount of time). In a deterministic system, the offered load is 100 percent of the service capacity. That is, the arrival rate exactly equals the service rate while the conveyor belt and the bottling machine are in operation. Stated yet another way, a deterministic system is capable of operating at full capacity.

When the arrivals or service take on random values, the situation changes markedly. For example, look back at Figure 10.2 and note that during some intervals the queue is empty, while during others the queue increases to relatively large values. For this example, the average arrival rate (denoted by the Greek letter lambda, λ) is the occurrence of a six once every six rolls of the single die. The average service time (T) before removing the roll of a six from the queue is five rolls of the dice. Thus, the average service rate (denoted by the Greek letter mu (μ)) is 1/5 of a removal from the queue for each roll of the die. Clearly, the average service time is inversely proportional to the average service rate (i.e., $T=1/\mu$).

A key parameter that characterizes a queuing system is the *offered load*. Throughout this book we refer to the load offered to a queuing system via the Greek letter rho (ρ) according to the following definition:

$$\text{Offered Load}(\rho) \; = \; \frac{\text{Average Arrival Rate } (\lambda)}{\text{Average Service Rate } (\mu)}$$

Hence, the offered load to the dice-rolling queuing system of Figure 10.2 is 5/6, or approximately 83 percent. Thus, although the system operates at less than full capacity, significant queues do indeed develop. Interspersed with these intervals of queuing are periods of no activity whatsoever. These phenomena of alternating busy and idle periods characterize waiting line systems in everyday experience and models the occurrence of congestion in IP and ATM networks. Note that offered load is dimensionless; therefore, the arrival and service rates must have the same units, for example, vehicles per minute, customers per hour, flights per day, or packets per second.

Queue Length and Waiting Time

Stable queuing systems exhibit average behavior over time intervals that are long with respect to the average interval between arrivals or the average service time. First, observe that the time a user spends in the queuing system T_s is the sum of the waiting (or queuing) time T_q and the average service time $T=1/\mu$ defined above. Or, in equation form, we have that the following average times are equal:

$$\text{Time in System } (T_s) = \text{Queuing Time } (T_q) + \text{Service Time } (T)$$

An important consequence of this result is that if we know the statistics of the number of users in the queue, then we can straightforwardly calculate the statistics of queuing time from this formula.

An important theorem in queuing theory known as *Little's Result* [1, 2] predicts that the average number of users in the queuing system is given by the following formula:

$$\text{Avg Number in System } (\overline{N}_s) = \text{Arrival Rate } (\lambda) \text{ Avg Time in System } (T_s)$$

Intuitively, this must be true because an arriving user must find the same average number of users in the system as a departing user. Before a user departs the system, an average of λT_s users arrive, which must equal the average number in the system. Since the time in the system is the sum of the queuing and service times, we can derive the average number of users in the queue from Little's result and obtain the following equality:

$$\text{Avg Number in Queue } (\overline{N}_q) = \text{Arrival Rate } (\lambda) \text{ Avg Queuing Time } (T_q)$$

We will use these results many times in the remainder of this book.

Effects of System Structure and Policy

The queuing system structure and service policy can have profound effects on the QoS performance observed by users. A commonly encountered example illustrates the reduced variability of waiting time achieved by systems with a single queue for multiple servers when compared with a system that employs a single queue per server. Figure 10.4 illustrates the two queuing systems under consideration for service systems implemented by two different banking establishments. The bank depicted in Figure 10.4a uses a separate queue for each clerk. Note that new arrivals must select one of two queues and wait for the clerk serving that queue. In our example, the arriving customer does not know whether to join the shorter queue with the customer having a large bag of money, or the longer queue where the clerk is occupied with an irate customer. A competing banking establishment shown in Figure 10.4b has a single shared queue from which the first available clerk serves the customer at the head of the line. In this system, arriving customers immediately join the single queue.

There is a difference in performance between these two queuing systems when offered traffic with the same arrival and service rates. The system with a separate queue for each server has a longer average waiting time than the shared queue system, mainly because of the wasted capacity when users queued at one server cannot jump over to an idle server. Furthermore, the variability in waiting time also differs markedly for these two systems. This result explains the frequent observation that the line we are in seems to move slower than the others do. Chapter 11 gives the formulas for the average waiting time, as well as the variability of waiting time.

Figure 10.4

Example of queuing systems with different structures and service policies.

a. Separate Queue for each Server

b. Shared Queue for all Servers

Queuing Theory Applied to IP and ATM Networks

This section describes the context and application of queuing theory to the design of networks of interconnected IP routers and ATM switches.

Quality of Service (QoS) Measures Calculated with Queuing Theory

Queuing theory analysis provides a quantitative means to assess QoS performance at the link level. Specifically, the remaining chapters in this part give relatively simple formulas for calculating the following QoS measures:

- Average delay
- Variation in delay
- Loss ratio (i.e., the probability that a queue is full)
- Delay statistics determined by queue occupancy probability

See Chapter 5 for definitions of these important QoS measures and the specific terminology employed in IP and ATM networks.

Multiplexed and Switched Traffic in Networks

The manner in which routers and switches multiplex and switch traffic from inputs to outputs results in traffic streams that often appear random. Hence, the concepts of probability theory and stochastic processes described in Part 3 apply. Let's take a look at an example with reference to Figure 10.5. Typically, networks of interconnected routers and/or switches (denoted as R/S in the figure) support end user devices like PCs, printers, and file servers. The interconnect technology may be either point-to-point links, or shared media like Ethernet or Token Ring Local Area Networks (LANs). End user devices generate traffic flows between them, for example, as illustrated via the dashed lines in the figure. It is this aggregated set of multiplexed and switched traffic that constitute the user population and arrivals in a generic queuing model for each router/switch interface or link.

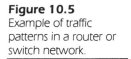

Figure 10.5
Example of traffic patterns in a router or switch network.

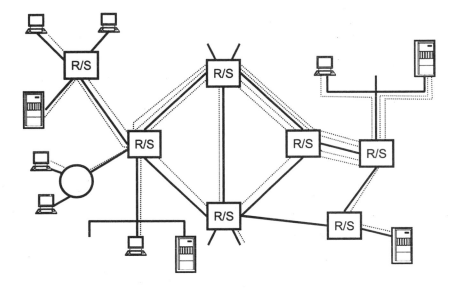

Router and Switch Architectures

In communications networks, Time Division Multiplexing (TDM) operates much like the deterministic bottling system described in the previous section. The framing format generates time slots into which TDM multiplexing and switching systems insert data. A TDM system can operate at full capacity (i.e., 100 percent load). In general, IP routers and ATM switches handle random traffic arrivals, whereas TDM switches require deterministic traffic patterns. Therefore, routers and switches must implement queuing (commonly called buffering) to average or smooth out fluctuations in the arriving traffic streams.

As described in Chapter 6, IP and ATM network devices implement a wide range of functions to deliver a specific QoS for a statistically defined traffic stream. These functions include policers, shapers, classifiers, buffers, and schedulers. Most queuing analysis simplifies the operation of a router or switch by adopting an abstract queuing model similar to that depicted in Figure 10.6. The traffic originating on other ports in the router/switch destined for a particular port acts as the user population that generates arrivals of packets/cells. The router/switch port takes the arriving packets/cells and places them into one or more queuing systems. The figure illustrates a simple single queue in the ports. The service policy engine then selects a specific packet/cell and transmits it on to the next router/switch (or end user device) over the communications link. The receive side of a router/switch port may also implement a queuing system and service

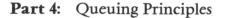

Figure 10.6
Abstract queuing model of a simple switch or router.

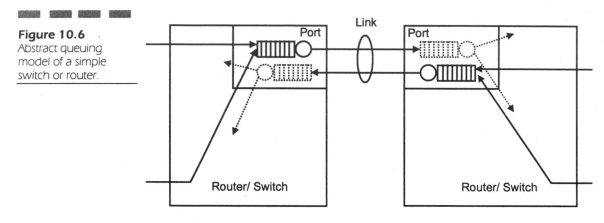

policy, as illustrated via dashed lines in the figure. The analysis of Chapters 11 and 12 covers the performance of queuing system implementations in router or switch ports. Hence, we say that queuing theory describes link-level performance. Part 6 extends these results by considering the performance of a network of interconnected queues.

Link-Level Queuing Model

The most basic application of queuing theory occurs at the link level in IP and ATM communication networks. Figure 10.7 illustrates more details of the unidirectional link-level queue on an IP router or ATM switch port. All of the link-level queuing models utilize the basic building block and concepts illustrated in this figure.

The next two chapters consider bursts of data independently of whether the underlying protocol is frame- or cell-based. In this general model, a burst may be anything ranging from a single fixed-length cell or packet to a train of variable-length packets. Starting from the left-hand side, bursts containing on average β bytes each arrive at a rate of λ to a queue (also called a buffer) capable of holding B

Figure 10.7
Abstract queuing model of an FIFO communication link.

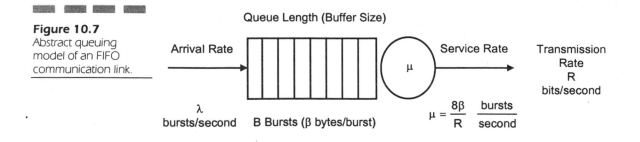

bursts. Thus, the service rate is μ=8β/R. A scheduler implements a specific service policy that removes bursts from the buffer at a rate μ over a transmission link operating at R bits/second, as shown in the right-hand side of the figure.

Queue Service Disciplines

Once a network element admits a connection or flow, and it satisfies the conditions of policing, then the IP packet or ATM cell is ready for transmission. At this point, the router or switch implements a particular queue servicing and scheduling mechanism.

First In First Out (FIFO) Queuing

The simplest queue service discipline is First Come First Served (FCFS), or First In First Out (FIFO). Just as the name implies, the scheduling algorithm services packets in the order that they arrive. Figure 10.8 illustrates an example of packet arrivals from three sources being serviced in FIFO order. The legend indicates each source via a different symbol. The figure plots a separate time line for each source, with arrivals from a particular source of a specified length shown below the line. The time that the queue service discipline serves the arrival is shown above the line. As seen from the figure, packets depart in the same order that they arrive.

Figure 10.8
Example of First In First Out (FIFO) queue service discipline.

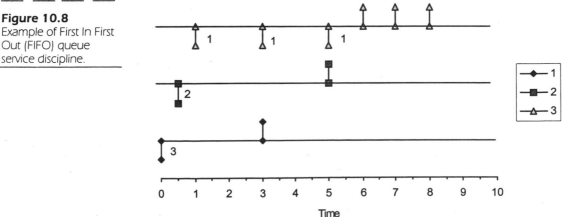

Prioritized Queuing

Priority queuing and weighted fair queuing [3, 4, 5] all basically implement multiple queues in the switch, such that delay-intolerant connections or flows can "jump ahead" of those that tolerate delay. IP routers and ATM switches employ *prioritized queuing* to meet different delay and loss priorities for different flows and connections. Switches and routers may perform either class-based queuing, or even implement a queue for each connection or flow. We describe prioritized queuing with reference to the block diagram of Figure 10.9. In our example, the prioritized queuing function conceptually resides on the output port of an IP router or ATM switch. The router/switch takes arriving packet/cell streams from multiple input ports, looks up an internal priority value, and directs the packets/cells to the queue on the output port corresponding to the class or individual flow/connection. The output side of the port serves the queues according to a particular scheduling algorithm.

A simple scheduling algorithm serves the highest-priority, non-empty queue to exhaustion and then moves on to the next-highest-priority queue. This process repeats for each successively lower-priority queue. This scheduling function ensures that the highest-priority queue has the least loss, delay, and delay variation. Consequently, lower-priority queues may experience significant delay variation, delays, as well as loss.

Actual switch designs may dedicate a set of buffers to each output port or split the buffers between the input and output ports. Some switches share memory between multiple priorities. Switches employing a shared memory approach usually limit the individual queue size for each port, service class, or in some cases, individual virtual connec-

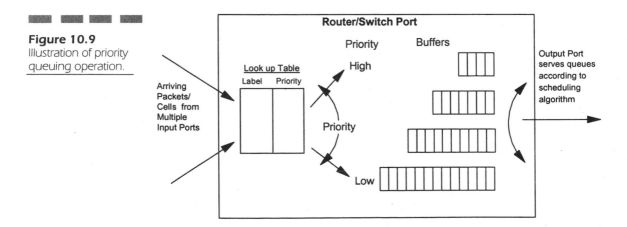

Figure 10.9
Illustration of priority queuing operation.

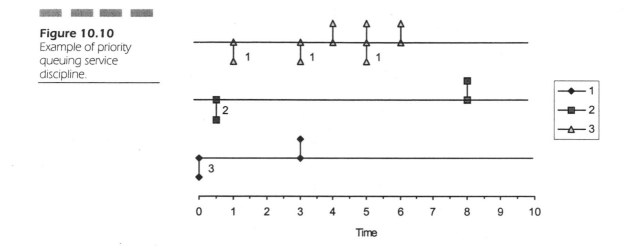

Figure 10.10
Example of priority queuing service discipline.

tions. Although theoretically ideal from a fairness point of view, per-connection queuing does add implementation complexity. The principal benefits of aggregating multiple connections or flows into a smaller number of classes are the reduction in the required amount of state information and hence reduced complexity. Most queue service disciplines are work-conserving, that is, if a packet or cell is in any queue, then the scheduler services it.

Figure 10.10 illustrates the operation of priority queuing for the same arrival pattern studied in the previous section with FIFO queuing. In this example, arrival sequence 3 has the highest priority, while arrival sequences 1 and 2 have the lowest priority. Since the packet of length 3 from sequence 1 arrives first, priority queuing services it first. This illustrates the phenomenon of a longer packet delaying a shorter, more urgent packet. However, now priority queuing services the packets from the high-priority sequence 3 ahead of those from the lower-priority sequence 2.

Weighted Queue Service Disciplines

Other scheduling algorithms spread out the variation in delay across the multiple queues. For example, a Weighted Fair Queuing (WFQ) scheduler sends out cells just before reaching the maximum delay variation value for cells in the higher-priority queues [6, 7, 8]. As we shall see, this action decreases delay variation in the lower-priority queues. The idealized Generalized Processor Sharing (GPS) model assumes that service can be broken down into infinitesimal amounts. A simpler explanation follows from the use of the notion of bit-by-bit service to express the units of a virtual clock. Packetized GPS (PGPS), commonly called WFQ, works on whole packet boundaries instead of the idealized bit-by-bit method described in this section.

The definition of GPS is closely tied to the definition of the token bucket defined in Chapter 3, which associates an average rate r_x and token bucket depth b_x with connection x. The router/switch port has an individual queue for each connection. A scheduler makes the rounds across all connection queues, one bit at a time. Thus, it is sufficient to keep time in terms of the current round $R(t)$ of the scheduler at time t as it moves through every queue. We can completely describe the service performed by defining the start time for packet i of connection x by defining the start time $S_{i,x}$ and the finish time $F_{i,x}$ in units of the round timer $R(t)$. The following simple recurrence formula for the finish time $F_{i,x}$ defines the operation of a GPS scheduler:

$$F_{i,x} = S_{i,x} + \frac{L_{i,x}}{\phi_x}$$

where $S_{i,x} \equiv Max[F_{i-1,x}, R(t_{i,x})]$ is the start time for packet i on connection x, $L_{i,x}$ is the length of packet i for connection x, $t_{i,x}$ is the arrival time of packet i on connection x, and ϕ_x is the scheduling weight for connection x.

If $N(t) > 0$ connections are active at time t, then the rate that the virtual clock $R(t)$ services each queue is inversely proportional to $N(t)$. The weight ϕ_x determines the guaranteed minimum service rate g_x for the queue servicing connection x as follows:

$$g_x = \frac{\phi_x}{\sum\limits_{i=1}^{N} \phi_i}$$

If $g_x \geq r_x$, then as shown in Chapters 14 and 18, the performance of GPS (and also WFQ) for a single node and a network of nodes has bounded delay with no loss. WFQ can also be applied to best-effort traffic in conjunction with performance guarantees available to connections with token bucket limited traffic.

Now we describe the operation of WFQ with reference to the example depicted in Figure 10.11. The arrival sequences are identical to those in the previous sections for the FIFO and priority queuing service disciplines. However, here, each flow has an equal service weight ϕ_x. Because this example represents idealized WFQ, the long packet from input sequence 1 does not delay the short packet of sequence 3.

In a packet-based WFQ system, of course, this would not occur and the long packet would delay the shorter packets as in the other examples.

Figure 10.12 illustrates the evolution of the WFQ round timer R(t) for the above example, which shows the arrival and departure instants for each of the input sequences. Note how the slope of R(t) decreases as the second and third sequences become active starting from t=0. As the second sequence completes service, R(t) increases again as expected.

The technical literature defines a number of variants of weighted queue service. A primary goal of these refinements involves reducing implementation complexity, controlling other performance parameters like jitter, or allocating different degrees of fairness to the served connections. See References 6, 7, and 8 for more information on weighted queue service disciplines.

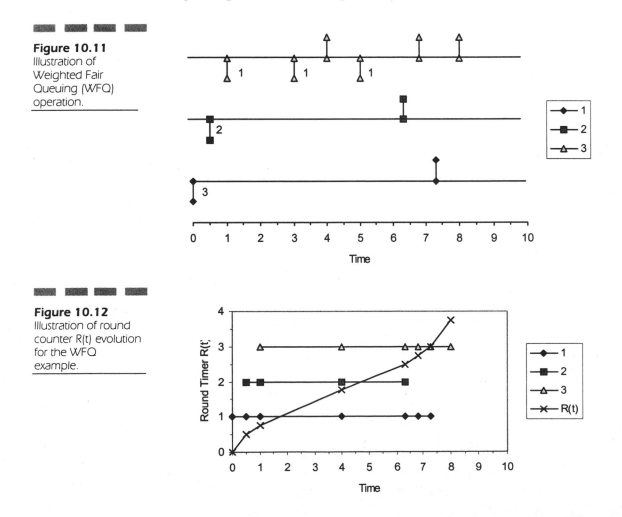

Figure 10.11
Illustration of Weighted Fair Queuing (WFQ) operation.

Figure 10.12
Illustration of round counter R(t) evolution for the WFQ example.

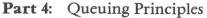

Figure 10.13
Illustration of discard
threshold operation.

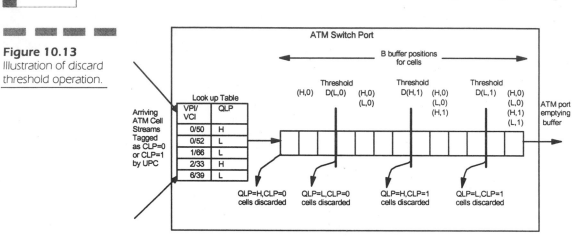

Discard Thresholds

On the router or switch port, each prioritized queue may also be seg-
mented into several regions via *discard thresholds.* Figure 10.13 illustrates the operation of discard thresholds within a single buffer. For
example, in ATM, arriving cell streams have the CLP bit set by either
the end user or the UPC/NPC at ingress to the network. The switch
port consults a lookup table to determine the Queue Loss Priority
(QLP) with a value of either High (H) or Low (L) based upon the
VPI/VCI combination in the cell header. The single buffer with B cell
positions has four thresholds in our example.

Starting from the right-hand side of Figure 10.13, the four thresholds determine the priority order for cell discard based upon buffer
occupancy as follows: discard QLP=L, CLP=1 cells first; discard
QLP=H, CLP=1 cells second; discard QLP=L, CLP=0 cells next; and finally discard QLP=H, CLP=0 cells only if the entire buffer is full.
Note that the buffer full condition is the implicit discard threshold
for QLP=H, CLP=0 cells in our example. Note that the selection of
discard thresholds in our example first give preference to CLP=0 traffic over CLP=1 traffic, then give preference to QLP=H traffic over
QLP=L traffic. Other choices of discard thresholds are possible. Thus,
cells with any combination of (QLP, CLP) may occupy the rightmost
portion of the buffer before the first discard threshold D(L,1), as
shown in the figure. For buffer occupancy greater than D(L,1), but
less than D(H,1), all cells except those of type QLP=L, CLP=1 may occupy the buffer. This partitioning of the buffer continues as we
move past successive thresholds towards the left until only cells with
QLP=H and CLP=0 may occupy the leftmost portion of the buffer
above the D(L,0) threshold.

Performance of Priority Discard Policies

Combinations of discard thresholds operating in each of several separate priority queues result in the capability to support a range of loss and delay QoS parameters. Simultaneously, the CLP discard thresholds provide a measure of congestion control as described in Chapter 14. Figure 10.14 qualitatively illustrates the combined effects of priority queuing and discard thresholds on the Cell Delay Variation (CDV) and Cell Loss Ratio (CLR) QoS parameters. The figure shows the resultant QoS values for a switch having four delay priority queues as shown in Figure 10.15, each with four discard thresholds, as shown in Figure 10.13. The values in this example are only a representative example of the type of CLR versus CDV plot resulting for such a system. The statistics and mix of the offered traffic for each delay and loss priority, the actual values of the discard thresholds, and the queue servicing algorithm all play roles in determining the actual QoS parameters; however, plots similar to the one in our example often result.

Note how the priority queuing supports differentiated QoS performance for applications that tolerate both increased CLR and CDV. In other words, lower-priority queues experience both higher loss rates and greater delay variation. Comparing Figure 10.14 with the plot of typical applications against the same CDV versus CLR scale in

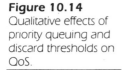

Figure 10.14
Qualitative effects of priority queuing and discard thresholds on QoS.

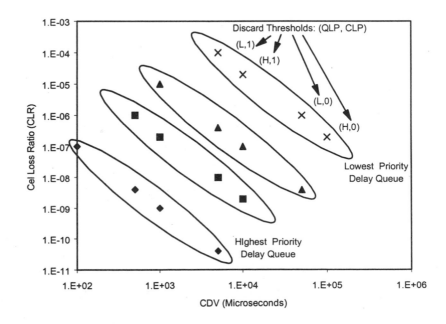

Chapter 5; observe that most applications require priority queuing. Fewer applications require the differentiation offered by discard thresholds, which offers increased CDV with decreased CLR. In general, many applications tolerate both CDV and CLR impairments equally well and cannot trade one off against the other.

Review

This chapter introduced the basic components of a queuing system: a user population, arrivals, a waiting room (or queue), and a service policy. The discussion drew analogies with transportation systems, shopping, and waiting for service in places like banks, airports, and shopping venues. The text then introduced the important properties of stability and loading and defined some basic terminology. The chapter continued with a description of how the queuing theory model addresses the subject of link-level performance in a network of interconnected routers and switches.

The text then introduced some commonly used service scheduling and admission policies. These included priority queuing, Weighted Fair Queuing (WFQ), and selective discard. We apply queuing theory in the next several chapters to describe traffic engineering for IP and ATM communication links.

References

[1]   L. Kleinrock, *Queuing Systems Volume I: Theory*, Wiley, 1975.

[2]   M. Tanner, *Practical Queuing Analysis*, McGraw-Hill, 1995.

[3]   D. Hong, T. Suda, "Congestion Control and Prevention in ATM Networks," IEEE Network, July 1991.

[4]   M. Katevenis, S. Sidiropoulos, C. Courcoubetis, "Weighted Round-Robin Cell Multiplexing in a General-Purpose ATM Switch Chip", *IEEE JSAC*, October 1991.

[5]   H. Kröner, G. Hébuterne, P. Boyer, A. Gravey, "Priority Management in ATM Switching Nodes," *IEEE JSAC*, April 1991.

[6]   A. Parekh, R. Gallager, "A Generalized Processor Sharing Approach to Flow Control in Integrated Services Networks: The Single-Node Case," *IEEE/ACM Transactions on Networking*, June 1993.

[7]   S. Keshav, *An Engineering Approach to Computer Networking*, Addison-Wesley, 1998.

[8]   W. Stallings, *High-Speed Networks — TCP/IP and ATM Design Principles*, Prentice-Hall, 1998.

11

Basic Queuing Theory Applied

"I am extraordinarily patient provided I get my own way in the end."

— Margaret Thatcher

This chapter summarizes the mathematical models employed in the analysis of queuing systems that are essential to understanding QoS performance at the link level in IP and ATM networks. Design problems answered by the application of queuing theory focus primarily on computing the QoS delivered by a specific implementation or determining resources like required buffer capacity or link speed to support a given load and deliver the desired QoS. Although queuing theory is mathematically involved, requiring mastery of the concepts of probability theory and stochastic processes detailed in the previous part, the application of the results is surprisingly straightforward. To emphasize this point, the treatment gives handy reference tables, computational aids, and example calculations readily amenable to spreadsheet implementation applied to the performance analysis of IP and ATM communication networks. The applications covered included computation of the blocking and queuing probabilities in connection-oriented networks, determination of required buffer capacity to meet a specific loss objective, and quantification of benefits achieved by integrating voice and data traffic.

Basic Queuing System Models

This section introduces the shorthand notation commonly employed to describe queuing systems. It then defines the solution technique and summarizes key results for the special case of Markovian queuing systems. Subsequent sections then apply these queuing theoretic results to the link-level design tradeoffs encountered in IP and ATM networks.

Kendall's Notation for Queuing Systems

Figure 11.1 depicts a widely used notation employed to categorize queuing systems. Hence, readers doing further research should become familiar with this notation originally attributed to Kendall. The notation designates arrival and service processes (denoted as A and B) as either M, for Markovian as described in Chapter 9; G, for General; or D for Deterministic. The required parameter s defines the number of "servers" in the queuing system; for example, in the case of communications networks the transmission link is a single server. The optional B and N parameters specify the buffer space (or waiting positions) for unserved arrivals and the source population, respectively. If either B or N is infinite, then the convention is to not include the parameter. For example, the Kendall notation M/M/1 denotes a single-server queuing system with Markovian arrival and service processes that has infinite buffer space and user population.

Birth-Death Processes

A special case of Markov chains of particular interest occurs when transitions occur only between adjacent states. Queuing theory texts give the special name *birth-death processes* to this class of Markov chains based upon the analogy of modeling the growth (or decline) of

Figure 11.1
Kendall's queuing
system notation.

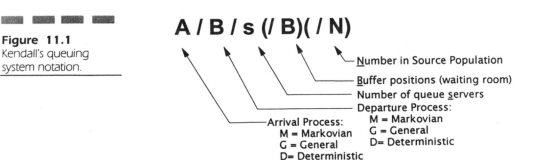

A / B / s (/ B)(/ N)

— Number in Source Population
— Buffer positions (waiting room)
— Number of queue servers
— Departure Process:
  M = Markovian
  G = General
  D= Deterministic
— Arrival Process:
  M = Markovian
  G = General
  D= Deterministic

a population where each birth (or death) occurs at a unique instant in time. As introduced in Chapter 9, the infinitesimal generator matrix for such a process has non-zero entries on the diagonal, as well as above and below the diagonal as follows:

$$
Q \equiv
\begin{bmatrix}
-(\lambda_0 + \mu_1) & \lambda_0 & 0 & \cdots & 0 & 0 \\
\mu_1 & -(\lambda_1 + \mu_2) & \lambda_1 & \cdots & 0 & 0 \\
0 & \mu_2 & -(\lambda_2 + \mu_3) & \cdots & 0 & 0 \\
\vdots & \vdots & \vdots & \ddots & \vdots & \vdots \\
0 & 0 & 0 & \cdots & -(\lambda_{n-2} + \mu_{n-1}) & \lambda_{n-1} \\
0 & 0 & 0 & \cdots & \mu_n & -(\lambda_{n-1} + \mu_n)
\end{bmatrix}
$$

These discrete-state, continuous-time Markov birth-death processes have a state-transition-rate diagram of the form depicted in Figure 11.2. The formulation of the steady-state solution for the birth-death process yields a particularly easy to use semi-graphical solution technique called *stochastic balance* [1, 2]. To illustrate this technique, we write down a few of the first and last terms of the steady-state solution of $\underline{\pi}Q=\underline{0}$ as defined in Chapter 9 as follows:

$$
\begin{aligned}
& -\lambda_0 \pi_0 & + \mu_1 \pi_1 & = 0 \\
\lambda_0 \pi_0 & -(\lambda_1 + \mu_1) \pi_0 & + \mu_2 \pi_2 & = 0 \\
\vdots \quad & \vdots & \vdots & \vdots \\
\lambda_{n-2} \pi_{n-2} & -(\lambda_{n-1}\mu_{n-1}) \pi_{n-1} & + \mu_n \pi_n & = 0 \\
\lambda_{n-1} \pi_{n-1} & -(\lambda_n + \mu_n) \pi_n & & = 0
\end{aligned}
$$

Rewriting these equations as follows, observe that the left-hand side is the total probability flow into the state, while the right-hand side is the probability flow leaving the state.

State	Flow in	=	Flow out
0	$\mu_1 \pi_1$	=	$\lambda_0 \pi_0$
1	$\lambda_0 \pi_0 + \mu_2 \pi_2$	=	$(\lambda_1 + \mu_1) \pi_0$
$\vdots$	$\vdots$	$\vdots$	$\vdots$
n-1	$\lambda_{n-2} \pi_{n-2} + \mu_n \pi_n$	=	$(\lambda_{n-1} + \mu_{n-1}) \pi_{n-1}$
n	$\lambda_{n-1} \pi_{n-1}$	=	$(\lambda_n + \mu_n) \pi_n$

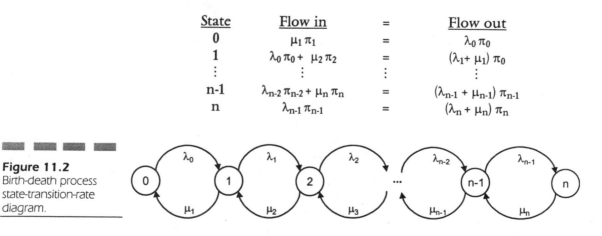

Figure 11.2
Birth-death process
state-transition-rate
diagram.

The conservation of flow inherent in the stochastic balance method allows us to write down the differential difference equations for the continuous-time Markov chain directly from the state-transition-rate diagram. Another way of looking at this is to draw an imaginary circle around each state, and add up the flows entering and leaving the state on the left- and right-hand side of the flow balance equation, respectively. One of these equations will always be linearly dependent. As in the discrete case, we arrive at the complete solution by using the theorem of total probability as the last equation.

Using this approach, the general solution for the long run, steady-state probability of being in state k for the Markovian birth-death process depicted in Figure 11.2 is:

$$\pi_k = \pi_0 \prod_{i=1}^{k} \frac{\lambda_{i-1}}{\mu_i} \tag{11-1}$$

where the symbol $\prod_{i=1}^{n} x_i$ denotes the product of the numbers x_i for i ranging from 1 to n, and the probability of being in state 0 is computed from the following formula:

$$\pi_0 = \left[1 + \sum_{k=1}^{n} \prod_{i=1}^{k} \frac{\lambda_{i-1}}{\mu_i} \right]^{-1}$$

Solutions for Markovian Queuing Systems

This section applies the generic solution technique of Equation (11-1) to the class of Markovian queuing systems with Kendall notation M/M/s/B/N. That is, the solutions for these systems have Markovian arrivals and service times with s identical servers, a waiting room of B buffer positions, and a population of N users. As shown in the following, selecting specific values of s, B, and N result in simpler solutions that correspond to Markovian queuing systems commonly encountered in the technical literature and traffic models [1].

First, we make the reasonable assumption that $N \geq B \geq s$. That is, the waiting room is never larger than the user population, and the number of servers is never larger than the waiting room. This means that N=n in the general solution of Equation (11-1). The usual assumption is a homogenous population of users who each generate bursts at an arrival rate of λ and a set of identical servers with a service rate μ.

Therefore, the arrival rate and service rate coefficients take on the following values:

$$\lambda_k = \begin{cases} (N-k)\lambda & 0 \le k \le B-1 \\ 0 & \text{otherwise} \end{cases}$$

$$\mu_k = \begin{cases} k\mu & 0 \le k \le s \\ s\mu & k \ge s \end{cases} \tag{11-2}$$

Substituting the specific definitions of the arrival and service rate coefficients from Equation (11-2) into Equation (11-1) yields the following equation for the steady-state probability that a M/M/s/B/N queuing system has k users present:

$$\pi_k = \begin{cases} \pi_0 \rho^k \binom{N}{k} & 0 \le k \le s-1 \\ \pi_0 \rho^k \binom{N}{k} \dfrac{k!}{s!} s^{s-k} & s \le k \le B \end{cases} \tag{11-3}$$

where $\rho \equiv \lambda/\mu$. Note that as N approaches infinity that the binomial term $\binom{N}{k}$ approaches unity.

As described in Chapter 8, the average number of users in the system is $E[k]$ and the variance is $\mathrm{Var}\,[k]$. Table 11.1 presents the results of simplifying Equation (11-3) for commonly encountered combinations of values for the number of servers (s), the buffer space (B), and the user population size (N) using the queuing system notation M/M/s/B/N.

As described in Chapter 10, the statistics for the waiting time are straightforwardly computed from the statistics of the number of users in the queuing system using *Little's result*. When the service order is First Come First Served (FCFS), the total average time in the system T (i.e., Waiting time W plus service time μ^{-1}) is equal to the average number of users $E[k]$ in the system divided by the arrival rate λ as follows:

$$T = W + \mu^{-1} = \frac{E[k]}{\lambda} \tag{11-4}$$

Rearranging this equation to yield the formula $\lambda T = E[k]$ shows that the product of the arrival rate and the average time spent in the system is equal to the average number in the system.

TABLE 11.1

Solutions for Markovian queuing systems of the form M/M/s/B/P for specific combinations of server (s), buffer (B), and population (N) parameters.

Queuing System	λ_k	μ_k	π_k	π_0	$E[k]$	$Var[k]$
M/M/1	λ	μ	$\pi_0 \rho^k$	$(1-\rho)$	$\dfrac{\rho}{1-\rho}$	$\dfrac{\rho}{(1-\rho)^2}$
M/M/1/B	$\lambda,\ k\leq B\text{-}1$	$\mu,\ k\leq B$	$\pi_0 \rho^k,\ k\leq B$	$\dfrac{1-\rho}{1-\rho^{B+1}}$	$\dfrac{\rho}{1-\rho}\left[1-\dfrac{(B+1)\rho^B}{1-\rho^{B+1}}\right]$	$\displaystyle\sum_{k=0}^{B} k^2\pi_k - E[k]^2$
M/M/1/N	$\lambda(N\text{-}k),\ k\leq N$	$\mu,\ k\leq N$	$\pi_0\dfrac{N!}{(N-k)!}\rho^k,\ k\leq N$	$\left[\displaystyle\sum_{k=0}^{N}\dfrac{N!}{(N-k)!}\rho^k\right]^{-1}$	$\displaystyle\sum_{k=0}^{B} k\pi_k$	$\displaystyle\sum_{k=0}^{B} k^2\pi_k - E[k]^2$
M/M/∞	λ	$k\mu$	$\pi_0\dfrac{\rho^k}{k!}$	$e^{-\rho}$	ρ	ρ
M/M/s Erlang C	λ	$\text{Min}(s,k)\mu$	$\pi_0\dfrac{\rho^k}{k!}\quad k\leq s$ $\pi_0\dfrac{\rho^k s^{s-k}}{s!}\quad k\geq s$	$\left[\displaystyle\sum_{k=0}^{s-1}\dfrac{\rho^k}{k!}+\dfrac{\rho^s}{s!}\dfrac{s}{s-\rho}\right]^{-1}$	$\rho+\pi_0\dfrac{\rho^s}{s!}\dfrac{s\rho}{(s-\rho)^2}$	$\displaystyle\sum_{k=0}^{B} k^2\pi_k - E[k]^2$
M/M/s/s Erlang B	$\lambda,\ k\leq s$	$k\mu,\ k\leq s$	$\pi_0\dfrac{\rho^k}{k!},\ k\leq s$	$\left[\displaystyle\sum_{j=0}^{s}\dfrac{\rho^k}{k!}\right]^{-1}$	$\rho(1-\pi_s)$	$\displaystyle\sum_{k=0}^{B} k^2\pi_k - E[k]^2$
M/M/s/s/N Engset	$\lambda(N\text{-}k),\ k\leq s\text{-}1$	$k\mu,\ k\leq s$	$\pi_0\binom{N}{k}\rho^k,\ k\leq s$	$\left[\displaystyle\sum_{j=0}^{s}\binom{N}{k}\rho^k\right]^{-1}$	$\displaystyle\sum_{k=0}^{B} k\pi_k$	$\displaystyle\sum_{k=0}^{B} k^2\pi_k - E[k]^2$
M/M/s/s/s	$\lambda(s\text{-}k),\ k\leq s$	$k\mu,\ k\leq s$	$\binom{s}{k}\left(\dfrac{\rho}{1+\rho}\right)^k\left(\dfrac{1}{1+\rho}\right)^{s-k}$	$(1+\rho)^s$	$\dfrac{s\rho}{1+\rho}$	$\dfrac{s\rho}{(1+\rho)^2}$

Solving Equation (11-4) for the waiting time W yields the following result for the waiting time Wμ normalized to units of average service time (i.e., μ^{-1}) employed in several examples later in this chapter:

$$\frac{W}{\mu^{-1}} = \frac{E[k]}{\rho} - 1$$

The remaining sections of this chapter apply these queuing system formulas to the traffic engineering of circuit-, packet-, and cell-switched networks. Of course, stability requires that the offered load $\rho=\lambda/\mu$ is less than the number of servers s. In some cases, the closed form expression for the mean or variance is rather complex. In these cases, the mean and variance can be readily evaluated numerically using the pdf (i.e., the values of π_k), as indicated in Table 11.1.

Blocking and Queuing in Circuit-Switched Voice Networks

This section looks at traditional traffic modeling derived from over a century of experience with telephone networks. The origin of this type of analysis is attributed to work published by the Danish Mathematician, A.K. Erlang in 1917.

Statistical Model for Call Attempts

Through extensive measurements, traffic-engineering experts know that the Markov process is a good model for telephone call attempts. The primary parameters are the call arrival rate λ, usually expressed in terms of Busy Hour Call Attempts (BHCA), and the average call holding time (i.e., call duration) $T=\mu^{-1}$. Without any blocking, the average number of calls in progress during the busy hour in such a system is λT. Traditionally, telephony engineers assign the units of offered *Erlangs* to this quantity, although, the measure is in fact unitless. In the following sections we refer to the average offered traffic load as (expressed in units of Erlangs) as follows:

$$\rho = \lambda T$$

In a real telephone network, blocking occurs with a certain probability B. Therefore, telephone engineers say that the system carries $\rho(1-B)$ Erlangs of traffic. Erlang also modeled systems that queue calls instead of blocking them. For example, a call answering system that places calling users on hold listening to music if all the operators are occupied effectively queues calls instead of blocking them via responding with a busy signal. We study these two types of systems — commonly referred to as blocked calls cleared and blocked calls held, respectively — in the next sections.

Implicit in the Erlang model is the assumption that the switching system under consideration supports a large number of telephone users. Furthermore, the model assumes that only some of these users are active during the busy hour.

Let's look at a simple numerical example with reference to Figure 11.3. A group of 1,000 subscriber lines originates an average of $\lambda=2,000$ call attempts during the busy hour. Each completed call lasts for 3 minutes on average, or $T=0.05$ hours. Thus, the offered load to the trunk on the telephone switch is $\rho=\lambda T=2,000\times0.05=100$ Erlangs. The interpretation of this model is that without any call blocking, on average only 100 of the subscribers are actually on the telephone at any point in time. This type of model applies to calls placed to a pool of dial-up modems via which subscribers attempt to access the Internet. Subsequent sections examine the performance when the switching system blocks or queues calls that exceed the trunk capacity.

Another note on historical terminology for telephone call attempt rates that you may encounter is that of the Call Century Seconds (CCS). The name CCS derived from the operation where a camera took a picture of the call peg counters on electromechanical switches once every one hundred seconds for billing purposes. If the counter advanced between photographs for a particular subscriber line, then the carrier assumed that the call was active for one hundred (a century) seconds, which explains the name CCS. Since an Erlang corre-

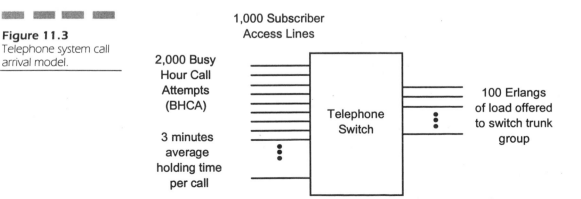

Figure 11.3
Telephone system call arrival model.

1,000 Subscriber Access Lines

2,000 Busy Hour Call Attempts (BHCA)

3 minutes average holding time per call

Telephone Switch

100 Erlangs of load offered to switch trunk group

sponds to a call with holding time equal to 3600 seconds, we have the relation that 1 Erlang is equivalent to 36 CCS. Prior to extended dial-up sessions on the web, a typical residential telephone line carried 3 to 6 CCS on average; that is, its average load was between 8% and 16%. Now, many residential lines carry 9 to 12 CCS.

Erlang's Blocked Calls Cleared Formula

A blocked calls cleared switching system has Markovian call arrivals, Markovian call durations and s servers (trunks or modems), and s waiting positions. Note that the s waiting positions correspond on a one-to-one basis to the servers. That is, there is no queuing room in such a system. Therefore, the M/M/s/s queuing system model from table 11.1 defines the blocking performance. For an average offered load of ρ Erlangs and s trunks, the following formula gives the probability that the system blocks a call attempt:

$$B(s,\rho) = \frac{\rho^s / s!}{\sum_{k=0}^{s} \rho^k / k!}$$

(11-5)

Typically, texts call Equation (11-5) the *Erlang-B* formula [1], [3]. Many older books contain tables for the values of the Erlang-B (lost calls cleared) probability. However, you can easily compute your own using the following simple recursion [3] in a spreadsheet:

$$B(s+1,\rho) = \frac{\rho B(s,\rho)}{s + 1 + \rho B(s,\rho)}$$

(11-6)

where $B(0,\rho)=1$.

This is a useful result to solve the commonly encountered problem of determining the number of trunks s, given an offered load ρ to meet an objective blocking probability $B(s,\rho)$. You can either write a spreadsheet macro, or define two columns of cells in the spreadsheet. The first column contains the values of s, starting at zero and incrementing by 1 for each successive row. The second column contains the value 1 in the first row corresponding to $B(0,\rho)$. Row k+1 contains the above formula for $B(k+1,\rho)$ coded to use the preceding row's result, $B(k,\rho)$, and the average offered load ρ.

Figure 11.4 illustrates the result of using this recursive method of calculation for some values of the Erlang-B blocking probability for various trunk/modem group sizes s versus the difference between the

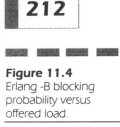

Figure 11.4
Erlang -B blocking
probability versus
offered load.

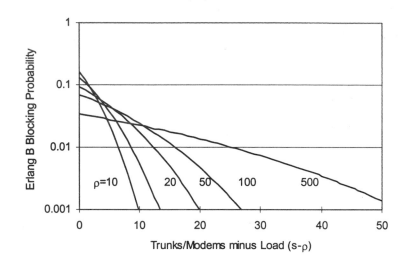

number of trunks and the offered load s-ρ. Note how the blocking probability decreases more rapidly when adding trunks/modems to serve smaller loads than it does when adding trunks/modems to serve larger loads. Intuitively, we expect this result since larger systems usually achieve an economy of scale.

One way of expressing economy of scale is to compare the percentage of required additional trunking that yields fixed blocking probability across a range of offered loads. We define this measure as the *overtrunking ratio,* which is simply the required trunks divided by the average offered load, namely s/ρ. For an overtrunking ratio of 100 percent, the number of trunks/modems exactly equals the average offered load yielding a particular blocking probability. For typical

Figure 11.5
Required overtrunking
ratio for various
blocking probabilities.

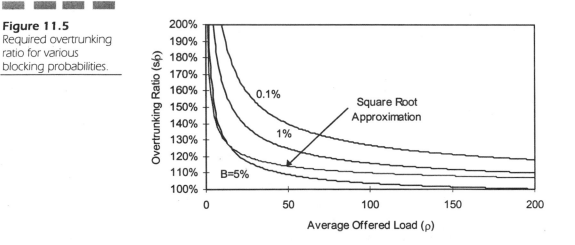

blocking probabilities in the range of 0.1 to 1 percent, the overtrunking ratio ranges between 110 and 120 percent for large values of offered load. Figure 11.5 illustrates the overtrunking ratio versus the average offered load for a set of representative values of blocking probabilities. Most commercial voice networks are engineered for a blocking probability ranging between 0.1 to 1 percent. Modem pools may be engineered for higher blocking probabilities in some networks. Also shown in the figure is the approximation $1+1/\sqrt{\rho}$ for the required overtrunking ratio.

If the population is finite, then the M/M/s/s/N model defined in Table 11.1 is more accurate. Commonly called the *Engset* model [1], it yields results similar to that of the Erlang-B formula for values of N much larger than the number of servers. For smaller systems, the Engset model generally predicts a larger number of required servers or a smaller carried load.

Erlang's Blocked Calls Held Formula

A blocked calls held switching system has Markovian call arrivals, Markovian call duration and s servers (e.g., operators), and an infinite number of waiting positions. Therefore, a M/M/s queuing system model defines the performance. For an average offered load of ρ Erlangs and s servers, using the definition of steady-state probability π_j, from Table 11.1 the following formula gives the probability that the system queues a call attempt:

$$\Pr[\text{Queuing}] = C(s,\rho) = \sum_{j=s}^{\infty} \pi_j = \frac{\dfrac{\rho^s}{s!} \dfrac{s}{s-\rho}}{\displaystyle\sum_{k=0}^{s-1} \dfrac{\rho^k}{k!} + \dfrac{\rho^s}{s!} \dfrac{s}{s-\rho}} \qquad (11\text{-}7)$$

Typically, texts call Equation (11-7) the *Erlang-C* formula [1, 3]. Many older books contain tables and plots for the values of the Erlang-C (lost calls held) probability. However, you can easily compute your own using the following simple formula [3] utilizing the Erlang-B recursion defined in the previous section:

$$C(s,\rho) = \frac{sB(s,\rho)}{s - \rho[1 - B(s,\rho)]}$$

Figure 11.6 illustrates some values of the Erlang-C formula for various server group sizes as a function of offered load. A trend similar

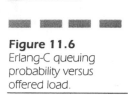

Figure 11.6
Erlang-C queuing
probability versus
offered load.

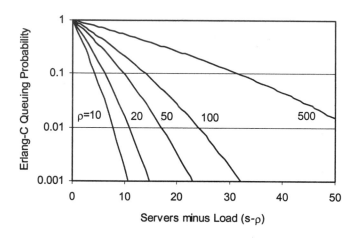

to that of blocking probability occurs when comparing the queuing
probability of a system with smaller offered load to a system with a
larger offered load. The fact that the queuing probability decreases
much more slowly with each additional server for larger systems than
it does for smaller ones results in an economy of scale similar to that
of blocking systems.

Performance of Separate Queues versus a Single Shared Queue

This section employs the Erlang-C formula to analyze the relative
performance of systems that employ a separate queue for each server,
as depicted in Figure 11.7a, versus that of a system where multiple
servers share a single queue, as shown in Figure 11.7b. An example of
a separate queue system is the checkout lines at a grocery store. An
example of a shared queue is the single waiting area for a number of

Figure 11.7
Illustration of separate
and single queue
service systems.

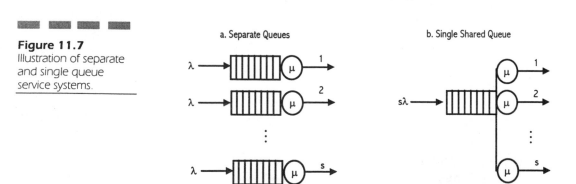

clerks at an airline check-in counter. The communication network analogs are statically allocated separate switch/router trunks versus dynamic load balancing across a set of trunks. The separate queue per server system is equivalent to s independent M/M/1 queuing systems, while the model for the shared queue is a single M/M/s system. The separate queue model assumes perfect load balancing, which in practice is difficult to achieve. Load balancing attempts to equally load each of the separate queues, using randomization based upon the IP packet header value, for example.

Using Equation (11-7), we can rewrite the expression from Table 11.1 for the expected number of users in the system (i.e., in service and queued for service) as follows:

$$E[k] = \rho + \frac{\rho}{s - \rho} C(s, \rho)$$

The first term then corresponds to average number of users in service, while the second term corresponds to the number of users in queue. Since the service time seen by an individual user is equivalent for both the separate queue and shared systems depicted in Figure 11.7, we analyze only the performance of the number in queue. Using the expressions for the probability density function from Table 11.1 for the M/M/s system yields a straightforward solution for the statistics on the number of users in queue defined as q=k-s. That is, no queuing occurs unless s or greater users are present in the system. For comparison purposes, we define the average utilization per server as u=λ/μ.

Table 11.2 presents the results of this calculation for the average number in queue E[q] and the variance of the number in queue Var[q]. Recall that the statistics of waiting time are directly proportional to the number in queue from Little's result. Before resorting to numerical comparisons, the formulas in Table 11.2 provide several insights. First, from Equation (11-7) observe that C(1,u)=u, which makes the results for s=1 equivalent, as they should be. Secondly, note that C(s,su)<u for s>1. This means that the mean and variance of waiting time are always less for the shared queue than separate queues.

	Statistic	Separate Queues (s × M/M/1)	Shared Queue (M/M/s)
TABLE 11.2	E[q], Average Number in Queue	$\dfrac{u^2}{1 - u}$	$\dfrac{uC(s, su)}{1 - u}$
Statistics of separate versus shared queuing systems.	Var[q], Variance of Number in Queue	$\dfrac{u^2(1 - u^2)}{(1 - u)^2}$	$\dfrac{uC(s, su)[1 - uC(s, su)]}{(1 - u)^2}$

Figure 11.8
Average number in
queue for separate
versus single queue
service systems.

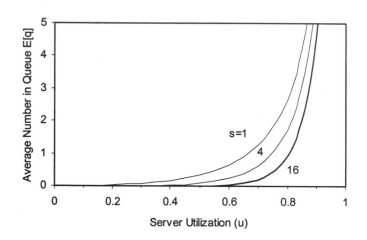

Figure 11.8
Average number in
queue for separate
versus single queue
service systems.

Figure 11.8 illustrates the numerical results for the average number in queue for separate queues (i.e., s=1) and systems with a single queue shared between s=4 and s=16 servers. At 85 percent utilization, the average waiting time for separate queues is over twice that of a 16-server system with a shared queue.

Buffer Design for Data Traffic

This section presents several models that determine the required buffer capacity to meet a specified loss objective.

Models for Buffer Overflow Probability

This section gives a simple approximation for the probability that traffic overflows a buffer. The analysis models the router or switch buffer as a M/M/1/B queuing system that has a finite buffer capable of holding B bursts of negative exponentially distributed length. Comparison of simulation results and exact analysis has shown this to be a reasonable approximation [4]. The probability of overflow for a M/M/1/B queuing system is equal to π_B. From Table 11.1, the exact and approximate buffer overflow probability is:

$$\Pr[\text{overflow}] \;\equiv\; \varepsilon \;=\; \frac{(1-\rho)\rho^B}{1-\rho^{B+1}} \;\approx\; \rho^B \qquad (11\text{-}8)$$

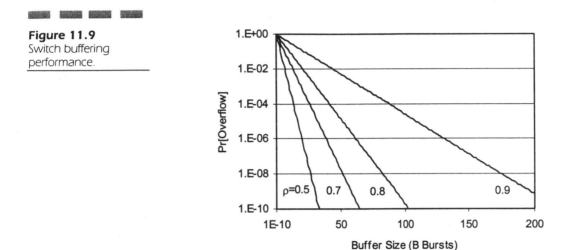

Figure 11.9
Switch buffering
performance.

The approximation is valid when $\rho^B \ll 1$. Figure 11.9 plots this approximate buffer overflow probability versus buffer size for various levels of offered load ρ. Of course, if the buffer has dimensions of cells, then you should multiply the x-axis by the average number of cells contained in a burst.

Typically, a network design requires a specific overflow probability objective. A curve of overflow probability versus buffer size varies as a function of the offered load, as shown in Figure 11.9. Note that for a given buffer size B, the overflow probability increases as the offered load ρ increases. This means that there is a maximum offered load that the queuing system operates at while still meeting a specified overflow probability ε.

We can solve Equation (11-8) to yield a simple guideline for the required buffer capacity B on a switch or router port serving Markovian traffic to yield a desired overflow probability. The result is the following:

$$B \approx \frac{\ln(\varepsilon)}{\ln(\rho)} \cong \frac{-\ln(\varepsilon)}{1-\rho} \tag{11-9}$$

The right-hand asymptotic result occurs as ρ approaches 100 percent load as derived from the series expansion for the natural logarithm.

We can compare the results for overflow probability ε and required buffer capacity B for self-similar traffic input using approximations for Fractional Brownian Motion traffic (see Chapter 9), as described in Reference 5. The probability of overflowing a buffer of size B_{ss} with self-similar traffic input characterized by an offered load ρ, Hurst parameter H is approximately:

$$\varepsilon \approx \exp\left[-\frac{1}{2}\left(\frac{1-\rho}{\rho H}\right)^{2H}\left(\frac{B_{ss}}{1-H}\right)^{2-2H}\right] \qquad (11\text{-}10)$$

Note that we omitted several factors from the more precise expression reported in Reference 5 for the sake of simplicity. Solving the above equation for the required buffer capacity for self-similar traffic input yields the following result:

$$B_{ss} \approx \frac{[-2\ln(\varepsilon)]^{2-2H}}{1-H}\left[\frac{\rho H}{1-\rho}\right]^{H/(1-H)} \qquad (11\text{-}11)$$

Recall from Chapter 9 that when the Hurst parameter H=1/2, the correlated self-similar process reduces to uncorrelated Brownian motion. Substituting H=1/2 into the above equation yields the following expression for the required buffer capacity:

$$B_{ss} \cong \frac{-2\ln(\varepsilon)\rho}{1-\rho} \quad \text{as } H \to \frac{1}{2} \qquad (11\text{-}12)$$

Comparing the above asymptotic result to the buffer dimensioning formula for a Markovian queuing system as ρ approaches unity from Equation (11-9), we see that the expressions have the same functional

Figure 11.10
Required buffers to achieve a specific overflow probability for Markovian and self-similar traffic inputs.

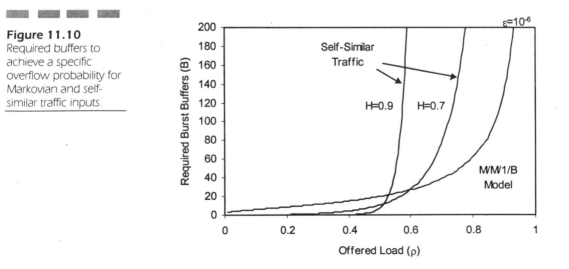

form. Based upon the preceding analysis, we are now in a position to compare the buffer requirements necessary to meet a particular overflow objective for a Markovian queuing system using Equation (11-9) against that of a queuing system driven by self-similar input traffic characterized by Hurst parameter H as described by Equation (11-11). Figure 11.10 plots the buffer capacity required to achieve an objective overflow probability for the Markovian system and systems driven by self-similar traffic for H=0.7 and H=0.9 for an overflow probability objective $\varepsilon=10^{-6}$.

This result teaches us several important lessons in traffic engineering. First, characterization of traffic is extremely important for buffer dimensioning. If you are designing an IP or ATM network for traffic best characterized by the self-similar model, the Markovian model will drastically underestimate the required buffer capacity. Chapter 21 describes practical methods for estimating the self-similar nature based upon actual traffic measurements. However, if the traffic in your network employs flow or congestion control, other factors influence the selection of an optimal buffer size, as described in the next part.

Shared versus Dedicated Buffer Performance

This section shows how a shared buffer scheme exhibits a marked improvement on buffer overflow performance. Since it is unlikely that all ports are congested at the same time, sharing a single, larger buffer between multiple ports is more efficient than statically allocating a portion of the buffer to each port.

The exact analysis of shared buffer performance is somewhat complicated [6]; therefore, we present a simple approximation based on the normal distribution. In the shared-buffer architecture, N switch ports share the common buffer, each having the M/M/1/B probability distribution requirement on buffer space as analyzed above. The sum of the individual port demands determines the shared-buffer probability distribution. The normal distribution approximates a sum of such random variables for larger values of N. The mean and variance of the normal approximation are then:

$$\text{Mean} = \frac{N\rho}{1-\rho} \quad , \quad \text{Variance} = \frac{N\rho}{(1-\rho)^2} \qquad (11\text{-}13)$$

Figure 11.11
Shared versus
dedicated buffer
performance.

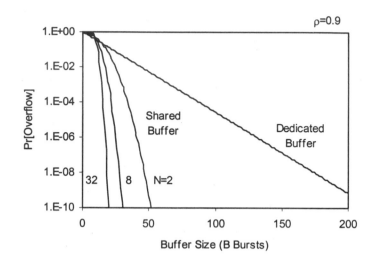

Figure 11.11 shows a plot of the overflow probability versus the equivalent buffer size per port for shared buffers on switches of increasing port size (N), along with the dedicated output buffer performance for large N from Figure 11.9 for comparison purposes. The offered load is $\rho=0.9$. The total buffer capacity on a shared buffer switch is N times the buffer capacity on the x-axis. Note that as N increases, the capacity required per port approaches a constant value. This result illustrates the theoretical efficiency of shared buffering.

Priority Queuing Performance

This section illustrates the capability of priority queuing to provide different delay (or loss) performance for two classes of traffic. Figure 11.12 illustrates traffic originating from two sources arriving to separate queues served by a priority scheduler with service rate μ. High-priority traffic arrives at rate λ_1, while low-priority traffic arrives at rate λ_2 according to the usual numbering convention for priorities

Figure 11.12
Illustration of priority
queuing system
operation.

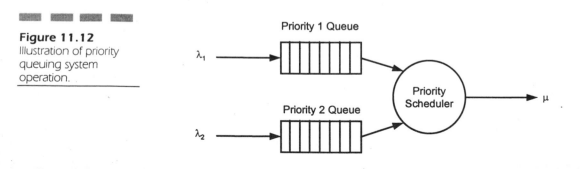

where the smaller number indicates higher priority. The priority scheduler services priority 1 traffic first, and only services priority 2 traffic when there is no priority 1 traffic. The priority scheduler completes service of any packet or cell before processing the next packet or cell. In other words, service is non-preemptive. In the following analysis, we assume that the queues are of infinite length. In a real switch or router, of course, the queues may overflow and create loss.

The following analysis assumes that both priority 1 and 2 traffic have a Poisson arrival rate of λ_1 and λ_2 bursts per second, respectively. All traffic has a negative exponentially distributed service time with mean μ^{-1}. The net effect of priority queuing is that the priority 1 traffic observes a delay as if the priority 2 traffic did not even exist. On the other hand, the priority 2 traffic sees delay as if the transmission capacity were reduced by the average utilization taken by the priority 1 traffic. The formulas for the average waiting time of priority 1 and priority 2 traffic in queue are [2]:

$$W_{q1} = E[\text{Priority 1 Bursts in Queue}] = \frac{\rho/\mu}{1-\rho_1} \qquad (11\text{-}14)$$

$$W_{q2} = E[\text{Priority 2 Bursts in Queue}] = \frac{\rho/\mu}{(1-\rho)(1-\rho_1)} \qquad (11\text{-}15)$$

where $\rho_1=\lambda_1/\mu$ and $\rho_2=\lambda_2/\mu$ are the offered loads for priority 1 and 2 traffic, respectively, and $\rho=\rho_1+\rho_2$ is the total offered load to the system. For comparison purposes, Table 11.2 gives the average number in queue for an M/M/1 system without any priority with $\rho=u$. The average waiting time $W_q=E[q]/\lambda$. Of course, the average waiting time for the system without any priority is equal to the weighted average of the waiting time for priority 1 and 2 users in the system as follows:

$$W_q = \frac{\rho/\mu}{1-\rho} = \frac{\rho_1 W_{q1} + \rho_2 W_{q2}}{\rho} \qquad (11\text{-}16)$$

Figure 11.13 illustrates the effect of priority queuing by plotting the average waiting time for a single-priority system according to the M/M/1 model against the average waiting time for priority 1 and priority 2 users. The figure plots the waiting times W_q normalized by multiplying by μ. This example assumes that 50 percent of the traffic is priority 1, that is, $\rho_1/\rho=0.5$. Observe that the priority 1 performance is markedly better than the single-priority system, while priority 2 performance degrades only slightly as compared to the system with

Figure 11.13
Priority queuing
performance example.

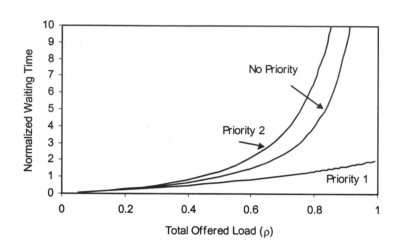

no priority. Thus, priority queuing provides an important means to deliver different levels of QoS to different traffic classes. When the high-priority traffic becomes a significant portion of the total traffic, the benefit of priority queuing diminishes.

Voice and Data Integration

This section gives a time-tested model for voice transmission statistics within an individual call for use in a simple statistical multiplexing gain model. Next, we use this model to estimate the savings resulting from integrating voice and data on the same transmission facility.

Voice Activity Traffic Model

Most people don't speak continuously in normal conversation; natural pauses and gaps create an on-off pattern of speech activity, as illustrated in Chapter 3. On average, people speak only 35 to 40 percent of the time during a typical phone call. We call this the speech activity probability p. Furthermore, the patterns of speech activity are independent from one conversation to the next. Therefore, the M/M/N/N/N queuing system defined in Table 11.1 is a good model for the probability that k people are speaking out of a total set of N conversations using the shared facility as follows:

$$\text{Pr[k out of N speakers active]} = \binom{N}{k} p^k (1-p)^{N-k} \qquad (11\text{-}17)$$

where $\binom{N}{k} \equiv \dfrac{N!}{(N-k)!k!}$. This corresponds to a M/M/N/N/N

Markovian queueing system with $p = \dfrac{\rho}{1+\rho}$.

The results of many studies performed since the introduction of digital telephony in the late 1950s show that most listeners don't object to a loss of approximately 0.5 percent of the received speech. Of course, the speech encoding and decoding mechanism determines the resulting quality in the event of loss — a very sensitive decoder can magnify small amounts of loss. The parameter of interest is then the fraction of speech lost, commonly called the *freezeout fraction* FF [7] defined by the following formula:

$$FF(N,C,p) = \frac{1}{Np} \sum_{k=C}^{L}(k-C) \binom{N}{k} p^k (1-p)^{N-k} \qquad (11\text{-}18)$$

This expression has the interpretation equivalent to the fraction of speech lost by an individual listener. What we need in the following analysis is a function which determines the capacity required C for a given number of speakers N, each with a source activity probability p. The subsequent analysis denotes this function as C(N, p, FF).

Statistically Multiplexing Voice Conversations

Satellite communication and undersea cable communication of voice has long used statistical multiplexing of many voice conversations to reduce costs. Devices performing this function are known as Digital Circuit Multiplication Equipment (DCME), since statistical multiplexing effectively packs multiple conversations into a single equivalent voice channel. ATM Adaptation Layer 2 (AAL2) will support the next generation of DCME, as well as integrated voice and data access. However, this gain occurs only when a system multiplexes enough voice conversations together. Unfortunately, the statistical multiplexing of voice reaches a point of diminishing returns after reaching a critical mass. Let's look at an example to see why this is true. First, the statistical multiplexing gain G(N,p,FF) for N conversations with voice activity probability p and a freezeout fraction objective FF is:

$$G(N,p,FF) = \frac{N}{C(N,p,FF)} \qquad (11\text{-}19)$$

where C(N,p,FF) is the largest number of channels C that satisfies Equation (11-18).

Figure 11.14 plots the results of the required capacity function C(N,p,FF) and the resulting statistical multiplexing gain versus the number of sources N. This example assumes that the voice activity probability p=0.35 and FF=0.5 percent for all sources. The curve is not smooth because the required capacity function returns integer values. This analysis illustrates several important points. First, until the number of sources reaches 5, there is no gain. After this point, the gain increases slowly and reaches a maximum value of 2. Indeed, for 128 sources the gain increases to only a factor of 2.2.

Voice/Data Integration Savings

The curious reader may now be thinking what gains remain for integrated voice and data transmission. Figure 11.15 illustrates the block diagram of an Integrated Voice/Data Multiplexer (IVDM). It has N voice channel inputs with activity probability p and freezeout fraction QoS parameter FF served by a link of capacity C(N,p,FF). The quantity determined in this section is the additional data traffic D(N,p,FF) that the IVDM can carry by utilizing the capacity unused by periods of voice inactivity.

The answer lies in the observation that although the voice multi-

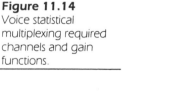

Figure 11.14
Voice statistical multiplexing required channels and gain functions.

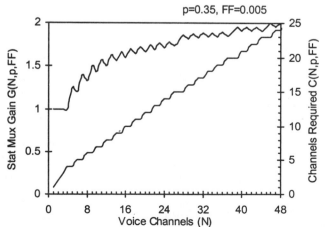

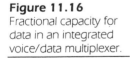

Figure 11.15
Block diagram of an integrated voice/data multiplexer.

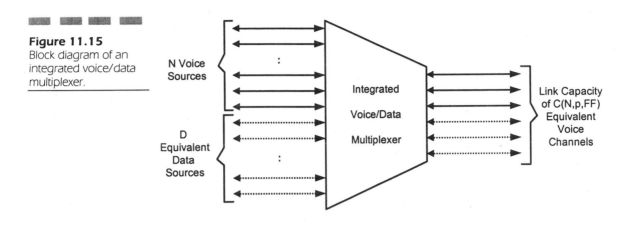

plexing system reserves capacity C(N,p,FF) for transmission of speech, the speech utilizes an average capacity equal to Np, the mean of the binomial distribution. Therefore, the fraction of additional data traffic D(N,p,FF) carried by an integrated voice/data system when compared with separate voice and data systems is bounded as follows [8]:

$$D(N,p,FF) \leq \frac{C(N,p,FF) - Np}{C(N,p,FF)} \qquad (11\text{-}20)$$

Figure 11.16 plots the fraction of additional data traffic supportable D(N,p,FF) versus the number of voice sources N for the same voice activity probability p=0.35 and FF=0.5 percent used in the previous example. For relatively small systems, integrating voice and data makes great sense, and ATM is the only standard way to implement it. Here again, however, a point of diminishing returns occurs as the number of voice sources increases above 30, where the additional capacity

Figure 11.16
Fractional capacity for data in an integrated voice/data multiplexer.

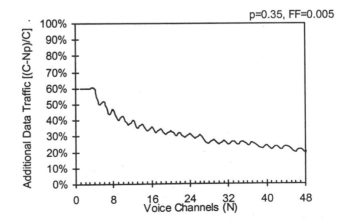

available for data is approximately 25 percent. For a system with 128 voice sources, savings decrease to 11 percent. Hence, don't expect an economy of scale when multiplexing large amounts of data and voice traffic.

This result indicates that the most benefit accrues when doing integrated voice/data multiplexing on access lines ranging from nxDS0 up to nxDS1 speeds. This offers the greatest benefits to medium-sized business locations because of reduced access line charges. Another benefit for carriers is better utilization of expensive transoceanic cables, satellite communications, and radio frequency networks via integrated voice and data multiplexing.

Review

This chapter summarized the general solution technique and presented important results for Markovian queuing systems commonly encountered in the design of circuit-, packet-, and cell-switched networks like IP and ATM. The chapter then applied these generic queuing theory results to the design of voice and data networks. Specifically, the text reviewed application of the famous Erlang formulas. The focus then turned to buffer dimensioning in data network elements like routers and switches. The text compared and contrasted the buffer requirements determined by classical Markov queuing theory against those determined by self-similar traffic models. The conclusion drawn from this analysis is that the type of traffic dramatically impacts required buffer capacity. We then presented an analysis that illustrates the increased efficiency of shared buffering over dedicated buffering. Finally, we covered the subject of voice statistical multiplexing gain, along with an assessment of the savings achievable in an integrated voice/data network.

References

[1]   L. Kleinrock, *Queuing Systems Volume I: Theory*, Wiley, 1975.
[2]   Gross, Harris, *Fundamentals of Queuing Theory*, Wiley, 1985.
[3]   R. Cooper, *Introduction to Queuing Theory, Second Edition*, North-Holland, 1981.
[4]   M. Schwartz, *Computer Communication Design and Analysis*, Addison-Wesley, 1977.

[5]   I. Norros, "On the Use of Fractional Brownian Motion in the Theory of Ethernet Traffic (Extended Version)," *IEEE JSAC*, August 1995.

[6]   M. Hluchyj, M. Karol, "Queuing in High-Performance Packet Switching," *IEEE JSAC*, December 1988.

[7]   B. Jabbari, D. McDysan, "Performance of Demand Assignment TDMA and Multicarrier TDMA Satellite Networks," IEEE JSAC, February 1992.

[8]   D. McDysan, "Performance Analysis of Queuing System Models for Resource Allocation in Distributed Computer Networks," *D.Sc. Dissertation*, George Washington University, 1989.

12

Intermediate Queuing Theory Applied

"The sublime and the ridiculous are often so nearly related, that it is difficult to class them separately. One step above the sublime makes the ridiculous, and one step above the ridiculous makes the sublime again"

— Thomas Paine

As seen from the previous chapter, basic queuing theory has a broad range of practical applications and provides significant insights into the behavior of traffic systems. However, Markovian random processes do not model a number of traffic phenomena very well. Therefore, intermediate queuing theory analyzes systems that have non-Markovian arrival or service processes. Unfortunately, the closed-form solutions become quite complex for all but the simplest properties of the traffic systems. This chapter reviews the important known results for these systems. We also analyze the statistics of the busy and idle periods observed in most real world traffic systems. This chapter also details a useful heuristic called *equivalent capacity* employed for admission control in routed and switched networks. Finally, we analyze the performance achieved when multiplexing a number of constant rate sources together.

The M/G/1 and G/M/1 Queues

This section summarizes results from intermediate and advanced queuing theory for queuing systems with non-Markovian service and arrival processes.

Introduction to the M/G/1 Queue

Chapter 11 studied queuing systems that had both Markov arrivals and departures. The Kendall notation for these systems with s servers, a buffer of length B, and a population of size N was M/M/s/B/N. This section summarizes the major results from intermediate queuing theory for systems that have either a Markovian arrival or departure process, but have a departure or arrival process that is general in nature. The Kendall notation for these systems is M/G/1 and G/M/1.

Several means exist to solve for the statistics of the M/G/1 queue. A popular technique is that of the *imbedded Markov chain* [1]. Central to this method is the fact that the statistics as seen by a user departing the queue are Markovian, allowing us to apply the solution techniques described in Chapter 9. The derivation is straightforward, yet lengthy. As described in Chapter 21, this technique is useful in simulation modeling. An important result for the M/G/1 queue is the following closed-form expression for the average number of users in the system, usually called the *Pollaczek-Khinchin mean-value formula*:

$$E[k] \; = \; \rho \; + \; \rho^2 \frac{(1 + C_b^2)}{2(1 - \rho)} \tag{12-1}$$

where $C_b^2 = \text{Var}[b] / E[b]^2$ is the squared coefficient of variation of the service time pdf b(t) and $\rho = \lambda E[b] < 1$ is the system load.

Let's look at some examples. For a Markovian service time distribution, $C_b = 1$. Therefore, the above equation reduces to $\rho/(1-\rho)$ which is precisely that of the M/M/1 system. For a queuing system with deterministic service time (i.e., an M/D/1 system), $C_b = 0$; that is, there is no variation in the service time, since it is a constant. Therefore, the mean number of users in an M/D/1 system is:

$$E[k] \; = \; \frac{\rho(2 - \rho)}{2(1 - \rho)}$$

Figure 12.1
Average number of
users in various
queuing systems.

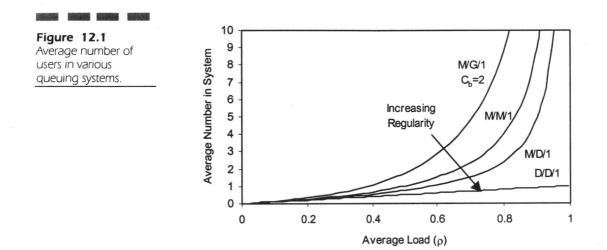

Thus, under heavy load as $\rho \to 1$, the average number of users in an M/D/1 system is approximately half that of an M/M/1 system. If $C_b>1$ in an M/G/1 system, then the average number in the system will be greater than that of an M/M/1 system with comparable load ρ. This is the case for self-similar traffic.

Figure 12.1 plots the average number of users for a range of queuing systems. The figure plots the above formulas for the M/M/1, M/D/1, and M/G/1 queues. For comparison purposes, the figure plots the average number of users in a D/D/1 system, which increases linearly since arrivals occur at a constant rate and service requires a fixed amount of time. As indicated in the figure, the average number in the system decreases under high load (i.e., $\rho \approx 1$) as the regularity of service increases. For example, in a D/D/1 queue, the average number in the system is 1 when $\rho=1$. See Reference 2 for more details on a related comparison technique that includes a comparison of the variance for these various queuing system models.

Pollaczek-Khinchin Transform Solution for the M/G/1 Queue

Other properties of M/G/1 systems like the distribution and higher-order moments are known only in terms of transform solutions. Typically, many intermediate and advanced queuing theoretic derivations begin with an intuitively appealing probabilistic description of the problem. The solution then involves reformulating the original problem in a transformed domain and then performing a series of tedious yet straightforward mathematical manipulations on the transformed equations. The final solution then involves inverting the manipulated, transformed equations back into the parameters of the original problem statement. Many important queuing theoretic results have been derived using these transform techniques. Unfortunately, the reader gains little insight into the physical properties through these exercises. Alternative approaches attempt to preserve the intuitive mapping to the original problem parameters.

One particularly elegant approach is called the *method of collective marks* [1], which we use to illustrate the transform method with reference to Figure 12.2. The notation employed in the figure depicts two horizontal time axes for the queue and the server. Vertical arrows labeled with the user number (i.e., U_n) depict user arrivals to the queue, movement from the queue to the server, and completion of service as shown. The waiting time w_n is the interval between the arrival of U_n and start of service as indicated in the figure. Similarly, b_n is the interval between the beginning of service for U_n and the time of service completion. The method of collective marks uses the concept of a fictitious "gremlin" that randomly marks other arrivals during U_n's time in the system. The first gremlin W^* marks arrivals during the time interval w_n, while the second gremlin B^* marks arrivals during the time interval b_n. These gremlins mark arrivals with probability $(1-z)$, which means they don't mark arrivals with probability z. Recalling that the arrival process is Markovian with average arrival rate λ, the probability that no arrivals during the interval w_n are marked using the above definitions and terminology is:

$$\Pr\begin{bmatrix} \text{none marked} \\ \text{in } w_n \end{bmatrix} = \sum_{k=0}^{\infty}\int_{0}^{\infty}\frac{(\lambda y)^k}{k!}e^{-\lambda y}z^k f_w(y)dy$$

$$= \int_{0}^{\infty}e^{-\lambda y(1-z)}f_w(y)dy$$

(12-2)

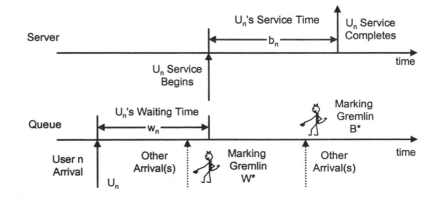

Figure 12.2
Terminology employed in the method of collective marks derivation of transform solutions.

where $f_w(y) \equiv dF[w_n = y] / dy$ is the waiting time probability density function (pdf). By definition, the *Laplace transform* of a pdf $f_x(x)$ is $X^*(s)$ as follows:

$$X^*(s) \equiv E[e^{-sx}] = \int_0^\infty e^{-sx} f_x(x) dx \qquad (12\text{-}3)$$

Using the above definition, $\Pr[\text{none marked in } w_n] = W^*(\lambda - \lambda z)$. Using similar reasoning, the derivation of the equality $\Pr[\text{none marked in } b_n] = B^*(\lambda - \lambda z)$ results. As seen from Figure 12.2, the time intervals w_n and b_n are non-overlapping, hence the Markovian arrivals are independent, and consequently, so are the marking events. Therefore, the probability of no marked arrivals in the combined time interval $w_n + b_n$ is:

$$\Pr\begin{bmatrix}\text{none marked} \\ \text{in } w_n + b_n\end{bmatrix} = \Pr\begin{bmatrix}\text{none marked} \\ \text{in } w_n\end{bmatrix} \Pr\begin{bmatrix}\text{none marked} \\ \text{in } b_n\end{bmatrix}$$
$$= W_n^*(\lambda - \lambda z) B_n^*(\lambda - \lambda z) \qquad (12\text{-}4)$$

The above equation reflects an important property of transform solutions: the transform of a sum of independent random variables is the product of the transforms of each of the random variables. The collective marks technique now proceeds by deriving a second expression for the probability of no marked customers in the interval $w_n + b_n$ using the theorem of total probability as follows:

$$\Pr\begin{bmatrix}\text{none marked} \\ \text{in } w_n + b_n\end{bmatrix} = \Pr\begin{bmatrix}\text{none marked} & U_{n+1} \\ \text{in } w_n + b_n & , & \text{marked}\end{bmatrix}$$
$$+ \Pr\begin{bmatrix}\text{none marked} & U_{n+1} \text{ not} \\ \text{in } w_n + b_n & , & \text{marked}\end{bmatrix} \qquad (12\text{-}5)$$

We now solve for each term on the right-hand side of the above formula separately. Clearly, from Figure 12.2 user $n+1$ cannot be marked when arriving in the interval $w_n + b_n$ and simultaneously have no marked arrivals in the same interval. Also, observe that the probability that U_{n+1} arrives after an interval $w_n + b_n$ is equal to the probability that no arrivals occur in the interval $w_n + b_n$. Furthermore, setting $z = 0$ in Equation (12-4) gives the probability that no users arrive in the interval $w_n + b_n$. Thus, the first term of Equation (12-5) is equal to

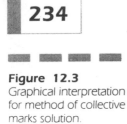

Figure 12.3
Graphical interpretation
for method of collective
marks solution.

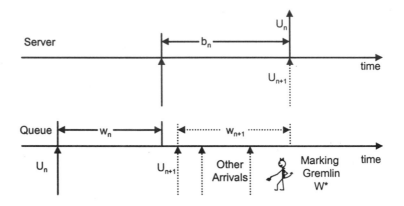

the probability that no arrivals occur in the interval w_n+b_n and that U_{n+1} is marked as follows.

$$\Pr\begin{bmatrix} \text{none marked} & U_{n+1} \text{ is} \\ \text{in } w_n + b_n & \text{marked} \end{bmatrix} = \Pr\begin{bmatrix} \text{no arrivals} \\ \text{in } w_n + b_n \end{bmatrix} \Pr\begin{bmatrix} U_{n+1} \text{ is} \\ \text{marked} \end{bmatrix} \quad (12\text{-}6)$$

$$= \dot{W}_{n+1}(\lambda)\,\dot{B}_{n+1}(\lambda)(1-z)$$

Now, let's address the second term in Equation (12-5). Looking at Figure 12.3, observe that since U_{n+1} is not marked, then we need only concern ourselves with other arrivals occurring during the waiting time of user n+1, namely the interval w_{n+1} as depicted in the figure. Since the probability that U_{n+1} is not marked is z by definition and Equation (12-2) gives the probability of no marked arrivals in a specific time interval, we have:

$$\Pr\begin{bmatrix} \text{none} & U_{n+1} \\ \text{marked} & \text{not} \\ \text{in } w_n + b_n & \text{marked} \end{bmatrix} = \Pr\begin{bmatrix} \text{none marked} \\ \text{in } w_{n+1} \end{bmatrix} \Pr\begin{bmatrix} U_{n+1} \text{ not} \\ \text{marked} \end{bmatrix} \quad (12\text{-}7)$$

$$= \dot{W}_{n+1}(\lambda - \lambda z)\,z$$

Now, substituting Equations (12-6) and (12-7) into (12-5) yields the sought after alternative expression for no marked users in the interval w_n+b_n as follows:

$$\Pr\begin{bmatrix} \text{none marked} \\ \text{in } w_n + b_n \end{bmatrix} = \dot{W}_{n+1}(\lambda)\,\dot{B}_{n+1}(\lambda)(1-z) + \dot{W}_{n+1}(\lambda - \lambda z)\,z \quad (12\text{-}8)$$

We now set the right-hand side of Equations (12-4) and (12-5) equal to each other, change some notation, and simplify as follows. In the long run, the random process converges to a steady state and $W^*(s) \cong W_n^*(s)$ as n approaches infinity. Furthermore, substituting $s = \lambda - \lambda z$ into the above equation yields the following result:

$$W^*(s)B^*(s) = W^*(\lambda)B^*(\lambda)(1-z) + W^*(s)z$$

From the definition of the Laplace transform in Equation (12-3), note that $W^*(\lambda)B^*(\lambda) = 1 - \rho$. Making this substitution into the above equation and solving for $W^*(s)$ yields the famous *Pollaczek-Khinchin transform equation*:

$$W^*(s) = \frac{s(1-\rho)}{s - \lambda + \lambda B^*(s)} \tag{12-9}$$

Believe it or not, the preceding derivation is the simplest means to derive this result! Most results of intermediate and advanced queuing theory are even more complex. Unfortunately, a closed-form solution for the waiting time distribution $f_w(w)$ cannot be found except for a few specific service time distributions $f_b(b)$ from Equation (12-9), for example, negative exponential or Markovian. However, this equation can be evaluated numerically to obtain higher-order moments by exploiting the following property of Laplace transforms:

$$E[x^k] = (-1)^k \left. \frac{d^k X^*(s)}{ds^k} \right|_{s=0} \tag{12-10}$$

Other probability and queuing theory texts define forms similar to Equation (12-10) and are called the *moment generating function* or *characteristic function*, since successive differentiation operations produce the next higher-order moment. Applying Equation (12-10) to (12-9) with k=1 yields the Pollaczek-Khinchin mean-value formula of Equation (12-1). Taking the derivative another time of this result and subtracting off the mean-value yields the variance of the number in an M/G/1 queuing system [2]:

$$Var[k] = \frac{\lambda^3 b_3}{3(1-\rho)} + \left(\frac{\lambda^2 b_2}{2(1-\rho)} \right)^2 + \frac{\lambda^2(3 - 2\rho)b_2}{2(1-\rho)}$$

where $b_k \equiv E[b^k]$ is the kth moment about the origin of a general service time distribution $f_b(b)$.

Most other results for the M/G/1 queue require numerical evaluation. We now study another interesting analytical measure of traffic burstiness in the form of statistics for busy and idle periods.

Busy and Idle Period Analysis

Most traffic systems experience intervals of high activity followed by intervals of inactivity. Queuing theory calls these intervals busy and idle periods, respectively. Figure 12.4 depicts a typical sequence of busy and idle periods for an M/M/1 queuing system with arrival rate of $\lambda=10$ bursts per second and a service rate of $\mu=20$ bursts per second. The uppermost plot depicts a time series of arrivals to a queue, which move on to the server. Departures occur from the server as shown at the top of the figure. After each arrival, the server has one more burst to complete. As the server transmits the packets or cells corresponding to the burst, the unfinished work decreases in a linear manner over time. The lower plot shows the unfinished work of the server over a 1-second interval. Busy periods occur where the unfinished work is non-zero, while idle periods occur where the unfinished work equals zero. A pattern of busy periods with a wide range of durations interrupted by idle intervals of correspondingly variable dura-

Figure 12.4
Busy and idle periods in a M/M/1 queuing system.

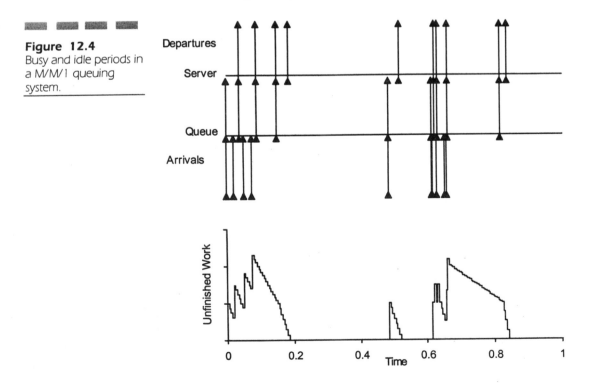

TABLE 12.1

Important statistics for the busy period of an M/G/1 queue.

Statistic	Expected Value	Variance
Duration of the Busy Period (T_{BP})	$\dfrac{E[b]}{1-\rho}$	$\dfrac{Var[b]+\rho E[b]^2}{(1-\rho)^3}$
Number Served in the Busy Period (N_{BP})	$\dfrac{1}{1-\rho}$	$\dfrac{\lambda^2 Var[b]+\rho}{(1-\rho)^3}$

tion is typical in real-world traffic systems. Let's look further at the statistics of the busy period to better understand this phenomenon.

A number of results for the busy period of an M/G/1 queue have been derived in closed form [1, 2]. Table 12.1 summarizes these results for the expected value and variance of the busy period duration T_{BP}, as well as the number of users served during the busy period N_{BP}. As before, $\rho=\lambda/\mu$ is the offered load, and E[b] and Var[b] are the average and variance of the service time pdf b(t), respectively.

These statistics provide insight into several important aspects of the busy period. First, the average duration of the busy period is independent of higher-order moments. In fact, the average duration and number served in the busy period are identical to that of the M/M/1 queue. Second, the $(1-\rho)^3$ term in the denominator for the variance of duration and numbers served during the busy period analytically models the high degree of variability observed in real-world traffic systems under heavy loads. To better understand this fact, consider the squared coefficient of variation of the busy period duration, defined as follows:

$$C_{BP}^2 \equiv \frac{Var[T_{BP}]}{E[T_{BP}]^2} = \frac{C_b^2 + \rho}{1-\rho}$$

where $C_b^2 \equiv Var[b]/E[b]^2$ is the squared coefficient of variation for the service time distribution. Let's consider some examples for a system under heavy load with $\rho=0.9$. For an M/M/1 system, $C_b^2=1$ and hence $C_{BP}^2=19$. Even for deterministic service, $C_b^2=0$, but the squared coefficient of variation for the busy period is $C_{BP}^2=9$, which means that the standard deviation of the busy period duration is three times larger than the mean. For self similar traffic, $C_b^2>1$, which means that C_{BP}^2 is even larger, implying even greater variability of the busy period.

The G/M/1 Queue

The G/M/1 queue has a general arrival process with pdf a(t) and Markovian service discipline. In a sense, it is the dual of the M/G/1 queue where the statistics of the arrival time distribution determine the waiting time statistics. In the G/M/1 case, the imbedded Markov chain occurs at the instants of user arrivals. For an average arrival rate λ and a Markovian service rate μ, the probability that an arrival finds the server busy is [1, 2]:

$$\Pr\begin{bmatrix} \text{Arrival finds} \\ \text{server busy} \end{bmatrix} \equiv \theta = A^*(\mu - \mu\theta)$$

where $A^*(s)$ is the Laplace transform of the arrival time pdf as defined in Equation (12-3). The value of θ is the solution to this equation, which generally requires numerical solution [2]. When the arrival time pdf is negative exponential (i.e., Markovian), $\theta = \rho$, and the G/M/1 queue reduces to the M/M/1 queue.

Interestingly, the probability of k users being in the system takes on a modified form of the geometric distribution with θ as the parameter as follows:

$$\pi_k = \begin{cases} 1 - \rho & k = 0 \\ \rho(1 - \theta)\theta^{k-1} & k > 0 \end{cases}$$

Note that for an M/M/1 system $\theta = \rho$ and the above equation and the moments are identical for the G/M/1 queue formulas, as they should. We can then compute the average number in the system in a straightforward manner directly from the pdf with the following result:

$$E[k] = \frac{\rho}{1 - \theta}$$

Similarly, the variance of the number in the system can be directly computed, resulting in the following formula:

$$\text{Var}[k] = \frac{\rho(1 + \theta - \rho)}{(1 - \theta)^2}$$

Unfortunately, as the reader surely has concluded by now, classical queuing theory becomes quite complex when attempting to model non-Markovian processes. Fortunately, researchers have developed a number of good approximations and approaches that are relatively simple to evaluate and provide deep insights that are not as complex. We turn our attention to application of these alternative solution techniques in the next section.

Fluid Flow Approximation and Equivalent Capacity

Equivalent capacity is a relatively simple analytical technique that models capacity requirements for variable-rate traffic sources [3, 4]. This model approximates the exact solution by combining two separate models, applicable for different regions of operation. For systems with a small number of sources, a fluid flow model considers each source in isolation, allocating a fixed amount of capacity to each source. Unfortunately, for larger systems the fluid flow model overestimates the required capacity because it fails to account for statistical multiplexing gain. In the case of larger systems, a model based upon the normal distribution accurately models the statistical benefits of capacity shared by a large number of sources. The equivalent capacity model is then the minimum of the capacity determined by the fluid flow model and the statistical multiplexing gain model. This section first covers the fluid flow model, followed by the normal distribution-based statistical multiplexing gain model, concluding with the equivalent capacity model.

This section uses a model with N identical traffic sources characterized by the following parameters:

Figure 12.5
Fluid flow capacity approximation.

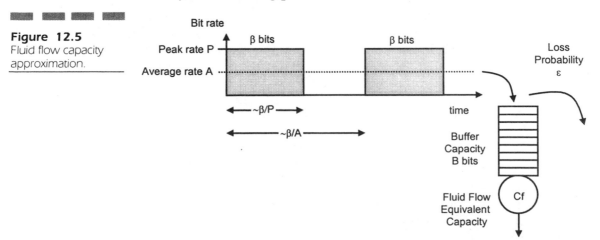

- Peak rate P (bps)
- Average rate A (bps)
- Average burst size β (bits)

The model is readily extended to a mix of different source types using the techniques described in References 3 and 5.

Fluid Flow Approximation

The fluid flow model treats each source independently, reserving bandwidth and buffer capacity to meet a specified loss probability. Conceptually, the model treats each source as a continuous-time two-state Markov process, each being in either an active (on) or an idle (off) state. In the active state, the source generates a burst of cells at a rate of P bps, with each burst containing an average of β bits. The model assumes that the switch or router allocates B bits in a buffer for each source. Figure 12.5 illustrates the concept of the fluid flow model.

The following formula for the fluid flow equivalent capacity depends largely upon the utilization of the source, $\rho=A/P$ and the ratio of the average burst size to the buffer capacity:

$$Cf \; = \; P \; \frac{z \; - \; 1 \; + \; \sqrt{(z-1)^2 \; + \; 4\rho \; z}}{2z} \qquad (12\text{-}11)$$

where $z \; = \; -\ln \; (\varepsilon) \; (1-\rho) \; \dfrac{\beta}{B}$.

Figure 12.6 plots the normalized fluid flow capacity (i.e., Cf divided by the peak rate P) versus the ratio of average burst size to buffer capacity, β/B, with the average source utilization ρ=A/P as the parameter. This normalized fluid flow equivalent capacity is the fraction of the actual source peak rate P required to achieve the required loss probability ε. Note that when the burst is very small with respect to the buffer (i.e., β/B=0.001), then the required equivalent capacity approaches the average source utilization ρ. However, as the size of the burst increases with respect to the buffer capacity (i.e., β/B>1) then the required equivalent capacity approaches 100 percent of the peak rate. Thus, if your application can tolerate wide variations in delay caused by large buffers, then you can run a network quite efficiently. However, if you're integrating voice and video along with this data, your network needs to do more than buffering.

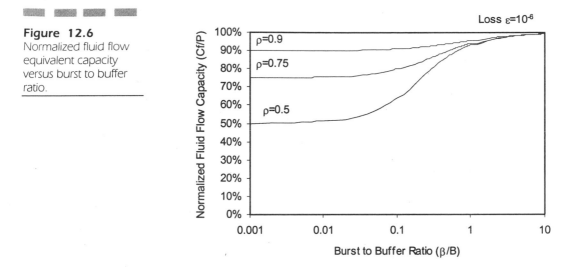

Figure 12.6
Normalized fluid flow equivalent capacity versus burst to buffer ratio.

Statistical Multiplexing Gain Model

Packet and cell switching enables statistical multiplexing, which exploits the on-off, bursty nature of many source types, as illustrated in Figure 12.7. In the left-hand side of the figure, N=4 sources generate bursts of data characterized by a peak rate P and average rate A. A statistical multiplexer combines these inputs, resulting in the multiplexed output stream shown in the right-hand side of the figure. In this simple example, the aggregate traffic normally require only two channels at any point in time. The statistical multiplexer either discards or buffers bursts in excess of the link rate L, as shown in the

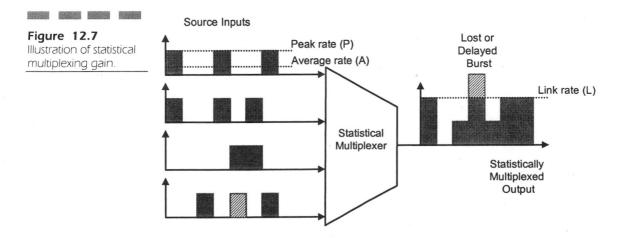

Figure 12.7
Illustration of statistical multiplexing gain.

figure. As the multiplexer combines more sources together, the statistics of this composite sum become increasingly more predictable. The statistical multiplexing gain G is the ratio of channels supported to the number of required channels, as indicated in the following formula:

$$G = \frac{\text{Number of Sources Supported}}{\text{Required Number of Channels}} \qquad (12\text{-}12)$$

Note that the gain is never less than one. Furthermore, G is significantly greater than one only if the number of sources supported greatly exceeds the number of channels required by individual sources. As described in Chapter 8, the pdf for N identical sources is given by the binomial distribution [6], and approximated by the normal distribution with the following parameters:

$$\text{Mean} = N\rho \quad \text{Variance} = N\rho(1\text{-}\rho)$$

The required number of channels for this Gaussian approximation, expressed in units of the number of peak rate sources, to achieve an objective loss probability $\varepsilon = Q(\alpha)$ is:

$$Cg \approx N\rho + \alpha\sqrt{N\rho(1-\rho)} \qquad (12\text{-}13)$$

where $Q(\alpha)$ is the probability that a zero-mean normal random variable takes on a value greater than α, as defined in Chapter 8.

Therefore, the statistical multiplexing gain G from Equation (12-12) is the ratio of the capacity required for the number of sources supported N divided by the required channels Cg. Equivalently, G is the sum of the peak rate for all sources NP divided by the link rate. Equating these expressions, we have:

$$G \equiv \frac{N}{C_g} = \frac{NP}{L} = N\eta \qquad (12\text{-}14)$$

where $\eta \equiv P/L$ is the peak-to-link-rate ratio.

Setting Cg in the above equation equal to the link capacity per source $L/N = 1/\eta$ yields a solution for N using the quadratic formula. Multiplying N by the parameter η results in the following formula for statistical multiplexing gain:

$$G \approx \frac{\eta \left(\sqrt{\alpha^2(1-\rho)+4/\eta} - \alpha\sqrt{1-\rho} \right)^2}{4\rho} \qquad (12\text{-}15)$$

Figure 12.8 plots the achievable statistical multiplexing gain G versus the peak-to-link ratio η with burstiness $b=P/A=1/\rho$ as a parameter for a loss of $\varepsilon=10^{-6}$. This figure illustrates the classical wisdom of statistical multiplexing. The ratio of any individual source with respect to the link rate η should be low, and the burstiness of the sources b must be high (or, equivalently, the source activity ρ must be low) in order to achieve a high statistical multiplexing gain G.

Note that the statistical multiplexing gain G never exceeds the source burstiness b, since $b=P/A$ is the maximum gain if only the average rate A were required for each source. Another way of looking at the performance is to consider the fraction of the link utilized on average. The link utilization U is the average rate A generated by N sources divided by the link rate L. We can rewrite U using the definition of G from Equation (12-14) by recalling that $b=P/A$ as follows:

$$U = \frac{NA}{L} = \frac{G}{b}$$

Figure 12.9 plots the utilization U achieved for the same parameters as in Figure 12.8 above. Note that the system achieves high link utilization only when the peak-to-link ratio, $\eta=P/L$, is very small. The reduction in statistical multiplexing gain results in a correspondingly lower utilization as peak-to-link ratio increases.

Figure 12.8
Achievable statistical
multiplexing gain.

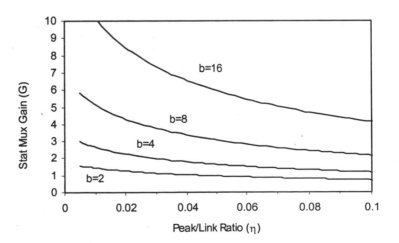

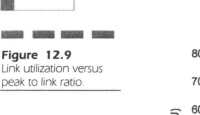

Figure 12.9
Link utilization versus
peak to link ratio.

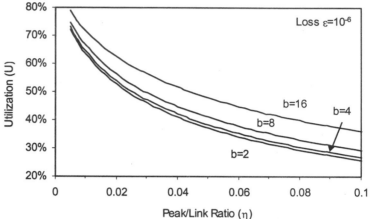

Implicit in the above expressions for statistical multiplexing gain and the associated utilization is that a certain number of sources R are multiplexed together. The required number of sources is simply G/η, where G is defined in Equation (12-15). Figure 12.10 illustrates the number of sources R that must be multiplexed together to achieve the statistical multiplexing gain and utilization predicted in the previous charts. This plot confirms the applicability of the following statistical multiplexing gain assumption. A large number of sources N with high burstiness b (or, equivalently, low source utilization ρ), along with a modest peak-to-link rate ratio η, must be multiplexed together in order to achieve a significant amount of statistical multiplexing gain G.

Figure 12.10
Required number of
sources to achieve
statistical multiplexing
gain.

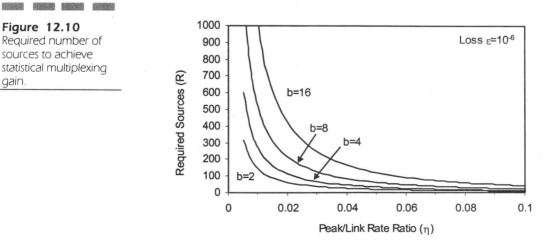

Equivalent Capacity Approximation

The preceding sections gave approximations that made different predictions. The fluid flow approximation predicts efficient operation when the burst size is much less than the buffer size. On the other hand, the statistical multiplexing model predicts higher efficiency when the source peak rate is much smaller than the link rate for a large number of sources. The equivalent capacity model combines these two models to yield the required equivalent capacity Ce according to the following formula [3]:

$$Ce = Min\{ N\ Cf, Cg\ P\}$$

where   Cf = fluid flow equivalent capacity from Equation (12-11)
          Cg = statistical multiplexing gain capacity from Equation (12-13)

Although the equivalent capacity approximation overestimates the required capacity, its computational simplicity makes it an attractive model to understand how the parameters of variable-rate traffic sources affect overall utilization and efficiency. Let's look at how these two approximations combine versus the parameters of peak-to-link ratio η and burst-to-buffer ratio β/B through several examples. All of these examples numerically compute the maximum number of identical sources that yield a loss of $\varepsilon=10^{-6}$.

Figure 12.11 plots utilization U versus the ratio of source peak rate

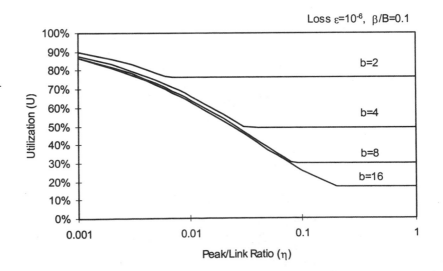

Figure 12.11
Utilization versus peak-to-link ratio, burst-to-buffer ratio = 10 percent.

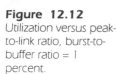

Figure 12.12
Utilization versus peak-to-link ratio, burst-to-buffer ratio = 1 percent.

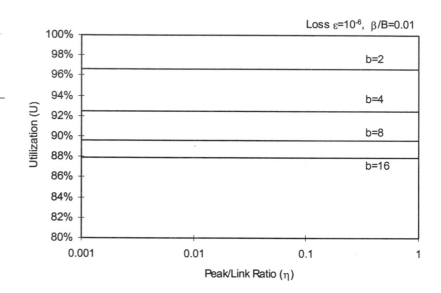

to link speed η=P/L for an average source burst size to switch buffer size ratio β/B of 10 percent with burstiness β=P/A as the parameter. This figure illustrates the point that the source peak rate should be much less than the link rate when multiplexing traffic with long bursts. As the peak-to-link ratio η increases, the asymptotic statistical multiplexing gain places a lower limit on utilization.

Figure 12.12 plots Utilization U versus the ratio of source peak rate to link speed for the same parameters, but now the average source burst size to switch buffer size ratio β/B is 1 percent. In other words, the buffers employed in the router or switch are ten times larger than those utilized in the previous chart. Note that the utilization is now independent of the source peak-to-link ratio, since the larger buffer smoothes out short-term fluctuations in source activity. Adaptive flow control, such as IP's slow-start TCP protocol or ATM's Available Bit Rate (ABR), would also achieve effects similar to the large buffer modeled in this example. This analysis stresses the importance of large buffers and/or small burst sizes in order to achieve high link utilization.

Figure 12.13 illustrates the effect of the ratio of average source burst size to switch buffer size β/B on utilization U. The PCR divided by the link rate η is now the parameter. The average source activity ρ is 50 percent in this example. For smaller values of burst-to-buffer ratio, the utilization is independent of the peak-to-link ratio. However, for larger values of burst-to-buffer ratio, the utilization approaches that of peak rate allocation. This graphic clearly illustrates the benefits of

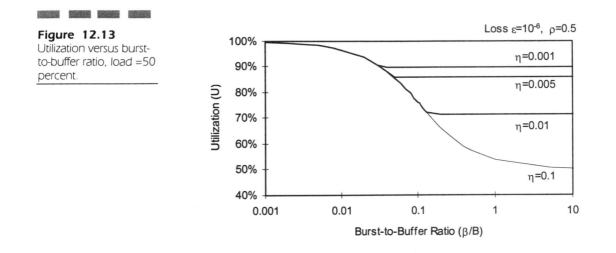

Figure 12.13
Utilization versus burst-to-buffer ratio, load =50 percent.

larger buffers, particularly when the peak-to-link ratio is larger than a few percent.

Multiplexing Deterministic Constant Rate Sources

The accurate loss performance measure of another very important traffic type that has a constant rate is relatively easy to calculate. Figure 12.14 illustrates the basic traffic source model. N identical sources emit a fixed-length burst once every T seconds, each beginning

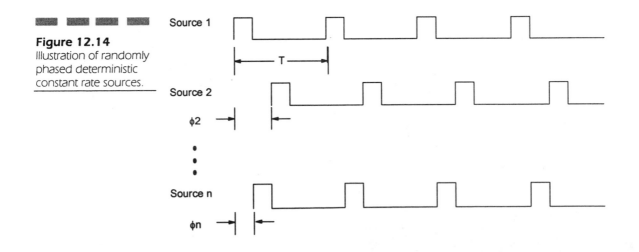

Figure 12.14
Illustration of randomly phased deterministic constant rate sources.

transmission at some random phase in the interval (0, T). For ATM, each cell is a burst of exactly $\beta=53\times8=424$ bits. Thus, even if the network allocates capacity according to the peak rate, the random phasing of the constant rate sources can still create overflow. This is most likely to occur in an IP router or ATM switch that has a large number of interfaces that can have simultaneous arrivals. A good approximation for the loss rate for such randomly phased constant rate traffic input is [7]:

$$\varepsilon \;=\; \text{Prob[Loss]} \;\approx\; \exp\left[-2B^2/n \;-\; 2B(1-\rho)\right]$$

where   n is the number of constant rate connections,
               B is the buffer capacity (in units of fixed-length bursts), and
               $\rho=nT$ is the offered load.

A closed-form solution for the number of buffers required to achieve a specified loss probability results by solving the above formula for the minimum buffer size B required to achieve a loss probability ε as follows [8]:

$$B_{req} \;\approx\; \frac{\sqrt{[n(1-\rho)]^2 \;-\; 2n\;\ln(\varepsilon)} \;-\; n(1-\rho)}{2} \qquad (12\text{-}16)$$

Figure 12.15 illustrates the results of this calculation by plotting the required buffers B_{req} versus the number of constant rate connections n for various levels of overall throughput ρ that achieves a loss objective of $\varepsilon=10^{-9}$. If the switch or router implements priority queuing,

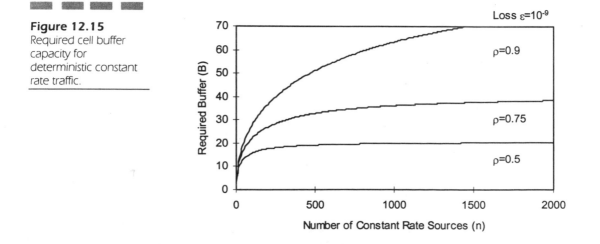

Figure 12.15
Required cell buffer capacity for deterministic constant rate traffic.

this performance measure applies independently of other perform-ance measures. Thus, in the example of Figure 12.15, constant rate traffic uses only the fraction ρ of the link overall capacity. The re-maining capacity is available for other service categories.

The actual delay variation Δ, measured in absolute time, delivered by the switch or router depends upon the packet size β and the link rate R. In general, delay variation increases in inverse proportion to the link rate. The worst-case delay variation occurs between the ex-tremes of the buffer being entirely empty and completely full. That is, the worst-case bound on delay variation is:

$$\Delta \le \frac{\beta B_{req}}{R}$$

A more accurate approximation for delay variation is the differ-ence between the buffer capacity B_{req} and the average number of bursts in the buffer [7] divided by the link rate, namely:

$$\Delta \approx \frac{\beta}{R} \left\{ B_{req} - \frac{\sqrt{n}}{2} \frac{1 - \Phi[(1-\rho)\sqrt{n}]}{\varphi[(1-\rho)\sqrt{n}]} \right\} \qquad (12\text{-}17)$$

where φ and Φ are the standard normal density and distribution func-tions, respectively, as defined in Chapter 8. The NORMDIST func-tion in Microsoft Excel implements the φ and Φ functions in the above formula.

Given the above solution for the required number of buffers B_{req} from Equation (12-16), we can utilize Equation (12-17) to compute the

Figure 12.16
Cell Delay Variation
(CDV) per switch
versus number of
connections.

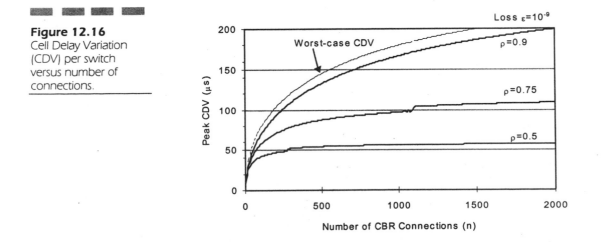

delay variation introduced by each node. For example, Figure 12.16 plots the resulting Cell Delay Variation (CDV) on a 149.76 Mbps OC3/STM-1 link versus the number of Constant Bit Rate (CBR) ATM connections n. The loss objective is $\varepsilon=10^{-9}$ and the overall link utilization ρ is the parameter. For large values of utilization ρ, the approximation and the worst-case bound yield comparable results. However, for lower values of utilization, the approximation predicts a much smaller CDV than the worst-case bound does.

Review

This chapter introduced the use of transform techniques using the method of collective marks and cited the known results for the mean and variance of the M/G/1 and G/M/1 queues. In particular, we showed how the variation of the service time distribution markedly impacts the statistics of the M/G/1 queue length. The text then presented an analysis of the busy and idle period statistics for an M/G/1 queue. These results analytically demonstrated the common experience of great variability in the duration of a busy or idle interval typical of many traffic systems. Next, the chapter detailed the equivalent capacity admission control model composed of a fluid flow approximation and a statistical multiplexing model. Through parametric analysis, we showed that significant statistical gain occurs only if the source rate is much less than the link rate. The model also demonstrated that routers or switches with buffers much larger than the source burst duration can achieve utilization approaching 100 percent. Finally, the chapter concluded with an approximate model regarding the multiplexing of a number of constant rate sources. The analysis determined the minimum buffer requirement, and hence maximum delay variation, required to achieve a specific loss objective.

References

[1]   L. Kleinrock, *Queuing Systems Volume I: Theory*, Wiley, 1975.
[2]   M. Tanner, *Practical Queuing Analysis*, McGraw-Hill, 1995.
[3]   R. Guerin, H. Ahmadi, M. Naghshineh, "Equivalent Capacity and Bandwidth Allocation," *IEEE JSAC*, Sept 1991.
[4]   M. Schwartz, *Broadband Integrated Networks*, Prentice-Hall, 1996.

[5] H. Ahmadi, P. Chimento, R. Guérin, L. Gün, R. Onvural, T. Tedjianto, "NBBS Traffic Management Overview," *IBM Systems Journal*, Vol 34, No. 4, 1995.

[6] Rasmusen, Sorenson, Kvols, Jacobsen, "Source-Independent Call Acceptance Procedures in ATM Networks," *IEEE JSAC*, April 1991.

[7] L. Dron, Ramamurthy, Sengupta, "Delay Analysis of Continuous Bit Rate Traffic over an ATM Network," *IEEE JSAC*, April 1991.

[8] M. Wernik, Aboul-Magd, Gilbert, "Traffic Management for B-ISDN Services," *IEEE Network*, September 1992.

5

Congestion Detection and Control

"Wisdom consists in being able to distinguish among dangers and make a choice of the least harmful."

—Niccolo Machiavelli

Now that we've seen the havoc that random traffic can wreak, an important question is, what can be done? First, note that traffic level and congestion go hand in hand. When traffic is light, there is no congestion. When traffic is heavy, there is moderate congestion. When traffic is at a standstill, congestion is severe.

Congestion control solutions respond differently to different traffic levels. The open-loop congestion control approach attempts to avoid congestion proactively by limiting admitted traffic selectively discarding lower priority traffic. A complementary approach reacts to severe congestion using closed-loop algorithms. Specifically, this part analyzes the performance of ATM's Available Bit Rate (ABR) and IP's Transmission Control Protocol (TCP).

13

Traffic Jam Up Ahead!

"Abandon all hope, you who enter here."

— Dante

Webster's New World Dictionary defines congestion as "filled to excess, or overcrowded, for example, highway congestion." This chapter begins by relating experiences from well-known congestion phenomenon in everyday life to communication networks. The text then defines congestion in terms specific to IP and ATM networks through use of a simple example. Depending upon the type of traffic, in conjunction with the capabilities of network elements and end user software, congestion control takes on one of two basic flavors: open loop or closed loop. We then discuss the principal performance measures of congestion control algorithms: throughput and delay.

Since reliable delivery via the use of retransmission protocols is a foundation of the Internet, this chapter introduces this important topic, detailing IP's Transmission Control Protocol (TCP). Retransmission schemes fall into two major classes: fixed and adaptive. We also summarize the operation of ATM's Available Bit Rate (ABR) closed-loop flow control algorithm. Finally, this chapter concludes with a descriptive taxonomy of congestion control protocols covered in Chapters 14 and 15.

Congestion Phenomena in Our Everyday Lives and in Networks

This section introduces the topic of congestion by drawing analogies with situations that many of us have experienced. We then apply analogies of these experiences to IP and ATM networks.

The Nature of Congestion

We experience congestion daily in the form of traffic jams, long checkout lines at stores, ticket lines, or just waiting for some form of service. Congestion is the condition reached when the demand for resources exceeds the available resources for an extended interval of time. Take the real-life example of a vehicular traffic jam. Congestion occurs because the number of vehicles wishing to use a road (demand) exceeds the number of vehicles that can travel on that road (available resources) during a rush hour (an extended time interval).

More specific to IP and ATM networks, congestion is the condition where the offered load (demand) from the user to the network approaches, or even exceeds, the network design limits for guaranteeing the Quality of Service (QoS) specified in a Service Level Agreement (SLA). This demand may exceed the resource design limit because the network incorrectly oversubscribed resources, because of failures within the network, or because of operational errors.

Congestion is inevitable in any expanding system. As traffic increases and the resources remain static, an overload eventually must occur. This pattern repeats itself in transportation systems around the world. The road systems once adequate for a quiet rural suburb of a large metropolitan area are jammed with commuters in areas with increasing population.

On the other hand, some systems seldom experience congestion, since other mechanisms or usage patterns keep demand below capacity. For example, some metropolitan centers experience little to no congestion during the evening hours and on weekends, since there are few residences or entertainment centers in the downtown area. Contrary to some articles in the popular press, the declining cost of transmission, memory chips, and computer processing power will not alleviate congestion. Changing cost structures frequently just move the bottleneck that causes congestion from one place to another.

Congestion is often a dynamic phenomenon caused by unpredictable events. Although the rush hour may be predictable on the freeway, an accident can cause an even more severe traffic jam at any time of day or night. Combine an unexpected event like an accident with a normal rush hour and the delays can stretch to hours.

Why are we concerned with congestion in networks? Because, as in transportation systems, shopping malls, and other areas where many people congregate: congestion is an unpleasant experience. In IP and ATM networks congestion causes excessive delay, loss, or both. Delay and loss reduce the quality of service provided to the end user application, often lowering productivity and sometimes rendering the application unusable.

Busy Seasons, Days, and Hours

Some days traffic is heavier than others. Usually, in transportation networks congestion occurs on a predictable basis at specific intersections or thoroughfares. Similar phenomena exist in many networks between specific communities of interest like clusters of geographic regions or departments in an enterprise. For example, Mother's Day is usually one of the busiest days in telephone networks.

A pattern typically called a *busy hour* exists in many networks much as it does during rush hour on the freeway. These observations of overall arrival rates averaged over many days during different seasons of the year differ from the random arrival model studied in the previous part. Instead of a single parameter describing the arrival process, a traffic pattern is modeled as an average arrival rate for a specific time of day, day of week, and season of the year. Similar busy hour and busy day traffic patterns also occur on Internet backbones [1].

At other times, exceptional conditions can create overloads in unexpected places at unusual times. Loads during the busiest intervals, or during abnormal periods of higher than usual activity create congestion in communication networks, much as overloads occur in transportation systems due to natural disasters or accidents. Occasionally, popular, newsworthy, or emergency events create overloads in telephone networks or on the Web.

Time Scales of Congestion

A number of application characteristics determine the impact of congestion, such as connection mode, retransmission policy, acknowledgment policy, responsiveness, and higher-layer flow control. In concert with the application characteristics, certain network charac-

Figure 13.1
Time scales of
congestion.

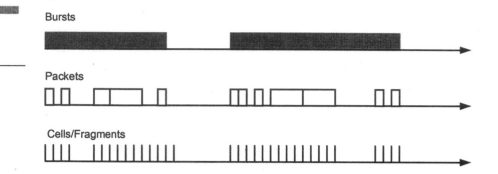

teristics also determine the response to congestion, such as: queuing strategy, service scheduling policy, discard strategy, route selection, propagation delay, processing delay, and connection mode.

As illustrated in Figure 13.1, congestion occurs on several time scales: at the burst level, the packet level, or at the ATM cell or fragment level for a specific flow or connection. See References 2, 3, and 4 for more on categorization of congestion time scales. The detection of congestion as a prelude to subsequent action is *congestion indication*, feedback, or notification. Traffic forecasts, utilization trends, buffer fill statistics, cell transmission statistics, or loss counters are all indications of congestion.

The reaction to indicated congestion occurs in either time or space. In *time*, reactive controls operate on either a cell-by-cell basis, on a packet (or burst) time scale, or at the call level. In *space*, the reaction can be at a single node, at the source, at the receiver, or at multiple nodes.

Introduction to Congestion Control

Although the best solution to congestion is to simply avoid situations where and when congestion is likely to occur, this strategy isn't always possible. Unfortunately, congestion occurs in many real world networking environments because there is always a bottleneck of some sort — a slow computer, a low speed link, an overloaded server or an intermediate switch or router with low throughput or excessive delay. This section provides an introduction to the basic concepts of congestion control techniques.

Examples of Congestion in a Network

In IP and ATM networks the congestable resources include buffers, transmission facilities, or processors. We call the resource where demand exceeds capacity the *bottleneck*, congestion point, or constraint. Figure 13.2 illustrates an example of congestion occurring along an end-to-end route from a server connected to node A to a user connected to node D. Links interconnect the nodes with thicker lines, indicating links with higher capacity. The number of dots next to each link indicates the rate of bursts (of cells or packets) being transferred by each link. In the following examples, a thick link can transfer at a rate of 3 bursts, while a thin link can transfer 1 burst per time interval.

Two points of congestion occur in the example of Figure 13.2. First, the high-speed link between nodes C and D is congested due to overload. As shown in the figure, the average input load to node C is 6 bursts, while the output link from C to D can carry only 3 bursts. If this overload of input rate exceeding output rate persists long enough, node C will drop packets or cells due to buffer overflow or depletion of other resources. The second point of congestion occurs on the low-speed link between node D and the user at the right-hand side of the figure. Congestion occurs because the low-speed link can support a rate of only 1 burst per time interval, while the server on the left-hand side of the figure is sending 2 bursts per time interval. Therefore, if this speed mismatch persists, node D must eventually discard packets or cells due to lack of resources.

Open- and Closed-Loop Congestion Control

Okay, once congestion occurs, what can be done? The next two examples illustrate the basic paradigms studied in the remainder of this part. Figure 13.3 illustrates the first case where voice communication users connected to nodes B and D share the congested link connecting nodes C and D. In this example, the voice bursts (shown as circles

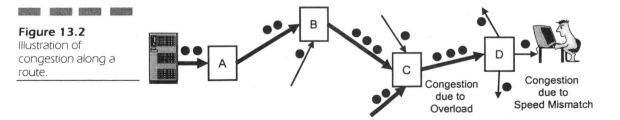

Figure 13.2
Illustration of congestion along a route.

Congestion due to Overload

Congestion due to Speed Mismatch

▬▬ ▬▬ ▬▬ ▬▬

Figure 13.3
Open-loop congestion
control — priority
service.

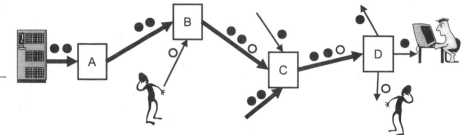

with white centers) have higher priority, and hence get through first. However, the communication link between C and D has limited capacity, hence the throughput of server to user connection between nodes A and D must decline. Thus, prioritization and ensuring that sufficient capacity exists on the selected route for high-priority traffic is one means of controlling congestion. Since this mechanism operates without any feedback, we call it *open-loop congestion control.*

Figure 13.4 illustrates the second major method of congestion control. Here, we have the same two congestion scenarios shown in Figure 13.2, but in this case the sender obtains feedback regarding the congested state of the flow. Since the feedback comprises a closed loop from the sender to the receiver and back to the sender again, we call this technique *closed-loop congestion control.* The most commonly used type of feedback is implicit. The Transmission Control Protocol (TCP) widely used in the Internet for the Web, E-mail, and file transfer employs this technique. Basically, TCP requires that the receiver acknowledge receipt of each packet to the sender. If the sender does not receive an acknowledgement after a time-out interval, then the sender implicitly determines that the unacknowledged packet was lost, and retransmits it. Furthermore, once the sender implicitly detects congestion via a time-out, it reduces the rate at which it transmits packets, thereby reducing congestion. Since TCP is so important in the Internet, we study it further in this chapter.

▬▬ ▬▬ ▬▬ ▬▬

Figure 13.4
Closed- loop
congestion control —
loss feedback.

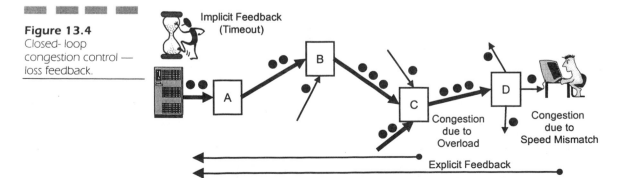

The arrows at the bottom of Figure 13.4 illustrate another type of feedback generated explicitly at the point of congestion. Since node C is aware that the link connecting C and D is congested, it could send feedback messages to the sources traversing the congested link. ATM's Available Bit Rate (ABR) closed-loop flow control technique uses this approach. Similarly, if the application running on user D's computer was the bottleneck creating congestion, it could explicitly signal the source to slow down. This technique addresses a problem that has existed since the earliest days of computer communications of interfacing a fast sender with a slow receiver. IP's source-quench protocol uses the explicit feedback technique.

Of course, there is another response to congestion suggested by our experience in transportation networks. Namely, if a particular route is congested, then choose an alternate route. Unfortunately, as in a roadway network, this doesn't help if you are already stuck in a traffic jam. Additionally, some of the design assumptions that trade off performance versus complexity in IP and ATM network routing algorithms restrict the degree of alternate routing available. Nonetheless, Part 6 addresses the topic of network level routing and covers the topic of alternate routing as a means of avoiding and recovering from congestion.

Tradeoff between Throughput and Delay in Congested Networks

Two basic measures define the degree of congestion experienced — throughput and delay. The file transfer and voice/video applications represent extremes of application requirements for throughput and delay. *Throughput* is the data transfer rate actually achieved by the end application. For example, if a File Transfer Protocol (FTP) application loses a packet, then it must retransmit that packet, and frequently in many implementations, all of the packets sent after it! Useful throughput is only those packets actually sequentially delivered to the end application without errors. Some applications like FTP, accept variable throughput, while others, like video, require a specific value of throughput to work acceptably.

Delay requirements differ by application type. Real-time traffic must be delivered within a fraction of a second, while for non-real-time applications that perform retransmission, delay takes on an additional dimension. When a protocol retransmits unsuccessfully delivered packets, the resulting delay is the time elapsed between the first unsuccessful transmission and the final successful reception of the packet at the destination.

Loss is another consideration in congestion control. Some applications, like video, can adapt their transmission rate and still deliver good performance if the network congestion control minimizes loss. Other activities, like Web-surfing, file transfer, and E-mail, recover from loss via retransmission, usually with little user impact.

Note that throughput, delay, and loss for some applications is identical to that of the underlying IP or ATM network. For example, voice or video coded to operate acceptably under loss conditions is not retransmitted, and hence experiences the same throughput and delay as the underlying IP or ATM network. In practice, voice and video coding only accept loss or delay up to a critical value; after which point the subjective perception of the image, or audio playback, becomes unacceptable.

Figure 13.5 plots effective throughput versus offered load. An ideal system has throughput that increases linearly until offered load reaches 100 percent of the bottleneck resource. A good congestion control protocol approximates the ideal curve. A poor congestion control scheme exhibits a phenomenon called *congestion collapse* [5]. As offered load increases toward 100 percent, throughput increases to a maximum value and then *decreases* markedly due to user application retransmissions caused by loss or excessive delay. Hence, we say that throughput collapses at the onset of congestion.

A key measure of the effectiveness of a particular congestion control scheme is how much delay or loss occurs under offered loads approaching or exceeding 100 percent of the bottleneck resource. Figure 13.6 illustrates the effective delay for the same three categories of congestion control systems described above. An ideal congestion control

Figure 13.5
Illustration of useful throughputs for congestion control schemes.

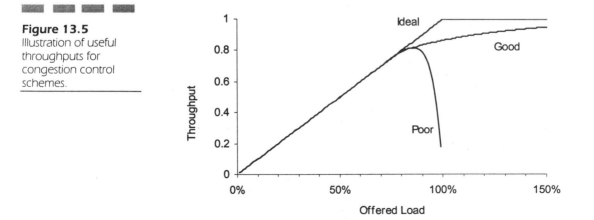

Figure 13.6
Illustration of effective
delay for congestion
control schemes.

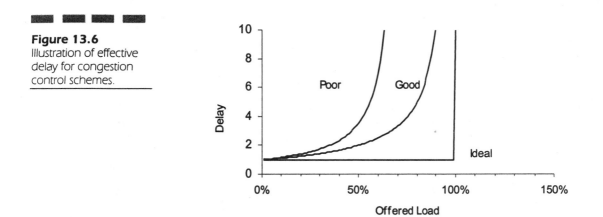

Figure 13.6
Illustration of effective
delay for congestion
control schemes.

system has bounded delay at all values of offered load up to 100 percent, at which point delay becomes infinite. A good congestion control protocol exhibits increased delay only as severe congestion occurs. A poor congestion control protocol has delay that increases markedly before the system reaches full utilization.

Clearly, achieving high throughput and low delay simultaneously is not possible. In order to optimize this tradeoff, traffic engineers devised the concept of queuing power [5]. Since the objective is to balance higher throughput while simultaneously achieving lower delay, queuing power is the following ratio:

$$\frac{\text{Queuing}}{\text{Power}} \equiv \frac{\text{Throughput}}{\text{Delay}}$$

Observe that queuing power trades off throughput against delay

Figure 13.7
Illustration of queuing
power for congestion
control schemes.

by comparing the ratio instead of absolute values. Figure 13.7 plots the queuing power for the ideal, good, and poor congestion control systems described above. The ideal system exhibits power that is optimal at 100 percent load. A good congestion control system has power that has an optimum value at a modest utilization level. A poor congestion control system has optimum power at a low utilization level. Hence, queuing power is a useful measure for comparing the relative performance of various congestion control schemes.

Retransmission Protocols

A commonly employed technique used in many computer communication networks to reliably transfer packet data uses the concept of error detection and retransmission, also called Automatic Repeat reQuest (ARQ) in classical work. This section introduces the basic concepts and techniques of this class of protocols.

Fixed Window Protocols

Figure 13.8 illustrates the basic concept of a fixed window retransmission protocol. A terminal on the left-hand side of the figure sends sequence numbered packets across a network. Because the network has delay, the sender transmits 3 packets at a time using a fixed-length window, and then stops before sending any more packets until it receives an acknowledgement. The receiver utilizes fields within the header to determine whether the packet is error-free, and then checks to ensure that the packet is the next in sequence. If the packet is error-free and in-sequence, then the receiver communicates this fact to the sender using an Acknowledgement packet ACK(0), as shown in the figure. The sender can then send another packet S(3), since it now has a free position in its fixed-size transmission window. This procedure repeats for packet S(1) and acknowledgement ACK(1), which results in the transmission of S(4).

If the network loses a packet (or the receiver detects an error), as shown by the line from the sender to the receiver with an X at the end for packet S(2), then the sender never receives an acknowledgement. Eventually, the sender times out and begins resending the last unacknowledged packet S(2). The example then repeats the same process described above, modeling the situation of a congested link within the packet network. Note that the sender transmits 5 packets,

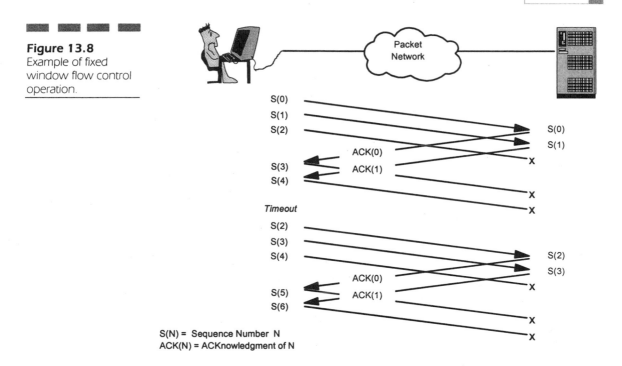

Figure 13.8
Example of fixed window flow control operation.

S(N) = Sequence Number N
ACK(N) = ACKnowledgment of N

however, the receiver successfully receives only 2 packets. Therefore, the effective throughput of this example is only 40 percent (i.e., 2/5). Chapter 14 studies the performance of fixed window type retransmission protocols.

IP's Transmission Control Protocol (TCP)

Figure 13.9 illustrates the version 4 TCP packet format as specified in RFC 793 [6] and RFC 1112 [7]. TCP employs the source and destination port numbers to identify a specific application program running in the source and destination hosts. The 16-bit port number in conjunction with the 32-bit host IP address comprise the 48-bit socket identifier. TCP uses a separate sequence number for each end of the session. The Sequence Number field identifies where the transmitted segment fits in relation to the other segments in this TCP session. The Acknowledgement Number field identifies the sequence number of the next byte expected at the receiver. The Data Offset field tells how many 32-bit words are in the TCP header. The default header length is five words, as shown in the figure. The code bits field contains six bits: URG, ACK, PSH, RST, SYN, and FIN. URG indicates that the Urgent Pointer is used. The ACK bit indicates that the Acknowledgement Number field is valid. The PSH (i.e., push) bit indicates that

Figure 13.9
TCP segment
format.

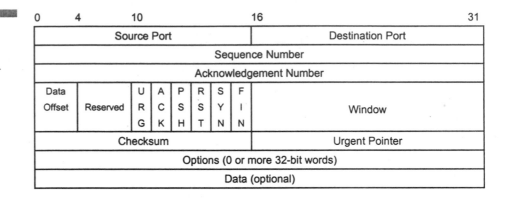

TCP should deliver the data to the destination port prior to filling an entire software buffer in the destination host. The RST bit indicates that the connection should be reset. TCP also uses the RST bit to reject invalid segments and refuse a connection attempt. TCP employs the SYN bit to establish connections and synchronize sequence numbers. The FIN bit releases a TCP connection. The 16-bit Window field identifies the amount of data the receiver is willing to accept, usually determined by the remaining buffer space in the destination host. The Checksum applied across the TCP header and the user data detects errors. The Urgent Pointer field specifies the position in the data segment where urgent data ends. The Options field is not mandatory, but provides additional functions, such as a larger window size field as specified in RFC 1323 [8]. Another popular option is selective retransmission as specified in RFC 1106 instead of the default go-back-N protocol — an important protocol difference that dramatically increases throughput on links with random bit errors or loss, as detailed in Chapter 14. The Options field may contain a padding field to align the TCP header to a 32-bit boundary for more efficient processing in hosts.

TCP is a connection-oriented protocol and therefore has additional, specific messages and a protocol for an application to request a distant connection, as well as a means for a destination to identify that it is ready to receive incoming connection requests.

TCP Slow-Start Congestion Control Protocol

TCP works over IP to achieve end-to-end reliable transmission of data. TCP flow control using a variable-length sliding window flow control protocol. The tuning and refinement of the TCP dynamic window flow control protocol has been the subject of a great deal of research.

The following example is a simple case of the Van Jacobson "Slow-Start" TCP algorithm [9, 10], an enhancement to the initial TCP implementation designed to dynamically maximize throughput and prevent congestion collapse. A TCP sender keeps track of a congestion window, which is never greater than the window size reported by the receiver in the TCP packet.

Figure 13.10 illustrates a simplified example of important concepts in the dynamic TCP window flow control protocol between a workstation and a server. The sender starts with a congestion window size equivalent to the length of one TCP packet, sends packet S(0), and then stops until it receives an acknowledgement. The IP network delivers S(0) to the destination server, which acknowledges receipt via the ACK(0) packet. The sending workstation then increases the congestion window size to two, sends packets S(1) and S(2), and stops again pending acknowledgement. When the destination acknowledges both of these segments, the sender increases the window size to four, doubling the window size for each received acknowledgment. At this point, congestion in the IP network causes loss of the fifth and sixth segments at this point (indicated in the figure by 'X's). The sender detects loss by starting a timer immediately after sending a packet. If the timer expires before the sender receives acknowledgement from the receiver, then the sender retransmits the packet. Upon such a re-

Figure 13.10
Example of TCP dynamic window flow control operation.

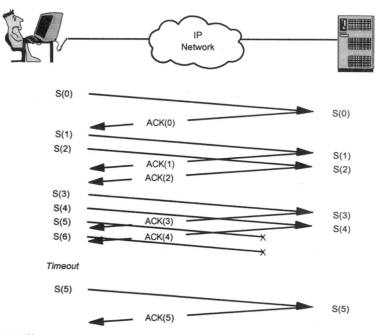

S(N) = TCP Segment N
ACK(N) = ACKnowledgment of N

transmission timeout, the sender resets its window size to one and begins the above process again. The time-out may be immediate, or typically, 500 milliseconds in an attempt to "piggyback" the acknowledgment onto another packet destined for the same TCP endpoint.

Note that TCP actually uses byte counts and not packet counts. Only if all packets are of the same size is our simple example accurate, but it illustrates the basic algorithm. Figure 13.11 illustrates the evolution of the TCP congestion window size versus time marked off in units of round-trip delay. Observe from the figure that TCP geometrically increases the window size (i.e., 1, 2, 4, 8, and so forth) during the initial startup phase. However, TCP congestion control has another function that limits the interval of geometric increase until the window size reaches a threshold of one-half the congestion window size achieved before the previous unacknowledged segment. After this point, TCP increases the congestion window by one segment for each round-trip time, instead of doubling it during the geometric growth phase as shown in the above example. This linear phase of TCP window growth is called *congestion avoidance*, while the geometric growth phase is called *slow start.*

Hence, during steady-state operation when there is a bottleneck in the IP network between the sender and the receiver, the congestion window size at the sender evolves according to a sawtooth-like pattern over time, as illustrated in Figure 13.11. This type of oscillating window behavior occurs when multiple TCP sources contend for a bottleneck resource in an IP network. Examples of such a bottleneck are a busy trunk connecting routers in the Internet or an access circuit connecting to a popular Web server. Since the World Wide Web's HTTP protocol runs over TCP, this phenomenon of oscillating throughput occurs during intervals of congestion on the Internet. Chapter 15 analyzes the performance of TCP slow start under con-

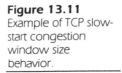

Figure 13.11
Example of TCP slow-start congestion window size behavior.

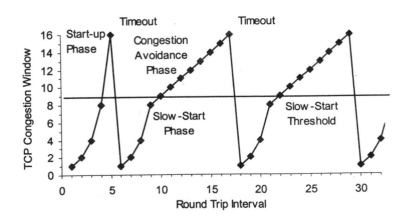

gested network conditions as a function of buffer size, round-trip delay, and number of connections.

TCP standard, RFC 2001 [9] describes further enhancements to TCP called *fast retransmit* and *fast recovery*. TCP generates a duplicate acknowledgment whenever it receives an out of order segment, since it is acknowledging the last byte received in sequence. Fast retransmit uses duplicate acknowledgements to detect a lost segment and attempts to avoid the throughput-robbing reduction of the congestion window size to one after a time-out by retransmitting only the lost segment. Fast recovery [11] follows after the transmitter sends the missing segment, reverting to the linear window size increase algorithm of congestion avoidance even if the transmitter is in the slow-start phase.

ATM's Available Bit Rate (ABR) Protocol

The ABR specification from the ATM Forum 4.0 specification [2] and ITU-T Recommendations I.371 [1] and I.371.1 [3] share a common goal: to make unused capacity available to cooperating end users in a fair, timely manner. Therefore, ABR targets the many existing applications with the ability to reduce their information transfer rate, such as TCP. As such, this objective goes well beyond that of today's best-effort LANs, where a single selfish, or "highly motivated," user can paralyze a shared network. If sources conform to the rules of ABR, then the network guarantees a Minimum Cell Rate (MCR) with minimal cell loss. The network may optionally penalize nonconforming sources, or enforce a policy that users not having transmitted recently lose any rights to access capacity at rates greater than MCR during periods of congestion.

On the other hand, TCP congestion control implicitly assumes everyone follows the same rules. For example, policing of TCP/IP conformance is limited to a professor's failing the graduate student who hacks the OS kernel to eliminate TCP's adaptive flow control and achieves markedly improved throughput at the expense of other TCP users sharing the same IP network. ABR's congestion control overcomes this problem by providing the means for an ATM switch to police users that do not conform to the mandated source behaviors. Hence, a rogue user who sends at a greater rate than that determined by the ABR protocol receives poorer performance than those ABR users that followed the rules. In the previous TCP scenario, the single rogue user achieves good performance while all the other honest users suffer. Hence, fairness is an important objective for any closed-loop congestion control protocol [13].

Although TCP sounds more like our daily lives and ABR seems to strive for a lofty, utopian goal, we now describe how ABR achieves fairly arbitrated congestion control. Let's begin by considering some simple analogies from everyday life that involve adaptive flow control.

ABR's binary mode is like the green/red lights at the entrance to congested freeways. The light turns green and another car (cell) enters the freeway (interface). Downstream sensors detect congestion and meter cars entering the freeway so that reasonable progress occurs. A police officer tickets vehicles that do not conform to this rule. By analogy, ATM switches indicate congestion using the EFCI bit in the ATM cell header in the forward direction. The destination end system employs a Congestion Indication (CI) field in a Resource Management (RM) cell in the backward direction to communicate the presence of congestion back to the source, which makes green-light/red-light type decisions regarding the source's current transmission rate. The recipient of the CI bit does not completely stop sending, but instead reduces its transmission rate by a fraction of the currently available cell rate.

The Explicit Rate (ER) mode of ABR operation adds another degree of complexity. Similar to the manner in which air traffic controllers control the speed of multiple airplanes (cells) converging on a crowded airport, ATM switches along the path of the end-to-end connection communicate an explicit rate for each source. In this way, the controller (RM cells) throttles back fast planes (user cells) during periods of congestion to yield a regular arrival pattern at the congested airport (interface).

The Virtual Source/Virtual Destination (VS/VD) mode is analogous to air traffic controllers and airline carriers coordinating the speed and route of aircraft (cells) as they approach airports (interfaces), making connections that maximize the number of seats filled — as well as customer satisfaction. Each airport-to-airport (virtual source-destination pair) route makes decisions with an awareness of congestion at other airports (other VS/VD pairs).

Of course, the details of ABR are more complex than these simple analogies; however, keeping these insights in mind may help the reader to grasp the essence of ABR as the following treatment proceeds into more abstract details. In a WAN environment, a key issue that a network ABR switch addresses is how to set the explicit rates to control the sources.

ABR specifies a rate-based, closed-loop flow control mechanism. A key objective of ABR is to fairly distribute the unused, or available, capacity to subscribing users while simultaneously achieving a low cell loss rate for all conforming ABR connections. All user data cells on ABR connections must have the CLP bit set to zero. The capacity allocated by the network to an ABR connection ranges between the Minimum Cell Rate (MCR) negotiated at connection establishment time and the Peak Cell Rate (PCR) depending upon network congestion and policy.

Users must conform to feedback provided via RM cells according to rules detailed in the ATM Forum's TM 4.0 specification [4]. ABR flow control occurs between a sending end system, called a *source*, and a receiving end system, called the *destination* connected via a bidirectional, point-to-point connection. Each of the terminals is both a source and a destination for each direction of an ABR connection. ABR specifies an information flow from the source to the destination composed of two RM flows, one in the forward direction and one in the backward direction, that make up a closed flow control loop. The forward direction is the flow from the source to the destination, and the backward direction is the flow from the destination to the source. In the following sections, we describe the information flow from the source to the destination and its associated RM flows for a single direction of an ABR connection; the procedures in the opposite directional are symmetrical, but may have different parameter values.

Binary Mode ABR

The binary mode, shown in Figure 13.12, involves ATM switching nodes setting EFCI in the forward direction so that the destination end station can set the CI field in a returned RM cell to control the

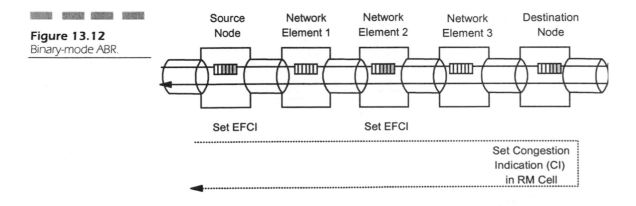

Figure 13.12
Binary-mode ABR.

flow of the sending end station. The binary mode ensures interoperability with older ATM switches which can only set the EFCI bit in the forward direction in response to congestion. This is the simplest mode; however, it experiences higher loss rates in certain situations, such as those where congestion occurs at multiple points in the network. Furthermore, unless the network elements perform per connection queuing, unfairness may result when sharing a single buffer.

The complexity in the end system rate control procedures compensates for the simple operation in the network in binary mode. An end system must tune over a dozen parameters to achieve good performance in this mode. The ATM Forum specification also defines a relative rate marking scheme using the Congestion Indication (CI) and No Increase (NI) bits in the RM cell to provide more granular adjustments of the source systems transmission rate.

Explicit Rate ABR

Figure 13.13 illustrates the Explicit Rate (ER) mode, where each Network Element (NE) explicitly sets the maximum allowed rate in RM cells looped back by the destination as they progress backward along the path to the source. The ATM Forum TM 4.0 specification gives examples of how switches may set the explicit rate in the feedback path in Informative Appendix I, leaving the implementation as a vendor-specific decision. Therefore, a key issue that a network ABR switch must address is how it to set the explicit rates to control the sources. The goal is that each user receives a fair allocation of avail-

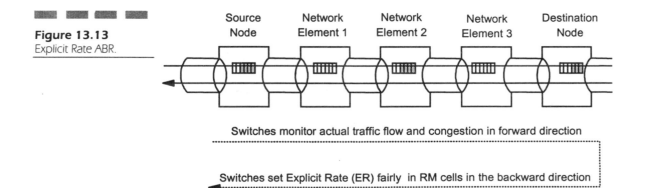

Figure 13.13
Explicit Rate ABR.

Figure 13.14
Virtual Source/Virtual
Destination (VS/VD)
ABR control loops.

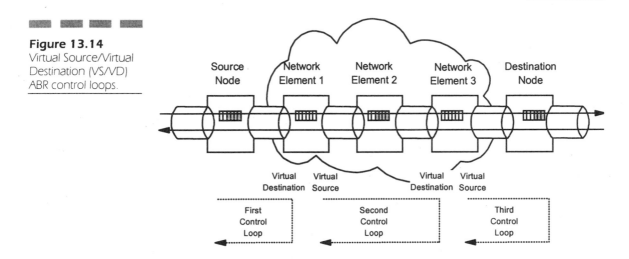

able capacity and buffer resources in proportion to their traffic contracts in a responsive manner. Simultaneously, the ABR service should operate at high utilization with negligible loss. This mode requires tuning of far fewer parameters, and hence is the preferred method in networks that are capable of supporting explicit rate ABR. Chapter 15 presents an analytical performance model that approximates ER ABR performance characteristics.

Virtual Source/Virtual Destination

Figure 13.14 illustrates an ABR virtual connection that incorporates segmentation using the concept of mated pairs of virtual sources and destinations. These sources and destinations form closed flow control loops across the sequence of network elements involved in an ATM ABR connection as shown in the figure.

A configuration where every switch on the path is a virtual source/destination is also called *hop-by-hop* flow control. The example in the figure shows the network elements using VS/VD mode to isolate the source and destination node control loops. The VS/VD scheme also provides a means for one network to isolate itself from nonconforming ABR behavior occurring in another network. On any network element, the virtual destination terminates the ABR control network for its corresponding source. The same device then originates the traffic on a virtual source for the next control loop that conforms to the end-to-end ABR traffic contract.

A Taxonomy of Congestion Control Approaches

Figure 13.15 depicts a taxonomy of congestion control approaches adapted from Reference 12. The first level of categorization is whether congestion control operates according to either an open-loop or closed-loop control system paradigm. Open-loop protocols include policing or fixed window retransmission schemes invoked at the source. At any node, open-loop schemes include priority service (e.g., weighted service, priority queuing, or selective discard. One specific open-loop control used in the Internet uses Random Early Detection (RED) of congestion. Chapter 14 covers these open-loop congestion control algorithms.

Moving to the right-hand branch of the tree, closed-loop control protocols have either explicit or implicit feedback. The premier example of a congestion control protocol employing implicit feedback is the Internet's Transmission Control Protocol (TCP). Under the class of algorithms employing explicit feedback, there are two subcategories: persistent and responsive. A persistent algorithm continuously generates feedback, while a responsive algorithm only generates feedback when congestion actually occurs. Either of these classes of algorithm may operate either locally or globally. The suite of ATM's Available Bit Rate (ABR) closed-loop flow control algorithms all operate using explicit feedback. Also, IP's source quench protocol is an example of an explicit feedback protocol operating locally. Chapter 15 analyzes the performance of closed-loop control algorithms.

Figure 13.15
A taxonomy of congestion control approaches.

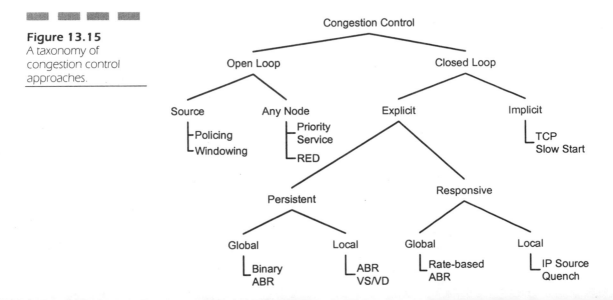

▬ ▬ ▬ Review

This chapter defined congestion via analogy with comparable phenomena in transportation and other waiting line systems. The text then gave the more precise definition of congestion as the event where offered load exceeds a bottleneck resource like buffer space or link capacity. Congestion occurs at multiple levels in time and space. In time, congestion occurs at the cell level, the packet level, or the burst level. In space, congestion occurs at a single node, multiple nodes, or across networks. We then gave examples of how congestion can occur at various points along a route. The chapter then extended this example to illustrate the two major types of response to congestion, namely, open-loop and closed-loop congestion control algorithms. The text gave a brief tutorial on the class of Automatic Repeat reQuest (ARQ) retransmission systems widely employed in computer communication networks. We defined the details of IP's Transmission Control Protocol (TCP) as background for the next two chapters. The text then summarized the operation of ATM's Available Bit Rate (ABR) closed-loop flow control protocol. The chapter concluded by categorizing congestion control schemes in terms of their general philosophy and approach. This resulted in a hierarchical taxonomy of the open- and closed-loop congestion control algorithms covered in Chapters 14 and 15.

▬ ▬ ▬ References

[1]   K. Thompson, G. Miller, R. Wilder, "Wide-Area Internet Traffic Patterns and Characteristics," *IEEE Network*, November/December 1997.

[2]   J. Hui, "Resource Allocation for Broadband Networks," *IEEE JSAC*, December 1988.

[3]   G. Awater, F. Schoute, "Optimal Queueing Policies for Fast Packet Switching of Mixed Traffic," *IEEE JSAC*, April 1991.

[4]   D. Hong, T. Suda, "Congestion Control and Prevention in ATM Networks," *IEEE Network Magazine*, July 1991.

[5]   R. Jain, K. Ramakrishnan, "Congestion Avoidance in Computer Networks with a Connectionless Network Layer: Concepts, Goals, and Methodology," Computer Networking Symposium, April 1988.

[6]   J. Postel, *Transmission Control Protocol*, RFC 793, IETF, September 1981.

[7]   R. Braden, *Requirements for Internet hosts - communication layers*, RFC 1122, October 1989.

[8]   V. Jacobson, R. Braden, D. Borman, *TCP Extensions for High Performance*, RFC 1323, May 1992.

[9] W. Stevens, *TCP Slow Start, Congestion Avoidance, Fast Retransmit, and Fast Recovery Algorithms*, RFC 2001, IETF, January 1997.

[10] M. Allman, V. Paxson , W. Stevens, *TCP Congestion Control*, RFC 2581, IETF, April 1999.

[11] S. Floyd , T. Henderson, *The NewReno Modification to TCP's Fast Recovery Algorithm*, RFC 2582, IETF, April 1999.

[12] C. Yang, A. Reddy, "A Taxonomy for Congestion Control Algorithms in Packet Switching Networks," *IEEE Network*, July/August 1995.

[13] S. Keshav, *An Engineering Approach to Computer Networking*, Addison-Wesley, 1998.

Open-Loop Congestion Control

"First, do no harm."

– Hippocrates

This chapter covers the subject of congestion control algorithms that operate without feedback regarding the current state of an end-to-end route. In other words, all information used to control traffic is statically preconfigured. The first class of algorithms analyzed is the policing and shaping functions introduced in Chapter 6. We summarize optimal delay and buffering bounds for a node with policed inputs. Next, the coverage moves to a simple performance analysis of open-loop fixed window size flow control techniques using commonly employed retransmission strategies. The text analyzes performance of these techniques in response to random and sustained loss.

Next, the chapter presents delay and loss performance results for a generic selective discard algorithm using a Markov Modulated Poisson Process (MMPP) model. Finally, the text describes the Random Early Detection (RED) congestion avoidance technique often employed by IP routers for TCP traffic.

Congestion Avoidance

Congestion avoidance attempts to ensure that the network never experiences congestion. For example, if we don't travel during rush hour, or wait until there are short lines for a particular service, we avoid congested times and places. Congestion avoidance protocols attempt to operate at the "knee" of the throughput versus load curve. This is analogous to life in the fast-paced modern world where we try to travel either just before or just after rush hour to avoid congestion.

Resource Allocation and Admission Control

The principal means that network designer employ to avoid congestion is proper resource allocation and the associated admission control. Resources subject to allocation and admission are:

- Physical transmission link capacity
- Buffer space
- Policing and shaping resources

The manner in which a network designer allocates resources to meet a balance between economic implementation cost and the degree of guaranteed QoS is an important decision. We studied the equivalent capacity model in Chapter 12 as a means to determine the maximum load supportable by a buffer served by a transmission link of a specified capacity to meet a particular loss objective. The resultant capacity was the minimum of that determined by a fluid flow model applied individually to each source and a statistical multiplexing model. The remainder of this section describes means to estimate the supportable load without loss for a router or switch with policed or shaped traffic inputs.

Closed Queuing System Model of a Shaper

One open-loop control mechanism that closely approximates the ideal throughput versus offered load curve studied in Chapter 13 is that of the shaper. As defined in Chapter 6, a simple token bucket traffic shaper implements the logic depicted in Figure 14.1. Starting from the left-hand side, arriving unshaped traffic enters a buffer of capacity b bits. If the buffer has insufficient space to admit the packet, it discards it. The decision logic checks to see if the number of tokens in

■ ■ ■ ■

Figure 14.1
Simple token bucket
shaper.

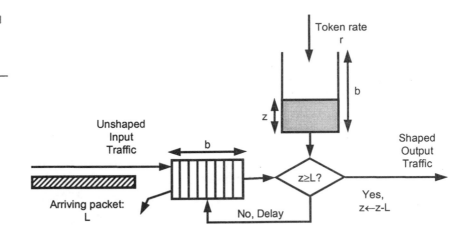

the bucket x is sufficient to admit the packet of length L bits. If not, the shaper delays the packet until there are sufficient tokens in the bucket. The token bucket fill rate is r token bits per seconds.

First, generalize the above shaper to operate in units of packets (or bursts). Then the buffer holds $X=b/L$ packets (or bursts) on average. Furthermore, consider tokens arriving at an average rate of $\mu=r/L$ packets (or bursts) per second to fill the bucket. We can then use the closed Markovian queuing system model depicted in Figure 14.2 to approximate the performance of this shaper [1]. The upper queue simulates arrivals occurring at a rate of λ packets (or bursts) per second. Note that arrivals can only occur if there are one or more packets in the queue. The lower queue simulates the operation of the token bucket shaper transmitting packets (or bursts) at an average rate of μ per second. This is only an approximation, since the actual packets (or bursts) may not have negative exponential distribution. At any point in time, the upper queue holds q_1 packets, while the lower queue contains q_2 packets. The constraint that $q_1+q_2=X$ models operation of the shaping buffer and token bucket. The throughput of the

■ ■ ■ ■

Figure 14.2
Closed queuing system
model of a simple
token bucket shaper.

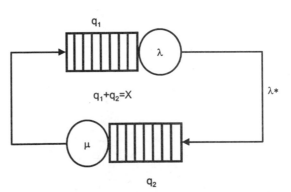

shaper given an offered load λ is the output of the upper queue, namely λ^{*}, which is:

$$\lambda^{*} = \lambda(1 - \pi_X)$$
(14-1)

where π_x is the probability that the upper queue is empty, or equivalently, the probability that the lower queue is full.

Note that the closed queuing system has a finite population X, and under the assumptions of Markovian arrival and service processes, the lower queue behaves as a M/M/1/X queuing system. From Table 11.1, the probability that such a queuing system is full is:

$$\pi_X = \frac{\rho^X (1-\rho)}{1-\rho^{X+1}}$$
(14-2)

where $\rho=\lambda/\mu$ is the offered load to the shaper.

Substituting Equation (14-2) into (14-1) and solving for the carried load ρ^{*} yields the following result:

$$\rho^{*} \equiv \frac{\lambda^{*}}{\mu} = \frac{\rho(1-\rho^X)}{1-\rho^{X+1}}$$

Figure 14.3 plots the carried load (i.e., effective throughput) ρ^{*} of the token bucket shaper versus values of offered load ρ for several values of the token bucket depth and shaping buffer capacity X. For comparison purposes, the figure also plots the ideal throughput versus load characteristic. Note how increasing the shaper's bucket/buffer

Figure 14.3
Carried load versus offered load for a simple token bucket shaper for various buffer sizes X.

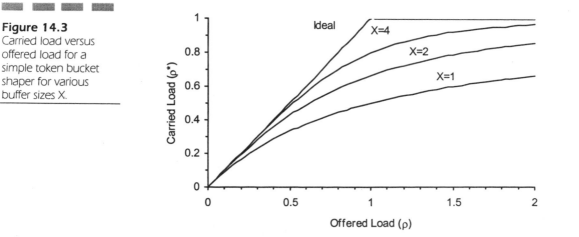

capacity X causes the throughput curve to approach the ideal characteristic. Of course, although the throughput approaches optimal values, delay also increases. Unfortunately, this simple model tells us nothing about the delay encountered by the original traffic stream arriving at rate λ.

Weighted Fair Queuing Model for Policing and Scheduling

As described in Chapter 6, policing acts as a traffic cop at the node connected to the user at the edge of the network and optionally at points where networks interconnect. Although IP and ATM employ different algorithms to define traffic policing parameters, they have similar semantics. In particular, we utilize the notation attributed to Cruz [2] of a token bucket regulator (or shaper) with token arrival rate r bps with a bucket depth of b bits. The following analysis does not include any delay encountered in the shaper.

Figure 14.4 depicts a nodal model of Packet-by-packet Generalized Processor Sharing (PGPS) commonly called Weighted Fair Queuing (WFQ) as defined by Parekh and Gallager [3], as introduced in Chapter 10. Starting on the left-hand side, N flows characterized by the traffic parameters r_i and b_i arrive to an individual queue Q_i via input links operating at a rate of R_i bps. A weighted scheduler services each queue at a proportion ϕ_i of the overall output link rate R of the node.

The net effect of the policing parameters is that the traffic delivered over an interval of time (0,T] by a conforming individual traffic stream $A_i(T)$ must satisfy the following inequality:

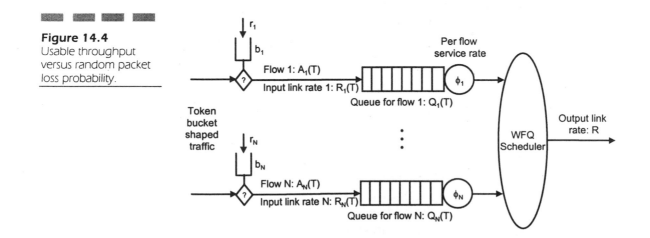

Figure 14.4
Usable throughput versus random packet loss probability.

$$A_i(T) \le b_i + \text{Min}[r_i T + L_i, R_i T]$$

where L_i is the maximum packet length for flow i.

Let $S_i(T)$ denote the amount of traffic served for flow i in a T second interval. The ϕ_i scheduling weights must be chosen to ensure that a backlogged flow i receives the following minimum guaranteed rate:

$$g_i \equiv \frac{S_i(T)}{T} \ge \frac{\phi_i}{\sum_{j=1}^{N} \phi_j} R \tag{14-3}$$

A feasible choice for the scheduling weights is $\phi_i = r_i$. Clearly, choice of the ϕ_i impacts the relative service rate, and hence the delay observed and the buffer space required by packet flow i. For example, choosing a value of ϕ_i such that $g_i > r_i$ results in lower delay for flow i. Of course, if a particular flow has no traffic, then the scheduler could serve other flows. If the only times when the link is idle is when there are no packets in queue, then we say that the scheduler is *work conserving*. In other words, a work-conserving scheduler must be busy if packets are waiting in the system [3].

Note that Equation (14-3) implies that the sum of the service rates across all of the backlogged queues be less than the link rate R in a stable system:

$$\sum_{i=1}^{N} g_i < R$$

For the case where the input links speeds are infinite (i.e., $R_i = \infty$) an important theoretical result from weighted fair queuing is that the worst case nodal delay Max[D_i] for traffic flow i shaped to the token bucket parameters (r_i ,b_i) is bounded by the following formula:

$$\text{Max}[D_i, \text{WFQ}] \le \frac{b_i}{r_i} + \frac{L_{max}}{R} \tag{14-4}$$

where $L_{max} \equiv$ the maximum packet length across all flows.

The first term of the above equation represents the worst-case delay specified the token bucket shaping parameters. Namely, a burst on flow i may have to wait for transmission until the last possible moment before the next burst arrives. The second term represents the impact of store and forward packet communication on delay when a long packet arrives just before the packet which the WFQ scheduler would have begun transmitting assuming ideal link sharing.

Although the proof of Equation (14-4) in References 3 and 4 is rather lengthy, simpler explanation results from considering the worst-case traffic pattern of an individual source introduced in Chapter 3. Basically, the maximum delay occurs under the worst-case arrival pattern, which turns out to be the case where all sources have been idle for a long time, and then begin transmitting all at once. Since source i can send no more than b_i bits in a burst, and the WFQ scheduler guarantees a service rate of r_i bps, Equation (14-4) applies for a bitwise WFQ scheduler. When operating with variable-length packets, the fact that the same result applies is not intuitive, but turns out to be true. Chapter 18 extends this nodal result to a network route.

This is a useful result since it bounds delay by the traffic parameters of the individual flow. Since WFQ effectively isolates the performance of each flow from every other one, we say it is fair. Note that WFQ does not minimize delay for higher-priority traffic. Instead, under conditions of heavy load it effectively serves each flow just in time to meet the conditions imposed by the token bucket parameters of an average rate of r_i bps and a bucket depth of b_i bits.

It is interesting to compare the performance of a lossless WFQ system with that of a Priority Queuing (PQ) system engineered to achieve a low loss probability, as described in Chapter 11. For a priority queuing system with buffer capacity B and link rate R, the maximum delay for a high-priority flow H is:

$$\text{Max}[D_H, PQ] \leq \frac{B}{R} + \frac{L_{max}}{R}$$

As described in Chapter 11, the required buffer capacity B (in units of the maximum burst size b_H) is a function of the loss probability ε and the offered load ρ. For the simplest case of Markovian traffic patterns, the ratio of the maximum delay for WFQ and PQ is approximately:

$$\frac{\text{Max}[D_i, WFQ]}{\text{Max}[D_H, PQ]} \approx \frac{R}{r_i} \frac{(1-\rho)}{-\ln(\varepsilon)}$$

Extension of the above result to self-similar traffic is a straightforward exercise using the buffer dimensioning techniques described in Chapter 11. The maximum delay ratio for WFQ and PQ has two terms. The first term is the ratio of the multiplexer link rate to the guaranteed source rate. The second term is a constant on the order of a fraction $-(1-\rho)/\ln(\varepsilon)$. Thus, sources with an average rate r_i on the order of a fraction of the link rate achieve comparable performance with

WFQ and PQ. Sources that have a rate on the order of the link rate achieve better performance with WFQ than PQ. Finally, sources with low average rates achieve better performance with PQ than with WFQ. Of course, a priority queuing system delivers better performance for higher-priority flows at the expense of poorer performance for lower-priority flows.

Note also that if the network element oversubscribes the outgoing link such that $\Sigma r_i > R$, then the WFQ bound on delay with zero loss does not apply, since loss may occur during periods of heavy load. In this case, the statistical methods described in Part 4 give estimates for delay and loss. As we study later in this chapter, a network element may employ an input policer and tag portions of non-compliant traffic flows instead of a traffic shaper as assumed for a WFQ system and still achieve good performance for the compliant portions of the traffic flows.

Buffering and Scheduling for Minimal Delay and Loss

If the user shapes traffic to a level less than or equal to that enforced by the policing function, then scheduling algorithms that deliver optimal delay with minimal buffer space exist [5]. Figure 14.5 depicts the interfaces and functions of a generic packet (or cell) multiplexer. On the left-hand side, a set of N token bucket shaped input streams feed the multiplexer. The memory block represents a set of buffer allocation designs A compared in the following. The multiplexer imple-

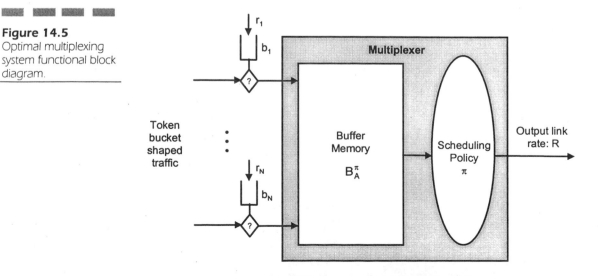

Figure 14.5
Optimal multiplexing system functional block diagram.

ments a scheduling policy π to assign packets from the inputs to the single outgoing link.

The analysis in Reference 5 compares the following three cases of buffer allocation design:

- Fixed Allocation (FI) — allocates a worst-case buffer to each flow
- Semi-Flexible Allocation (SE) — allocates a buffer to each flow using knowledge of the flow parameters (r_i, b_i)
- Flexible Allocation (FL) — implements a completely shared memory buffer

The symbol B_A^{π} represents the required buffer capacity for allocation method A under scheduling policy π. As would be expected, the buffer requirement decreases as the flexibility of the scheduling policy increases, namely:

$$B_{FI}^{\pi} \geq B_{SE}^{\pi} \geq B_{FL}^{\pi}$$

Of course, the price paid for better buffer utilization is increased scheduling policy complexity. The scheduling policies considered in Reference 5 are a Non-Preemptive Earliest Deadline First (NPEDF) and a Tracking policy based upon Preemptive Earliest Deadline First (T(PEDF)). These are more general policies than GPS or WFQ. Choosing a policy π* that minimizes buffer space yet still results in bounded optimal delay results in the following inequalities for each of the buffer allocation methods. First, for the fixed allocation case (FI), the required buffer capacity is $O(N^2)$ as follows:

$$B_{FI}^{\pi^{*}} \geq N^2 L_{max} + N \sum_{i=1}^{N} b_i \qquad (14\text{-}5)$$

where L_{max} is the maximum packet size across all flows.

The T(PEDF) policy results in a buffer allocation requirement for a minimized semi-flexible (SE) buffer allocation as follows:

$$B_{SE}^{\pi^{*}} \leq 2NL_{max} + 2 \sum_{i=1}^{N} b_i \qquad (14\text{-}6)$$

Finally, any work-conserving service policy achieves the following performance for a full flexible (FL) buffer allocation strategy:

$$B_{FL}^{\pi^{*}} \leq NL_{max} + \sum_{i=1}^{N} b_i \qquad (14\text{-}7)$$

Figure 14.6
*Relative buffer
requirements for an
optimal multiplexing
system with various
buffer allocation
strategies.*

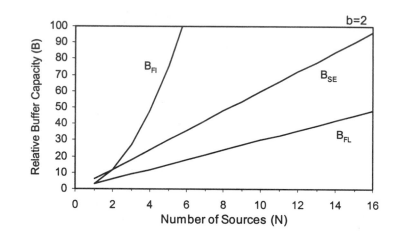

Note that the buffer requirement of a fully flexible system is half that of a semi-flexible system, but is considerably harder to implement than a semi-flexible allocation method. Figure 14.6 illustrates the relative buffer requirements for fixed (FI), semi-flexible (SE), and fully flexible (FL) allocation methods by setting $b_i=b$ and $L_{max}=1$ in Equations (14-5), (14-6), and (14-7). Effectively, this selection of parameters equates the units of buffer capacity to the maximum packet size, Lmax. That is, the units of the parameter b are equivalent to a burst of maximal-length packets. The plot in the figure assumes that the token bucket burst parameter b=2. The inefficient use of buffers via a fixed allocation policy is evident in this plot. Furthermore, the relatively small improvement of fully flexible allocation versus semi-flexible allocation is also clear.

Performance of Selective Discard

IP routers and ATM switches can recover from congestion by selectively discarding traffic. This section covers the following examples of congestion recovery:

- Selective Discard of Lower-Priority Traffic
- Early/Partial Packet Discard (EPD/PPD)
- Random Early Detection

Identifying Lower-Priority Traffic

As studied in Chapter 6, policing allows the ingress network node to either discard traffic that fails to conform to the traffic parameters, or else mark non-conforming traffic at a lower priority. The ATM cell header used the Cell Loss Priority (CLP) bit to indicate whether a cell is of high priority (CLP=0) or low priority (CLP=1). The IP diffserv standard allows implementations to selectively mark non-conforming packets. The experimental field in the MPLS header may also support selective tagging of non-conforming packets. Additionally, the IP integrated services architecture document [6] recommends tagging non-conforming packets if such a means is available.

Selective discard gives preferential treatment to higher-priority cells or packets over lower-priority cells or packets during periods of congestion. ATM Standards define selective cell discard as the mechanism where the network may discard lower-priority flows while meeting Quality of Service (QoS) for higher-priority flows. In ATM, selective discard is an important standardized network equipment function for recovering from severe congestion. The network may use selective discard to ensure that compliant flows receive a guaranteed QoS. If the network is not congested, then the network may provide higher throughput by also transferring non-compliant traffic, but never less than the reserved amount.

The application may also tag packets or cells as lower priority if it considers them to be of lesser importance. However, user tagged packets or cells create an ambiguity because intermediate network nodes have no way to discern whether the user or the network policer

Figure 14.7
Illustration of selective
cell discard function.

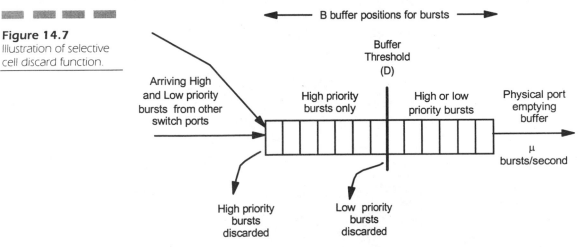

set the priority indication. If the user sets the priority indication, and the network policer performs tagging, then it may not be possible to guarantee a loss probability for low-priority flows.

Figure 14.7 shows an example implementation of the selective discard mechanism. The router or switch fills a single buffer having B burst positions with high- and low-priority bursts arriving from the left. The physical layer empties the buffer at a rate of μ bursts per second from the right. When clumps of arrivals occur from other ports, the buffer becomes congested. One simple way of implementing selective discard is to set a threshold above which the port discards any incoming low-priority traffic, but still admits high-priority traffic. Note that high-priority traffic may occupy any buffer position, while low-priority traffic may only occupy the portion of the buffer to the right of the threshold as indicated in the figure. Therefore, by controlling the buffer threshold, the network controls low-priority loss performance. A refinement of this idea involves flushing out low-priority traffic after crossing another threshold [7].

Discard Threshold Performance Model

This section presents a tractable, Markovian model of a buffer resource control strategy that models the selective discard congestion recovery method described above. Figure 14.8 shows the state transition rate diagram for a model of a buffer with a threshold. This is similar to the M/M/1/B Markovian model analyzed in Chapter 11, but with a change in the state transition rate coefficients at the discard threshold D. The high- and low-priority burst arrival processes are Markovian with arrival rates of λ_1 and λ_2 respectively. All bursts have an negative exponentially distributed distribution with average service time of μ^{-1} as determined by the burst size and the port interface speed.

In the following, we denote the total load as $\omega=(\lambda_1+\lambda_2)/\mu$. The fraction of the load that is high priority is defined as $x=\lambda_1/(\lambda_1+\lambda_2)$, which means that the high-priority load is $x\omega$. Applying the flow balance technique from Chapter 9 yields the following steady-state solution

Figure 14.8
Priority discard
Markovian queuing
system model.

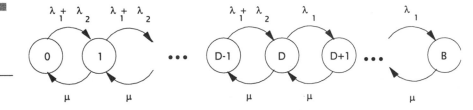

for the Markov chain of Figure 14.8 for the probability that k bursts are in the buffer:

$$\pi_k = \begin{cases} \omega^k \pi_0 & ,0 \le k \le D \\ \omega^k x^{k-D} \pi_0 & ,D < k \le B \end{cases}$$

Enlisting the closed form expressions for finite geometric series, the normalizing constant π_0 is:

$$\pi_0 = \left[F(\omega,D) + \omega^D \; F(x\omega, B+1-D) \right]^{-1}$$

where $\quad F(z,N) = \displaystyle\sum_{i=0}^{N-1} z^i = \begin{cases} \dfrac{1-z^N}{1-z} & ,z < 1 \\ N & ,z = 1 \\ \dfrac{z^N - 1}{z-1} & ,z > 1 \end{cases}$

By definition, the probability of loss for the high-priority traffic ε_1 is the probability that the buffer is full, namely:

$$\varepsilon_1 = \pi_B = \omega^B x^{B-D} \pi_0$$

Similarly, the probability of loss for the low priority traffic ε_2 is the probability that the buffer contains D or more bursts as follows:

$$\varepsilon_2 = \sum_{i=D}^{B} \pi_i = \omega^D \pi_0 F(x\omega, B+1-D)$$

After some algebraic manipulation, the closed-form expression for the average number of frames in queue $E(n) = \displaystyle\sum_{n=0}^{B} n\pi_n$ results:

$$E(n) = \pi_0 \left\{ G(\omega, D+1) + \omega^{D+1} x \; \left[G(x\omega, B-D) + (D+1)F(x\omega, B-D) \right] \right.$$

where $G(z,N) = \displaystyle\sum_{i=0}^{N-1} iz^i = \begin{cases} \dfrac{z + z^N[(N-1)z - N]}{(1-z)^2} & ,z < 1 \\ \dfrac{N(N-1)}{2} & ,z = 1 \\ \dfrac{z + z^N[z(N-1) - N]}{(z-1)^2} & ,z > 1 \end{cases}$

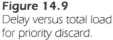

Figure 14.9
Delay versus total load
for priority discard.

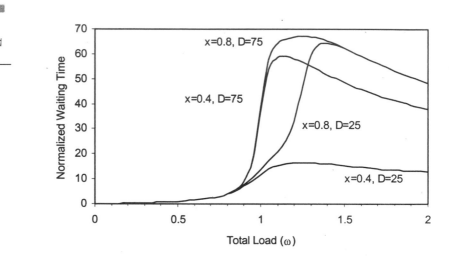

Let's look at some numerical examples. The above formulas are straightforwardly coded as spreadsheet macros to obtain results like those shown in the plots below. The buffer size is B=100 packets, or bursts in the following examples. Figure 14.9 plots the normalized average waiting time for the thresholded discard queuing system versus total load ω for values of the fraction of high-priority traffic x of 40 percent and 80 percent for a buffer threshold D of 25 and 75. For a high-priority load fraction of 40 percent (x=0.4) note how the threshold D limits the average delay for very high loads by discarding the lower-priority traffic. For a high-priority load fraction of 80 percent (x=0.8) the discard threshold does not have as much of an effect because the majority of the traffic is high priority. After a total load of ω=1.25, where xω=1, the average delay approaches the threshold size because the buffer is full most of the time. Therefore, the region of design interest focuses around the region between the points where total load is slightly below to slightly over 100 percent.

Figure 14.10 illustrates the normalized average waiting time for the priority discard system versus the fraction of the load x that is high priority x. The curves correspond to a total load ω of 95 percent and 105 percent for buffer thresholds D of 25 and 75 with a buffer size B=100. For a total load of 95 percent, the average waiting time is largely independent of the discard threshold. On the other hand, when the system is in overload with total load of 105 percent, the discard threshold has a profound effect on limiting average waiting time. However, as the fraction of high-priority traffic increases toward 100 percent, waiting time converges towards a common value determined by the discard threshold D.

Figure 14.10

Delay versus fraction of
high-priority traffic.

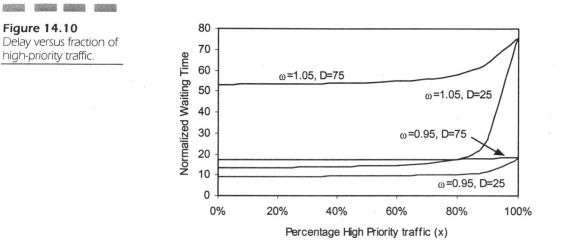

Figure 14.10

Delay versus fraction of
high-priority traffic.

Figure 14.11 illustrates the loss priority for the high-priority and low-priority traffic as ε_1 and ε_2 respectively versus the buffer threshold D for a fraction of high-priority traffic x and total load ω selected to yield a total high-priority load of $x\omega\approx75$ percent, as indicated on the figure. For both cases of total offered load (ω) the high-priority traffic loss probability ε_1 increases, while the low-priority traffic loss probability ε_2 decreases as the buffer threshold D increases. This makes sense because the increased threshold allows more traffic into the buffer.

Usually, a loss objective for the high-priority traffic determines a maximum value of the buffer threshold D. For example, a discard threshold of D=75 yields a loss probability ε_1 of approximately 10^{-6}. A smaller threshold is feasible if it still meets the loss probability objec-

Figure 14.11

Loss by priority versus
buffer threshold.

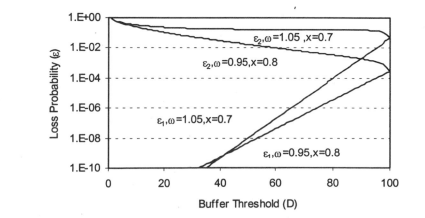

tive for low-priority traffic, which results in a lower average number in the system and hence lower delay. For example, a threshold of D=50 reduces ε_1 to approximately 10^{-9}, but ε_2 increases to approximately 10 percent.

These results demonstrate how selective discard acts as a congestion recovery mechanism in an overloaded state by selectively discarding lower-priority traffic. In extreme overload situations (i.e., $x\omega>1$) even high-priority traffic is lost, and other congestion recovery mechanisms must be employed.

Early/Partial Packet Discard (EPD/PPD)

Typically, the loss of a single cell results in the ATM Adaptation Layer 5 (AAL5) Segmentation and Reassembly (SAR) process losing an entire packet. A number of studies and tests show that a more effective reaction to congestion is to discard at the frame level rather than at the cell level [8, 9]. Therefore, the ATM Forum TM 4.0 specification specifies an intelligent frame discard function as an optional congestion recovery procedure. The situation where intelligent frame discard helps the most occurs when many sources congest a particular resource, such as an output queue on an ATM switch serving a heavily utilized link. Significant performance degradation occurs when a network element discards cells that are portions of many packets. The objective of intelligent frame discard is to maximize the number of complete packets transferred.

An ATM device may treat user data as frames only if the user indicates so in a signaling message or at PVC subscription time. Once the user negotiates frame level discard service with the network using either of these means, the ATM switches use the Payload Type Indicator (PTI) in the ATM cells to detect the last cell of an AAL5 PDU. The commonly used industry terminology for the intelligent frame discard capability is the following two actions:

- Early Packet Discard (EPD) occurs when a device in a congested state discards every cell from an AAL5 PDU. EPD prevents cells from entering the buffer, reserving remaining buffer capacity for the cells from packets already admitted to the buffer.
- Partial Packet Discard (PPD) occurs when a device discards all remaining cells, except the last one, when it discards a cell in the middle (i.e., not the first or last cell) of an AAL5 packet. PPD acts when some cells from a packet have already been admitted to the buffer.

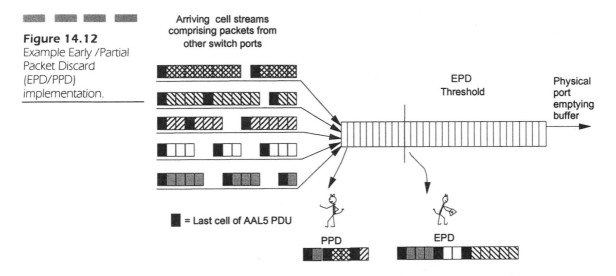

Figure 14.12
Example Early /Partial Packet Discard (EPD/PPD) implementation.

Figure 14.12 shows a representative implementation of EPD/PPD using a single shared buffer. Cells from multiple frame level sources arrive at the switch buffer from other ports on the switch, as indicated on the left hand side of the figure. Once the buffer level exceeds the EPD threshold, the EPD gremlin selectively discards cells from entire frames. Once the buffer reaches capacity, or some other discard action occurs, such as selective cell discard dropping a CLP=1 cell within a frame, the PPD gremlin takes over, discarding the remaining cells of the frame. PPD improves overall throughput because if the network loses even one cell from a frame, the end user loses the entire frame. For example, a maximum size Ethernet data frame of 1500 bytes requires 32 cells. When applied in the context where many sources contend for a common resource, EPD/PPD can improve useable throughput significantly on ATM interfaces in routers and switches.

Fixed Window Retransmission Protocols

Loss is an enemy of data communication protocols. Many protocols utilize error detection and retransmission to combat loss. This section describes the operation of these protocols and analyzes the performance in typical network environments.

Strategies — Go-Back-N and Selective Reject

Loss or excessive delay results in a time-out or negative acknowledgment in a higher-layer protocol (e.g., TCP), which then retransmits one or more packets. Therefore, operation of retransmission protocols over networks with loss or excessive delay can result in significant performance degradation. First, capacity usage becomes less efficient because the protocol must send some packets multiple times. Second, delay increases markedly when the sender retransmits data only after a long round-trip delay time. Finally, either additional retransmission or buffering at the receiver is necessary to ensure in-sequence delivery of packets to the higher-layer application.

Higher-layer protocols recover from detected errors, or time-outs, by one of two basic methods, called Go-Back-N and selective reject. The *Go-Back-N* strategy retransmits the packet that resulted in the detected error or time-out followed by all other packets sent afterwards. If the transmitter has sent N packets upon detecting a lost packet or time-out; then it must retransmit these same N packets again, hence the name Go-Back-N. The technical literature sometimes calls this approach a cumulative acknowledgment strategy.

The *selective reject* strategy retransmits only those packets that were actually lost or timed out. Obviously, this is superior to the Go-Back-N strategy that potentially retransmits packets that the destination already received correctly, since the transmitter resends only the selectively rejected packets. On the other hand, this method requires greater complexity in the receiver and sender protocols. First, the higher-layer protocol must explicitly identify the lost or timed-out packet. Second, the receiver must buffer all received packets and only deliver them to a higher-layer application only after selective retransmission fills in any gaps in the original sequence. Standards call this a selective reject, selective retransmission, or selective acknowledgment strategy. The ATM Service Specific Connection Oriented Protocol (SSCOP) details a sophisticated selective reject algorithm [10]. The IETF defines optional selective acknowledgment strategy as extensions to TCP [11] in support of communication over long delay paths; however, few implementations support it.

Figure 14.13 presents space-time diagrams for the Go-Back-N and selective reject retransmission strategies. Figure 14.13a shows a Go-Back-N example where a sender transmits sequence numbered packets to a receiver over a network with a one-way delay of τ seconds. In the example, the network successfully transfers packets numbered 0 and 1, but loses packet number 2, as indicated via the dashed line in the figure. Since the round-trip delay 2τ is relatively long with respect to the packet transmission time T, the sender continues operating in the absence of any feedback by sending packets 3 and 4. The receiver sends packets acknowledging the receipt of packets 0 and 1, as shown via the ACK messages, but sends no further acknowledgements, since it never receives packet 2, and packets 3 and 4 are received out of sequence. Eventually, the sender times out at some point after the expected arrival of an ACK for packet 2. At this point, the sender goes back 3 packets, resending the time-out-generating packet 2 and all unacknowledged packets sent afterwards, namely packets 3 and 4 in our example. Fortunately, the network delivers both packets 2, 3, and 4 to the receiver, which acknowledges their receipt.

Figure 14.13b shows a similar example using the selective-reject protocol. The example begins as before with the network successfully delivering packets 0 and 1, but losing packet 2, but now things are different. When the receiver successfully gets packet 3, it recognizes a gap in the sequence, namely that packet 2 is missing. The receiver communicates this information to the sender in a Selective REJect (SREJ) message that communicates the identity of the missing packet(s). While the SREJ message returns to the sender, the receiver gets packet 4 and stores it in its buffer of unsequenced packets along with packet 3. Upon receipt of the SREJ message, the sender then only sends the missing packet(s), namely packet 2 in this example. Note that the receiver then acknowledges the latest sequence number

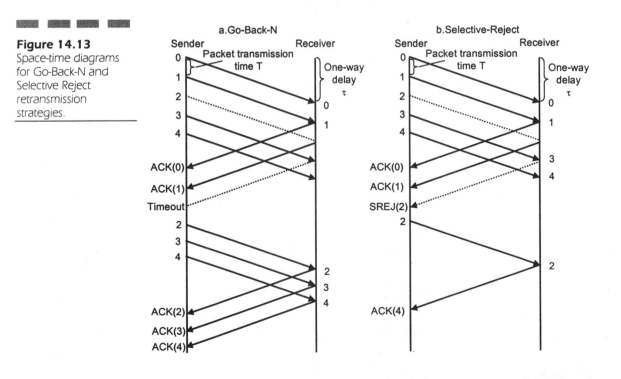

Figure 14.13

Space-time diagrams for Go-Back-N and Selective Reject retransmission strategies.

of all packets received so far, in this case packet 4.

In this simple example, the Go-Back-N strategy required the sender to transmit 8 packets to deliver 5 packets to the receiver achieving an effective throughput of 62.5 percent. On the other hand, the selective reject approach required that the sender only transmit 6 packets to deliver the same 5 packets to the receiver, achieving an effective throughput of 83.3 percent. Furthermore, selective reject delivered these 5 packets in less elapsed time. Let's look at how well these two retransmission strategies perform in the face of typical loss patterns experienced in IP and ATM networks.

Performance with Random Loss

The classical analysis of retransmission protocols assumes that lost packets occur randomly with probability π. Typically, these analyses assume that the source of packet loss is due to random errors corrupting the received packet. The analysis also applies to networks that lose packets randomly in an uncorrelated manner.

Observe that packets transferred from the sender to the receiver experience a one-way delay τ, followed by acknowledgements of these same packets arriving at the receiver τ seconds later. Since it takes $8P/R$ seconds to transmit a P byte packet at R bps, the maximum window of packets (of length P) that can be sent before receiving an acknowledgement is:

$$W_{max} \equiv \frac{\text{Round} - \text{trip delay}}{\text{Packet transmit time}} = \frac{2\tau}{8P/R} \qquad (14\text{-}8)$$

If a sender's packet transmit window is less than W_{max}, then throughput must be less than 100 percent since the sender must stop and wait for acknowledgements before proceeding. In the example of Figure 14.13, W_{max} is approximately 10 packets. The following analysis assumes a greedy sender. That is, the sender continues sending packets up to its fixed unacknowledged packet window size W.

In the Go-Back-N strategy, if a single packet is in error at the beginning of a window of W packets, then the sender must retransmit the entire window of W packets. For the Go-Back-N retransmission strategy, the effective throughput η(Go-Back-N) is approximately the inverse of the average number of times the entire window must be resent, which is approximately [12, 13]:

$$\eta(\text{Go Back N}) \approx \begin{cases} \dfrac{1-\pi}{1+\pi W} & W \geq W_{max} \\[4mm] \dfrac{W(1-\pi)}{(W_{max}+1)(1-\pi(W-1))} & W < W_{max} \end{cases}$$

In the selective-reject retransmission strategy, if a single packet is in error, then the sender retransmits only that packet. For the selective reject retransmission strategy, the usable throughput η(Selective Reject) is approximately the inverse of the average number of times any individual packet must be sent, which is [12, 13]:

$$\eta(\text{Selective Reject}) \approx \begin{cases} 1-\pi & W \geq W_{max} \\[2mm] \dfrac{W(1-\pi)}{W_{max}+1} & W < W_{max} \end{cases}$$

The above formula applies to more-sophisticated protocols that can retransmit multiple packets within a round-trip delay interval, such as ATM's Service Specific Connection Oriented Protocol (SSCOP) [10] used for reliable transport of signaling messages and high-performance satellite links. The factor $W/(W_{max}+1)$ in the above formulas accounts for the fact that senders with window size W smaller than the value W_{max} required for maximum throughput experience proportionately lower effective throughput.

Figure 14.14 plots the effective throughput η for Go-Back-N and selective reject retransmission strategies for an OC3/STM-1 rate R of 150 Mbps, a packet size P of 1500 bytes, and a one-way delay τ equal to 30 ms. The resulting maximum window size W_{max} is approximately 1500 packets, as seen from Equation (14-8). Both retransmission protocols have nearly 100 percent usable throughput up to a packet loss rate of

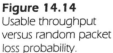

Figure 14.14
Usable throughput versus random packet loss probability.

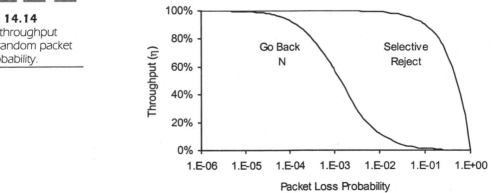

10^{-5}. As the loss rate increases, however, the effective throughput of the Go-Back-N protocol decreases markedly because the probability that an individual window is error free decreases markedly. As the loss rate increases above 10 percent, the probability of individual packet loss dominates the overall performance, and the selective reject protocol's effective throughput falls off as well.

These examples illustrate the importance of the QoS loss parameter on acceptable effective throughput η. Since most IP Transmission Control Protocol (TCP) implementations use a Go-Back-N type of protocol, low loss rates due to errors are essential to good performance. However, errors are only one source of loss. In fact, on fiber optic networks, loss due to errors is a relatively rare occurrence. The next section examines retransmission strategy performance in the face of a more commonly encountered situation, namely congestion.

Performance with Resource Contention

As we have seen, when multiple flows converge at a port in an IP or ATM node, congestion can occur. When the flows employ a window-based retransmission strategy, interesting things happen in response to overload conditions that result in buffer overflow on a router or switch port. Figure 14.15 presents a simple model of N sources, each with a fixed window size W_i sending packets to a network node, which has a finite buffer of capacity B. The sources all send at the same rate R. The node's transmission link also drains the buffer at rate R. The one-way propagation delay from each source to the network node is τ seconds. Note that the units of W_i, B, and R must be consistent. An example choice of units is bits for W_i and B and bits per second for R. Another convenient choice of units is the average number of packets for W_i and B and packets per second for R.

In the interest of simplicity in the following analysis, we assume that $W_i = W$ for all sources. An important parameter in the perform-

Figure 14.15
Retransmission performance model under overload conditions.

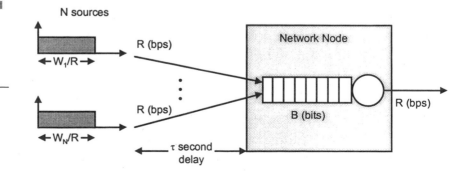

ance of window flow control protocols is bandwidth-delay product defined as

$$\Gamma \equiv 2R\tau$$

Since the minimum round-trip delay is 2τ, maximum throughput occurs only if $W \geq \Gamma/N$ bits.

The specification of the problem is still incomplete. The additional information needed is the relative transmission time and patterns for each source. We consider two cases that bound the performance of the entire range of scenarios. First, in the best-case scenario of Figure 14.16a, we assume a uniform distribution of transmission start times across the entire 2τ second interval. This choice of transmission starting times minimizes overlap, and hence minimizes the amount of traffic that builds up in the buffer. If the sum of the source window sizes (NW) exceeds the optimal value Γ, then the buffer will overflow, as shown in the figure. If $W=\Gamma/N$, then the sources never interfere and no traffic ever accumulates in the buffer. Note that in this scenario, the buffer overflow impacts only those sources that transmitted later in the round-trip delay cycle. Thus, the sources that transmitted earliest achieve maximum throughput, while the later transmitting sources receive no throughput.

The second scenario depicted in Figure 14.16b is the worst-case. This occurs when all sources begin sending their windows at the same time.

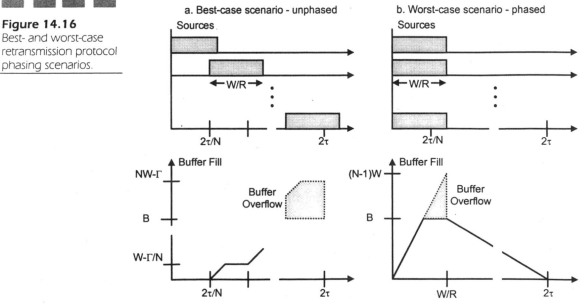

Figure 14.16
Best- and worst-case retransmission protocol phasing scenarios.

Typically, the literature refers to this alignment of senders as *synchronization*, or *phasing* [14]. Here, the buffer drain rate is no match for the sustained overload, and hence rapidly fills, and overflows if $W>2\tau/N$, as shown in the figure. However, in this case the buffer overflow impacts traffic from multiple flows. Since the last sequence of packets is lost from every flow, the Go-Back-N and selective-reject retransmission strategies would perform equivalently. Fortunately, the sources all stop sending at the same time, and the buffer has some time to drain. Note that if the traffic patterns cause backlog in the buffer, then the round-trip delay that sources experience waiting for acknowledgements also increases.

Other scenarios with other phasing of the sources and even transmission at less than the line rate R are feasible. However, as demonstrated by these examples, the choice of optimal window and buffer size depends upon not only the propagation delay τ, the transmission rate R, and the number of sources N, but on the phasing of the sources themselves. Hence, optimal selection of a fixed window size is a viable congestion control technique only in a simple, static network. Of course, there is a better way — dynamically control the window size, an approach that the next chapter explores.

Phasing has a significant impact on the buffer required to achieve maximum throughput without loss. Examining the plot of 14.16a, the fraction of traffic lost is:

$$\text{Loss(unphased)} = \begin{cases} \dfrac{NW - \Gamma - B}{NW} & B \le NW - \Gamma \\ 0 & \text{otherwise} \end{cases}$$

Thus, lossless operation occurs for unphased sources if $B \ge NW-\Gamma$. Similarly, for phased sources, the fraction of traffic lost for phased sources is easily computed from Figure 14.16b as follows:

$$\text{Loss(phased)} = \frac{NW - B}{NW}$$

The buffer requirement for lossless operation with phased sources increase by Γ to NW in this case. This occurs because the uniform distribution in time for the unphased sources makes the bandwidth-delay product Γ act as additional buffering capacity. Since phasing makes such a marked difference in required buffer capacity and the resulting variation in delay, avoiding phasing has been an important area of optimization in dynamic congestion control algorithm design.

Random Early Detection (RED)

As the two scenarios for fixed window congestion control in the previous section illustrated, a first come, first served strategy does not always result in a fair distribution of throughput across all user flows. Furthermore, when operating with automatically adjusted window sizes the phenomenon of synchronization or phasing occurs all too frequently in real IP networks. In order to avoid congestion at router or switch ports, researchers at Berkeley invented an algorithm called Random Early Detection (RED) [15]. The objective of this algorithm was to fairly distribute the effects of congestion across multiple user flows competing for a congested resource.

Figure 14.17 illustrates the operation of the basic RED algorithm defined in Reference 15. On the right-hand side, a transmission link serves a buffer that has two thresholds: min and max. The node keeps a low-pass filtered average using the current queue length q by implementing the calculation shown in the lower right-hand corner with the parameter x<1 controlling how much past memory the average retains. Before admitting arriving packets to the buffer, the node first performs a series of tests. If the low-pass average is less than the minimum threshold, then the node admits the packet. If the average exceeds the maximum threshold, then the nodes discards every incoming packet, and hence avoids buffer overflow. Finally, if the average is between the minimum and maximum thresholds, the node randomly drops (or marks as a lower priority) selected packets with the following probability:

$$\Pr[\text{drop}] \;=\; p_{max}\,\frac{avg - min}{max - min}$$

were p_{max} is the maximum drop probability.

Other refinements and enhancements of the RED algorithm include dropping all packets from a randomly identified flow, imple-

Figure 14.17
Random Early
Detection (RED)
algorithm operation.

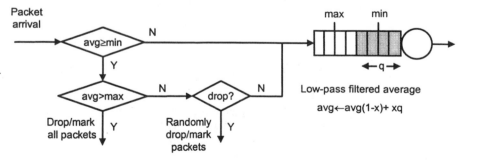

menting thresholds on a per-flow basis, and weighting the drop probability based upon prioritization across different flows. For more information, see the papers cited in Reference 16. Of course, RED applies only to dynamic window flow controlled protocols like TCP.

Review

This chapter analyzed the approaches to avoiding congestion based upon knowledge of the traffic obtained beforehand. Since this class of algorithms does not employ feedback regarding actual network state, we called them open-loop congestion control techniques. First is the use of policing and shaping first introduced in Chapters 3 and 6. We summarized the important results from Weighted Fair Queuing (WFQ) regarding bounded delay without loss for policed inputs presented to a network node. The text then compared the performance of WFQ with that of priority and FIFO queuing.

Next, the chapter covered another method of avoiding congestion when traffic of different priorities overloads a network resource. We presented a simple Markovian model for selective discard that predicts the loss and delay performance for a thresholded buffer serving high- and low-priority traffic. This method applies to sources that have prioritized traffic, either marked by policers at network ingress, or marked via applications like video.

Finally, the text delved further into the operation of retransmission protocols that employ a fixed window size. We summarized the classical results of Automatic Repeat reQuest (ARQ) protocol performance in the face of random errors or loss. The text then considered what happens to ARQ protocols when a number of sources contend for a common buffer resource. The next chapter continues this thread when analyzing TCP's dynamic windowed flow control protocol. Finally, the chapter concluded with a description of a congestion avoidance technique commonly employed by IP routers called Random Early Detection (RED).

References

[1]   M. Schwartz, *Broadband Integrated Networks*, Prentice-Hall, 1996.

[2]   R. Cruz, "A Calculus for Network Delay, Part I: Network Elements in Isolation," *IEEE Transactions on Information Theory*, January 1991.

[3]   A. Parekh, R. Gallager, "A Generalized Processor Sharing Approach to Flow Control in Integrated Services Networks: The Single-Node Case," *IEEE/ACM Transactions on Networking*, June 1993.

[4]   A. Parekh, R. Gallager, "A Generalized Processor Sharing Approach to Flow Control in Integrated Services Networks: The Multiple Node Case," *IEEE/ACM Transactions on Networking*, April 1994.

[5]   L. Georgiadis, R. Guérin, A. Parekh, "Optimal Multiplexing on a Single Link: Delay and Buffer Requirements," IEEE Transactions on Information Theory, September 1997.

[6]   R. Braden, D. Clark, S. Shenker, *Integrated Services in the Internet Architecture: An Overview*, RFC 1633, IETF, June 1994.

[7]   H. Kröner, G. Hébuterne, P. Boyer, A. Gravey, "Priority Management in ATM Switching Nodes," *IEEE JSAC*, April 1991.

[8]   Fore Systems, "ForeThought Bandwidth Management," http://lina.vis.com.tr/fore/FTBMWP.html.

[9]   N.E.T., "Advanced Traffic Management for Multiservice ATM Networks," http://www.net.com/techtop/adtmatm_wp/white.html.

[10]   ITU-T, B-ISDN *ATM Adaptation Layer — Service Specific Connection Oriented Protocol (SSCOP)*, Recommendation Q.2110, July 1994.

[11]   V. Jacobson, R. Braden, "TCP Extensions for Long-Delay Paths," RFC 1072, October, 1988.

[12]   W. Stallings, *High-Speed Networks — TCP/IP and ATM Design Principles*, Prentice-Hall, 1998.

[13]   D. Bertsekas, R. Gallager, *Data Networks — Second Edition*, Prentice-Hall, 1992.

[14]   S. Floyd, V. Jacobson, "The Synchronization of Periodic Routing Messages," IEEE/ACM Transactions on Networking, April 1994.

[15]   S. Floyd, V. Jacobson, "Random Early Detection Gateways for Congestion Avoidance," IEEE/ACM Transactions on Networking, August 1993.

[16]   S. Floyd, "References on RED (Random Early Detection) Queue Management," http://www.aciri.org/floyd/red.html.

15

Closed-Loop Congestion Control

"When one door closes another door opens; but we often look so long and so regretfully upon the closed door that we do not see the ones which open for us."

— Alexander Graham Bell

As described in the preceding chapter, selection of the optimal window size for a retransmission protocol depends upon a number of parameters. Real applications cannot statically configure these parameters. Therefore, IP- and ATM-based applications utilize adaptive flow control techniques to dynamically set the window size or transmit rate, respectively. Since these techniques utilize feedback, we call them closed-loop congestion control schemes. After presenting some general design guidelines, this chapter summarizes some foundational results from control theory applied to rate-based closed-loop congestion control algorithms. The text develops the theory, and gives an example for ATM's Available Bit Rate (ABR) protocol. Next, the coverage moves on to the subject of window-based congestion control. Finally, the chapter concludes with an analysis of TCP performance, addressing the impact of buffer size and the number of TCP sources on performance.

Principles of Adaptive Closed-Loop Congestion Control

Many data communications applications hungrily utilize as much available bandwidth as possible, thereby creating the potential for congestion. The basic idea of closed loop congestion control is to reduce offered load before significant loss occurs in the network, thus maximizing useable throughput.

Ideally, the network should fairly dole out bandwidth to contending users. In other words, no one user should get all of the available bandwidth of a bottleneck resource if several users equally contend for it. Additionally, conforming users should be isolated from the effects of non-conforming or abusive users.

The generic name given to this balancing act is *adaptive flow control.* In essence, the objective is to control traffic to achieve a throughput close to that of the maximum resource capacity, with very low loss. Such protocols require close cooperation between users and the network. For example, when the network notifies users of congestion, end applications should reduce traffic accordingly. On the other hand, when the network is not congested, applications should be free transmit as much as they wish.

A closed-loop control system can only address congestion if it persists for intervals substantially greater than the round-trip delay; otherwise, the congestion abates before any feedback control can act. The worst-case scenario for such a feedback scheme would be that of periodic input traffic, with a period approximately equal to the round-trip time.

A realistic scenario that can result in long-term overload would be that of major trunk and/or nodal failures in a network during a busy interval. This will likely result in congestion that persists for the duration of the failure, in which case feedback control can be an effective technique for avoiding congestion and splitting the impairment fairly across different sources.

Closed-loop congestion control algorithms use one of two basic methods — either rate- or window-based control. Each of these methods strives to meet the common goal of controlling the flow from the sender to maximize throughput, yet minimize loss, hence dynamically avoiding congestion. As we shall see, each method differs in the way it detects congestion indication as well the response taken to avoid congestion.

The next section begins with a control system model of a rate-based control system. ATM's Available Bit Rate (ABR) rate-based flow con-

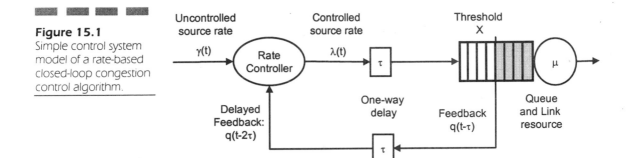

Figure 15.1
Simple control system model of a rate-based closed-loop congestion control algorithm.

trol dynamically adapts the source's transmit rate in response to explicit feedback from the network. The remainder of the chapter focuses on the analysis of window-based algorithms. The Internet's Transmission Control Protocol (TCP) employs an adaptive window-based flow control that limits the amount of data a source may transmit using a dynamically sized transmit window size based upon detected loss and timeouts. The TCP closed-loop flow control algorithms is extremely important to operation of Internet applications.

Rate-Based Control System Model

A model for closed-loop congestion control algorithm performance comes from the discipline of control system theory [1]. As depicted in Figure 15.1, the principal objective of such a control system is to take an uncontrolled source and use feedback about the bottleneck buffer resource to derive a controlled source rate $\lambda(t)$ to optimize a particular performance objective. This model represents the congestion along a path of nodes as a single queuing system, which could be either a congested link or node or a representation of multiple congested resources along an end-to-end route. Examples of desirable performance are minimal loss or maximum throughput. As seen from the figure, there is a time lag of τ seconds from the point when the source sends bits and the bottleneck queue receives these bits. As we shall see, this time delay plays a critical role in the design and optimization of congestion control algorithms. This model is the *rate-based*, which is the technique used in the ATM ABR algorithm.

The one-way delay τ in the system defines the number of bits in transit before a control action can take place. The number of bits in transit, commonly called the *bandwidth-delay product*, is:

$$\Gamma \;=\; 2\mu\tau \qquad\qquad (15\text{-}1)$$

Typically, analyses consider the worst-case scenario of greedy sources. A greedy source always has data to send, or in other words, the uncontrolled source rate $\gamma(t)=\infty$. We can analyze the time evolution of the closed-loop congestion control system of Figure 15.1 by first writing down the differential equations that determine the operation of the rate controller and the rate of buffer fill [2]. The next two sections summarize the important points of this derivation for a simple linear model and a more realistic model that captures additional characteristics of the TCP and ABR closed-loop congestion control algorithms.

Simple Linear Model

In this simplest case, the differential equation for the rate controller has a linear increase and linear decrease rate α as follows:

$$\frac{d\lambda(t)}{dt} = \begin{cases} \alpha & q(t-\tau) < X \\ -\alpha & q(t-\tau) \geq X \end{cases} \tag{15-2}$$

Notice how the above formula delays the feedback signal by τ seconds when comparing the queue level $q(t-\tau)$ to the threshold level X. Observe that the queue grows only if the input rate $\lambda(t)$ exceeds the service rate μ. Therefore, the differential equation for the queue occupancy $q(t)$ is:

$$\frac{dq(t)}{dt} = \begin{cases} 0 & \lambda(t-\tau) < \mu, \ q(t) = 0 \\ \lambda(t-\tau)-\mu & \text{otherwise} \end{cases} \tag{15-3}$$

Now, we can straightforwardly solve for the time evolution of the closed-loop congestion control system using Equations (15-2) and (15-3) with reference to Figure 15.2 for the case where $X=0$.

Assuming that the system is operating in the steady state, that is, at $t=0$, $\lambda(t)=\lambda_{min}$ and $q(t)=0$, the evolution of the controller output rate and queue level is as follows:

$$\left.\begin{array}{rcl} \lambda(t) &=& \alpha t \\ q(t) &=& 0 \end{array}\right\} \quad 0 \leq t \leq t_{max} - \tau \tag{15-4}$$

where $t_{max} = \dfrac{\mu - \lambda_{min}}{\alpha} + 2\tau$.

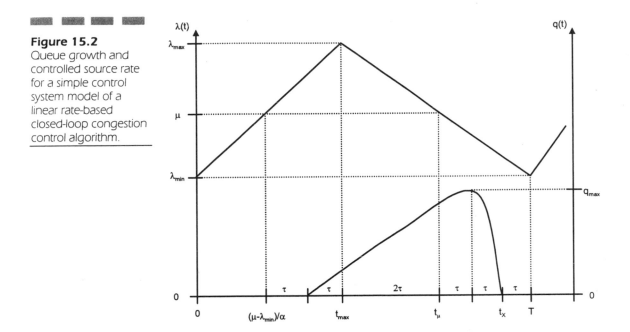

Beginning at time t_{max} -2τ, the source rate exceeds the queue service rate μ. Hence, τ seconds later the queue begins growing according to the following formula during the interval from t_{max}-τ to t_{max}+τ

$$q(t) = \int_{t_{max}-\tau}^{t} [\lambda(t-\tau) - \mu]dt \qquad (15\text{-}5)$$

Of course, τ seconds after the queue begins to grow, feedback that the queue has crossed the threshold X=0 reaches the source controller at time t_{max}, at which point the source rate reaches a maximum value:

$$\lambda_{max} \equiv \lambda(t_{max}) = \mu + 2\alpha\tau \qquad (15\text{-}6)$$

After time t_{max}+τ the queue continues growing until it reaches a maximum value q_{max} some τ seconds after the source rate $\lambda(t_\mu)$ exceeds the queue service rate μ at time t_μ, as illustrated in Figure 15.2. Solving Equation (15-2) yields the result t_μ=t_{max}+2τ. Next, the solution for the maximum queue size at time t_μ+τ from Equation (15-5) is:

$$q_{max} \equiv q(t_\mu + \tau) = 4\alpha\tau^2 \qquad (15\text{-}7)$$

Since $q(t_X)$=0 from Figure 15.2, we obtain from Equations (15-5) and (15-7) the solution $t_X = t_\mu + (1 + 2\sqrt{2})\tau$. Since the cycle repeats every

$T = t_X + \tau$ seconds as shown in Figure 15.2, we then have a closed-form solution for the minimum arrival rate:

$$\lambda_{min} = \mu - \left(2 + 2\sqrt{2}\right)\alpha\tau \qquad (15\text{-}8)$$

This in turn determines the value of t_{max} from Equation (15-4), which then specifies the cycle period T as:

$$T = 4(2 + \sqrt{2})\tau = 2t_{max}$$

Throughput and Delay

This section examines the implications of the control system parameter α on throughput and delay. The amount of data transferred during a cycle of duration equal to T seconds is:

$$D \equiv \int_0^T \lambda(t)dt = \left[\mu - \sqrt{2}\alpha\tau\right]T \qquad (15\text{-}9)$$

Therefore, the throughput η of the linear control system is the data transferred D divided by the cycle period T as follows:

$$\eta \equiv \frac{D}{T} = \mu - \sqrt{2}\alpha\tau \qquad (15\text{-}10)$$

As expected, the maximum throughput of the system is μ. In the following analysis, we consider the throughput relative to this maximum by considering the utilization $\rho \equiv \eta/\mu$. Therefore, throughput decreases as the parameter α increases. This result provides important insight into the design of a closed-loop congestion control system. A larger value of α means that the controlled source rate $\lambda(t)$ oscillates frequently between the minimum and maximum values. A smaller value of α means that the controlled source rate $\lambda(t)$ changes less frequently, and achieves a higher average throughput. Indeed, Equation (15-8) implies that the source rate factor α must satisfy the following inequality to ensure that the minimum rate λ_{min} is non-negative:

$$\alpha \leq \frac{\mu}{\left(2 + \sqrt{2}\right)\tau} \qquad (15\text{-}11)$$

Thus, we see from Equation (15-11) that a control capable of increasing the source rate to its maximum value within a few round-trip times drives throughput toward zero. Thus, we conclude that any closed-loop congestion control system must act at a rate slower than the bottleneck rate μ divided by the round trip time 2τ to achieve acceptable throughput performance.

Since the model assumes greedy sources, the concept of statistical queuing delay described in Part 4 does not apply because the system is always in the overload state. Instead, we consider a system that matches the offered load to the achievable throughput. Specifically, assume that a burst of traffic of size D arrives starting at the beginning of a cycle. The principal source of delay for such an arrival burst is the transient response time of the congestion control algorithm. The transient response time T_0 is the amount of time required for the rate controller to increase the source rate to the maximum value λ_{max} given in Equation (15-6):

$$T_0 \ = \ \frac{\mu}{\alpha} \ + \ 2\tau \qquad\qquad (15\text{-}12)$$

Clearly, transient response time improves with increasing α. Let's look at some numerical examples to better understand the operation of the linear congestion control system. Figure 15.3 plots the results of two scenarios using different values of the control parameter α for the controlled source rate $\lambda(t)$ and the queue fill $q(t)$ for the following set of ATM-specific parameters:

- One-way delay $\tau=0.01$ seconds, or one tick on the horizontal axis
- Queue service rate of $\mu=100,000$ cells/second
- Queue threshold of X=0 packets

Figure 15.3a shows the results for an increase rate of $\alpha=10^6$, while Figure 15.3b plots the results for $\alpha=2\times10^6$ cells/second/second. As expected, scenario a has less fluctuation about the long-term average μ than scenario b does, as predicted by Equations (15-6) and (15-8). Also, scenario a has a smaller maximum queue fill than scenario b as predicted by Equation (15-7). In summary, scenario a has fewer oscillations and lower variability in queuing delay. On the other hand, the transient response time T_0 for scenario a is twice as long as scenario b, as predicted by Equation (15-12).

Figure 15.3
Illustration of the rate
controller parameter
α's effect on transient
response time and
oscillation.

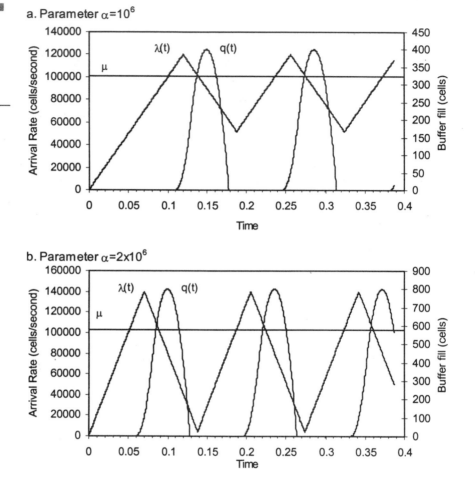

a. Parameter $\alpha = 10^6$

b. Parameter $\alpha = 2 \times 10^6$

This simple example illustrates several important principles of closed-loop congestion control algorithms. The system reaches a steady state after an initial transient of one cycle. In the steady state, the source rate oscillates above and below the queue service rate μ over time due to the delay between the source controller and the controlled queue resource. Note that the oscillation that reduces throughput creates greater variation in delay. The delay variation Δ is the difference between the maximum delay and the minimum delay as follows:

$$\Delta = \frac{1}{\lambda_{min}} - \frac{1}{\lambda_{max}}$$

Thus, a tradeoff exists between throughput and delay variation as a function of the control system parameter α. Figure 15.4 plots the

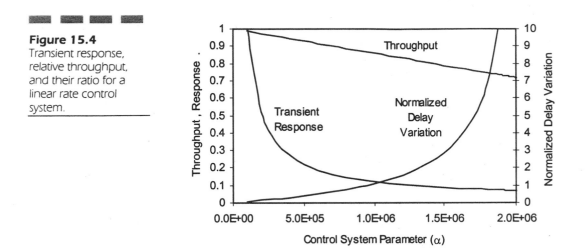

Figure 15.4
Transient response, relative throughput, and their ratio for a linear rate control system.

transient response time T_0, relative throughput ρ, and the normalized delay variation $\Delta\mu$ for the parameters of our example system as a function of the control system parameter α. Note that as discussed above, throughput gradually decreases as α increases due to oscillation of the controlled source rate. On the other hand, the transient response decreases markedly, and then levels off as α increases. Finally, note how the normalized delay variation $\Delta\mu$ increases markedly with increasing control parameter α. Hence, selection of the control system parameter largely centers on the tradeoff between transient response time and delay variation.

Realistic Linear Increase, Multiplicative Decrease Model

While the simple linear model of the previous section afforded some crucial insights, most real-world closed-loop congestion control algorithms use a controller that has an additive increase and a multiplicative decrease, as proposed in Reference 3. Both TCP and ABR essentially follow this rule. Specifically, if the feedback signal indicates that the buffer fill is less than the threshold X, then the controller increases the additive rate α; otherwise, the controller decreases the rate by the multiplicative factor β. Therefore, the differential equation for the rate controller in this case is:

$$\frac{d\lambda(t)}{dt} = \begin{cases} \alpha & q(t - \tau) < X \\ -\beta\lambda(t) & q(t - \tau) \geq X \end{cases} \qquad (15\text{-}13)$$

The differential equation for the queue occupancy $q(t)$ is still given by Equation (15-3). We can now straightforwardly solve for the time evolution of the closed-loop congestion control system using Equations (15-13) and (15-3) with reference to Figure 15.5 for the case where $X=0$.

Up until time $t_{max}+\tau$, the arrival rate and queue occupancy evolves in precisely the same manner as the linear system described in the previous section. Afterward, however, according to Equation (15-13), the controller decreases its source rate in a multiplicative fashion until τ seconds after the queue fill falls below the threshold X at time t_X, as shown in Figure 15.5, as follows:

$$\lambda(t) \;=\; \lambda_{max}e^{-\beta(t-t_{max})} \quad, t_{max} \leq t \leq t_X + \tau \qquad (15\text{-}14)$$

where $\lambda_{max}=\mu+2\alpha\tau$ as in the linear case.

The cycle then repeats after $T=t_X+\tau$ seconds. At the beginning of each cycle, the value of the source rate reaches a minimum value:

$$\lambda_{min} \;=\; \lambda_{max}e^{-\beta(T-t_{max})}$$

Numerical solution is required for the value of t_{max} from the following equation obtained by computing the slope in the linear region of source rate increase, from the starting value of λ_{min} given above:

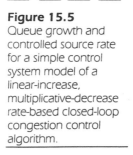

Figure 15.5
Queue growth and controlled source rate for a simple control system model of a linear-increase, multiplicative-decrease rate-based closed-loop congestion control algorithm.

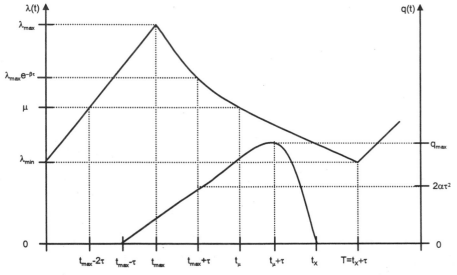

$$t_{max} = \left(\frac{\mu + 2\alpha\tau}{\alpha}\right)\left(1 - e^{-\beta(T-t_{max})}\right) \qquad (15\text{-}15)$$

After time $t_{max}+\tau$ until time t_X, the queue continues growing until it reaches a maximum value q_{max} some τ seconds after the source rate $\lambda(t_\mu)$ exceeds the queue service rate μ at time t_μ, as illustrated in Figure 15.5. Solving Equation (15-14) for t_μ yields the following result:

$$t_\mu = t_{max} - \frac{1}{\beta}\ln\left[\frac{\mu}{\lambda_{max}}\right]$$

Now, solving for the maximum queue size at time $t_\mu+\tau$ yields the following result:

$$q_{max} \equiv q(t_\mu + \tau) = 2\alpha\tau^2 + \frac{2\alpha\tau}{\beta} + \frac{\mu}{\beta}\ln\left[\frac{\mu}{\lambda_{max}}\right]$$

Setting $q(t_X)=0$ and solving for $z\equiv T-t_{max}-2\tau$ results in the following equation:

$$1 - e^{-\beta z} = \frac{\beta\mu}{\lambda_{max}}z - \frac{2\alpha\beta\tau^2}{\lambda_{max}}$$

The solver tool in Microsoft Excel easily solves for the value of z, which then allows straightforward solution for T and t_{max} from Equation (15-15). The amount of data transferred D in a T second cycle is then:

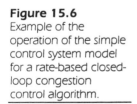

Figure 15.6
Example of the operation of the simple control system model for a rate-based closed-loop congestion control algorithm.

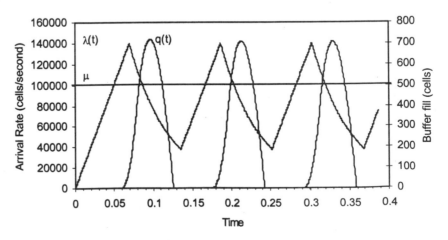

$$D \equiv \int_0^T \lambda(t)dt = \alpha t_{max}^2 + \lambda_{min} t_{max} - \frac{\lambda_{max}}{\beta}[1 - e^{-\beta(T-t_{max})}]$$

Figure 15.6 plots the results of the controlled source rate $\lambda(t)$ and the queue fill $q(t)$ for the same set of ATM specific parameters presented in the previous section with a multiplicative exponential decrease factor of $\beta=20$. Numerical solution is necessary to compute the throughput, transient response time, and delay variation for this system.

Window-Based Flow Control

When the bandwidth-delay product Γ is large with respect to the packet size, the rate-based models of the previous section is a good approximation of a window-based system. One simply substitutes packets for bits in the units for the parameters. Because cells are so short, the rate-based model applies well to ATM. An analysis of the performance of a series of nodes using a dynamic window-based flow control protocol under the case of heavy load provides some interesting insights [2].

7 Figure 15.7 illustrates the closed-loop queuing system model for a flow control protocol with a window size equal to W packets. The network has N nodes, each modeled as a separate queue with service rate of μ packets per second. The model lumps the delay between each of the nodes in the forward direction with the feedback path into one element, with a total latency of 2τ seconds, as shown at the bottom of the figure. In the forward direction, this simplification is accurate. In the backward direction, this model assumes that the acknowledgement responses do not encounter queuing delays. This simple model does not consider loss.

In this closed-loop queuing system, the packets (or their acknowledgements) must be in one of the nodes or in the feedback delay

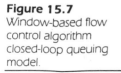

Figure 15.7
Window-based flow control algorithm closed-loop queuing model.

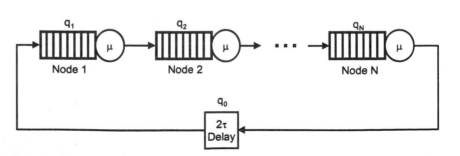

element. The term q_k represents the number of packets (or ACKs) in element k, as shown in the figure. The closed-loop queuing system model forces the sum of the q_k to equal the window size W. The exact solution for the q_k is computed recursively [2]. Several results regarding the window size that maximizes queuing power and the resulting response time and throughput are interesting.

In a closed-loop queuing model, throughput increases as window size increases. This occurs because the packets in the queues in the forward direction represent transfer in the forward direction, while those in the feedback delay element represent packets queued at the source pending acknowledgements that will open the transmit window again. The optimum window size has the following value:

$$W_{opt} \approx \Gamma + \frac{1}{2}\sqrt{\frac{\Gamma}{N}}$$

where $\Gamma \equiv 2\mu\tau$ is the bandwidth-delay product.

The expected value of the round-trip response time T is the sum of the transmission delay 2τ and a queuing delay. It has the following average value at the optimal window size when $\Gamma \gg 1$:

$$E[T] \approx 2\tau\left[1 + \sqrt{\frac{N}{\Gamma}}\right]$$

From Little's theorem, the queuing delay component of T is the product of the average number in queue at each node $E[q_k]$ times the response time 2τ summed across all N nodes. Hence, the average number of packets in queue is:

$$E[q] \approx \sqrt{\Gamma/N}$$

The variance of the number of packets in queue at each node is:

$$Var[q] \approx \frac{\Gamma}{N+1}$$

The relative throughput ρ at the optimal window size is:

$$\rho \approx 1 - \sqrt{\frac{N}{\Gamma}}$$

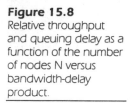

Figure 15.8
Relative throughput and queuing delay as a function of the number of nodes N versus bandwidth-delay product.

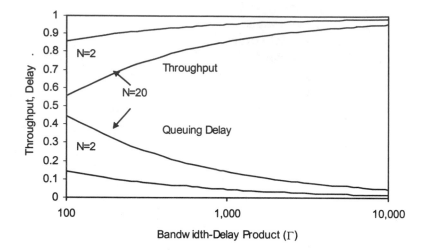

Figure 15.8 depicts the relative throughput and queuing delay (normalized by dividing by 2τ) versus the bandwidth-delay product Γ for a network with a number of nodes along the path of N=2 and N=20. Note that as the bandwidth-delay product increases, the throughput approaches 100 percent, while normalized queuing delay approaches zero. To understand this effect, realize that for a fixed round-trip delay 2τ, increasing values of Γ mean that the link rate μ is becoming larger. At lower values of bandwidth-delay product, the number of nodes in the path N has a significant effect on performance. A basic consequence of these results to network design is that networks traversing a large number of nodes over long distances should use high-speed transmission links.

TCP/IP Model

This section describes the effect of window size on performance, the interaction of interfering traffic streams, and the impact of router or switch buffer size.

TCP Window Size Impact on Throughput

Network congestion resulting in loss affects end-to-end transport layer performance (e.g., TCP), and ultimately application layer (e.g., HTTP) performance. Since standard TCP implementations only support a 64-Kbyte window size, applications running over TCP cannot sustain transmission at 10-Mbps Ethernet speeds across one-way WAN distances greater than approximately 2,500 miles. For applications capable of transmitting at 100 Mbps, the standard TCP window size limits the distance over which maximum throughput is achievable to 250 miles. To achieve higher throughput over networks with large bandwidth-delay products, look for devices that implement TCP window scaling extensions defined in IETF RFC 1323 [4].

A general rule of thumb is that the total throughput of TCP increases with the window size linearly up to the point where either the maximum window size is reached, or the window equals the product of the round-trip delay and the bottleneck bandwidth. IP routers and ATM switches should have large buffers, sized to be on the order of the product of the round-trip delay and bandwidth bottleneck when supporting TCP. As described in Chapter 13, TCP's adaptive windowing protocol dynamically acts to fill the available bandwidth, if application demand is high enough. Thus, a packet- or cell-switched network infrastructure supports TCP's ability to fill in bandwidth unused by higher-priority multimedia traffic like voice and video.

Discrete TCP/IP Performance Model

This section defines a model for the performance of a number of greedy TCP/IP sessions contending for a common buffer in a router or switch. The following treatment analyzes the effective TCP throughput for the case where the buffer admission and service logic either allows source phasing, or works to prevent it. As studied in

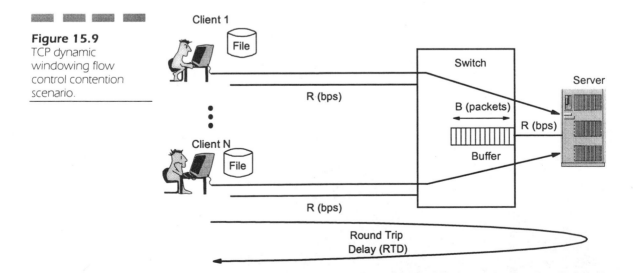

Figure 15.9
TCP dynamic windowing flow control contention scenario.

Chapter 14, the Random Early Detection (RED) method attempts to break up phasing. Additionally, ATM switches should implement Early/Partial Packet Discard (EPD/PPD) to minimize phasing, as described in Chapter 14.

Figure 15.9 illustrates the scenario where N TCP clients simultaneously transfer data to a single server attached to a switch egress port and buffer. All hosts connect to the switch via transmission lines running at R bits per second. A single trunk line also running at R bps empties a buffer that has a capacity of B packets. All clients have the same Round-Trip Delay (RTD). Since this configuration is completely symmetric, congestion causes all sources to begin retransmission simultaneously. As studied in Chapter 13, this phenomenon is called phasing, or source synchronization.

Figure 15.10 illustrates the effect of two (N=2) contending, identical sources on the TCP window size (measured in packets here) and the buffer fill versus the horizontal axis measured in units of RTD. The figure shows the window size by squares on the figure every RTD time. Recall from Chapter 13 that the TCP slow start protocol effectively doubles the window size each RTD until it reaches a value of one-half the previous maximum window size. After passing the one-half value, TCP linearly increases the window size linearly by one packet for each RTD interval. The figure indicates the number of packets sent in each RTD interval by a horizontal line. Once the buffer overflows, TCP fails to receive an acknowledgement. In our example, we assume that TCP times out after one RTD interval. When the time-out occurs, TCP decreases the window size to one.

Figure 15.10
TCP dynamic windowed flow control window size and buffer fill.

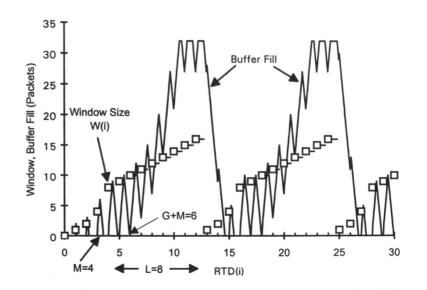

The buffer fill plot in the figure depicts the worst-case situation where each TCP source generates packets in phase. Notice how the buffer fill returns to zero when the window size is short during the slow-start interval, but then accumulates as the window size increases in the congestion avoidance region. In this example the buffer capacity is B=32 packets, which overflows on the 14th, 15th, and 16th RTD intervals, as shown in the figure. The maximum number of packets "on the fly" (F) is 20 in this example.

The net effect of this protocol is that each TCP session on average gets about half of the egress port bandwidth. This sawtooth type of windowing pattern is typical for TCP when operating over routers or switches that have large buffers.

The following analytical model approximates TCP slow start performance using the following variables:

M   = Number of RTDs in the multiplicative increase interval
L   = Number of RTDs in the linear increase interval
P   = Packet size (Bytes)
R   = Link Rate for each sender (bits/second)
N   = Number of sources
B   = Buffer size (in cells)
RTD   = Round-Trip Delay (seconds)

The rate from each transmitter determines the number of packets on the fly during an RTD time is as follows:

$$F = \frac{R}{P} \frac{RTD}{8}$$

Translating the TCP slow-start algorithm into a formal expression, the window size (in packets) in the ith RTD interval is:

$$W(i) = \begin{cases} 2^{i-1} & 1 \le i \le M \\ L+i & M < i < M+L+1 \end{cases}$$

Since TCP transitions from exponential to linear increase when the window size crosses half of the previous maximum value, we infer that $L \le 2^{(M-1)}$. In the example of Figure 15.10, M=4 and $L=8=2^{(M-1)}$. Note that unlimited buffer growth occurs at RTD interval G+M in the linear region when the packets from all sources exceed the capability of the bottleneck link to empty the buffer in an RTD (which is F packets), namely:

$$N(G+L) > F.$$

This implies that the point where unlimited growth occurs is $G \approx F/N\text{-}L$. Buffer overflow occurs as growth accumulates in the linear increase region after the Gth RTD interval until the (L+M) interval. The total packets arriving minus those transmitted by the link serving the buffer determines the following balance equation:

$$N \sum_{i=G+M}^{L+M} W(i) \;-\; (L-G+1)F \;=\; B$$

Solving the above equation for buffer overflow for the linear increase interval comprised of L -G+1 RTD time segments yields:

$$L \approx \frac{F}{2N} + \sqrt{\frac{B+F}{2N}}$$

The effective TCP throughput η, or "goodput," is the ratio of good frames transferred to the total frames that could have been sent in a sequence of (M+L) RTD intervals as follows:

$$\eta \approx \frac{N \sum_{i=1}^{M+L} W(i)}{F(M+L)} = \frac{N \,(3L^2/2 \;+4L \;-\Delta)}{F(\log_2 L + L)}$$

The Δ term models the case where the network device employs phasing avoidance, and the case where it does not. When the device implements phasing avoidance, Δ=2L, while when it does not, Δ=4L. This is true because in the best case the TCP sources must lose at least N×L packets to cause the retransmission time-out plus N×L unproductive packet transmissions that must be re-sent. In the case where the device does not implement phasing avoidance, the destination fails to receive even fewer packets. This model made a number of approximations to yield the relatively simple expression above. Therefore, beware that when the buffer size exceeds the packets on the fly number F, this model may return values of throughput η greater than 100 percent due to the approximations made.

Buffer Size Impact on Performance

Figure 15.11 illustrates the results of the above model compared with simulation results and an actual measurement over an ATM network.

The figure plots the effective TCP throughput with and without phasing avoidance. For this example, N=2 sources, R=40 Mbps corresponding to operation over DS3 PLCP, the RTD is 70 ms, and the packet size P=4096 bytes. For these parameters, M is 5 and L is approximately 25. This means that a complete TCP slow-start dynamic window cycle takes over 2 seconds to complete. The network devices in the measurement and the simulation did not implement phasing avoidance. The correspondence between the analytical approximation and the measured and simulated results is relatively good for this set of parameters.

The simple analytical model does not address a situation that occurs in devices with very small buffers, but which the measurements in Figure 15.11 illustrate. When the buffer size of the ATM switch is less than the packet size, then when two packets arrive nearly simultaneously, one or more cells from both packets are lost and both must be retransmitted, resulting in very low throughput, as shown by the measurements in the figure. When the buffer size is increased so that two packets can arrive simultaneously, throughput increases markedly. As the buffer size increases further, the throughput increases, but not nearly as dramatically. Similar results occur in a local area for switches with buffers that are small with respect to the packet size, as reported in [5].

Figure 15.12 illustrates another example where R=150 Mbps corresponding to operation over an OC3/STS-3c, the RTD is 40 ms, and the packet size P=1500 bytes. Approximately 14,000 cells are on the fly for these parameters. The figure plots the effective TCP throughput ver-

Figure 15.11
TCP effective throughput versus buffer size.

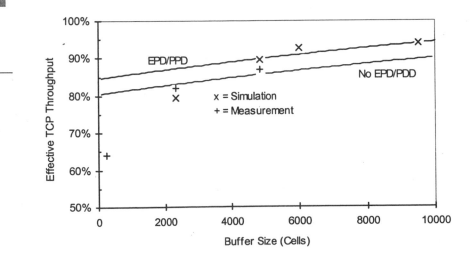

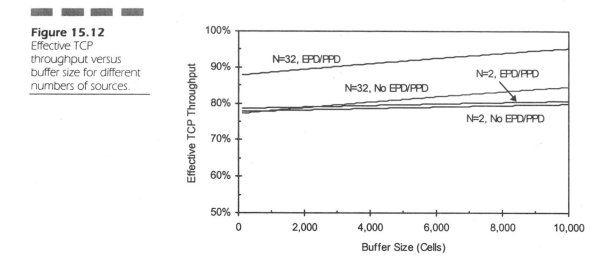

Figure 15.12
Effective TCP
throughput versus
buffer size for different
numbers of sources.

sus buffer size B (in cells) as before for the two cases where the device does and does not implement phasing avoidance. However, the figure plots the throughput for two values of the number of sources, namely: N=2 and N=32. For the case where N=2, M is 7 and L is approximately 120. This means that a complete TCP slow-start dynamic window cycle takes over 5 s to complete. On the other hand, for N=32 M is 4 and L is approximately 10, meaning that a complete TCP congestion cycle completes within less than half a second. Note how the throughput improves for a larger number of sources N. Even without phasing avoidance, the performance improves because of the sources spending relatively more time in the productive congestion avoidance interval. Note that the impact of phasing avoidance is small when N=2. The next section addresses the impact of the number of sources N on TCP/IP throughput.

Number of Sources Impact on Performance

Figure 15.13 illustrates the same example where R=150 Mbps corresponding to operation over an OC3/STS-3c, the RTD is 40 ms, and the packet size P=1500 bytes, as covered in the previous section. This figure plots the effective TCP throughput versus the number of sources N for a fixed buffer size of 10,000 cells for a device with and without phasing avoidance. This plot clearly shows the benefit of phasing avoidance as the number of sources increases. This effect occurs because phasing avoidance spreads the loss evenly over the sources by discarding the largest-possible portions of single packets. In LAN en-

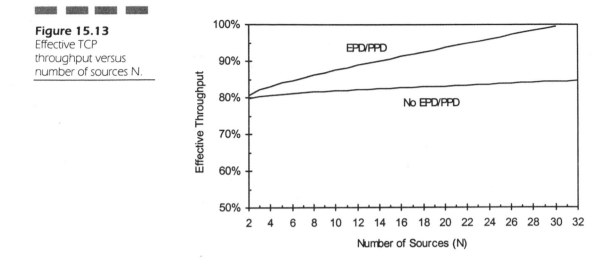

Figure 15.13
Effective TCP throughput versus number of sources N.

vironments, the performance improvement of EPD/PPD phasing avoidance is even greater. However, the approximations in our simple model are not accurate for small values of TCP multiplicative increase interval M typically encountered in LAN environments.

TCP over ATM: UBR and ABR

This section examines some additional considerations involved when carrying TCP traffic over the ATM Unspecified and Available Bit Rate (UBR and ABR) service categories. TCP/IP is the most common data traffic running over ATM networks today. During congestion conditions and subsequent loss of cells, the ATM network device does not notify the sender that retransmission is required — instead higher-layer protocols, like TCP, must notice the loss via a time-out and retransmit the missing packets. Not only does one cell loss cause the missing packet to be retransmitted, but all packets after it up to the end of the transmit window. Excessive packet discards within a TCP window can degrade the recovery process and cause host time-outs — causing interruptions on the order of many seconds to minutes. Loss also touches off TCP's slow-start adaptive windowing mechanism, further reducing throughput. If you plan to operate TCP/IP over UBR, be sure that your ATM switches or service provider support Early/Partial Packet Discard (EPD/PPD), as defined in Chapter 14. The EPD/PPD functions ensure that the switch discards entire packets during periods of congestion. This is especially important when a relatively large number of TCP sources contend for a particular bottleneck.

Possibly, the best ATM service category for TCP traffic is ABR, since it is effectively lossless. However, in order to realize the full benefit of ABR, the TCP source must control its transmission rate in response to feedback from the ATM network.

Review

This chapter began by discussing some general issues involved in dynamic closed-loop congestion control. The text then presented a simple linear control system model of a rate-based control system. We then summarized some tradeoffs between transient response, throughput, and delay variation performance of rate-based protocols. The text continued with a description of a more accurate non-linear control system model that captured important attributes of ATM's Available Bit Rate (ABR) protocol. We then presented a theoretical model for the optimum window size in a network. Next, the coverage provided an in-depth look at the factors that affect performance of the Internet's popular Transmission Control Protocol (TCP) over ATM. The topics covered were, impact of buffer size and performance as a function of the number of network users, as well as the effect of ATM service category on performance. Finally, the chapter concluded with some practical considerations involved in optimizing the operation of TCP/IP over ATM.

References

[1]   S. Mascolo, M. Gerla, "An ABR Congestion Control Algorithm Feeding Back Available Bandwidth and Queue Level," 1998 IEEE ATM Workshop Proceedings.

[2]   M. Schwartz, *Broadband Integrated Networks*, Prentice-Hall, 1996.

[3]   R. Jain, K. Ramakrishnan, "Congestion Avoidance in Computer Networks with a Connectionless Network Layer: Concepts, Goals and Methodology," Computer Networking Symposium, 1988.

[4]   V. Jacobson, R. Braden, D. Borman, *TCP Extensions for High Performance*, IETF, RFC 1323, May 1992.

[5]   A. Romanow, "Dynamics of TCP Traffic over ATM Networks," IEEE JSAC, May 1995.

Routing and Network Design

"There is nothing so powerful as truth, — and often nothing so strange."

— Daniel Webster

This part moves into yet another level of complexity, namely an interconnected set of traffic systems, moving a step closer to the real world of networks comprised of many switches or routers. Here, analogies between transportation networks and networks of IP routers and ATM switches interconnected via communication links apply. We call the process of selecting a path *routing*. When there is more than one choice of path, routing frequently becomes a difficult problem. In particular, traffic engineers must optimize routing to satisfy particular quality requirements and minimize economic cost. Furthermore, routing must also fairly allocate available capacity to traffic flows to deliver the required level of quality. Next, we expect that routing provide a certain degree of restoration in response to link or nodal failures. The following chapters formulate these problems and summarize the important analytical results in the field of routing.

CHAPTER **16**

Routing Background and Concepts

*"Two roads diverged in a wood, and I took the one less travelled by,
And that has made all the difference."*

— Robert Frost

Although the analogy of Internet traffic and urban rush-hour gridlock may be exaggerated, one thing is certain — enterprises relying on the Internet to disseminate information, advertise, and conduct mainstream activities cannot tolerate productivity impairing traffic jams. This chapter begins by recapping the lessons learned from planes, trains, and automobiles as an introduction to the concepts of shortest path routing, constraint-based routing, and traffic matrices. The chapter describes the workings of the widely used link-state routing protocols employed by IP and ATM networks through a simple example, augmented to illustrate the operation of constraint-based routing. Finally, the chapter concludes by describing how routing performs network restoration, and the relevant efficiency of one approach over another.

Introduction to Routing

This section introduces the concepts of routing algorithms and how they relate to QoS and traffic management. The next two chapters cover these subjects in detail.

Some Transportation Analogies

As an illustration of the bandwidth reservation and routing problem encountered in connectionless routing protocols like IP's Open Shortest Path First (OSPF), consider the following example of booking a flight reservation from Boston to Los Angeles [1]. The problem stems from the fact that the routing algorithm advertises a single metric — in this example, the distance between airports. First, the agent informs you that the shortest path connects through Chicago and Denver. The agent then tells you that there is good news and bad news. The good news is that a seat is available on the flight from Boston to Chicago. The bad news is that the OSPF reservation system doesn't know if or when seats are available on the Chicago-Denver or Denver-Los Angeles segments, since only information on the flight distance is available. Advertising the number of seats available on each flight would be an additional metric. Furthermore, a longer path exists through Dallas and has an available seat on the Boston-Dallas segment, but the availability of seats on the Dallas-Los Angeles segment is also unknown. This occurs because routers running OSPF only know about the status of the directly connected links. Even if you tried to make a first-class reservation (i.e., equivalent to priority queuing), this doesn't help the situation. A router running OSPF can't tell if there are any "seats" available except on directly connected links.

This phenomenon occurs because simple routing algorithms optimize a single parameter. Usually, descriptions call this optimization criterion cost or distance. The objective is to minimize this criterion, hence the common descriptions of shortest path or least cost routing. Solutions to routing problems with multiple parameters or constraints require algorithms that are much more complicated. An analogy with multiple-parameter routing involves selecting a route from your house to the grocery store. One route takes more gas yet takes less time, and the other route takes less gas yet takes more time (e.g., because of construction delays). Each route has a different set of costs (time and money). You choose the cost measure most important to you — that is, do you want to minimize time spent or gas used — and you take that route choice.

A relevant analogy to routing is that when caught in a particularly bad traffic jam, you might take an alternate route or pull off the road and do something else while waiting for congestion to abate. Also, when we attempt to access a particular service, and find that the line is too long — we may leave and decide to try again later if conditions allow us to do so. Alternate routing and time varying routing are important techniques in optimizing IP and ATM networks.

Another way to address congestion and fairness is to move the resources closer to the sources requesting it. In transportation and commerce networks, planners attempt to place new schools, services, and shopping close to the community that requires these facilities. A similar distribution of resources occurs on the Web via the use of server sites that shadow the same content at servers around the world.

Shortest-Path or Least-Cost Routing

Routers employ connectionless protocols using an elegant algorithm to pick the "shortest" path. Sometimes, texts call the measure of "shortness" cost instead. The terms shortest-path and least-cost routing are equivalent. Figure 16.1 depicts a simple five-node network used to illustrate the differences between shortest-path and constraint-based routing. The five nodes labeled A through E shown in the figure are interconnected by DS3 links, which each have capacity of approximately 45 Mbps. This example concerns the routing of 10-Mbps flows from a port on node A to a port on node B. For purposes of simplicity, we assume that no other flows are active and that the shortest path is the one with the least number of hops.

Shortest path routing directs all of the flows over the shortest path, namely A-C-B. This action creates an overload on this route. If the

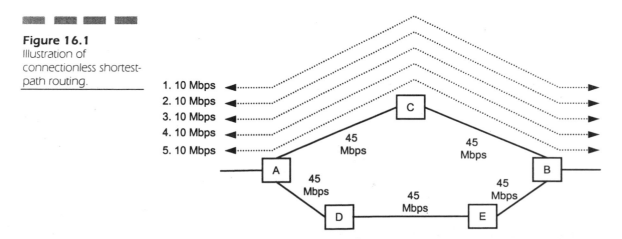

Figure 16.1
Illustration of connectionless shortest-path routing.

traffic flows employ a higher-layer congestion control protocol like TCP, then the flows experience reduced throughput. If, however, the flows require a certain level of capacity (e.g., a video conference or voice conversation), then the overload will likely result in unacceptable performance. This situation can occur with shortest-path routing because the optimization considers only one parameter — the path length — and does not consider other constraints, such as required capacity.

Routing Subject to Constraints

Connection-oriented protocols handle capacity-constrained routing naturally. Typically, they assign connections to the best path until it is full. They then assign connections to the next-best path. If no path can support the connection request; then the network blocks the attempt. Figure 16.2 illustrates the same network as used in the previous example, but now employing connection-oriented capacity constrained routing. As the first four requests arrive for 10-Mbps connections between A and B, the network chooses the shortest path, namely A-C-B, as shown at the top the figure. However, the network cannot route the fifth connection request on the shortest path, because it is full. Therefore, connection-oriented routing selects the next-best path with available capacity, namely A-D-E-B, as shown at the bottom of the figure.

At best, connection-oriented routing makes the optimal routing decision based upon the state of the network at the time of the request. However, the routing in a connection-oriented network can become suboptimal when supporting connections with long holding times. Consider the example Figure 16.2 again, where the five connections

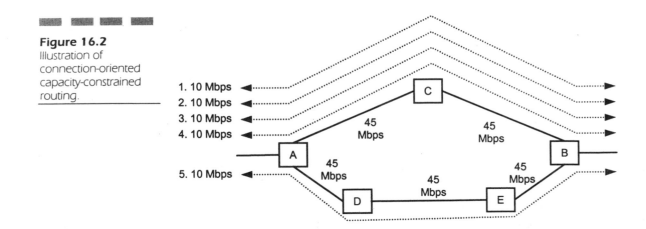

Figure 16.2
Illustration of connection-oriented capacity-constrained routing.

are active. After a period of time, connections 1 through 4 release, leaving connection 5 on a suboptimal path. If other connection requests arrive; for example, four connections between D and E each requiring 10 Mbps, the network will block one of these requests. One way around this issue is to periodically rearrange long-duration connections in a relatively non-disruptive manner. However, as detailed in the next chapter, rearrangement adds complexity to connection-oriented routing and processing and also creates interruptions in service.

Traffic Patterns and Communities of Interest

In most traffic systems, a community of interest or pattern of traffic flow between network nodes arises. In highway systems, the busiest periods of vehicular traffic typically occur in the direction from the suburbs to the downtown area in the morning, and in the reverse direction in the evening. Indeed, much of the efforts of transportation engineers involve measuring the demand for travel between geographic points and then planning for the construction of highways, scheduling of airline flights, or dispatching of trains to serve the forecasted demand. Network designers analyzing traffic patterns perform similar tasks when they collect a matrix of offered traffic between nodes within a network. Furthermore, network designers look for predictable levels of traffic that frequently occur at different times of the day, week, and season between communities of interest.

In transportation networks, minimizing some measure of economic cost is of paramount importance. Good network designers also seek to minimize the overall network cost, which is comprised of the equipment, transmission facilities, and operating expenses. This text focuses primarily on the equipment and transmission components of the overall economic equation. As described in the next chapter, design techniques similar to transportation problems apply to the selection of nodal sites, and connection of these nodes via communication links. Additionally, specification of routing policies and parameters also help to minimize overall network cost.

Let's look at the example of Bob surfing the Web, but now from the network point of view with reference to Figure 16.3. Of course, many users attach to an Internet service provider (ISP) network. Hence, network routers and switches serve many users, and therefore the overall aggregate traffic offered between geographically diverse locations drives the traffic in the network backbone. The figure

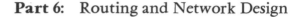

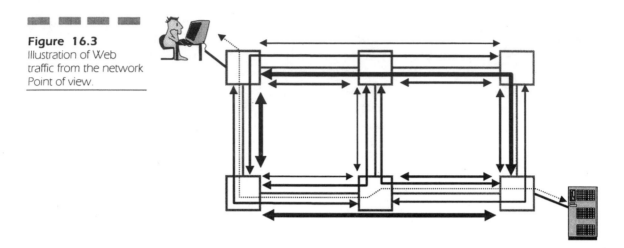

shows a network of six nodes arranged in a lattice pattern, which is typical of many network topologies. The thin dashed arrow shows the flow of traffic between Bob's computer and the server with which he currently has a Web session. The thicker solid arrows indicate the relative volume of aggregate traffic between other nodes in the network resulting from the interaction of many other clients and servers. The network routing algorithm determines the specific path taken by aggregate traffic flows. As we shall see, routing and load balancing in a network is a complex traffic-engineering problem.

Routing Algorithms

This section examines the principal attributes of routing algorithms used in IP and ATM networks.

Background

Routing algorithms exchange information about the topology, that is, the links that are connected and their associated costs employing one of two generic methods [2, 3]. The first is a *distance vector* algorithm, where neighbor nodes periodically exchange vectors that describe the distance to every destination subnetwork. This process eventually converges on the optimal solution. In the second method, each router learns the entire *link-state* topology of the entire network. This technique floods only the changes to the link-state topology throughout the network. Flooding involves a node broadcasting topology state change messages such that every other node receives exactly one copy of the message. The link-state approach is more complex, but converges much more rapidly than the distance vector approach. When the topology of the network changes due to addition or failure of a link or node, or because of a link metric change, the flooding protocol must disseminate this information to every other node. The *convergence time* is the interval required for updating all nodes in the network about the topology change.

The early ARPAnet employed a distance vector method, which the Internet's Routing Interchange Protocol (RIP) still employs. A principal advantage of the distance vector protocol is its simplicity. A major disadvantage of the distance vector protocol is that the topology information message grows larger with the network, and the time for it to propagate through the network increases as the network grows. Therefore, the convergence time of a distance vector algorithm is poor. Another disadvantage of the distance vector algorithm is that it uses hop count instead of a weighted link metric. Minimum hop routing leads to some pathological route choices in certain network topologies.

Link-state advertisement is a more recent development designed to address the scalability issues of the distance vector technique. The Internet first began using link-state routing in 1979. A fundamental tenet of the approach is to reliably flood an advertisement throughout the network whenever the state of one or more links change. Note that the state of a node is equivalent to the state of all links connected to it. Examples of link-state change are adding a new link, deleting a link, and an unexpected link failure. Thus, each node obtains complete knowledge of the network topology in the convergence time t (usually several seconds). After any change, each node computes the least-cost routes to every destination using an algorithm such as the Dijkstra algorithm, as detailed in Chapter 17. Since every node has the same topology database, they all compute consistent next hop forwarding tables. Examples of link-state routing protocols are the Internet's Open Shortest Path First (OSPF) [4] and the OSI IS-IS Routing Protocol [2], where IS stands for Intermediate System. Key advantages of these protocols are reduction of topology update information and decreased convergence times when compared with distance vector approaches. A disadvantage is the increased complexity of these methods, and the consequent challenge in achieving interoperability between different vendor implementations.

Routing is a complicated subject, and we describe only enough for our purposes. Readers interested in more detail should consult Reference 2 for OSI-based routing and References 3, 5, 6, 7, and 8 for IP-based routing.

Link-State Routing and Topology Discovery

Routers implementing a link-state protocol perform the following four basic functions [6]:

1. They say hello to their neighbors, learn addresses, and collect routing "cost" or "distance" information.
2. They collect state information from all their links and place these in link-state packets.
3. They reliably and efficiently "flood" the link-state packets throughout the network such that every router quickly converges to an accurate view of the entire network's topology.
4. They compute the least-cost path to every other router in the network.

Let's look into each of these steps a little further with reference to the simple example in Figures 16.4 and 16.5. Neighboring routers run a "hello" protocol once they boot up or once a link activates, as shown in Figure 16.4a. The hello protocol messages contain routing "cost" information, which may be economic information about the link, or may reflect some other information such as distance, latency or the capacity of a particular link. Routers also detect link failures when they stop receiving the periodic "heartbeat" of the hello protocol messages from a neighbor.

Each network node assembles its view of the current link states into a packet and forwards it to each of its neighbors, as shown in Figure 16.4b. In general, the node need only transmit the information that

Figure 16.4
Example of hello
protocol and link-state
packets.

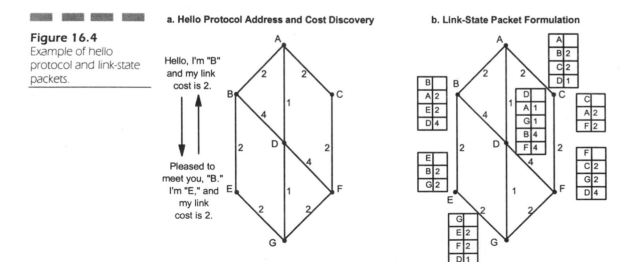

a. Hello Protocol Address and Cost Discovery

b. Link-State Packet Formulation

has changed since its last broadcast. The link-state packet identifies the source router in the first line, and the destination routers and link costs in each of the subsequent lines in the figure. Routers send link-state packets at start-up time or whenever a significant change occurs in the network. Examples of significant changes are a link or nodal failure, a link or node restart, or a change in the routing cost metric or reachability advertised by an adjacent network.

Intermediate nodes flood link-state packets to every other node in the network, as illustrated in Figure 16.5a for router A. *Flooding* involves replicating the link-state packets in an efficient and reliable manner such that each node quickly and reliably obtains an identical copy of the link-state topology for the entire network. Nodes receiving multiple copies of the link-state packets discard duplicates. Additional fields in the link-state packets contain a sequence number and an aging count that eliminate duplicate packets and handle other error scenarios. Since each router must have the identical topology database, the link-state protocol acknowledges flooded packets.

Finally, each router computes the least-cost path to every other router in the network. Figure 16.5b illustrates the result of this calculation for router A in the thick solid lines. The net effect of the routing calculation, using the Dijkstra algorithm (as detailed in the next chapter) is a minimum spanning tree rooted at each node, as shown by the upside-down tree rooted in router A in the figure. This concept embodies the essence of routing. Whenever a link or node fails, a new node or link is added, or a link or node is deleted; then the above procedure repeats. We call the time for this entire process to complete the *convergence time.* Current link-state routing algorithms converge within seconds in moderately sized networks. Rapid conver-

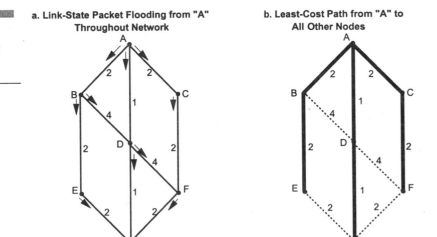

Figure 16.5
Example of flooding and least-cost route determination.

a. Link-State Packet Flooding from "A" Throughout Network

b. Least-Cost Path from "A" to All Other Nodes

gence to a common topology database in every network node is critical to achieving consistent end-to-end routing decisions. If nodes have different topology databases, then they may create routing loops. Since routing transients will inevitably occur, IP explicitly handles the possibility of routing loops through the Time To Live (TTL) field in the IP packet header, which prevents a packet from circulating indefinitely.

Constraint-Based Routing Algorithms

A network that selects the least-cost or shortest path is important in terms of engineering economics or propagation delay. However, a complete solution must also provide sufficient capacity to meet QoS objectives like loss and delay variation. The literature calls this more complicated problem *constraint-based routing*. Constraints may take on a number of forms, including limits on QoS parameters, sufficient capacity, avoidance (or exclusive use of) particular link types like satellites or fiber optic facilities, or any of a number of policy-related parameters. In the following simple example we consider a constraint-based routing algorithm that operates in a manner similar to the Private Network-Network Interface (PNNI) defined by the ATM Forum [9]. This example considers the constraint of available capacity.

Figure 16.6a illustrates a network where the flooding protocol distributes not only the link cost, but the available capacity on the link as well. Since the nodes continually allocate and release capacity in response to connection request and release messages, the available capacity portion of the topology database is at best an estimate. In Figure

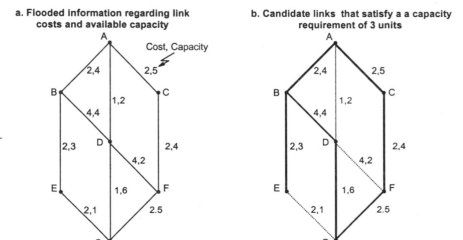

Figure 16.6
A network topology database augmented with available capacity information pruned to meet a specific capacity requirement.

16.6b, Node A receives a connection request with destination Node G requiring 3 units of capacity. Node A removes all links that fail to meet the capacity constraint of 3 units. We say that the algorithm prunes the links with insufficient capacity from the topology database, as illustrated by dashed lines in the figure.

Now, Node A can run a shortest-path algorithm on the pruned topology database to find the path with the least cost. As shown by the arrow in Figure 16.7a, this is the path ACFG. The PNNI signaling protocol uses an explicit routing mechanism called a Designated Transit List (DTL). A DTL is a stack computed by the source node that lists the sequence of node addresses on the specified path from the source to the destination. PNNI and token ring networks call this technique *source routing*. As the nodes pass the signaling message along, they move a pointer illustrated by the underlined node letter in the figure. The pointer identifies the next node along the explicit route. The signaling message retains the entire path in case the request encounters insufficient capacity along the route, in which case the nodes employ the full path to *crankback* the request to the source node, which can then specify an alternate route. Figure 16.7b illustrates the network topology database some time after allocating capacity to the connection between nodes A and G. An important consideration in the design of the network flooding algorithm with capacity constraints involves balancing the desire for an accurate topology database against the requirement to keep topology update traffic within the bounds of the nodal route processors. Typically, these implementations only flood topology updates if a significant change occurs in a constraint, like available capacity. Additionally, the algorithms also set a minimum time interval between updates to keep flooding traffic at or below an acceptable level. Since the topology database may be out of

Figure 16.7
Explicit source routing and topology database update reflecting changed capacity usage.

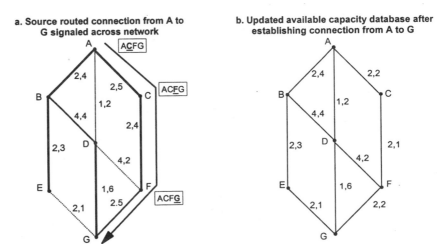

synch with actual network state, a procedure like crankback is essential.

There is a basic mathematical reason for why the OSPF routing algorithm is well defined and widely implemented, while the constraint-based ATM/label switching routing algorithm is still undergoing standardization. Minimizing a single parameter, such as minimum distance has a relatively simple optimal solution that the Dijkstra algorithm solves in an optimal amount of time. Adding a like available capacity makes the problem considerably more complex. Hence, design of suboptimal, yet still relatively efficient, constraint-based routing algorithms is an important challenge for scaling the Internet backbone or a large ATM network. Chapter 17 addresses this subject in greater detail.

IEEE 802.1d Bridging — The Spanning Tree Protocol (STP)

Early bridged LAN implementations simply broadcast MAC frames on every port except the one upon which they received the frame. Soon, network designers found that this basic form of bridging had several problems [2]. The broadcast bridges worked fine as long as the LAN physical network topology had only a single path between any bridges. Unfortunately, if a single link or bridge failed, then the bridged network was down. The IEEE's 802.1d Spanning Tree learning bridge Protocol (STP) [10] solved this problem and delivered reliable, automatically configuring network bridging. The Spanning Tree Protocol dynamically discovers network topology changes and modifies the forwarding tables to automatically recover from failures and revert to an optimized configuration as the topology changes.

The 802.1d Spanning Tree Protocol provides reliable networking by utilizing an algorithm that determines a loop-free topology within a short time interval. The STP algorithm runs continuously to react to link failures, as well as automatically add and delete stations and LANs. The resulting path through the bridged network looks like a tree rooted at the bridge with the lowest numerical MAC address. All other bridges forward packets up the tree toward this root bridge. Intermediate nodes then forward packets back down the tree to the destination leaf. The destination bridge then simply transmits the frame onto the destination LAN.

Figure 16.8 illustrates a simple example of this property of the spanning tree algorithm. Figure 16.8a illustrates the physical topology of seven LANs, labeled A through G, interconnected by five bridges,

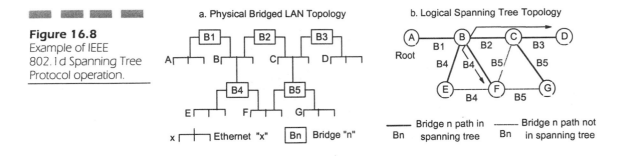

Figure 16.8
Example of IEEE
802.1d Spanning Tree
Protocol operation.

labeled B1 through B5. Observe that the physical topology has multiple paths between LANs B through G. However, the spanning tree algorithm resolves to a single logical topology of a tree rooted in the port on LAN A in Bridge 1 (B1) as shown in Figure 16.8b. Note that traffic in such a bridged network often does not take the most direct path. For example, LAN frames between LANs F and D will not flow through B5 and B3, but instead flow through B4, B5, and B3. Designers can control which links the STP bridge chooses when multiple parallel paths connect bridges by setting administrative costs in the STP algorithm. In addition, network designers can choose the MAC address utilized by the bridges to control the resulting topology to a certain extent. However, WAN network designers should carefully employ these techniques to minimize traffic flowing across the WAN in the spanning tree.

Routing, Traffic Engineering, and Restoration

This section addresses some important aspects of routing scalability and restoration from failures.

Routing Paradigm Scalability

A fundamental attribute of any network is the basic routing paradigm: connection-oriented or connectionless. ATM and RSVP use a connection-oriented paradigm similar to that employed by the telephone network. Here, each node must maintain the state for each connection along the end-to-end path. A connection-oriented paradigm must maintain state for every flow, which is on the order of 100,000 flows on an OC3 carrying Internet traffic [11]. Each of these flows might last 30 seconds. If the network attempted to establish a connection for each flow, it would require connect setup rates on the order of 10 million attempts per hour. Currently, the largest telephone switches process calls at rates on the order of 1 million attempts per hour. Clearly, a connection-oriented approach cannot support the current mix of Internet traffic on a large backbone.

The Internet solves this problem by using a connectionless paradigm where devices use the header within each packet to determine the next hop towards the destination. Connectionless routing protocols require tables on the order of 100,000 entries that contain a next hop forwarding port for every address prefix in the global Internet. Hence, the connectionless design scales better than the connection-oriented paradigm for Internet traffic composed of a large number of short-lived flows. The essential difference is aggregation of addresses in the connectionless design.

Physical Layer Restoration

Let's look at a simple example of a four-node network to better understand the efficiency of routing and restoration. Each node has an equal amount of traffic destined for every other node. We call this a uniform traffic distribution. Figure 16.9 illustrates a network where four SONET rings connect the nodes. Each SONET ring dedicates one physical circuit between nodes for restoration, hence the network operates at 50% efficiency. A major advantage of a SONET ring network is that restoration after a failure occurs within 50 milliseconds or less. Another advantage is that the router or switch requires fewer ports, an important consideration with the port-limited routers or switches offered by some manufacturers.

A similar result occurs if we consider a SONET ring connecting an Add Drop Multiplexer (ADM) at each site, as depicted in Figure 16.10.

Figure 16.9
Example of SONET ring routing/restoration in a network with multiple rings.

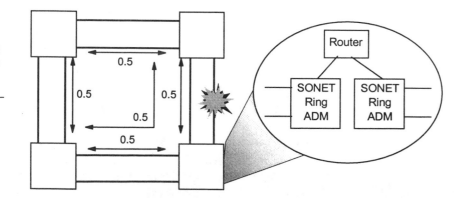

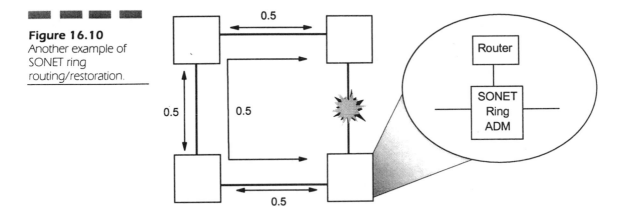

Figure 16.10
Another example of
SONET ring
routing/restoration.

Here too, each link can only carry traffic equal to 50 percent of the link capacity while providing for complete restoration in the event of any single link or node failure. When a break occurs, the traffic between the pair of nodes adjacent to the cut is sent in the opposite direction around the ring. Furthermore, the granularity of restoration in the limited by the TDM multiplexing hierarchy, as described in Chapter 2.

Network Layer Restoration

Figure 16.11 illustrates the case of restoration performance when IP operates directly over SONET links. The IP/SONET design requires the deployment of Big Fast Routers (BFRs). The example shows the response of a BFR network running the OSPF protocol in response to the same failure. Since OSPF picks the shortest path, rerouting results in only 50% efficiency, since each working circuit has a corresponding protection circuit. An advantage of IP/SONET versus SONET ring

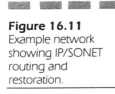

Figure 16.11
Example network
showing IP/SONET
routing and
restoration.

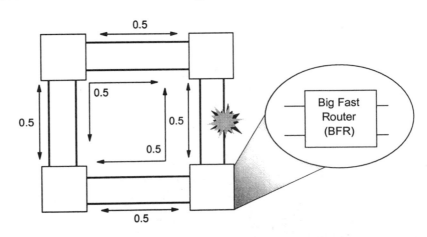

restoration is the ability to statically load-balance traffic across equal cost routes, as shown in the figure. This technique offers less traffic to each link, which means fewer intervals of congestion.

Hierarchical Restoration

Figure 16.12 shows the case where IP operates over an ATM or a label switched infrastructure. The figure illustrates the rerouted traffic loads in response to the same failure scenario for an ATM or label switch-based network. If the ATM- or label-based routing algorithm is aware of required bandwidth, the design improves efficiency by 50%, resulting in 75% utilization. ATM's PNNI algorithm won't necessarily yield this performance in all situations, but could come close. Note from the figure how the constraint-based routing algorithm splits traffic across both the shortest and longer paths to achieve this goal. Therefore, although IP over SONET achieves improved link-level efficiency (due to less overhead) as studied in Chapter 3, the loss in network-level efficiency requires that the routing algorithm changes as well before migrating off of ATM. The IETF has defined the Multi-Protocol Label Switching (MPLS) standard for this very reason.

Review

This chapter introduced the concept of routing by analogy with transportation networks. The text presented the concept of routing optimization against a single metric, like distance or cost via several examples. We also introduced the real-world routing problem subject

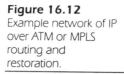

Figure 16.12

Example network of IP over ATM or MPLS routing and restoration.

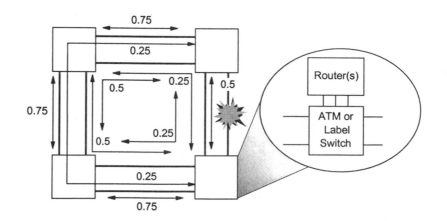

to the constraint of the route having sufficient capacity for the traffic flow. The text then covered an example of link-state based shortest-path routing for a simple network. The coverage then expanded the example to include a capacity constraint and illustrated the operation of explicit routing. We summarized the operation of the spanning tree algorithm commonly used in bridged Ethernet networks. The chapter concluded with examples illustrating the operation of constraint-based routing that provide traffic engineering as well as a restoration response to network failures.

References

[1]   M. Ladham, "MPOA versus MPLS," ICM L2/L3 Interworking Workshop, April 1998.

[2]   R. Perlman, *Interconnections*, Addison-Wesley, 1992.

[3]   J. Moy, *OSPF — Anatomy of an Internet Routing Protocol*, Addison-Wesley, 1998.

[4]   J. Moy, *OSPF Version 2*, RFC 1247, IETF, July 1991.

[5]   D. L. Comer, *Interworking with TCP/IP - Volume I Principles, Protocols and Architecture*, Prentice Hall, 1991

[6]   A. Tannenbaum, *Computer Communications, Third Edition*" Prentice-Hall, 1996.

[7]   C. Huitema, *Routing in the Internet*, Prentice-Hall, 1995.

[8]   M. Streenstrup, *Routing in Communication Networks*, Prentice-Hall, 1995.

[9]   ATM Forum, *Private Network-Network Interface Specification Version 1.0*, af-pnni-0055.00, March 1996.

[10]   IEEE, *IEEE Standards for Local and Metropolitan Area Networks: Media Access Control (MAC) Bridges*, Std 802.1d-1990, March 1991.

[11]   K. Thompson, G. Miller, R. Wilder, "Wide-Area Internet Traffic Patterns and Characteristics," *IEEE Network*, November/December 1997.

17

Routing Algorithms

"Out of chaos comes order."

— Nietzche

This chapter describes some important aspects of routing algorithms used in IP and ATM networks. The coverage begins with a short primer on graph-theoretic terminology used to describe the topology of networks. We then turn our attention to the study of algorithms that optimize the selection of routes, or paths, through an interconnected network of nodes. Our discussion includes considerations involved in centralized and distributed implementations. The text then introduces the practical concepts of constraints, focusing primarily on the need to serve a specific traffic pattern using links with a finite capacity. The coverage continues by detailing the specific operation of a constraint-based routing algorithm. Although no optimal solution is currently known, the text summarizes relevant theoretical results and practical guidelines. We describe how rearrangement can optimize some traffic flows. The chapter concludes with a brief introduction to mathematical programming techniques defined in the operations research discipline applied to optimal routing and network design.

Graph Theory Applied to Networks

This section introduces the graph-theoretic terminology commonly employed in the analysis of network routing.

Basic Terminology

The representation of networks in graphical form has a mathematical basis in graph theory [1, 2, 3, 4]. Figure 17.1 represents a network of abstract *nodes* connected via *links*. Note that the graph-theoretic term for node is *vertex* and the term for link is *edge* or *arc*. We use these terms interchangeably. The weight w_{ij} for the link connecting node N_i to node N_j may have a component in each direction, which may not be equal. In this case, a set of directed links connect each pair of nodes. However, in many real-world networks, the link weights are symmetric.

We indicate each directed edge by an ordered pair of node numbers inside angle brackets. That is, the directed edge from node N_i to node N_j has representation <i,j> with weight w_{ij}. The set $\mathfrak{N}$ contains all N nodes and $\mathfrak{L}$ is the set of all L links in the graph. A graph $\mathfrak{G}$ is defined by the set of nodes $\mathfrak{N}$, and the set of links $\mathfrak{L}$.

The network *topology* is the pattern of links that connect the nodes. We say that two network graphs are topologically equivalent if we can move the nodes around (and the associated interconnecting links) to yield the same graphical representation. In other words, topology defines only the nodes and their interconnections, not the precise location of nodes and links as drawn on a map.

Figure 17.1
Graph-theoretic model
of a network.

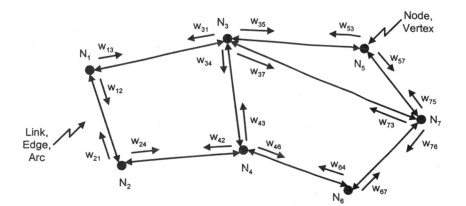

Matrix Representations of Network Graphs

Graphical methods provide intuitively appealing displays. However, such visual representations rapidly become cluttered when performing computer modeling of networks. Instead, we represent the networks and parameters associated with each node and link using vectors and matrices. This notational representation lends itself more readily to computer evaluation.

An important consideration in network routing is the relative desirability of selecting one link over another. Graph theory defines a weighted adjacency matrix A, with the element a_{ij} being the ith row and jth column of the matrix to represent the relative weight of links in a graph as follows:

$$a_{ij} \quad = \quad \begin{cases} w_{ij} & <i,j> \in \mathcal{L} \\ \infty & \text{otherwise} \end{cases} \qquad (17\text{-}1)$$

For example, the weighted adjacency matrix for the network graph of Figure 17.1 is:

$$A \; = \; \begin{bmatrix} \infty & w_{12} & w_{13} & \infty & \infty & \infty & \infty \\ w_{21} & \infty & \infty & w_{24} & \infty & \infty & \infty \\ w_{31} & \infty & \infty & w_{34} & w_{35} & \infty & w_{37} \\ \infty & w_{42} & w_{43} & \infty & \infty & w_{46} & \infty \\ \infty & \infty & w_{53} & \infty & \infty & \infty & w_{57} \\ \infty & \infty & \infty & w_{64} & \infty & \infty & w_{67} \\ \infty & \infty & w_{73} & \infty & w_{75} & w_{76} & \infty \end{bmatrix}$$

The *degree* of a network node is the number of links that exit the node. For example, in Figure 17.1, nodes N_1, N_2, N_5, and N_6 have degree 2, nodes N_4 and N_7 have degree 3, and node N_3 has degree 4. Note that nodes with higher degree have a greater amount of connectivity.

A graph is *connected* if every node is reachable from any other node. Generally, network design deals only with connected graphs. Furthermore, we say that a pair of nodes is k-connected if the removal of any k-1 nodes (excluding the pair of nodes under consideration) results in a graph that is still connected [3]. We say that a graph is k-connected if every pair of nodes is k-connected.

In addition to providing basic terminology, graph theory provides a means to analyze connectivity generated by concatenating several links and nodes [2]. A binary adjacency matrix B is one where a value of $b_{ij}=1$ indicates that a link joining connects nodes i and j, and a zero otherwise. The following are then true for the non-zero elements in the matrices resulting from operations on B:

- B represents the direct connectivity for each node
- $B \times B \equiv B^2$ represents the connectivity for all two-hop paths
- B^n represents the connectivity for all n-hop paths

Note that this method eventually generates paths that traverse the same node more than once, forming a *cycle*, or a routing loop. In general, the occurrence of cycles in network routing is undesirable because it wastes resources. Typically, routing designs use the notion of spanning trees to avoid cycles.

Trees and Spanning Trees

A tree is a special type of network graph. Intuitively, a tree is a graph without any cycles that has exactly N-1 links. A tree graph $\mathfrak{T}$ is a set of nodes $\mathfrak{N}$ and links $\mathfrak{L}$ such that [5]:

1. One node is designated the root.
2. All remaining nodes can be partitioned into some number $m \geq 0$ disjoint sets $\mathfrak{T}_i$ such that each $\mathfrak{T}_i$ is also a tree with exactly one link adjacent to the root node. A tree $\mathfrak{T}_i$ is called a subtree of $\mathfrak{T}$.

Recursively applied, the above definition unambiguously defines a tree. Because of this definition, a tree has no cycles and has a unique path from the root node to every other node.

A subgraph $\mathfrak{T}$ of a graph $\mathfrak{G}$ is called a *spanning tree* if it includes all of the nodes of $\mathfrak{G}$ and satisfies the definition of a tree given above. For example, Figure 17.2 uses solid lines to depict the links in one possible spanning tree rooted at node N_1 for the network graph of Figure 17.1. The figure depicts the links not included in the spanning tree as dashed lines. Note that the spanning tree satisfies all of the properties of a tree described above. In this example, N_1 is the root node, nodes N_5, N_6, and N_7 are leaf nodes, and nodes N_3 and N_4 are branch nodes.

Frequently, the weights w_{ij} of the adjacency matrix A represent an economic cost, transmission delay, or some other measure that we wish to minimize. A pivotal problem in network routing is then finding the spanning tree subgraph $\mathfrak{T}$ that results in a minimum total weight of every subgraph in $\mathfrak{T}$. This means that the resulting paths defined by the minimum spanning tree are the least-weight paths from the root node to every other node in the network graph. Since

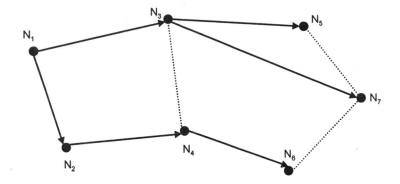

Figure 17.2
Spanning tree for the
network graph of
Figure 17.1.

the link weight often is associated with a distance (or cost) metric, many texts state the problem of finding the minimum spanning tree as that of finding the shortest (or least-cost) path.

Shortest-Path Algorithms

This section discusses the general network routing problem of finding the shortest path from a root node to every other node.

The General Problem

The design of techniques that quickly and efficiently determine the shortest path from one node to another has been an area of intense research and development. This section summarizes the general problem and then describes two popular algorithms. The following examples employ the network topology of Figure 17.1. In particular, Figure 17.3 depicts the example network with specific numeric values assigned to the link weights w_{ij}.

Figure 17.3
Adjacency weight
assignments for the
network graph of
Figure 17.1.

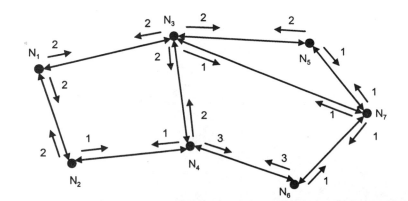

The problem now is to find the shortest path from any one node to every other node. This problem has been widely studied in a variety of disciplines: operations research [6, 7], computer science [5], graph theory [1], and network routing [3,4,9,8]. Algorithms that implement this calculation may be centralized or distributed. The centralized algorithms are simpler to analyze because a basic premise is that global knowledge of the network topology and state is available. The performance of distributed algorithms approach the optimality of their centralized counterparts only during steady-state conditions. The principal difference is in how various distributed algorithms react to transient changes in the network topology or state.

The Dijkstra Algorithm

The literature attributes the following simple algorithm for finding the shortest path from one node to every other node to Edsger Dijkstra [3]. Define a set S that will contain the nodes for which the algorithm has found the shortest path. Initialize this set to contain only the source (i.e., root node), for example, $S \equiv \{1\}$ when N_1 is the root. Finally, define a parameter d_i to hold the current estimate of the distance from the root to each node N_i. Initialize this distance estimate as follows:

$$d_i = \begin{cases} 0 & i = 1 \\ w_{1j} & \text{otherwise} \end{cases}$$

Given the above definitions and initialization, the *Dijkstra algorithm* then consists of the following steps:

1. Select the next-closest node N_k by finding a node for which the shortest path has yet not been found ($k \notin S$), which has the smallest distance estimate d_k ($d_k = \underset{j \notin S}{\text{Min}} (d_j)$).
2. Add node N_k to the set of nodes S with shortest path already found ($S \leftarrow S \cup \{k\}$).
3. If a shortest path is known for every node ($S = \mathfrak{N}$), then stop: the algorithm has completed.
4. Update the distance estimates for all nodes not in S by the new shortest link value if the new path is shorter than the previous one ($d_j \leftarrow \text{Min}[d_j, w_{kj} + d_k]$, $\forall j \notin S$).
5. Go to step 1.

Steps 1 and 4 embody two powerful concepts that make the algorithm work. We say that this is a greedy algorithm because step 1 selects the shortest distance from those currently known. When the algorithm begins, the distance estimates d_i, contain the one-hop distances to all of the direct neighbors of node N_1. The last part of step 1 effectively makes the link weights unique if it breaks ties in a deterministic, predictable manner. This is an essential property for a distributed routing algorithm. If there is a tie for the minimum distance, the algorithm requires a tiebreaker that results in a consistent outcome. An example of such a tiebreaker is selecting the link that has the highest numbered node as an endpoint.

As the algorithm progresses, the logic in step 4 updates the distance estimates to reflect the best cumulative path to every other node for which the shortest path is not already known. Since the algorithm selects the shortest path at each step, it traces out the shortest path in only N-1 iterations for an N node network. Note that the Dijkstra algorithm requires at worst N computations in each iteration to sort the distance estimate. Hence, the worst-case level of computation is on the order of N^2, expressed as $O(N^2)$ [3]. Using the heap sort technique to reduce the number of computations per iteration reduces the computation to $O((N+L)\log(N))$ [9].

Figure 17.4 depicts the results of the shortest-path spanning tree from a root node N_1 to every other node using the weights defined in Figure 17.3. For clarity, the figure replaces the directional arrows and weights with a single digit. Note that this spanning tree differs from another possible spanning tree for this graph as depicted in Figure 17.2.

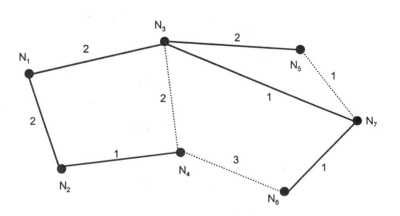

Figure 17.4
Shortest path from node N_1 to every other node for the weighted network graph of Figure 17.3.

The Bellman-Ford Algorithm

The *Bellman-Ford algorithm* uses another approach to find the shortest path. It is useful if a maximum number of hops is a constraint. This algorithm maintains a parameter d_i^h that contains the cumulative distance from a root node (i.e., N_1 in the following description) to node N_i for an h-hop path. Initially, the algorithm sets $d_1^h = 0$ for all h, sets $d_i^h = \infty$ for all i≠1, and sets h=1. Next, the algorithm executes the following steps:

1. Update cumulative distance for the current hop value h ($d_i^h = \underset{j}{Min}[w_{ji} + d_j^h]$ for all i≠1).

2. If there is no change in the cumulative distance counts ($d_i^h = d_i^{h-1}$ for all i), then stop: the algorithm has completed.

3. Increment the hop count (h←h+1).

4. Go to step 1.

This algorithm eventually traces out the same shortest-path spanning tree as the Dijkstra algorithm does if ties are broken in the same manner. It does so using an approach that begins at the root node, and then branches out toward all destinations in a parallel fashion in an increasing radius of hops away from the root node. Thus, when implemented in a distributed manner it acts as a distance-vector routing algorithm. The amount of calculation required for the Bellman-Ford algorithm is O(mL) [3], where m is the maximum number of links in a shortest path and L is the number of links in the network graph. In the worst case, the computation required in the Bellman-Ford algorithm is between $O(N^2)$ and $O(N^3)$ since m≤(N-1) and (N-1)≤L≤N(N-1). Note that for sparsely connected networks, the required level of computation can be considerably less than $O(N^3)$.

Considerations in Centralized and Distributed Implementations

If all nodes have the same knowledge of the network topology and link weights, then they can all execute a shortest-path routing algorithm and construct the same spanning tree from each node to every other node. Thus, an important component of a distributed routing algorithm is the protocol that reliably floods the topology state information to every node in a timely manner [12, 13]. Another consideration is stability. If the topology or link weights change too frequently, then the routing algorithm does not have time to converge and problems may develop like transient routing loops or large numbers of lost packets. In the late 1990s distributed routing algorithms in large internetworks converged to a stable solution within minutes. Ongoing research has the objective to reduce convergence time.

Having performed this global calculation, then each node need only set up its forwarding table to implement its portion of the overall shortest-path spanning tree. This relatively simple concept is at the heart of Internet routing. This solid theoretical foundation of shortest-path routing is one important reason that the Internet is able to continue its rapid pace of growth.

Constraint-Based Network Routing and Design

This section introduces the concepts of link and traffic constraints and some of the basic techniques involved in real-world IP and ATM network routing.

Link Capacity Constraint

The Dijkstra and Bellman-Ford algorithms efficiently determine the shortest path according to a single metric w_{ij} administratively assigned to each link. Unfortunately, most network designers must optimize network performance according to several parameters and constraints. A common network routing objective is to route traffic over the path with minimum delay. In the early days of the Internet, the routing algorithm implemented a scheme that dynamically updated the link weights based upon measured delay values. The experience taught an important lesson. The dynamic delay updates caused the routing algorithm to update its calculations and send traffic to where delay had previously been low. Unfortunately, the resulting onslaught of congestion caused delay to increase on the popular route and decrease on the previously unpopular routes. When the routing algorithms ran again using updated delay measurements, they chose the path that currently had the least delay, which was actually the same path the algorithms had just moved the traffic away from in the previous iteration. The movement of traffic back and forth between routes created instability and poor throughput due to packet loss caused by frequent rerouting.

An undesirable property of shortest-path algorithms is that they create congestion on links with low weights. This is unavoidable since the algorithm operates only on a single parameter without knowledge of any other parameters or constraints. Thus, the problem a network designer faces is that of minimizing cost subject to the constraint that routing does not offer traffic to any link in excess of its capacity. Thus, we now have two parameters for each link $<i,j>$: a routing weight w_{ij} and a link capacity c_{ij}.

Continuing with the same network topology used in the previous examples, Figure 17.5 assigns a numerical weight w_{ij} and link capacity c_{ij} to the link connecting nodes N_i and N_j. The example uses symmetric link weights and capacities as indicated in the figure. If no connection exists between nodes, then the link capacity $c_{ij} \equiv 0$. As we shall see, the addition of the capacity parameter complicates the routing problem considerably.

Maximum-Flow, Minimum-Cut Set

One measure that is relatively easy to compute is the maximum flow possible from one node to another. The maximum-flow-minimum cut theorem [6, 10] defines the procedure to determine this measure. A i-j *cut* is a set of links that when removed completely partitions a connected graph into two separate graphs, one containing node N_i and the other containing node N_j. The minimum i-j cut has the smallest sum of capacity values (i.e., the c_{mn}) for the removed links. The important result of the theorem is that the minimum i-j cut defines the maximum flow between nodes N_i and N_j.

Figure 17.5
Symmetric weights and link capacities for the weighted network graph of Figure 17.3.

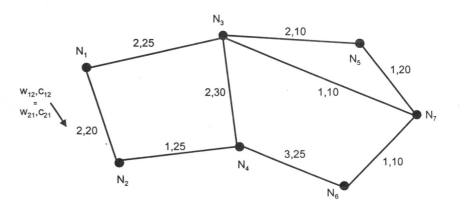

Figure 17.6 illustrates the minimum-cut-maximum-flow for our example network between nodes N_1 and N_7. The minimum cut involves the links $\langle 5,7 \rangle$, $\langle 3,7 \rangle$, and $\langle 6,7 \rangle$. The flow is 40 capacity units across this cut. Therefore, the maximum traffic flow between nodes N_1 and N_7 is also 40 units. However, this result only considers the community of interest between a pair of nodes in the absence of all other traffic. Therefore, the next constraint we introduce is that of a traffic matrix that considers the traffic patterns between all nodes.

The Traffic Matrix Constraint

The final part of the mathematical formulation of the constraint-based routing problem involves specifying the traffic offered between each pair of nodes. Denote the traffic from node N_i destined to node N_j as t_{ij} expressed in the same units as the c_{ij} link capacities. Collecting the t_{ij} into matrix form yields a traffic matrix T as follows:

$$
T = \begin{bmatrix}
0 & t_{12} & t_{13} & t_{14} \\
t_{21} & 0 & t_{23} & t_{24} \\
t_{31} & t_{32} & 0 & t_{34} \\
t_{41} & t_{42} & t_{43} & 0
\end{bmatrix}
\tag{17-2}
$$

In general, the traffic matrix contains an entry for every pair of nodes. Furthermore, the traffic may be asymmetric. The traffic matrix elements contain point-point and well as multicast and broadcast traffic. The usual convention is to indicate intranodal traffic (i.e., the diagonal t_{ii} elements) as zero since it does not require link capacity. Note, however, that intranodal traffic is important in nodal capacity sizing.

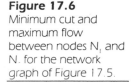

Figure 17.6
Minimum cut and maximum flow between nodes N_1 and N_7 for the network graph of Figure 17.5.

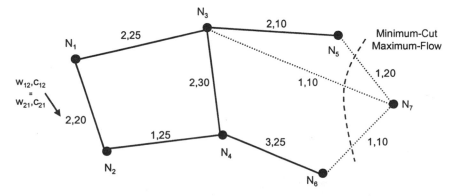

As a first step in network design, the min-cut-max-flow theorem determines whether a particular network can support each of the t_{ij} in isolation, as described earlier. If this fails, then the network designer should augment link capacities of add links such that the network at least meets the min-cut-max-flow constraint for each t_{ij} traffic pair.

A common assumption is that the underlying IP or ATM network is capable of directing the flows between pairs of nodes along paths that may not necessarily be the shortest in order to satisfy a link capacity constraint. ATM does this naturally because it is a connection-oriented protocol. Many IP networks run over ATM networks to realize the benefits of constraint-based routing. As discussed in Chapters 2 and 3, the IETF-defined MultiProtocol Label Switching (MPLS) protocol offers the same basic constraint-based routing infrastructure that ATM employs, without the cell and adaptation layer overhead.

Least-Cost Network Design

When the w_{ij} weights in the adjacency matrix A represent the cost of provisioning a unit of capacity between nodes N_i and N_j, then we can design a network to support offered traffic as defined by the traffic matrix T in Equation (17-2). This type of design is an approximation for a Virtual Private Network (VPN) constructed out of carrier facilities that provide dedicated capacity at a fine level of granularity based between nodes. One example is ATM PVC service provided by common carriers [14]. Although real services have a finite granularity, primarily for simplicity and reduction in operational complexity, the growth of most networks makes precise design less critical. For facility or private line-based networks, the granularity of this approximation is usually too coarse.

Basically, the least-cost design results from determining the minimum cost spanning tree rooted at each source node with offered load for each link determined by the row of the traffic matrix T corresponding to the source node. Let's look at our network example again for the minimum-cost spanning tree rooted at source node N_1 with the following normalized traffic load from the traffic matrix row of Equation (17-2):

$$< t_{11}, t_{12}, t_{13}, t_{14}, t_{15}, t_{16}, t_{17} > \ = \ < 0,1,2,3,1,3,2 >$$

Figure 17.7 depicts the resulting link capacity requirement C for the traffic originating from node N_1 to all other nodes using the above offered load and the minimum-cost spanning tree of Figure 17.4.

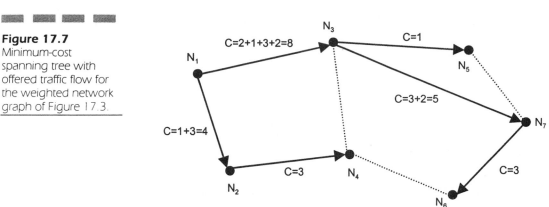

■■■ ■■■ ■■■ ■■■

Figure 17.7
*Minimum-cost
spanning tree with
offered traffic flow for
the weighted network
graph of Figure 17.3.*

Starting at the leaf nodes, the required link capacity C is simply the capacity generated by root node N_1 for that node. Moving backward toward the root node, the required link capacity includes the offered traffic for downstream leaf nodes in addition to traffic destined for intermediate branching nodes. The overall capacity required on each link direction is the sum of the required link capacities across the minimum cost spanning trees rooted at each node.

Equivalently, we could have defined a tree in the opposite direction with the branches serving the traffic from every other node to one node. This corresponds to using a column from the traffic matrix instead of a row as employed in the above example. Indeed, this is precisely how IBM's Aggregate Route-based IP Switching (ARIS) [17, 18] contribution to the IETF's MPLS standard defines the problem. In either the case of a source- or destination-rooted tree, the optimal network capacity design is the sum of the link capacities determined by a forest of such minimum-cost trees, one rooted at each node.

Planning for Failures

Another complication involved in the design and planning of real networks is engineering the node and link capacities to account for failure of one or more nodes or links. This aspect of network design directly relates to the QoS metric of availability. If traffic engineering does not consider the impact of failures, then sufficient capacity may not be available to serve the offered traffic. When insufficient capacity exists, then other QoS metrics like loss, delay, and delay variation also degrade, as described in the next chapter.

One commonly used technique simulates a candidate network design and routing algorithm under the conditions of any single link failure [21]. If the network design is still able to support the offered traffic load under the condition of any single link failure, then it meets at least a first-level test of resiliency. This type of design is valid only if the physical routing of every link is completely diverse from the physical routing of every other link. In practice, this is difficult to achieve. Hence, realistic simulations account for single points of failure like a fiber cut or a disaster that disables an entire node. If these failure simulations indicate that the candidate network design does not provide adequate capacity under failure scenarios, then the designer must augment network capacity and rerun the simulation.

One technique for reliable network planning involves finding primary and alternate paths that have no links in common. We call these *link disjoint* paths. Without any other constraints, one such algorithm employs using a shortest-path algorithm to find the primary route. The link disjoint algorithm then prunes the topology database of the links in the primary route. We then run the shortest-path algorithm against the pruned topology database to determine the best alternate path. After performing these steps, the primary and alternate paths have no links in common. A straightforward extension to this algorithm can generate paths that have no nodes in common by pruning the topology database of nodes used in prior steps instead of links.

Constraint-Based Routing and Design Algorithms

This section examines some specific algorithms that attempt to handle one or more of the previously defined constraints.

The Need for Heuristic Algorithms

At this point, the algorithmic theory of network routing becomes significantly more complex. No known routing algorithm yields an optimal solution for routing in a network with link capacity, traffic, or failure constraints using less computation than a brute force comparison of all possible alternatives. However, a number of heuristic algorithms yield a nearly optimal solution for many network topologies. The principal differences between these algorithms are the underlying service paradigm and required computation.

As discussed in Chapter 2, IP and ATM represent the two extremes of forwarding paradigms: connectionless and connection-oriented. A connectionless protocol like IP has difficulty handling constraints. For example, early experience in the ARPANET, the precursor to today's Internet, which attempted to dynamically estimate delay and adjust routing weights, led to unstable forwarding behavior. On the other hand, ATM employs a set of heuristic connection-oriented routing and signaling protocols based upon techniques proven in the circuit-switched telephone network, LANs, and the Internet. The differentiated services (diffserv) and MultiProtocol Label Switching (MPLS) protocols draw upon a similar toolkit to address the challenging problem of constraint-based routing.

The shortest-path routing algorithms studied earlier require a deterministic on the order of polynomial time to complete — that is, $O(n^k)$ in the commonly employed order notation. In the theory of algorithms, the constraint-based routing problem requires on the order of a non-deterministic polynomial time to complete, hence this problem is often called *NP-complete* [20]. Generally, experts consider an algorithm that has deterministic polynomial execution time tractable, while optimal solution of a NP-complete problem is intractable, requiring an approximate or heuristic solution instead.

Topology Pruning

The ATM Forum's Private Network-Network Interface (PNNI) specification [11] describes a well-known heuristic algorithm for implementing constraint-based routing. As done in other distributed routing algorithms, PNNI employs a reliable flooding procedure such that every node has an up-to-date view of the network topology and available capacity on each link. The topology database may also contain other link and node metrics and attributes, such as the ATM service categories supported, administrative link weight, and QoS parameters. Since ATM is connection-oriented, the PNNI algorithm processes a request for each connection. The basic procedure is to prune the overall network graph to eliminate links that either have insufficient capacity or else have a metric or attribute that fails to meet a requirement for the connection request.

Figure 17.8 illustrates our example network with each link labeled with a symmetric weight w_{ij} and available capacity a_{ij}. This example makes the available capacity symmetric in each direction in the interest of simplicity. A connection request arrives at node N_1 with a destination served by node N_7 that requires 3 units of capacity in each direction. Node N_1 examines its topology database, and prunes it of links that have available capacity less than 3 units, as indicated by dashed lines in the figure. Node N_1 then examines the administrative

Figure 17.8
Network topology
pruned of links that fail
to meet a capacity
constraint.

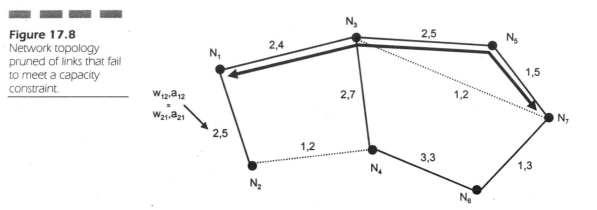

weight of the remaining links in the topology and selects the route traversing nodes N_1, N_3, N_5, and N_7, as indicated by the two-headed arrow in the figure.

Explicit Routing, Route Pinning, and Crankback

After the PNNI algorithm determines the shortest path, it issues a connection setup message that contains information defining the end-to-end path from the source to the destination. The literature calls the description of the end-to-end path either a *source route*, or an *explicit route*. Intermediate nodes use the explicit route to determine the next hop on the route toward the destination. The proposed constraint-based routing algorithms for IP diffserv and MPLS also employ the concept of explicit routes [15, 16]. An explicit route may be strictly defined in terms of a set of nodes that the path must include, or may be more loosely specified as a candidate set of nodes.

IP routing protocols can dynamically change the route of particular flows based upon topology changes. Therefore, for loosely specified explicit routes, the technique of *route pinning* forces a flow to remain on the same path that met capacity and QoS requirements at establishment time.

If a race condition occurs and the setup request finds insufficient capacity available on an intermediate link, then the network returns the setup request back to the source. The intermediate node "cranks back" the failed request to the source node with information identifying the reason for failure. The source node then removes the link with insufficient capacity (or other elements that fail to meet the required constraint) from its topology database and repeats the topology pruning and explicit routing procedure. The network should reject the connection request only if all possible routes are unable to meet the constrained routing requirement.

Suboptimal Routing and Rearrangement

The connection-oriented heuristic routing algorithm described above has the potential to block new connection attempts even though sufficient network capacity may exist as determined by some other algorithm. This behavior occurs despite the fact that the algorithm makes an optimal decision at establishment time for each connection. This occurs under conditions of heavy or focused network overload, as illustrated by the following example. Figure 17.9 depicts the available capacity of our example network topology after completing the connection from node N_1 to node N_7 using the shortest path with sufficient capacity. Note that the available capacity elements along the route highlighted by the double arrow have 3 units deducted from the values shown in Figure 17.8 to account for the capacity allocated to the connection between nodes N_1 and N_7.

We continue our example by considering how the network handles a new connection request from node N_4 to node N_7 requiring four units of capacity. The dashed lines in Figure 17.9 depict the topology pruned of the links that have less than 4 units of available capacity. Unfortunately, no route exists between nodes N_4 and N_7 with the constrained topology pruned of all links with insufficient capacity.

A key to understanding the suboptimal nature of this network state lies in noting that there is a way to rearrange the capacity used by the connections such that the network could support this additional connection request. Figure 17.10 illustrates this principle. It shows the available link capacity restored to the values shown in Figure 17.8 prior to making the connection between nodes N_1 and N_7

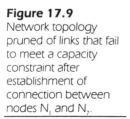

Figure 17.9
Network topology pruned of links that fail to meet a capacity constraint after establishment of connection between nodes N_1 and N_7.

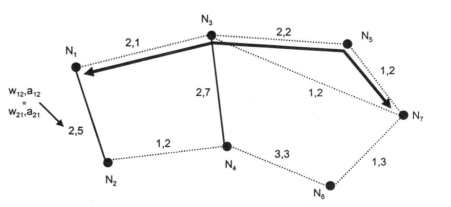

with the dashed lines indicating pruned links that have less than 3 units of capacity.

Finding configurations like this that involve two or more source-destination pairs requires a leap in algorithmic complexity. For a simple network like this, a trial and error procedure shows that routing the connection from node N_1 to N_7 to along the higher cost route traversing nodes N_1, N_3, N_4, N_6, and N_7 frees up sufficient capacity to accommodate the connection between nodes N_4 and N_7. Indeed, the challenge in developing such a rearrangement algorithm is significant, since to add additional connections, the number of required rearrangements may be quite large.

Unfortunately, the rearrangement approach has some problems. Rearrangement creates a disruption, or requires additional overhead and resources to proceed with minimal disruption. Time Division Multiplexed (TDM) networks employ a rearrangement technique similar to that described above to support private line service using Digital Cross-connect Systems (DCS). TDM systems perform rearrangement with intervals of disruption less than 50 ms. These systems accomplish this feat via broadcasting the signal over separate paths at one end of the connection and switching from one path to the other at the destination. Sometimes, the literature calls this technique "patch and roll," or "head-end broadcast and tail-end switching."

Note that even perfectly coordinated switching results in some disruption if the information transfer delay of the paths differ. If rearrangements are infrequent enough, then this is a viable strategy to optimize a quasi-static network. Otherwise, the routing algorithm designer must trade off optimal use of network capacity versus the interruption caused by rearrangement. Some rearrangement is acceptable for traditional packet-switched applications carrying non-real-time traffic like file transfer, Web browsing, and the like. Real-time applications, like voice and video, don't tolerate interruptions caused

Figure 17.10
Network topology showing a rearrangement of the connection between nodes 1 and 7 to accommodate a new connection between nodes 4 and 7.

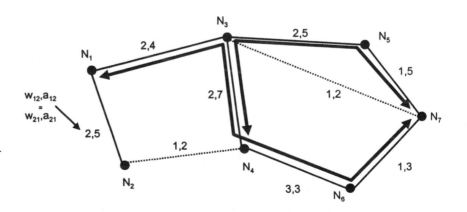

by unnecessary rearrangements nearly as well.

Viewed in another way, the example illustrated in Figure 17.8 through 17.10 illustrates the sensitivity of a connection-oriented routing algorithm to the order of connection attempts. Note, however, that in our example, simply reversing the order of the connection attempts fails to admit both requests. In other words, individually routing each request to achieve the least cost results in connecting only one or the other request.

Mathematical Programming Applied to Networks

A solution to a problem similar to constraint-based routing exists in the discipline of Operations Research (OR), which calls this a transportation problem with transshipment nodes [6,7,19]. The solution may have finely divisible units of capacity or discrete units. These mathematical programming techniques fall under the general headings of linear programming for finely grained units of capacity or integer programming for discretely defined units of capacity. As of this writing, engineers employ these techniques in the network design and optimization phase of IP and ATM networks. Seldom do real-time routing algorithms use these techniques due to the high degree of algorithmic complexity and correspondingly long computing times.

The linear programming approach requires division of the internodal flows into a number of smaller flows in order to efficiently pack traffic onto links. Otherwise, a knapsack-type problem occurs with integer programming when larger traffic bundles won't fit into the remaining capacity on a link. Practically, however, the capacity required by a particular flow places a lower limit on granularity. Furthermore, handling a larger number of flows increases complexity.

The remainder of this section works out a simple example of linear programming using the Microsoft Excel solver tool to illustrate the technique. To fit the example on one spreadsheet page, we consider a simple 4-node network. Figure 17.11a depicts the link weights and capacities of the example network. In order to set up the problem, we select a simple indexing method for the unidirectional links shown in Figure 17.11b. The matrix L forms the mapping to a link number Y as the directed link from node N_i to node N_j according to the formula $Y=L(i,j)$.

Now all that remains to completely specify the problem is the traffic matrix $T \equiv X[t_{ij}]$, where X is a multiplicative factor applied to every

Figure 17.11
Simple four-node
network example link
weights and capacities
and a link numbering
scheme.

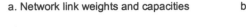

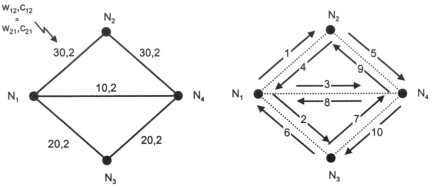

a. Network link weights and capacities   b. Network link numbering scheme

element in the traffic matrix. Separating out the X factor allows us to evaluate how much the traffic level can grow while still fitting within the capacity of the network. The upper part of Figure 17.12 illustrates the entry of the traffic matrix T, multiplicative factor X, weight matrix W, capacity matrix C, and link mapping matrix L as ranges (highlighted by a box) assigned a name in the spreadsheet.

The remainder of the spreadsheet lists all possible routes using the index K between each pair of nodes I and J in terms of the link numbers defined in Figure 17.11b. That is, if route K from node I to node J contains link Y, then $R(K,Y)=1$; otherwise, it equals zero, as shown in the body of the spreadsheet. The spreadsheet highlights the first row of a series of rows defining routes from one node to another via light shading. One may generate these routes manually for a small network such as this, or via a macro for larger networks. The list of routes may include all possible routes or only those routes that are candidates for the optimization algorithm. For example, the tabulation may only contain the S shortest routes. Thus, the number of rows required for routing is then no more than the quantity SN(N-1).

The column labeled $P(K,I,J)$ is the fraction of traffic between nodes I and J assigned to route K. The index K is an arbitrary number for a specific route between nodes I and J. Therefore, a mapping I(K) and I(J) exists as shown in the spreadsheet that uniquely determines the source node I and the destination node J. The percentage traffic assigned to a particular route $P(K,I,J)$ is the variable manipulated by solver's mathematical programming algorithm subject to the constraints described below.

First, we have the constraints that $0 \leq P(K,I,J) \leq 1$ for all values of I,J, and K. That is, the fraction of traffic offered to any route must be non-negative and no more than 100 percent. The column labeled S(I,J) defines the constraint that the traffic across all routes between nodes

I and J must total 100 percent. That is, the S(I,J) represent the following N constraints:

$$S(I,J) \equiv \sum_{a=I,b=J} P(K,a,b) = 1 \qquad (17\text{-}3)$$

The rows labeled C(I,J), W(I,J), I, and J in the middle of the spreadsheet are included for ease in indexing the values associated in each

Figure 17.12

Illustration of constraint-based optimization of the simple four-node network using the linear programming method in a Microsoft Excel spreadsheet using the Solver tool.

#	A	B	C	D	E	F	G	H	I	J	K	L	M	N	O	P
1	X		1.5													
2	T		1	2	3	4	L		1	2	3	4				
3		1		0.5	1	2		1		1	2	3				
4		2	0.5		0.5	0.5		2	4			5				
5		3	1	0.5		1		3	6			7				
6		4	2	0.5		1		4	8	9	10					
7																
8																
9	W		1	2	3	4	C		1	2	3	4				
10		1		30	20	10		1		2	2	2				
11		2	30			30		2	2			2				
12		3	20			20		3	2			2	INDEX(C,M17,M18)			
13		4	10	30	20			4	2	2	2			INDEX(W,O17,O18)		
14																
15						C(I,J)	2	2	2	2	2	2	2	2	2	2
16						W(I,J)	30	20	10	30	30	20	20	10	30	20
17	X*INDEX(T,B20,C20)					I	1	1	1	2	2	3 (Link Y=L(I,J))	3	4	4	4
18						J	2	3	4	1	4	1	4	1	2	3
19	K	I(K)	J(K)	X*T(I,J)	P(K,I,J)	S(I,J)	1	2	3	4	5	6	7	8	9	10
20	1	1	2	0.75	1	1	1									
21	2	1	2	0.75	0											
22	3	1	2	0.75	0											
23	4	1	3	1.5	1	1		1								
24	5	1	3	1.5	0											
25	6	1	3	1.5	0											
26	7	1	4	3	0.6667	1			1							
27	8	1	4	3	0.2917											
28	9	1	4	3	0.0417											
29	10	2	1	0.75	1	1				1						
30	11	2	1	0.75	0											
31	12	2	1	0.75	0											
32	13	2	3	0.75	0.5	1										
33	14	2	3	0.75	0.5											
34	15	2	3	0.75	0											
35	16	2	3	0.75	0											
36	17	2	4	0.75	1	1					1					
37	18	2	4	0.75	0											
38	19	2	4	0.75	0											
39	20	3	1	1.5	1	1						1				
40	21	3	1	1.5	0											
41	22	3	1	1.5	0											
42	23	3	2	0.75	0.5	1										
43	24	3	2	0.75	0											
44	25	3	2	0.75	0.5											
45	26	3	2	0.75	0											
46	27	3	4	1.5	1	1							1			
47	28	3	4	1.5	0											
48	29	3	4	1.5	0											
49	30	4	1	3	0.6667	1								1		
50	31	4	1	3	0.2917											
51	32	4	1	3	0.0417											
52	33	4	2	0.75	1	1									1	
53	34	4	2	0.75	0											
54	35	4	2	0.75	0											
55	36	4	3	1.5	1	1										1
56	37	4	3	1.5	0											
57	38	4	3	1.5	0											
58	Carried Load F(Y)						2	2	2	2	2	2	2	2	2	2
59	Leftover Capacity G(Y)						-1E-06	0	1E-06	-1E-06	-1E-06	3E-14	0	1E-06	-1E-06	3E-14
60	Weighted Usage H(Y)					440	60	40	20	60	60	40	40	20	60	40

Callout annotations shown in the spreadsheet:

- R(K,Y)
- SUM(E39:E41)
- SUMPRODUCT($D20:$D57,$E20:$E57,J20:J57)
- K16*K59
- N15-N58
- H=SUM(G60:P60)

link in subsequent calculations. Each row in the body of the spreadsheet contains a value of 1 if the link numbers defined by the matrix L are on the route from node I to node J. The last three rows of the spreadsheet form the final constraints and the optimization criteria. The row labeled F(Y) is the load carried by link Y according to the following formula:

$$F(Y) \equiv X \sum_K T(I(K), J(K)) \, P(K, I, J) \, R(K, Y)$$

Thus, the leftover capacity for link Y in the direction from node I to node J is $G(Y) \equiv C(I,J)\text{-}F(Y)$ where $Y \equiv L(I,J)$. We then have the final set of constraints that $G(Y) \geq 0$. That is, no link can be overloaded.

Finally, the last row forms the optimization criterion of the sum of the carried load weighted by the metric $w_{a,b}$ for the link Y connecting node a to node b as determined by the function Y=L(a,b) as follows:

$$H \equiv \sum_Y H(Y) = \sum_{Y=L(a,b)} w_{a,b} G(Y)$$

To perform the optimization, select Tools and then Solver from the menu bar in Microsoft Excel, enter the Target Cell as F60 (i.e., H), and select the Min radio button for minimization. Next, identify that Solver can change the cells in the range E20:E57 (i.e., the P(K,I,J)) to achieve this goal. Then we must enter each of the constraints described above. Note that Solver allows entry of constraints as a range. Finally, click on the Solve button, and the Solver tool will begin calculations and indicate status as it performs iterations. It will complete and indicate that it has found a feasible solution, or else indicate that it cannot find a feasible solution. A feasible solution means that the network can serve the offered traffic. If Solver indicates that no feasible solution exists, then the network has insufficient capacity to serve the offered load. In this case, try augmenting the capacity for the fully occupied links. The Solver tool has a number of options to control the accuracy of the result, the number of iterations, reporting, and algorithm employed. See the help screens in the Microsoft Excel spreadsheet program for further information.

In the example of Figure 17.12, the offered traffic with a multiplier of X=1.5 completely fills the example network capacity, as seen by examining the small values of remaining link capacity on the line labeled G(Y). It does so by spreading the traffic across the links using the values of the routing parameter P(K,I,J). These values are not intuitively obvious even in this simple example.

This was only a simple example. This spreadsheet technique will handle networks containing no more than 10 to 20 nodes depending upon the network topology and the number of routes considered. The field of optimal constraint-based routing is relatively new. The reader interested in further details should consult periodicals in the field of OR and mathematical programming, in addition to the textbooks cited at the beginning of this section.

Review

This chapter defined the basic terminology from graph theory applied to networks of nodes and links. We detailed an important concept from graph theory widely used in network routing — that of trees, in particular, a tree that spans an entire network with minimum cost. The text then described some of the most frequently encountered algorithms employed by routing algorithms to determine the shortest path using a minimum spanning tree. We then defined the concept of optimal routing subject to constraints and demonstrated why this becomes such a difficult problem. The chapter described an example of a heuristic constraint-based algorithm based upon the ATM Forum PNNI specification. Finally, the chapter concluded with an example illustrating how the mathematical programming technique from operations research applies to optimal routing and network design.

References

[1]   G. Chartrand, *Introductory Graph Theory*, Dover, 1977.
[2]   J. Tremblay, R. Manohar, *Discrete Mathematical Structures with Applications to Computer Science*, McGraw-Hill, 1975.
[3]   D. Bertsekas, R. Gallager, *Data Networks — Second Edition*, Prentice-Hall, 1992.
[4]   W. Stallings, *High-Speed Networks — TCP/IP and ATM Design Principles*, Prentice-Hall, 1998.
[5]   D. Knuth, *The Art of Computer Programming — Volume 1/Fundamental Algorithms, 3rd Edition*, Addison-Wesley, 1997.
[6]   F. Hillier, G. Lieberman, *Introduction to Operations Research*, McGraw-Hill, 1995.
[7]   R. Vanderbei, *Linear Programming — Foundations and Extensions*, Kluwer, 1997.
[8]   R. Perlman, *Interconnections*, Addison-Wesley, 1992.

[9]   M. Streenstrup, *Routing in Communication Networks,* Prentice-Hall, 1995.

[10]   L. Kleinrock, *Queueing Systems — Volume II: Applications,* Wiley, 1976.

[11]   ATM Forum, *Private Network-Network Interface Specification Version 1.0,* af-pnni-0055.00, March 1996.

[12]   A. Tannenbaum, *Computer Communications, Third Edition,* Prentice-Hall, 1996.

[13]   J. Moy, *OSPF — Anatomy of an Internet Routing Protocol,* Addison-Wesley, 1998.

[14]   D. McDysan, D. Spohn, *Hands-On ATM,* McGraw-Hill, 1998.

[15]   B. Jamoussi, *Constraint-Based LSP Setup using LDP,* IETF, draft-ietf-mpls-cr-ldp-01.txt, February 1999.

[16]   C. Semeria, *Traffic Engineering for the New Public Network, Juniper Networks,* January 25, 1999
       http://www.juniper.net/leadingedge/whitepapers/TE_NPN.pdf.

[17]   A. Viswanathan, N. Feldman, R. Boivie, R. Woundy, *ARIS: Aggregate Route-based IP Switching,* IETF draft-viswanathan-aris-overview-00.txt, March 1997.

[18]   N. Feldman, A. Viswanathan, *ARIS specification,* IETF, draft-feldman-aris-spec-00.txt, March 1997.

[19]   F. Hillier, G. Lieberman, *Introduction to Mathematical Programming,* McGraw-Hill, 1995.

[20]   T. Cormen, C. Leiserson, R. Rivest, *Introduction to Algorithms,* McGraw-Hill, 1990.

[21]   R. Cahn, *Wide Area Network Design — Concepts and Tools for Optimzation,* Morgan-Kaufmann, 1998.

CHAPTER 18

Performance of Networks

"...a computer is just a glorified pencil."

— Karl Popper

This chapter extends the results of the previous chapter by describing the analytical technique of Jackson networks to model sets of independent queuing systems interconnected via a network of links. The resulting product form of the nodal queue occupancy probability density makes calculation of end-to-end QoS performance measures feasible. We carry through an analysis of the delay variation QoS metric for various queue service disciplines, including weighted fair queuing and priority queuing. We provide numerical results applied to IP and ATM networks. The text outlines how to apply these methods in a generic reference configuration to calculate end-to-end QoS performance measures in general networks. The analysis of general networks is quite involved, as covered in the next part. As an introduction to this subject, this chapter concludes by analyzing the performance of a special class of symmetric networks with uniform traffic. Specifically, the text presents results on the average routing hop distance and the traffic-carrying efficiency of mesh and tree network topologies.

Networks of Queues

This section extends the results of the previous chapter to model networks of interconnected routers or switches.

Generic Switching and Queuing Model

As described in Part 4, the conventional traffic engineering model for each directed link in a graph is a queuing system. Thus, a network is a set of interconnected switching and queuing elements, each implementing its own complex traffic management and QoS decisions. Making this substitution into the graph-theoretic model of the previous chapter, the result is a network of queues as shown in Figure 18.1. Now, the terms in the traffic matrix represent the stochastic properties of the point-to-point traffic between every pair of nodes. This characterization may be as simple as a Poisson arrival rate between each node pair with an identical packet service distribution, or as a complex as a set of parameters describing the traffic flow and queue service discipline.

Jackson Network Model

Due to the complexity of this problem, a common assumption is that the traffic is Poisson. This simplifies matters, because as studied in

Figure 18.1
Network of interconnected switching and queuing elements.

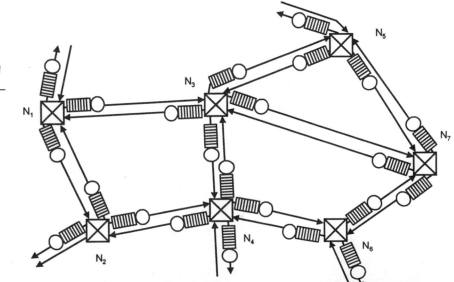

Chapter 8, merging or splitting a Poisson process results in yet another Poisson process. An important theorem attributed to Jackson provides the theoretical basis for the analysis of networks of queues [1, 2, 3]. The theorem makes some simplifying assumptions and uses some specific terminology that we now define with reference to the example 5-node network shown in Figure 18.2. The following parameters define the rate of Markovian processes at various points in the network. The parameter λ_i denotes the average arrival rate of external traffic to node i, while the parameter ω_i denotes the average rate of traffic departing node i as shown in the figure. As a result of randomized routing described below, the parameter γ_{ij} denotes the traffic offered from node i to node j, while the parameter μ_{ij} denotes the service rate of the link connecting node i to node j. The queues in this model have infinite capacity.

The Jackson theorem utilizes the concept of randomized routing. Specifically, a routing matrix $R=[r_{ij}]$ defines the nodal routing decisions. We call the elements of R routing probabilities because r_{ij} represents the probability that switch i routes an arrival from any incoming link to outgoing link j. In effect, this random routing creates the random merging of Poisson processes that preserve the Markovian nature of the arrival processes across the entire network. The blown-up view of node 2 (N_2) in Figure 18.2 illustrates the operation of the routing probabilities. The drawing in the insert omits loopbacks for simplicity, although the following formulation permits traffic coming in from one link to exit on the same link in the opposite direction. The probability that node i delivers an arrival to a locally connected user,

Figure 18.2
Example illustrating Jackson network terminology.

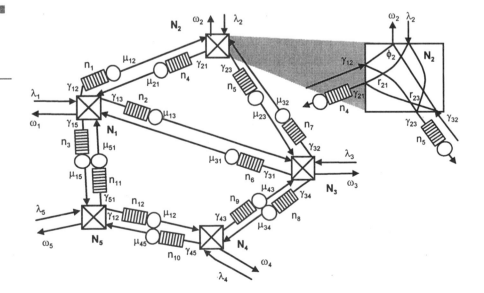

that is, the probability that a packet leaves the network, is:

$$\phi_i = 1 - \sum_{j=1}^{N} r_{ij}$$

Note that the above equation implies that the r_{ij} sum to a value no more than unity. We are interested in the queue occupancy statistics for each link in an L-link network. To do this, we effectively model each link as an independent queuing node. Using the flow balance technique, the average load offered to the link directed from node i to node j is:

$$\gamma_{ij} = \left[\lambda_i + \sum_{k=1}^{N} \gamma_{ki} \right] r_{ij} = T_i r_{ij} \qquad (18\text{-}1)$$

where T_i is the total traffic entering node i (i.e., externally and from adjacent nodes), which can also be expressed as follows using the above definitions:

$$T_i = \sum_{j=1}^{N} \gamma_{ji} = \lambda_i + \sum_{j=1}^{N} T_j r_{ji} \qquad (18\text{-}2)$$

The routing probabilities must satisfy the constraint that no link is overloaded, namely $\gamma_{ij} \leq \mu_{ij}$, to yield a stable queuing system solution. Similarly, the traffic leaving node i is $\omega_i = T_i \phi_i$. Furthermore, the r_{ij} routing probabilities must also satisfy the condition that the total traffic entering the network equals that leaving the network, namely:

$$\lambda \equiv \sum_{i=1}^{N} \lambda_i = \omega \equiv \sum_{i=1}^{N} \omega_i$$

A constraint-based routing technique, as described in the preceding chapter, can generate a routing matrix R that meets the above constraints. Then, along with the values of the external arrival rate λ_i at each node, Equation (18-2) defines N simultaneous linear equations solvable for the average load offered to each node T_i. Equation (18-1) then defines the γ_{ij} link level loads in terms of the T_i nodal load values and the r_{ij} routing probabilities.

We now have a problem formulated in terms of the arrival rate offered to a link connecting nodes i and j, γ_{ij}. In order to simplify notation, define a link mapping index y(i,j) that assigns a unique number to each link. The link level traffic is then γ_y. We also use the inverse mapping $\underline{x}(y)=<i,j>$, which returns the ordered pair of node numbers indexed by the link number y.

Product Form Probability Density

Let $\mathbf{n_k}$ be a random variable that denotes the number of packets in queue on the kth link as shown in Figure 18.2. The joint probability density of queue occupancy across all L links in the network is:

$$\Pr[\mathbf{n_1}, \mathbf{n_2}, ..., \mathbf{n_L}] \equiv \pi(n_1, n_2, ..., n_L)$$

Jackson's theorem states that this joint probability density factors into a product form of the individual link queue densities as follows:

$$\pi(n_1, n_2, ..., n_L) = \pi(n_1)\pi(n_2)...\pi(n_L)$$

In the simplest case, each link is a single-server M/M/1 queue with average utilization $\rho_k \equiv \gamma_k/\mu_k$. The joint probability density of link queue occupancy for the entire network of link-level queues then has a geometric density as follows:

$$\pi(n_1, n_2, ..., n_L) = (1-\rho_1)\rho_1^{n_1}(1-\rho_2)\rho_2^{n_2}...(1-\rho_L)\rho_L^{n_L} \qquad (18\text{-}3)$$

The fact that each queue behaves independently greatly simplifies analysis. Note that this model does not accurately model a real network of packets flowing through routers or switches, since the packet lengths do not change randomly. A number of simulations show that the random mixing and splitting of traffic in real networks yield results closely approximated by the Jackson network model [3]. Although the independence assumption is much simpler than a correlated traffic model, beware because it may yield overly optimistic results in some circumstances. When the traffic and interaction of the queues exhibit significant correlation, the only recourse is simulation of the network using the techniques summarized in Part 7.

End-to-End Performance

This section gives several models for the performance experienced by a flow of packets or cells traversing a network of IP routers or switches from one endpoint to another.

Jackson Network Model Predictions

The user application experiences the end-to-end performance delivered by the sequence of queues along the route. The resulting performance is the combined queuing delay experienced by the sequence of L links as shown in Figure 18.3. Similar results apply for the loss and delay QoS parameters to those described in the following sections for delay variation. Frequently, standards call this technique allocation of impairments in a reference connection model. The probability density of queue occupancy of Jackson networks allows us to compute statistics for delay across the entire network, or along a particular route, using the techniques from basic probability theory described in Part 3. The key to computing any statistics is the product form of the queue occupancy density given in Equation (18-3).

The total average number of packets in the queue for the kth link is $E[n_k]=\rho_k(1-\rho_k)^{-1}$. Hence, the average delay spent in queue and in service on link k, $E[t_k]$, is readily determined from Little's formula as follows:

$$E[t_k] \quad = \quad \frac{E[n_k]}{\gamma_{x(k)}}$$

where $\gamma_{x(k)}$ is the offered load for link k.

By virtue of the independence of queue occupancy density for each link, the average delay along a particular route is simply the sum of the average delays of each link on the route. An expression for average delay for all packets traversing the network $E[t]$ results from applying Little's formula to the entire network as follows [4]:

$$E[t] \quad = \quad \frac{\sum_{k=1}^{L} E[n_k]}{\lambda}$$

where $\lambda = \Sigma \lambda_i$ is the arrival rate for the entire network.

We can also determine the distribution of the end-to-end delay on a route via adding up the independent random variables. The prob-

Figure 18.3
End-to-end
performance model for
a path traversing a
series of nodes.

ability density of the time t_k spent by a packet in the M/M/1 queue for link k is [1,3]:

$$f_{t_k}(t_k) \;=\; \mu_k(1-\rho_k)e^{-\mu_k(1-\rho_k)t_k} \tag{18-4}$$

where ρ_k is the average utilization and μ_k is the service rate for link k.

The probability density of the delay along an L link route is the probability density of the sum of independent random variables corresponding to the delay encountered in each queue. Let $s_2=t_1+t_2$ be the sum of two independent random variables t_1 and t_2 with identical negative exponential densities as given by Equation (18-4) with $\rho_k=\rho$ and $\mu_k=\mu$ for all values of k. The probability density of s_2 is then the convolution of the individual densities, computed according to the following definition:

$$f_{s_2}(s_2) \;\equiv\; \int_{-\infty}^{\infty} f_{t_1}(s_2 - t_1)f_{t_2}(t_1)dt_1$$

. The result of convolving two independent random variables with identical negative exponential densities with parameter α is:

$$f_{s_2}(s_2) \;\equiv\; \alpha^2 s_2 e^{-\alpha s_2}$$

where $\alpha=\mu(1-\rho)$ for the packet delay. Let s_n be the sum of the delay values for n identical links. The probability density of the delay s_n encountered after traversing n identical links is found by successively convolving n negative exponential densities, which yields the famous Erlang distribution of order n [5]:

$$f_{s_n}(s_n) \;\equiv\; \frac{\alpha(\alpha s_n)^{n-1}}{(n-1)!}e^{-\alpha s_n}$$

The central limit theorem states that the probability density of a sum of independent random variables with an arbitrary density tends toward a normal distribution [6]. Figure 18.4 illustrates the density for the delay encountered after traversing 1, 2, 3, 4, and 5 links, each having a negative exponential pdf, for a normalized parameter $\alpha=1$. Notice how the density becomes increasingly similar to the bell-shaped normal density as n increases. Thus, we can use a normal distribution to approximate the delay variation accumulated along a route due to random contention and consequent queuing.

The expected value and variance of s_n, the sum of the n independent negative exponentially distributed delays encountered along a route with n hops, are:

$$E[s_n] \; = \; \frac{n}{\mu(1-\rho)} \qquad , \qquad Var[s_n] \; = \; \frac{n}{\mu^2(1-\rho)^2} \qquad (18\text{-}5)$$

Note how the delay variation increases as the number of hops in the path n increases. This means that the tail of the delay probability density for packets traversing many networks of nodes can be substantial unless intermediate nodes take specific measures to constrain the amount of delay that each node introduces. First, however, let's quantify the delay variation impact on a playback buffer.

Accumulation of Delay Variation

Typically, end equipment absorbs the delay variation accumulated by packets or cells traversing an IP or ATM network via a playback buffer as described in Chapter 4. Therefore, ensuring that delay variation seldom exceeds a specific value is an important admission control decision. Furthermore, each IP router or ATM switch also adds a fixed delay $\tau \equiv E[s_i]$ for all i. A simple result follows from the assumption that the probability density of delay for each link obeys a normal distribution with mean τ and standard deviation σ. The resulting delay distribution after traversing n links is the sum of n independent, identically distributed normal random variables. Thus, the density of the sum is the convolution on the individual densities,

Figure 18.4
Probability density of the delay after traversing 1, 2, 3, and 4 links.

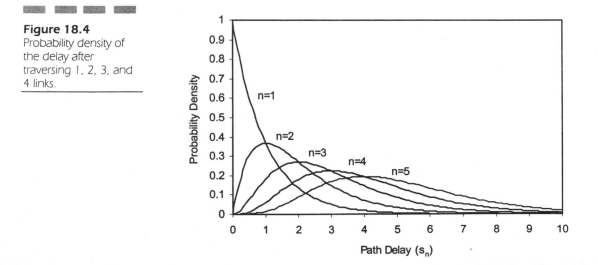

which is another normal random variable s_n with the following mean and variance [6]:

$$E[s_n] = n\tau \qquad , \qquad Var[s_n] = n\sigma^2$$

Because the standard deviation is the square root of the variance, it increases as $\sqrt{n}$ instead of linearly with n as the average delay does.

The probability ε that the end-to-end accumulated delay exceeds a playback threshold θ is simply the area under the tail of the normal distribution using the Q function defined in Chapter 8:

$$\varepsilon \equiv Pr[s_n \geq \theta] \approx Q\left(\frac{\theta - n\tau}{\sqrt{n}\sigma}\right) = Q(\alpha)$$

Solving for the playback threshold θ we obtain from the above formula yields the following result:

$$\theta \approx n\tau + \sqrt{n}\alpha\sigma \qquad (18\text{-}6)$$

This equation states that end-to-end delay variation is less than the threshold θ with probability 1-ε. The reason that the accumulation of variation is less than linear is that congestion is unlikely to occur simultaneously at every node. For example, while the variation is high in one node, it may be low in another node. Correlation between the traffic traversing multiple nodes makes this model overly optimistic, as described in informative Appendix V of the ATM Forum's Traffic Management 4.0 specification [7].

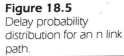

Figure 18.5
Delay probability
distribution for an n link
path.

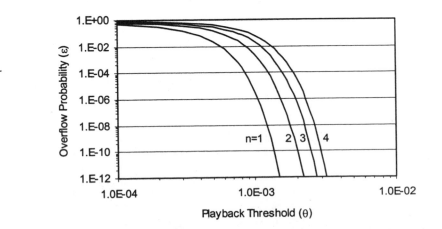

Figure 18.5 plots the overflow probability ε that the delay exceeds a certain value θ after traversing n nodes for a mean delay per link of τ=100 μs and delay variation standard deviation of σ=200 μs. As discussed in Chapters 4 and 5, the absolute magnitude of the accumulated delay and delay variation are critical QoS parameters for real-time applications.

Weighted Fair Queuing Performance Across a Network

When the input traffic is policed or shaped to ensure conformance to a traffic contract and the network nodes employ the Weighted Fair Queuing (WFQ) service discipline, a simple bound on the end-to-end delay results [8, 9]. As defined in Chapter 11, we assume a traffic flow characterized by an average rate r with token bucket regulator depth b and a maximum packet length L. Letting L_{max} denote the maximum packet length across all flows, the maximum delay experienced on a path of K links is:

$$Max[t] \leq \frac{b + 2(K-1)L}{r} + \sum_{i=1}^{K} \frac{L_{max}}{R_i}$$

where R_i is the bit rate of the ith link.

Note that the right-hand term of the above equation is insignificant for high-speed links (i.e., $R_i >> L_{max}$). However, if the path contains low-speed links, then the possibility of the extended transmission of a large packet delaying a shorter packet substantially does indeed exist. Note that the above formula reduces to the single node delay bound defined in Chapter 11 when K=1. For lower-speed flows, keeping a

Figure 18.6
WFQ delay variation bound for IP and ATM networks.

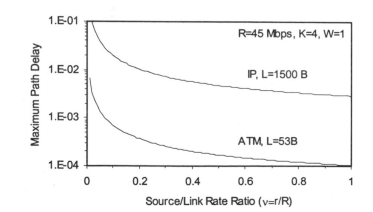

reasonable value of L/r is essential to keep delay variation low. For high-speed flows (r>>L) traversing a path of high-speed links (R_i>>Lmax), the maximum delay tends toward b/r.

Let's see how these parameters apply to IP and ATM networking through a simple example. If we let L_{max}=L and define the token bucket parameter to allow W maximum-length packets, then b=WL, where W≥1, since the token bucket must be able to admit at least one maximum-length packet. Furthermore, assume that R_i=R for all links on the path. Finally, let v≡r/R be the ratio of the source rate to the link rate. Using these assumptions, the bound on the path delay for WFQ service is:

$$\text{Max}[t_{WFQ}] \leq \frac{[W + 2(K-1) + Kv]}{v} \frac{L}{R} \tag{18-7}$$

Figure 18.6 plots the maximum delay variation from the above equation for representative parameters used in IP and ATM networks. Specifically, the example sets the maximum packet size to L=53×8=424 bits for ATM and L=1500×8=12,000 bits for IP. The example assumes that all K=4 links operate at a rate of R=45 Mbps and that W=1. As seen from the form of Equation (18-7), the term L/R multiplies the maximum delay Max[t_{WFQ}]. Hence, since the maximum packet sizes for IP and ATM differ by approximately an order of magnitude, the delay variation bound also differs by the same ratio. Recall from Chapter 4 that interactive applications should have one-way delay on the order of 100 ms. Leaving some allowance for propagation delay, this choice of parameters illustrates the fact that IP network backbones must operate at greater than DS3 speeds to serve interactive applications at the efficiency achieved with large maximum packet sizes. When operating over a larger number of links, we must increase the link rate R in direct proportion to keep the path-level delay variation at comparable levels. Operation at lower link speeds requires that the network break large packets into smaller segments like ATM does. Packet fragmentation standards also support this QoS-preserving capability.

Comparative Performance of Queue Service Disciplines on a Network Path

How does WFQ stack up against other queue service disciplines? This section computes delay variation bounds for FIFO queuing and priority queuing along a K-link path for comparison with the WFQ bounds given in the previous section. The model assumes a series of Jackson FIFO queues which substitutes the mean and variance from Equation (18-5) into the accumulated normal delay variation bound of Equation (18-6) with $\mu=R/L$. Hence, the delay variation bound for a path of K queues each using a FIFO discipline is:

$$Max[t_{FIFO}] = \frac{KL}{R(1-\rho)}\left[1 + \alpha\sqrt{K}\right] \qquad (18\text{-}8)$$

A delay bound when each node employs a Priority Queuing (PQ) service discipline substitutes the priority queuing service time defined in Chapter 11 for the FIFO service time as the mean and variance into Equation (18-6) with $\mu=R/L$. The resulting delay bound for the high-priority traffic is:

$$Max[t_{PQ}] = \frac{KL(1-\rho_1+\rho)}{R(1-\rho_1)}\left[1 + \frac{\alpha L(1-\rho_1+\rho)\sqrt{K}}{R(1-\rho_1)}\right] \qquad (18\text{-}9)$$

where ρ_1 is the utilization of the high-priority traffic of link capacity.

Figure 18.7 compares the resulting delay-bound performance for FIFO and PQ as given in Equations (18-8) and (18-9), respectively, versus the total link load ρ for a path traversing K=4 links. The example assumes the same parameter values used in the WFQ analysis in the previous section. The example assumes a utilization of high-priority traffic of $\rho_1=0.2\rho$ and a loss ratio of $\varepsilon=10^{-6}$. This choice of parameters yields a delay for IP less than 100 ms for typical operating parameters as was done in the WFQ example above. As seen in the WFQ analysis, the minimum delay differs by the ratio of the maximum packet size

Figure 18.7

Comparison of delay variation bounds for the FIFO and Priority Queuing (PQ) service disciplines in IP and ATM networks.

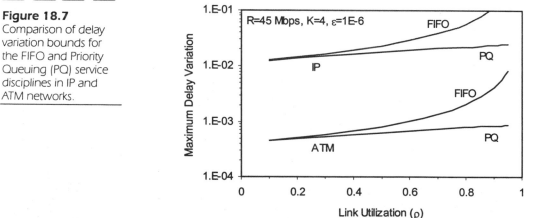

L for IP and ATM, which is approximately 30 in our example. As seen in many such systems, the FIFO service discipline has a delay curve that increases sharply as the offered load approaches 100 percent (note that delay has a logarithmic scale here). On the other hand, simple priority queuing has nearly flat path delay when the fraction of high-priority traffic is modest.

Comparing the delay-bound results for WFQ from Figure 18.6 with those of FIFO and PQ from Figure 18.7 along with the associated equations yields some interesting observations regarding relative performance. For high link utilization ρ and values of source-link ratio $v>0.1$, WFQ yields better delay variation than FIFO or PQ does. For values of source-link ratio $v<0.1$, PQ yields superior delay variation performance when the fraction of high-priority traffic is significantly less than 100 percent. This occurs because WFQ delays traffic with a low average rate to provide consistent delay to all traffic flows, while PQ services all high-priority traffic before serving any lower priority traffic. Note that other choices of parameters may yield conclusions with different numerical crossover points.

Hierarchical Access/Backbone Performance

In a typical network, a routed path traverses links that have a wide range of bit rates. Figure 18.8 depicts a model commonly encountered in large IP and ATM networks involving a hierarchy of node sizes and link speeds. Typically, the access links connecting a switch/router to the end user are of the lowest speed, ranging from 10 kbps to several Mbps. Access switches and routers collect traffic from many users and multiplex the aggregate onto higher-speed feeder trunks connect-

Figure 18.8
Typical hierarchical structure of a large IP or ATM network.

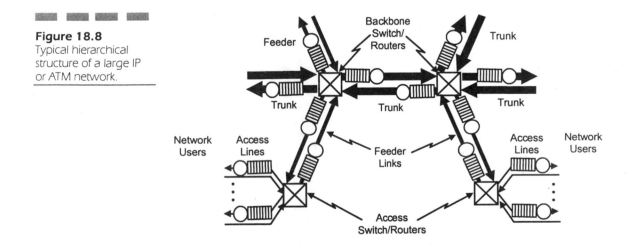

ing to larger-backbone switch/routers. Depending upon traffic demand, feeder links operate in the range of 10 Mbps to 1 Gbps. High-speed trunks then interconnect these backbone nodes at speeds ranging from 1 Gbps to 10 Gbps and more.

Since absolute delay and delay variation are the principal QoS parameters of interest, we must pay close attention to the store and forward delay of packet switching on low-speed links, in particular the low-speed access lines. Typically, queuing delay dominates backbone performance, while packet or cell transmission delay dominates access line performance in networks where the link speeds differ by orders of magnitude.

Analytical Routing Models

Other constraints or objectives often placed on network routing involve QoS performance parameters like delay and loss. Some constraints specifically apply only to connectionless networks like IP and others apply only to connection-oriented networks like ATM. Fairly distributing the loss probability across all traffic flows is important in the design of a connectionless network. On the other hand, a prime consideration in the design of a connection-oriented network is the probability of blocking a new connection attempt.

These are difficult metrics to compute for networks with general topologies and traffic patterns. The analysis of networks with simple topologies and regular traffic patterns provide some insight into the tradeoffs involved in network design [10]. This type of analysis best applies when engineering a network where the equipment port costs dominate overall expenditures — for example, in a LAN environment or when using carrier services that do not have a distance-sensitive cost component and where a hop count is the most important criterion.

Symmetric Networks with Uniform Traffic

This section analyzes the performance of networks possessing a high degree of symmetry with a traffic matrix that has a uniform load between every pair of nodes. The simplest such network to analyze is a fully meshed one. Specific networks with lesser connectivity are often impossible to analyze in closed form, and require computer solution using analytical, simulation, or optimization techniques as described in Part 7. As a prelude to that discussion, we consider a simple bound on symmetric networks with uniform traffic.

The following discussion references the terminology used for symmetric networks illustrated in Figure 18.9. For networks with a number of nodes N, a fully meshed graph has a routing distance to any other node of exactly one hop. The network graph is *balanced* [11] because the degree is D=N-1 links impinging on each node. The average routing distance d=1 for a fully meshed graph as shown in the figure. Deleting sets of links from the fully meshed graph that keep the nodal degree D balanced, larger values of average routing distance d result as shown by the examples in the figure. The largest routing distance occurs in a ring network. When the graph is symmetric, the average routing distance d is relatively easy to compute. It is simply the sum of the distance for each shortest-hop route from any one node to every other divided by the number of routes from one node to all others (i.e., N-1). For example, for a network with N=8 nodes in the ring configuration, the average routing distance d is:

$$d = \frac{1+1+2+2+3+3+4}{7} = \frac{16}{7}$$

In general, for a balanced N-node graph where each node has identical degree D, the formula for the average routing distance for N≥2 is:

$$d(N,D) = \frac{\sum_{i=1}^{M} iD + (M+1)(N-1-MD)}{N-1} \tag{18-10}$$

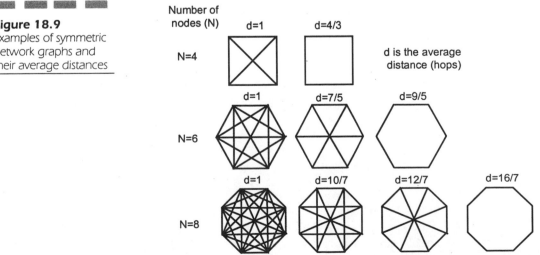

Figure 18.9
Examples of symmetric network graphs and their average distances

Number of nodes (N)

N=4   d=1   d=4/3

d is the average distance (hops)

N=6   d=1   d=7/5   d=9/5

N=8   d=1   d=10/7   d=12/7   d=16/7

where $M \equiv \left\lfloor \dfrac{N-1}{D} \right\rfloor$ with $\lfloor x \rfloor$ defined as the largest integer $\leq x$.

For larger, sparsely connected networks, a simpler approximation is useful. Specifically, when $N \gg 1$ and $N \gg D$, the average routing distance is approximately:

$$d(N,D) \cong \frac{N}{2D} \tag{18-11}$$

The number of the links in an N-node symmetric network where each node has degree D is simply:

$$L(N,D) = \frac{N \times D}{2} \tag{18-12}$$

Capacity and Design Considerations

Let ω denote the unidirectional traffic destined between every pair of nodes — that is, $t_{ij} = \omega$ for all i and j in the traffic matrix. Then the total bi-directional network traffic is:

$$\Omega = \frac{N(N-1)\omega}{2}$$

The traffic offered to each link is proportional to the average distance $d(N,D)$ defined in Equation (18-10) times the traffic offered by all nodes that flow along that link as follows:

$$\rho(N,D) = \frac{\Omega}{L(N,D)} d(N,D)$$

For large sparsely connected networks, the approximation of Equation (18-11) applies, and hence the offered link load is approximately:

$$\rho(N,D) \cong \frac{\Omega}{D^2} \tag{18-13}$$

As studied in Chapter 6, an admission control or network design algorithm utilizes a function $C(\rho,\varepsilon)$ to determine the required link capacity to service a load ρ to meet a QoS parameter objective ε, for example the probability of buffer overflow, connection blocking, or a bound on delay variation. The following simple model results for a capacity function determined by the normal distribution when both the mean and variance equal the traffic load parameter ρ:

$$C(\rho,\varepsilon) \;=\; \rho \;+\; \alpha\sqrt{\rho}$$

where $\varepsilon = Q(\alpha)$ is the probability that a unit variance normal random variable exceeds the value of α as detailed in Chapter 8.

Therefore, the total required network capacity Ψ is the product of the number of links in the network given in Equation (18-12) times the link capacity function $C(\rho,\varepsilon)$, namely:

$$\Psi(N,D) \;=\; L(N,D)\;\; C(\rho(N,D),\varepsilon)$$

Enlisting the normal approximation for the offered load from Equation (18-13) and rearranging terms yields the following expression for the total required network capacity:

$$\Psi(N,D) \;\cong\; \frac{N\Omega}{2D}\left[1 \;+\; \frac{\alpha D}{\sqrt{\Omega}}\right] \qquad\qquad (18\text{-}14)$$

Analysis of the above formula confirms several common-sense facts about networking. First, the required capacity increases linearly with the number of nodes N. Therefore, good designs keep the number of nodes as small as possible while balancing other factors. These factors include available switch size and link costs or QoS metrics (like delay and delay variation) that increase with greater link lengths and number of switching hops.

Second, the required capacity depends upon the degree D, offered load Ω and the parameter α. Although a ring network with D=2 has the smallest number of links, it actually has the largest required capacity Ψ. The optimal design of ring networks is analogous to the traveling salesman problem discussed in Chapter 20. For a network designed only for the average load (i.e., α=0), the required capacity decreases for increasing degree D.

The final observation regarding network economy of scale results by looking at the ratio of the carried load Ω divided by the required capacity Ψ, which results in the following formula:

$$\frac{\Omega}{\Psi} \;\cong\; \frac{2D}{N}\left[\frac{\sqrt{\Omega}}{\sqrt{\Omega} \;+\; \alpha D}\right] \qquad\qquad (18\text{-}15)$$

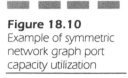

Figure 18.10
Example of symmetric network graph port capacity utilization

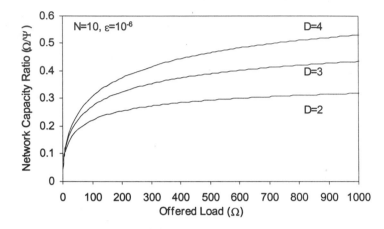

The ratio Ω/Ψ is a measure of how efficiently the network design utilizes port capacity. A higher value of this ratio indicates that the network utilizes capacity more efficiently. Figure 18.10 plots the capacity ratio Ω/Ψ from Equation (18-15) versus the offered load Ω for a network with N=10 nodes and QoS parameter $\varepsilon=10^{-6}$ ($\alpha\approx5$) for several values of node degree D. The capacity ratio approaches the maximum value of 2D/N as the offered load becomes much larger than $(\alpha D)^2$.

Symmetric Tree Networks

Another important class of networks involves trees. In a manner similar to mesh networks, we can derive relatively simple closed-form results for regularly structured tree networks. This study has application in other disciplines, in particular, computer science involving the amount of processing time required to search a tree-structured database [11]. In the area of networking, it applies to the analysis of bridged subnetworks as described in Chapter 16, as well as MPLS forwarding and VC merge-type algorithms in support of IP networks. Furthermore, use of a tree topology is common in access and local area networks that don't require resiliency.

Figure 18.11 illustrates a complete D-ary tree where the degree of each node is balanced with value of D=3. The tree's height H is the number of branching levels in the graph, which in this example is H=3. The tree is complete if every position in the hierarchy contains a node. In other words, a complete tree of degree D and height H must contain precisely N nodes as determined by the following formula:

$$N \equiv \sum_{i=0}^{H} D^i = \frac{D^{H+1}-1}{D-1} \qquad (18\text{-}16)$$

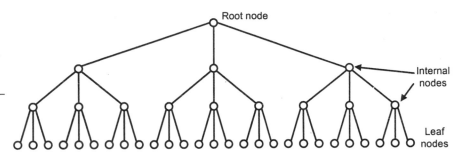

Figure 18.11
Illustration of a complete D-ary tree for degree D=3 and height H=3

As observed in Chapter 17, a tree has only N-1 links, while a balanced network graph analyzed in the previous section has N links. Hence, a tree has the lowest total link cost, which may be significant for smaller values of N. As described in Chapter 16, an Ethernet 802.1d-bridged spanning tree algorithm directs all traffic up to the root before sending it back down the tree to the destination. Therefore, the average routing distance increases because traffic from leaf and internal nodes must flow up the tree toward the root before it can progress toward the destination.

Thus, an important performance measure for trees is the sum of the hop distances from every leaf and internal node back to the root node. The special case for complete trees reduces the general solution of the sum of hop distances S [11] to the following expression:

$$S(H,D) = \frac{D^{H+1}[H(D-1)-1]+D}{(D-1)^2}$$

Since in the worst case, a bridged subnetwork sends data from one node to any other via the root and there are N-1 possible destinations as defined in Equation (18-16), the average routing distance for a tree with degree D and height H is:

$$d(H,D) = \frac{2\,S(H,D)}{N-1} = \frac{2\left[D^{H+1}[H(D-1)\,-\,1]\,+\,D\right]}{\left(D^{H+1}-D\right)\,(D-1)}$$

Assuming the same definitions of uniform offered traffic ω between each node pair and total network traffic Ω used in the previous section, the total required capacity for tree network using bridging is:

$$\Psi(H,D) = \Omega\,d(H,D)$$

Thus, the capacity ratio of a complete tree network using root node bridging is:

$$\frac{\Omega}{\Psi} = \frac{1}{d(H,D)}$$

Note that this analysis did not consider the effect of the capacity function in the interest of simplicity. In a real bridged network, the links closer to the root must have higher capacity or higher utilization than the links nearest the leaf nodes.

Figure 18.12 plots the capacity utilization ratio Ω/Ψ versus the tree height H for degree D=2 and D=4 trees. Thus, as expected, a star network (i.e., H=1) is the most efficient. The nodal degree does make much difference in the capacity ratio, but, of course, results in much larger networks, as indicated in Equation (18-16). Observe how the utilization declines rapidly as tree height H increases. When link utilization is not a significant cost factor, as it is in Ethernet-based local area network design, this inefficiency does not greatly impact overall cost. However, in networks where link costs are greater, a designer should avoid bridged networks that have a tree topology.

Review

This chapter extended the results of networks of queues constructed to model the operation of switches and routers. An important simplification in analysis results if one considers Poisson traffic. The resulting Jackson network queuing model is the foundation of many real-world QoS impairment allocation and admission control algorithms.

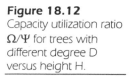

Figure 18.12
Capacity utilization ratio Ω/Ψ for trees with different degree D versus height H.

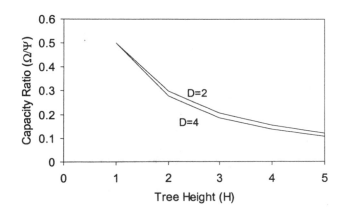

We then applied these theories to the calculation of QoS performance along a route of queuing nodes. The analysis compared the resulting delay variation performance of weighted queuing versus that of prioritized queuing, describing the relative advantages and disadvantages of each. Finally, the chapter concluded by analyzing a special class of networks that have symmetric topologies and uniform traffic as a prelude to the analysis of real-world networks addressed in the next part where asymmetries abound.

References

[1]   Gross, Harris, *Fundamentals of Queuing Theory — Third Edition*, Wiley, 1998.

[2]   M. Tanner, *Practical Queuing Analysis*, McGraw-Hill, 1995.

[3]   L. Kleinrock, *Queuing Systems Volume I: Theory*, Wiley, 1975.

[4]   W. Stallings, *High-Speed Networks — TCP/IP and ATM Design Principles*, Prentice-Hall, 1998.

[5]   E. Suhir, *Applied Probability for Engineers and Scientists*, McGraw-Hill, 1997.

[6]   A. Papoulis, *Probability, Random Variables and Stochastic Processes, Third Edition*, McGraw-Hill, 1991.

[7]   ATM Forum, *ATM Forum Traffic Management Specification, Version 4.0*, af-tm-0056.000, April 1996.

[8]   A. Parekh, R. Gallager, "A Generalized Processor Sharing Approach to Flow Control in Integrated Services Networks: The Multiple Node Case," *IEEE/ACM Transactions on Networking*, April 1994.

[9]   M. Schwartz, *Broadband Integrated Networks*, Prentice-Hall, 1996.

[10]   B. Devi, "Some Results on Estimation and Modeling of Switch Transit Traffic in a Backbone Network," IC^3N Conference, October 1998.

[11]   D. Knuth, *The Art of Computer Programming — Volume 1/Fundamental Algorithms, 3rd Edition*, Addison-Wesley, 1997.

7

Putting It All Together

"You can only find truth with logic if you have already found truth without it."

— G. K. Chesterton

This final part summarizes some important considerations involved in the design and traffic engineering of networks. Chapter 19 summarizes some important considerations in the design of scalable networks. It then provides an overview of the network design and planning process, summarizing the properties of network design tools. Chapter 20 then covers some additional network design topics. It summarizes some theoretical results in the area of hierarchical network design and dynamic routing. This chapter also discusses the important consideration of engineering economics in network design. Chapter 21 concludes the book by introducing the techniques of simulation and measurement. We summarize the application of event-based simulation tools to traffic engineering problems. The book concludes with a summary of areas of active research, along with some speculation about the application of QoS and traffic management in IP and ATM networks of the future.

CHAPTER **19**

Traffic Engineering Applied

"I waited for the idea to consolidate, for the grouping and composition of themes to settle themselves in my brain. When I felt I held enough cards I determined to pass to action, and did so."

— Claude Monet

The preceding chapters covered a number of theoretical results, applying them to various aspects of the overall communication network. This chapter pulls these topics together by describing approaches involved in the design of scalable IP and ATM networks. Specifically, we outline the historical design of IP networks over an ATM infrastructure and why the new MPLS label switching paradigm will likely replace it in large networks. The text also applies the notion of hierarchy and decomposition of a large network design problem into a set of smaller related problems. We also summarize two other design techniques for large networks, namely address summarization and flow aggregation. The chapter then summarizes the important steps involved in the network design and planning process. The discussion includes an overview of the principal functions implemented in modern network design tools.

Network Design for Scalability

This section surveys several techniques and issues involved in building large IP and ATM networks.

Hybrid IP/ATM Networks

Beginning in the middle 1990s, Internet service providers constructed IP backbones using high-end enterprise routers interconnected via a network of ATM switches that provided full-mesh connectivity. While this approach provided the initial infrastructure for the public Internet, there is always room for improvement. Indeed, in response to the tremendous growth of the Internet, MultiProtocol Label Switching (MPLS) targets this very issue [1]. As described in Chapter 2, MPLS is a particular type of label switching specifically designed for connectionless networks. Therefore, MPLS has all of the potential traffic engineering and routing control benefits that ATM does. Although one could construct a network from conventional routers interconnected by MPLS switches, a machine called a Label Switch Router (LSR) can do so more effectively [2].

The improvement in performance of LSRs over a hybrid IP/ATM architecture derives from several factors. First, frame-based MPLS achieves a 10 to 15 percent improvement in link-level utilization over ATM due to reduced overhead, as analyzed in Chapter 3. Second, an IP router network overlaid on an ATM network that provides a full mesh of N(N-1)/2 PVCs makes every router appear to be only one hop away from every other router, as illustrated in Figure 19.1. This in-

Figure 19.1
Hybrid network of IP routers connected via ATM switches.

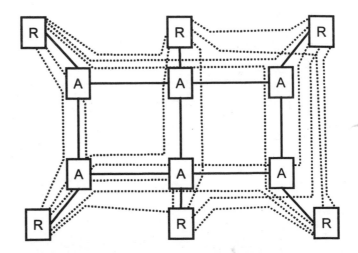

creases the load on routing processors due to the operation of the flooding algorithm, which inherently limits the scalability of an IP/ATM hybrid network [3]. Additionally, although ATM provides good traffic engineering support for the full mesh of virtual connections between the routers, the administration of this virtual mesh is done separately from the process of IP routing. The LSR allows the label switching and routing decisions to be made in a coordinated fashion, instead of the independent, "ships in the night" approach employed in an IP over ATM network.

MPLS Label Switch Router Networks

MPLS aims to improve the situation for IP routing by combining the traffic engineering function of ATM PVCs with the operation of topology flooding. Running IP over ATM has advantages related to traffic management, as cited in the IETF's draft MPLS requirements. In fact, the MPLS work draws directly on several important concepts from ATM. The MPLS label and the ATM cell header both have a similar semantic interpretation. Indeed, MPLS label switching replaces the function of ATM cell header-based forwarding. Since the semantics of layer 2 label switching are identical, ATM connection-oriented signaling and routing protocols can be applied to different hardware. There is no reason that ATM user and control plane protocols can't run over a frame-based protocol. As studied in the last chapter, at backbone speeds greater than DS3 rates, the benefits of the small cell size to preserving QoS diminish in inverse proportion to the trunk rate.

Figure 19.2 depicts the same example network as above with LSRs instead of a separate router and ATM switch at each site. Observe that the routing protocol has fewer adjacencies, and hence will have less processing to perform on flooded topology update messages. In fact, the routes are identical to the physical topology. A further advantage of this tighter integration is the potential to integrate the traffic engineering aspects more closely with that of network routing. As stud-

Figure 19.2
Network of MPLS Label
Switch Routers (LSRs).

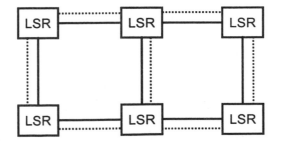

ied in the next chapter, this is not a trivial problem, since an ideal routing algorithm must simultaneously meet constraint-based routing, traffic engineering, and restoration requirements [4].

Hierarchical Access/Backbone Networks

Another commonly used technique for building very large networks involves partitioning the problem into several smaller, more readily solvable problems. Telephone networks have employed this technique for decades, resulting in the designation of central offices according to classes ranging from 5 at the lowest local level to a class 1 office at the largest tandem level [5]. A number of heuristic algorithms support the topological design of data networks with the aim of minimizing the overall economic cost using hierarchical design techniques [6, 7, 8].

The basic problem is to design a network of the least cost that connects a given set of traffic sources and sink locations, such as those depicted in Figure 19.3. These design techniques require definition of the community of interest between these sites by a traffic matrix. Furthermore, we must know the economic costs and capacity for interconnecting these sites with candidate transmission technologies or carrier services to design a least-cost network. When the number of nodes becomes large, the optimal design of such a network becomes quite complex. A traditional approach is to break the design problem into two hierarchical components, namely a set of access subnetworks that feed a set of interconnected backbone network nodes.

Figure 19.4 depicts a typical result generated by a hierarchical network design algorithm focused on achieving a minimized overall network cost. The figure indicates backbone nodes via solid-filled circles and backbone trunks via solid lines. The open circles represent access nodes and the dashed lines indicate feeder links that connect access nodes to backbone nodes or each other. Depending upon the reliability requirement of particular nodes, the access subnetwork

Figure 19.3
Set of traffic source and sink sites requiring an optimal economic design.

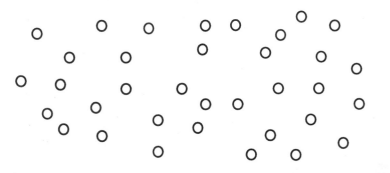

Figure 19.4
Hierarchical access and
backbone network
design.

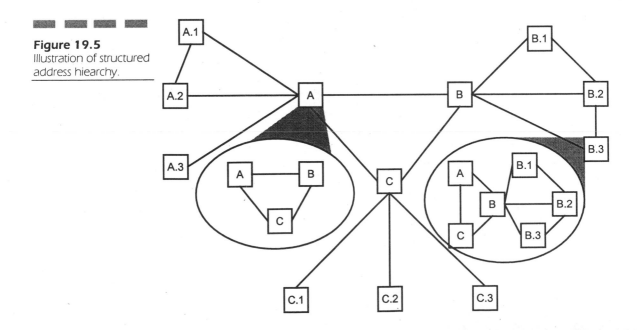

Figure 19.4
Hierarchical access and
backbone network
design.

may employ dual homing to backbone nodes or a ring topology as
indicated in the figure. These heuristic techniques employ principles
of optimal network design described in this part. The major simplification of this approach is that it decomposes the design of a complex
network into a set of simpler traffic engineering problems involving
the nodes and links indicated via the shaded regions in the figure.

Address and Topology Summarization

Routing protocols utilize the technique of structured address fields to
manage the routing table size component of scalability. Network operators must configure routing nodes to understand which high-order
bits correspond to a particular address prefix and associated grouping

Figure 19.5
Illustration of structured
address hiearchy.

of nodes. ATM's PNNI is the mother of all routing protocols, supporting up to 105 levels of hierarchy [9]. IP's OSPFv2 supports two levels of hierarchy [10]. Figure 19.5 illustrates the use of a structured address level hierarchy. The three nodes identified by the letters A, B, and C are top-level hierarchical nodes. The nodes labeled by a letter followed by a period and a number (e.g., A.1, B.3, C.2) are lower-level nodes. Note that node identifiers that begin with a letter are in the same higher-level peer group.

These concepts are readily extensible to multiple levels of hierarchy, limited only by the address field size. The notation of a series of identifiers separated by periods, for example, A.1.b, indicates three levels of addressing hierarchy.

Virtual Paths/Channels and Label Stacking

ATM and IP's MPLS both allow design of hierarchical traffic aggregation. ATM's fixed-format cell header allows only two levels of hierarchy: the Virtual Path (VP) and Virtual Channel (VC). MPLS, on the other hand, allows for an essentially unlimited level of hierarchy using label stacking. Nodes in MPLS and ATM networks employ label switching as defined in Chapter 3. This means that the packet header labels need only be unique on an individual link. Recall that label switching involves mapping an incoming label to an outgoing label on a per-connection basis. An end-to-end connection is then a con-

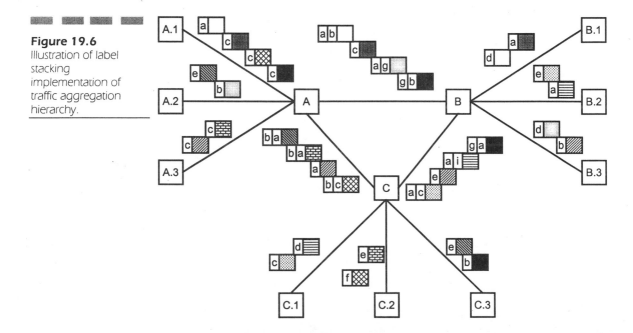

Figure 19.6
Illustration of label stacking implementation of traffic aggregation hierarchy.

catenation of such label-switching actions. Label stacking occurs when a switch maps a number of connections into another aggregate connection at a higher hierarchical level. Thus, the next higher-level flow contains the aggregate of many lower-level flows.

Figure 19.6 illustrates the operation of label stacking for a simple network. This example illustrates the operation of label stacking and the attendant flow aggregation. The shading and pattern of the packets illustrate the end-to-end connections between lowest-level nodes. Highest-level nodes can either encapsulate multiple lower-level flows within a common label, or else handle the flow without stacking any labels (see the flow from A.1 to B.1 via nodes A and B). Such flow aggregation eases the task of network routing and traffic engineering by reducing the number of required connections.

Overview of the Network Planning and Design Process

This section summarizes the network design and planning process. When done properly, this process is a closed recurring cycle of measurement, forecasting, design, analysis, implementation, and then beginning with measurement again, as depicted in Figure 19.7. These steps in the process feed each other, but also require external inputs, as shown in the figure. The following sections describe this process further and place these activities in the overall context of network planning and design.

Network Design Approaches and Modeling Philosophy

There are several approaches to network design. As always, one approach is to do nothing proactive at all. That is, simply wait and see what happens and react. While this may be acceptable for smaller networks without stringent quality requirements, it is not appropriate for QoS-aware applications or networks that provide service to multiple customers. Network designers need some way of predicting network performance; otherwise, users complain and productivity declines.

An essential aspect of traffic engineering philosophy relates to the required accuracy of the model. As expected, the more complicated

Figure 19.7
Flow diagram for the
network design and
planning process.

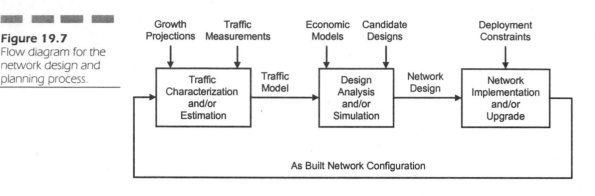

the model, the more difficult the results are to calculate. A good
guideline is to make the accuracy of the switch and network model
comparable to the accuracy of the traffic model.

If you only know approximate, high-level information about the
offered traffic, then an approximate, simple switch and network
model is appropriate. The old computer science adage — garbage in
garbage out — applies here. If you know a great deal of accurate information about the traffic, then investment in an accurate switch
and network model, such as a detailed simulation, is appropriate. Using a detailed traffic model in conjunction with an accurate switch
and network model yields the most realistic results. Beware that detailed models are quite complex and require simulation via a high-
performance computer system.

When neither traffic nor network details are available, approximations are the only avenue that remains. Approximate modeling is
usually simpler, and often requires only the analytical methods described in the body of this book. One advantage of the analytical
method is that insight into relative behavior and tradeoffs is much
clearer. One word of caution remains, however: these simplified
models may yield overly optimistic or pessimistic results, depending
upon the relationship of the simplifying assumptions to a particular
real-world network. Therefore, modeling should be an ongoing process. As you obtain more information about traffic characteristics,
switch/router performance, and quality expectations, feed this back
into the modeling effort. For this reason, modeling has a close relationship to the performance measurement aspects of network management.

Measuring Traffic and Performance Data

In order to apply the techniques described in this book, the designer
must select a traffic model. The best way to determine the appropriate

statistical model is via measurement. External measurement devices can collect detailed performance data [11, 12, 13]. These tools provide the most detailed information possible, since they examine the header of every packet or cell traversing an interface on a specific switch or router. Thus, we have the entire time series of the actual traffic and can estimate a number of statistical parameters like the mean, variance, and correlation. Chapter 21 describes some basic tests useful to determine whether your traffic data meets a particular statistical model. In particular, we summarize the popular procedures employed to determine the degree of self-similarity of specific traffic patterns. Unfortunately, these tools can result in reams of data that make determination of higher-level patterns quite difficult to discern.

Another technique involves collection of statistical data through standard Management Information Bases (MIBs), such as the IETF RMON MIB. This provides higher-level summary information about a number of switch or router interfaces. Unfortunately, collecting statistics like the number of packets or cells handled by an interface over a number of minutes reduces our knowledge to the average value of the offered traffic. Other parameters like the number of dropped packets or cells due to buffer overflow indirectly imply other parameters about the traffic if we know the buffer capacity and queue service policy of the switch or router.

Collecting information about the traffic matrix is a difficult problem. Traditionally, analysis of call records from telephone networks yielded one means of developing a traffic matrix. A similar method is applicable for ATM SVC networks. For connection-oriented ATM PVC networks, the MIB or external traffic monitoring device method performs best, since the source and destination endpoints are fixed. Similarly, statistics from MPLS Label Switched Paths (LSPs) provide a source of a traffic matrix data. For connectionless IP networks, an external traffic monitor is the best method, but may be impractical to deploy on a wide scale.

Candidate Network Design Development

Depending upon the nature of your application and the existing equipment in your enterprise, the first decision is selection of an IP- or ATM-based network. Frequently, the maturity of the technology or support for the specific application mix determines the network equipment requirements. At the time of this writing, experts generally acknowledged that ATM was a more mature technology than IP for implementing QoS and traffic management functions. However, as described throughout this book, IP-based techniques borrow heavily from the experience gained through ATM, extending and refining capabilities in certain areas. Since the principal user interface will likely be IP-based for many applications, most experts predict that market forces will drive toward mature IP-based QoS and traffic management solutions in the early part of the twenty-first century.

Analyzing and Simulating Candidate Networks and Technology

Typically, network designers base decisions upon long-term, historical trending and projections of traffic characteristics. This method applies to private as well as public networks. The types of decisions involved range from deciding on a replacement network technology to selecting sites that require upgraded switches or routers to changing the homing or installing additional transmission capacity.

A number of commercially available network analysis tools exist that implement many of the analytical models described in this book, as well as a number of heuristic design techniques. See Reference 14 for a survey of these tools. Typically, these tools require that the user enter some information about traffic patterns, volumes, and characteristics. Most of these tools also include the means to input economic data about the cost of switch/routers, transmission capacity and other charges. These network planning tools then provide answers to "what if" questions regarding candidate network designs, upgrades, or changes using analytical methods. In the end, the economic considerations involved in network design are a pivotal decision point for most enterprises.

Another class of tool is the event-based simulation model. This tool allows a network designer to model the operation of a network or even the discrete components of a switch or router at any level of detail desired. However, beware that modeling at low levels of detail re-

Figure 19.8
Network design
quadrants: intuitive
explanation, analysis,
simulation, and
measurement.

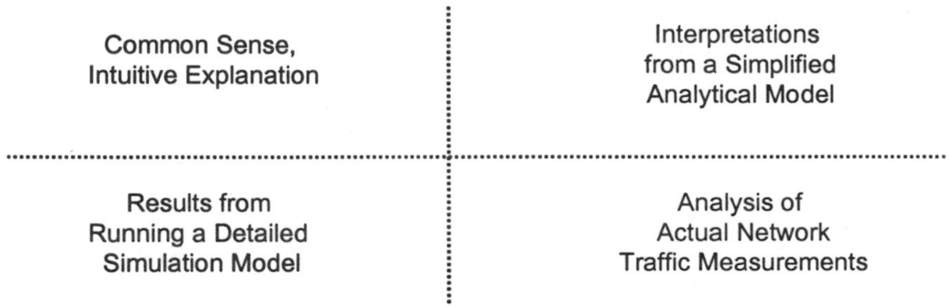

Common Sense, Intuitive Explanation	Interpretations from a Simplified Analytical Model
Results from Running a Detailed Simulation Model	Analysis of Actual Network Traffic Measurements

quires extensive computing resources to simulate even small periods of real time. Therefore, a practical compromise is to simulate components of a network element and then analyze networks of such elements using approximations that take less computer time to perform. A number of commercial tools exist that operate using the event-driven simulation paradigm.

Practice Makes Perfect

Frequently, the designer must make a tradeoff between cost and performance. For example, a more expensive network may accommodate all traffic during the busy period with high quality, even in case of failures. On the other hand, a less expensive network may deliver lower quality during busy periods and intervals when failures disrupt part of the network. However, the job doesn't end after the network design is done.

Developing a plan to continuously monitor network performance during the network design phase is not enough. You must collect the measurement data and analyze it to truly optimize a network. When acceptable QoS and capacity requirements are critical to your enterprise, proactively monitoring actual performance and comparing it against the design objectives is a critical step in completing the cycle. Careful analysis of actual performance helps immeasurably when tuning network parameters, planning for network upgrades, or identifying problem areas. Furthermore, keeping on top of your network's performance frequently means happier users and greater productivity for your enterprise. Keep in mind the concept of continuous improvement. As your experience grows, so will the effectiveness of your decision making. In a growing network, each incremental reduction in cost or improvement in productivity returns an increasingly larger return as traffic volume grows.

Ideally, you should strive to explain, justify, and validate your design decisions using the four quadrants of network design illustrated in Figure 19.8. If all of these views are consistent, then you should have high confidence that your plan will work. This book focused on the quadrants of intuitive explanation and analysis, which are typically the first steps in the design process. The next section provides an overview of analysis and simulation tools. Chapter 21 highlights some of the important attributes of simulation tools and the underlying principles that they employ. It also introduces some of the statistical techniques involved in the analysis of traffic measurements.

▬▬ ▬▬ Network Design Tools

Designing a network is a complex task. The spreadsheet tools used in the examples in this text are useful in analysis of individual nodes, sets of links, and simple network topologies. However, spreadsheets become cumbersome for networks comprising more than a dozen nodes or so. Furthermore, a real-world model must support economic analysis of various alternatives. The next step is either purchase an off-the-shelf tool [14], start with a public domain program and modify it [6], or write your own. Most of these tools have the following attributes:

- A Graphical User Interface (GUI) for managing the topology database of network topology and economic information and displaying results.
- A set of functions for manipulating and generating offered traffic scenarios.
- The capability to model a particular admission, policing, and routing algorithm for the network configured in the topology database.
- The means to compute and display the results predicted by the analytical and/or simulation model for a set of scenarios specified by the user.
- A set of utilities for managing database versions of topology, economic data, "what if" scenarios, and results.

The following sections summarize the important attributes for each of the above items. For an inexpensive introduction to network design tools, Reference 6 describes a number of examples using the downloadable "Delite" network design tool that illustrates many of these concepts. The author provides periodic updates and bug fixes to the program on the Web site identified in the book.

Design Tool Graphical User Interface (GUI)

The GUI provides for data entry and display of results. Figure 19.9 shows a representative view of such a tool. The format typically involves symbols that indicate nodes, with specific shapes and/or colors indicating the type of equipment at that location and its status. Frequently, the tool allows the user to move nodal symbols around to make the overall topology less cluttered than an accurate geographical map would depict. The other principal component of the GUI is

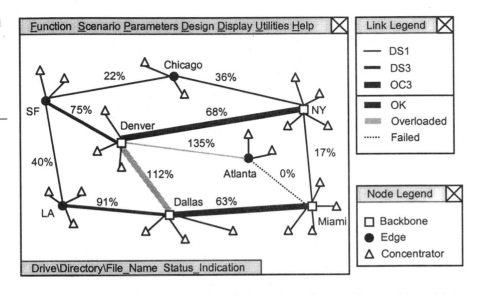

Figure 19.9
Illustration of a typical Graphical User Interface (GUI) provided by a typical network design tool.

links interconnecting the nodes. The color, line style, and/or thickness of the lines often have particular meaning. For example, green lines may indicate links with sufficient capacity, while red lines may indicate links with insufficient capacity. Most tools also display text or numbers next to nodes and links indicating parameters associated with these network elements. Additionally, most tools have a menu of some sort, for example, a bar at the top of the screen, as shown in the figure. Finally, the tools also must have some means for data entry, such as a separate screen, or a pop-up menu, as shown in the figure. Note that all of these tools assume that the user is familiar with the basic concepts of probability, queuing theory, and traffic engineering described in this book.

Specifying Design Scenarios

Models implement the capability for users to specify a number of generic classes of scenarios, including:

- Definition of traffic growth projections to determine scalability of an existing network design
- Specification of link and nodal failure scenarios for testing network reliability
- Alternative selections for nodal and link locations.

Usually, network design is not a static problem. Typically, traffic grows, or in some cases, declines. Traffic rarely stays at a constant level. Therefore, a conscientious network designer must diligently determine if performance will suffer due to growth and recommend incremental capacity at the most economical level. Increasingly, network availability in the event of failures is an important design criterion. Finally, selection of new or changed nodal sites and choice of links can have significant economic and performance impact.

Modeling Network-Specific Capabilities

An important aspect of a design tool is the accuracy that it models the specific functions and performance of the actual switch/routers, links, and any other functions in the network design. These include:

- Parameters that determine the operation of admission control algorithms implemented by the nodes
- Capacity, efficiency, availability, and error rate of links that connect nodes
- Information that controls the operation of the routing and signaling algorithms implemented by network nodes
- The maximum capacity and detailed configuration rules of vendor-specific switch/routers and other network elements

Some commercial network design tools often accurately model the admission control and routing algorithms in conjunction with configuration rules for popular vendor equipment. Therefore, be certain to investigate if a specific tool models the vendor(s) in your network. Some parameters like capacity, protocol efficiency, and error rate are generic, and hence vendor independent. In some cases, if vendors implement a standard algorithm like OSPF or PNNI, then a generic tool is sufficient. In some cases, vendors offer design tools or consulting services tailored to model their equipment.

Displaying and Comparing Results

There are three principal types of results that network design tools generate:

- The least-cost network topology that meets the constraints specified for a particular design scenario.
- The predicted performance and cost for the specified network topology subjected to the offered traffic load under the conditions of the user-specified scenario.

■ Cost and performance comparisons of a number of heuristically derived network topologies.

Unfortunately, algorithms exist that compute optimal topologies for only the simplest networks under very simple assumptions. Most real-world network design problems fall under the second or third categories. Many tools simply predict performance for an existing network or planned upgrades. Other tools allow the network designer to trade off cost versus performance. Typically, lower-cost networks have greater delays and lower availability than a well-designed higher-cost network. In general, achieving the lowest cost simultaneously with high performance is not possible. The approach that does work is to set realistic performance objectives and then design the network that just meets these requirements at the lowest-possible cost.

Review

This chapter began by summarizing considerations involved in building large networks. This included a comparison of IP/ATM and the MPLS approach for constructing Internet backbones. The text also summarized the hierarchical network design approach that breaks a large network into a set of access networks feeding a single backbone network. The text then covered some other topics relating to hierarchical network design. We summarized the concept of address summarization employed in IP and ATM networks. The treatment also described the technique of traffic aggregation used in MPLS and ATM networks to aid traffic management of large networks. Finally, the chapter introduced the overall network design and planning process. This description centered on how to use functions commonly found in network design tools over the life cycle of a network.

References

[1]   E. Rosen, A. Viswanathan, R. Callon, *Multiprotocol Label Switching Architecture*, IETF, draft-ietf-mpls-arch-04.txt, February 1999.

[2]   C. Semeria, *Multiprotocol Label Switching: Enhancing Routing in the New Public Network*, Juniper Networks, March 17, 1999, http://www.juniper.net/leadingedge/default.htm.

[3]   C. Semeria, *Traffic Engineering for the New Public Network*, Juniper Networks, Jan. 25, 1999, http://www.juniper.net/leadingedge/default.htm.

[4]   D. Awduche, J. Malcolm, J. Agogbua, M. O'Dell, J. McManus, *Requirements for Traffic Engineering Over MPLS*, IETF, draft-ietf-mpls-traffic-eng-00.txt, October 1998.

[5]   G. Ash, *Dynamic Routing in Telecommunication Networks*, McGraw-Hill, 1997.

[6]   R. Cahn, *Wide Area Network Design — Concepts and Tools for Optimzation*, Morgan-Kaufmann, 1998.

[7]   D. Bertsekas, R. Gallager, *Data Networks — Second Edition*, Prentice-Hall, 1992.

[8]   J. McCabe, *Practical Computer Network Analysis and Design*, Morgan-Kaufmann, 1998.

[9]   ATM Forum, *Private Network-Network Interface Specification Version 1.0*, af-pnni-0055.00, March 1996.

[10]   J. Moy, *OSPF Version 2*, RFC 1247, IETF, July 1991.

[11]   M. Petrovsky, *Optimizing Bandwidth*, McGraw-Hill, 1998.

[12]   J. Apisdorf, K. Claffy, K. Thompson, R. Wilder," OC3MON: Flexible, Affordable, High Performance Statistics Collection," INET'97 Conference, June 1997.

[13]   K. Claffy, G. Miller, K. Thompson, "The Nature of the Beast: Recent Traffic Measurements from an Internet Backbone" INET'98 Conference, April 1998.

[14]   D. Spohn, *Data Network Design*, McGraw-Hill, 1997.

CHAPTER

Designing Real World Networks

"Flaming enthusiasm, backed by horse sense and persistence, is the quality that most frequently makes for success."

— Dale Carnegie

This chapter covers some more-detailed aspects of network design, beginning with hierarchical network design. We first analyze the scaling properties inherent in a tiered, or hierarchical, network. These include the concepts of address and flow aggregation. Next, the text describes the bursty nature of overflow traffic in a connection-oriented hierarchical network. The text summarizes important results from classical hierarchical telephone network engineering generalized to ATM or label-switched networking. The chapter then moves on to review the subject of dynamic routing. Summarizing the relevant history from telephone networking again, we illustrate the benefits of dynamic routing over that of static routing through use of a simple example. The text outlines the method necessary to compute the benefits of dynamic routing for general configurations. Finally, we introduce the topic of economical network design through the simple example of designing a least-cost ring network.

Hierarchical Network Design

This section covers the mathematical background for aspects of network design related to hierarchical network design.

Scaling via Levels of Hierarchy

The maximum network routing protocol scaling achieved via levels of hierarchy is nearly identical to the number of nodes in a complete tree as studied in Chapter 18. Figure 20.1 depicts a simple network hierarchy with D=3 nodes per domain and H=3 levels of hierarchy. This network has 13 domains, each with 3 nodes, for a total of 39 nodes.

In general, for a network defined by a complete tree with H levels of hierarchy and D nodes per domain, the number of nodes in the network for a complete hierarchy is:

$$N \equiv \sum_{i=1}^{H} D^i = \frac{D^{H+1} - D}{D - 1} \tag{20-1}$$

When D>>1, then $N \cong D^H$. Note that this is a bound on the number of nodes in a real network, since not all domains may have D nodes. Therefore, observe that if the number of nodes possible per domain is large, then a large network requires relatively few levels of hierarchy. On the other hand, if D is small, then more levels of hierarchy are necessary to build a network of comparable size. Typically, network routing protocols can support between 100 and 1,000 nodes per domain.

Figure 20.2 plots the number of nodes N in a network with H levels of hierarchy for D=100 and D=1,000 nodes per domain. Global networks like the telephone network and the Internet have at least 4 levels of hierarchy: local, regional, national, and international. As seen from the figure, these networks must have at least 4 hierarchical levels in order to support subscriber populations on the order of a billion or more.

Figure 20.1
Illustration of a balanced hierarchical network.

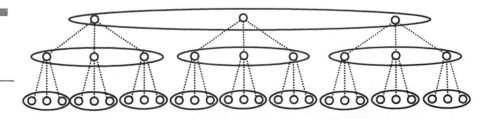

■ ■ ■ ■

Figure 20.2
Nodes in a network N
versus number of
hierarchical levels H for
D nodes in a domain.

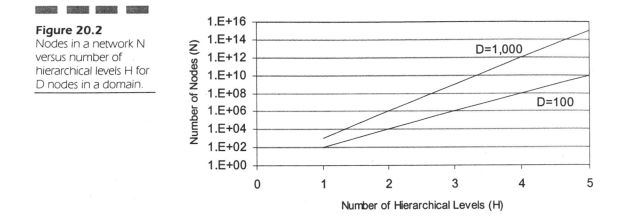

Figure 20.2
Nodes in a network N versus number of hierarchical levels H for D nodes in a domain.

Overflow Traffic and the Equivalent Random Method

Often a network has a combination of direct and indirect, or tandem, links between pairs of nodes. The long history involved in the design of telephone networks gives us a set of tools to optimize the number of direct and tandem links in hierarchical connection-oriented networks [1, 2, 3]. Although developed for telephone networks, the philosophy of these techniques applies to hierarchical ATM, RSVP, and MPLS networks as well. An example of such a capability would be an on-demand, switched video delivery service. The fact that all connections operate at the same rate considerably simplifies the analysis of telephone networks, as compared with ATM or MPLS networking, which may deal with connections operating across a wide range of rates and QoS categories.

A simple network involves three nodes as shown in Figure 20.3a, where D direct trunks connect nodes 1 and 2, and T tandem trunks connect nodes 1 and 2 to tandem switching node 3. Offered traffic load is symmetric between all nodes, with a units of traffic offered between nodes 1 and 2, and b units of traffic between node 3 and the other nodes. Any traffic arrivals between nodes 1 and 2 that find all D trunks occupied overflow to the tandem route via node 3 as shown by the dashed arrows in the figure. Figure 20.3b is a traffic flow diagram for this simple network. The tandem trunks with capacity T have two sources of offered load, one with b Erlangs and the other the overflow traffic from the direct trunk group with capacity D. Chapter 11 defined the units of Erlangs as the product of the arrival

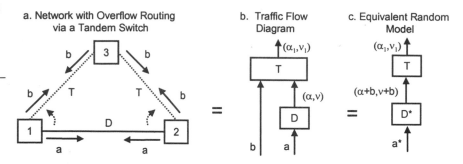

a. Network with Overflow Routing via a Tandem Switch
b. Traffic Flow Diagram
c. Equivalent Random Model

rate and the average connection duration, which by Little's theorem is the average number of users present in a queuing system with infinite capacity. Since the direct trunk has finite capacity D, the overflow traffic has average value equal to the offered load times the blocking probability defined in Chapter 11 for Poisson arrivals to a system with a finite number of servers, namely:

$$\alpha \;=\; aB(D,a) \tag{20-2}$$

where $B(D,a) = \dfrac{a^D / D!}{\displaystyle\sum_{k=0}^{D} a^k / k!}$ is the Erlang-B blocking probability.

As shown in Figure 20.3b, the overflow traffic from the direct trunk group of capacity D has a variance:

$$v \;=\; \alpha\left[1 \;-\; \alpha \;+\; \frac{a}{D+1+\alpha-a}\right] \tag{20-3}$$

Solving the above formula for the number of direct trunks D yields the following result:

$$D \;=\; \frac{a(\alpha + z)}{\alpha + z - 1} \;-\; \alpha \;-\; 1 \tag{20-4}$$

where $z = v/\alpha$ is the peakedness of the overflow traffic.

The peakedness of Poisson traffic is $z=1$, since the mean equals the variance. The peakedness of overflow traffic can be quite large, as illustrated in the numerical calculations shown in Figure 20.4 involving Equations (20-2) and (20-3). The plot shows how the peakedness z increases markedly when the normalized overload of the direct trunk becomes significant. The normalized overload is the average load in excess of the direct trunk capacity (a-D) divided by the average load a,

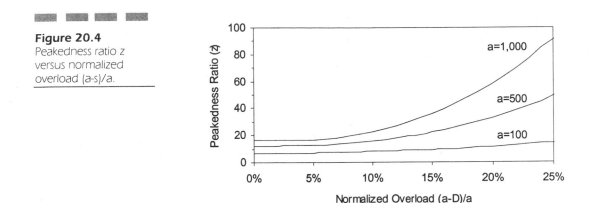

Figure 20.4
Peakedness ratio z
versus normalized
overload (a-s)/a.

namely (a-D)/a. When the normalized overload is near zero, the peakedness is still significant, taking on higher values for larger values of offered load a. As the normalized overload ratio increases, the peakedness ratio z grows nonlinearly. As seen from the figure, the peakedness ratio becomes quite large for higher values of offered load a under conditions of significant overflow. Thus, overflow traffic in a connection-oriented network shows the characteristic of a heavy-tailed distribution.

Given the value of the offered load a and the number of direct trunks D, computation of the variance v and hence peakedness z is straightforward, yet requires numerical evaluation as done in the plot above. Figure 20.3c illustrates the equivalent random method which has average overflow $\alpha_1 = a^* B(T+D^*, a^*)$, where a^* is the equivalent random offered load and D^* is the number of direct trunks that yields equivalent performance. The *Rapp approximation* [1] gives a simple expression for the equivalent random load in terms of the variance v and peakedness z as follows:

$$a^* \; = \; v \; + \; 3z(1-z) \tag{20-5}$$

The equivalent random approximation involves computing the average load as the sum of the averages and the variance as the sum of the variances, for example, as shown for the simple network example of Figure 20.3c. Typically, real networks have a number of direct routes that overflow to a tandem switch, as depicted in Figure 20.5. The figure considers the analysis from the perspective of node 1. The computation for the other nodes involves the same procedure. Equations (20-2) and (20-3) give the average offered load α_k and the variance v_k, and consequently the peakedness $z_k = v_k/\alpha_k$, of the load offered to the tandem trunk as overflow from direct route k with capacity D_k.

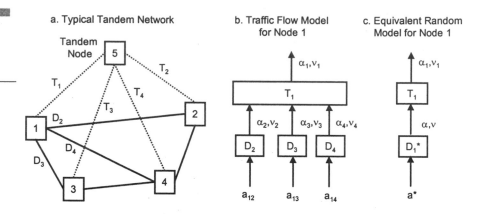

a. Typical Tandem Network

b. Traffic Flow Model for Node 1

c. Equivalent Random Model for Node 1

Summing the average load and variance yields the description of the offered load to the tandem trunk T_1 as follows for a network of N directly connected nodes:

$$\alpha \equiv \sum_{k=1}^{N} \alpha_k \quad , \quad \nu \equiv \sum_{k=1}^{N} \nu_k \qquad (20\text{-}6)$$

Equation (20-5) then gives the equivalent offered load a^* while Equation (20-4) gives the equivalent number of direct trunks D_1^* connected to node 1 for the equivalent random load a^*. The remaining unknown quantity is the required T_1 tandem trunks connecting node 1 to tandem switching node 5 that achieves a specific blocking probability. Note that the blocking probability is simply the ratio of the traffic overflowing the tandem trunk T_1 divided by the equivalent offered random load a^*, namely:

$$\Pr[\text{blocking on } T_1] \equiv \frac{\alpha_1}{a^*} = B(T + D_1^*, a^*) \qquad (20\text{-}7)$$

Now, we can use the above equation and the numerical techniques defined in Chapter 11 to solve for the value of s that yields the desired value of Erlang-B blocking probability $B(s,a)$. The required number of tandem trunks is then simply $T_1 = s - D_1^*$.

Economical Hierarchical Network Design

The analysis of the preceding section considered the design of the required tandem node trunks assuming a given number of direct trunks. However, the goal of a network designer is often to optimize the overall cost, which involves the optimal selection of both the direct and tandem trunk capacities, taking the cost of each into consideration. Historically, Truitt first analyzed this type of problem in the 1950s using a technique called Economic Call Century Seconds (ECCS) [1, 2, 3]. As described in Chapter 11, the term *call century second* referred to the means used to capture usage every 100 seconds via photographing peg counters in telephone switches of the pre-electronic era. Although this technique is quite old, the basic principles still apply today.

Figure 20.6a illustrates the basic economic model of a direct route between nodes 1 and 2 with offered load and capacity D. The overflow traffic flows through tandem node 3, which has trunks with capacity T that also serve other overflow traffic. The cost C_D applies to each additional trunk on the direct route while a cost of C_T accrues for each additional trunk on the tandem route. These costs include not only the transmission links but the switch ports as well.

Hence, the overall cost $C is the sum of the direct and tandem trunk costs as follows:

$$\$C = D \times \$C_D + T \times \$C_T \qquad (20\text{-}8)$$

The objective, of course, is to minimize the overall cost $C. First, however, we must investigate the cost of adding trunks to the tandem route in more detail to derive the model.

As studied in the previous section, the link to the tandem node carries traffic resulting from the overflow of traffic from several direct routes. Thus, the concept of the traffic carried by the last trunk in a group is a good approximation to the marginal traffic carried by adding a trunk to the tandem link. Thus, the additional traffic carried by the last trunk in a group designed to yield a specific blocking probability $\varepsilon = B(s,a)$ for an offered load a is:

$$\gamma = a\left[B(s-1,a) - B(s,a)\right] \qquad (20\text{-}9)$$

Figure 20.6
Economic model of direct and tandem network routing.

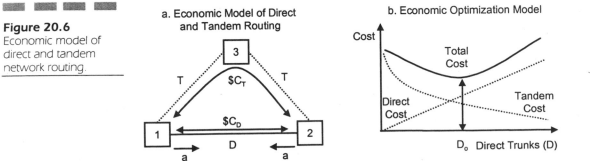

a. Economic Model of Direct and Tandem Routing

b. Economic Optimization Model

Figure 20.7 plots the load carried by the last trunk γ versus the equivalent offered random load a˙ with various values of blocking probability ε as the parameter. The plots are not smooth because the Erlang-B function is discrete valued. Note that the load carried by the last trunk approaches a constant value when the trunk has high values of offered load. This simplification is critical to the following analysis. Note also that this result illustrates the economy of scale achieved via larger trunk groups. Thus, although the cost of the tandem route typically exceeds that of the direct route, the traffic carried by a larger trunk group can be much greater than that of a smaller trunk group. Remember that the equivalent offered load to an overflow trunk group is proportional to the variance of the overflow traffic as defined by the Rapp approximation in Equation (20-5). As seen from Figure 20.4, the peakedness z indicates that the effective offered load could easily be an order of magnitude greater than the average overflow load.

Using the assumption that the traffic carried by each additional trunk in the tandem trunk group is a constant γ determined approximately by Equation (20-9), the total cost equation is approximately:

$$\$C(D) \;\approx\; D \times \$C_D \;+\; \frac{aB(D,a)}{\gamma} \times \$C_T \qquad (20\text{-}10)$$

The traffic carried by the last trunk and the nonlinear nature of the Erlang-B function determines the overall nature of the total cost equation, as shown in Figure 20.6b. Obviously, the direct cost in-

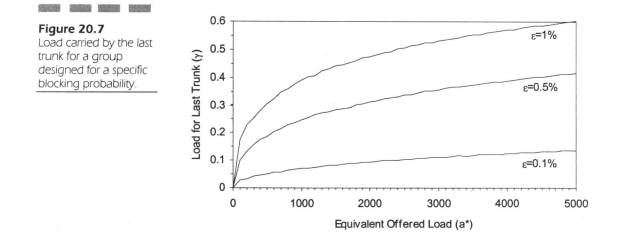

Figure 20.7
Load carried by the last trunk for a group designed for a specific blocking probability.

creases in a linear fashion with the direct trunk capacity D. However, the cost of tandem route capacity decreases markedly with increasing D, since the amount of overflow traffic declines rapidly, as determined by the Erlang-B B(D,a) blocking probability term in the above formula. See the plots in Chapter 11 for more insight into the non-linear nature of the Erlang-B function. The sum of the direct and tandem costs is the total cost, which has a minimum value at the optimum number of direct trunks D_o. This optimum occurs by setting the finite difference in the cost function to zero at the optimum value D_o, which implies that $\$C(D_o)=\$C(D_o-1)$. Using this result and the definition of the total cost from Equation (20-10) yields the following important relationship:

$$a\left[B(D_o-1,a) - B(D_o,a)\right] \geq \gamma\frac{\$C_D}{\$C_T} \tag{20-11}$$

Recalling the definition of the load carried by the last trunk from Equation (20-9), observe that the optimal operating point occurs when the load carried by the last trunk in the direct group equals the expression on the right-hand side. The expression on the right-hand side is simply the ratio of the costs of the direct to tandem routes $\$C_D/\$C_T$ times the load carried by an incremental trunk γ in the large tandem trunk group. Texts frequently call the optimum direct trunk value D_o determined by Equation (20-11) the *ECCS operating point*.

It is interesting to compare the cost savings of the tandem hierarchical approach with that of a direct-routing approach. The required number of trunks when using direct routing exclusively is the smallest value of D_{dir} such that $B(D_{dir},a)\leq\varepsilon$. We can then compare the fractional cost savings of the optimized combine direct-tandem design over that of a direct-only design using Equation (20-10) as follows:

$$\frac{\$C_DD_{dir} - \$C(D_o)}{\$C_DD_{dir}} = 1 - \frac{D_o}{D_{dir}} - \frac{aB(D_o,a)}{\gamma\,\$C_D\,/\,\$C_T} \tag{20-12}$$

In telephone networks, the cost ratio $\$C_D/\$C_T$ is on the order of 0.6. For the numerical example of the cost savings from the above equation shown in Figure 20.8, we also assume that the blocking probability ε is 1 percent. The traffic carried by the last overflow trunk γ is determined from Equation (20-9) using the equivalent random load, which we assume to be quite large for the tandem trunk because of the peakedness of overflow traffic. For a blocking probability of 1 percent, the load carried by additional overflow trunks is $\gamma\approx0.6$ for a large tandem trunk. In general, the percentage cost savings is greatest

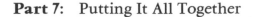

Figure 20.8
*Percentage cost savings
of a hierarchical design
over that of a direct-
only design.*

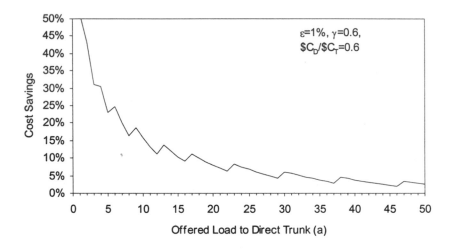

for smaller values of offered load. Note that if the load carried by the last trunk via the tandem network γ is not large enough, then cost savings may not exist at all.

Dynamic Routing

So far, the routing algorithms described in Parts 6 and 7 have been static. That is, the analyses assumed that the traffic patterns have been constant. This section summarizes some techniques that improve network utilization when traffic patterns vary with time and community of interest.

The Nature of Variable Traffic Loads

Fixed hierarchical routing does provide some savings over direct trunks when we know the offered traffic load precisely. When traffic levels are not well known, or are variable, then other routing techniques frequently perform better. One example involves time-of-day variation in traffic loads. In traditional telephone networks, traffic levels vary by time of day, generally in alignment with the local time zone. Figure 20.9 plots such an arrival pattern typical of telephone networks. Typically, telephone traffic peaks during busy hours of around 10 AM and 2 PM local time corresponding to the busiest portions of the business day. Increasingly, telephone networks

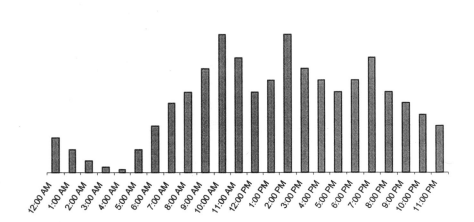

Figure 20.9
Illustration of a typical
telephony traffic Pattern
for a business day.

also see an evening busy hour corresponding to users dialing up their Internet service providers. Business and Internet traffic also follow similar patterns [4]. Although the ideal usage pattern is full utilization over all hours of the day, real networks tend to exhibit some type of daily usage patterns such as this.

Consider the data center that performs its backups during the wee hours of the early morning. These are the busiest times for these networks. Typically, the busy period traffic patterns drive the network design. The busy period may be a season, week, day, hour, minute, or even second. The network designer should collect historical data to ensure the best fit to the offered traffic load.

Non-Coincident Busy Hours and Cluster Busy Hour Design

The preceding section described how traffic levels vary over the hours in a typical day between two endpoints. Frequently, the traffic patterns also differ between endpoints. Often this occurs because the endpoints are in different time zones. Figure 20.10 illustrates a simple 3-node network that has varying traffic levels between each pair of nodes over each of five separate time intervals. The figure introduces notation utilized in subsequent analysis. There are 3 source-destination pairs, 1-2, 2-3, and 1-3, as well as three links identified as A, B, and C.

A static routing algorithm cannot readily take into account the fact that traffic loads may not have coincident busy hours. One such simplifying network design technique assumes that the point-to-point traffic occurs during the same hour. This design technique ensures

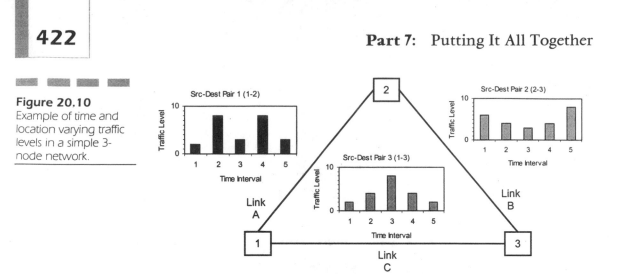

Figure 20.10
Example of time and
location varying traffic
levels in a simple 3-
node network.

that the network achieves the desired blocking probability, however, at the expense of additional capacity if the busy hours are non-coincident. For the simple three-node network example above, the busy hour design results by sizing each of the direct trunks appropriately (if the direct trunks are indeed the least expensive). This means that each link must be sized for a capacity of 8 units. The next section investigates the efficiency achievable if the routing differs during each of the time intervals.

Dynamically Controlled Routing

Telephone network designers have long realized that additional efficiency can result by designing more-complex routing that takes into account time-varying traffic patterns between different network nodes [1]. Specific implementations deployed in real networks include Dynamic Non-Hierarchical Routing (DNHR) and Dynamically Controlled Routing (DCR). These techniques work in connection-oriented networks when the holding time is short with respect to the time scale over which traffic load varies. Recent analyses of traffic on ISP backbones indicate that similar savings also apply to Internet traffic when using an MPLS Optimized Multipath (OMP) design technique [5]. This technique utilizes a randomized hashing technique to direct variable fractions of connectionless traffic along different routes. This will cause some performance impact due to rearrangement, as discussed in Chapter 17, but can significantly reduce capacity requirements. We illustrate the benefits of dynamic routing using the simple 3-node network topology and time-varying traffic profiles from the previous section with reference to the spreadsheet shown in Figure 20.11.

The example uses a technique similar to that described in Chapter 17 using the Microsoft Excel Solver tool. The spreadsheet includes a set of rows corresponding to each possible route for each possible source-destination pair for each time interval. Let $\rho(i,t)$ be the offered load for source-destination pair i during interval t on route r and $x(i,t,r)$ be the fraction of the traffic $\rho(i,t)$ directed along route r during

Figure 20.11

Example of optimal dynamic routing in a simple 3-node network.

	A	B	C	D	E	F	G	H	I
1	Optimal Multihour Dynamic Routing Design								
2			Offered	Routed					
3	Src-Dest		Load	Load		A	B	C	Link (L)
4	Pair (i)	Interval t	$\rho(i,t)$	$x(i,t,r)$	Constraint	1	1	1	Cost c(L)
5	1	1	2	62%	1	1			
6	1	1	2	38%	=SUM(D5:D6)		1	1	
7	2	1	6	35%	1		1		
8	2	1	6	65%		1		1	
9	3	1	2	85%	1			1	
10	3	1	2	15%		1	1		
11	1	2	8	19%	1	1			
12	1	2	8	81%			1	1	
13	2	2	4	0%	1		1		
14	2	2	4	100%		1		1	
15	3	2	4	100%	1			1	
16	3	2	4	0%		1	1		
17	1	3	3	0%	1	1			
18	1	3	3	100%			1	1	
19	2	3	3	17%	1		1		
20	2	3	3	83%		1		1	
21	3	3	8	63%	1			1	
22	3	3	8	37%		1	1		
23	1	4	8	19%	1	1			
24	1	4	8	81%			1	1	
25	2	4	4	0%	1		1		
26	2	4	4	100%		1		1	
27	3	4	4	100%	1			1	
28	3	4	4	0%		1	1		
29	1	5	3	8%	1	1			
30	1	5	3	92%			1	1	
31	2	5	8	39%	1		1		
32	2	5	8	61%		1		1	
33	3	5	2	97%	1			1	
34	3	5	2	3%		1	1		
35		Interval t			Cost C(L,t)	A	B	C	
36		1				5.02	5.48	3.13	
37	F$4*SUMPRODUCT($C5:$C10,$D5:$D10,E5:E10)					5.50	5.50	6.50	
38		3				5.50	5.50	6.50	
39		4				5.50	5.50	6.50	
40		5				5.28	5.19	5.93	Total
41					=MAX(F36:F40)/F$4	=SUM(F36:H40)			Cost C
42					Capacity R(L)	5.50	5.50	6.50	17.50

interval t for the source-destination pair i. The constraint that all traffic must be routed along some path during every interval is formulated in the column labeled "constraint" in the spreadsheet according to the following formula:

$$\sum_r x(i,t,r) \; = \; 1 \tag{20-13}$$

We denote the cost of link L as c(L). Furthermore, let P(i,r,L)=c(L) if link L is included in route r for source-destination pair i, and P(i,r,L)=0 otherwise. The cost of the load carried on link L during interval t, C(L,t), is then:

$$C(L,t) \; = \; \sum_i \sum_r x(i,t,r) \;\; \rho(i,t) \;\; P(i,r,L) \tag{20-14}$$

The optimal network design is the one that minimizes the cost C over all links over all time intervals. That is, the following equation defines the target cell I42 as the cost C used for minimization by the Solver tool:

$$C \; = \; \sum_L \underset{t}{\text{Max}} \;\; C(L,t) \tag{20-15}$$

After running Solver, note how the routed load fraction x(i,t,r) varies for the various time intervals for the same source-destination pairs. You may have to run the Solver tool several times in order to converge on the best solution. Also, note how the cost of the carried load C(L,t) on each of the links shown at the bottom of the spreadsheet is relatively flat. The last row in the spreadsheet reports the required capacity for link L, R(L), which has the following value:

$$R(L) \; = \; \underset{t}{\text{Max}} \;\; \left[C(L,t) / c(L) \right] \tag{20-16}$$

Since c(L)=1 in this simple example, the network capacity for the links equals the cost. Note that the dynamic network requires a total capacity of only 17.5 units, as compared with the worst-case busy hour design required capacity of 24 units, a savings of almost 30 percent! Savings on the order of 10 to 20 percent are typical when comparing dynamic routing with that of static worst-case routing in telephone networks [1].

Least-Cost Network Design

This section introduces the topic of economical design using a simple example. In Chapter 17, we studied the design of an economical design given a previously designed network topology. Another commonly encountered network design problem is selecting links to form an interconnection topology given a set of previously selected nodes that results in the least economic cost. Usually, minimum economic cost is an important criterion in most networks. In general, economical network design is an extremely complex problem except for the simplest of the networks — the tree network design problem studied in Chapter 17. To illustrate the complexity involved in only moderately complex networks, this section considers the design of one of the simplest networks — a ring network.

As studied in Chapter 17, a ring network has the fewest number of links that can restore traffic in case of any link failure. The problem statement is as follows, with reference to Figure 20.12. Given a set of N nodes and a set of economic costs for candidate links that could connect them, select a set of N disjoint links that result in a connected network that has the least-possible economic cost. Furthermore, we insist that our traveler can visit each node only once. In networking terms, this means that the design is resilient to any single link or node failure. The study of operations research has long studied this problem as the *traveling salesman problem* [6]. Graph theory denotes this same problem of visiting each node only once while traversing links with minimal cost as an optimal tour [6], or a Hamiltonian cycle [7].

Figure 20.12
Optimal ring design —
the traveling salesman
problem analog.

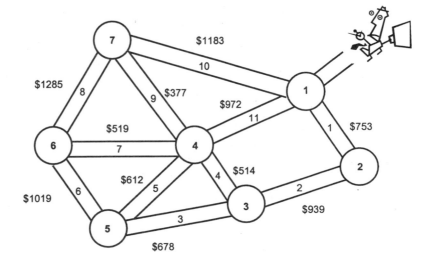

Figure 20.13
Optimal ring design —
the traveling salesman
problem analog.

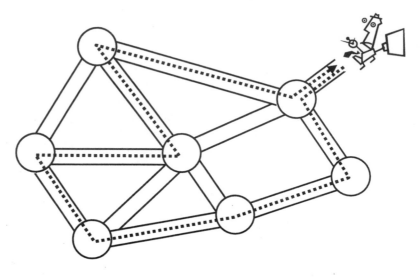

Interestingly, for some network graphs, a feasible solution does not exist. For example, Leonhard Euler first proved this fact in the eighteenth century by showing that the problem of crossing the seven bridges of Königsberg only once to return to the origin had no solution [7]. Some simple heuristic approaches that make sense on the surface can result in substantially suboptimal designs [6]. For example, one simple strategy would be to always take the least-cost next hop link. After all, this approach worked well for a tree network, as long as we could backtrack and pick the best route later.

Unfortunately, no known theoretically optimum solution exists for the traveling salesman problem. In fact, this problem has been shown to be NP-complete. Instead, the network designer must rely on heuristics [6, 8], or in the case of relatively small problems such as this, an exhaustive search. Figure 20.13 illustrates the optimal tour for our traveling salesman problem analog to ring design obtained by exhaustive search. Several facts from graph theory are useful in computing such a search. Specifically, the degree of every node is exactly 2, and the tour must have exactly N links.

As the reader might expect, the economical design of an even more complex network topology does not have a known optimal solution either. Indeed, this is the case, and hence has created a market and demand for heuristic network design tools to address this need, as summarized in Chapter 19.

▰▰ ▰▰ Review

This chapter began by showing how a hierarchical architecture enables the construction of extremely large networks. Indeed, part of the reason for the scalability of the Internet lies in these fundamental results. The text then summarized some important results for traditional telephone traffic engineering that used hierarchy to reduce overall costs. These concepts also apply to ATM and MPLS network design. Next, the chapter introduced the subject of dynamic routing. Typically, traffic patterns vary by time-of-day between various communities of interest. A routing design that exploits these patterns can significantly reduce the cost of a real network. Finally, we introduced the topic of economic network design by considering the simple example of constructing a least-cost ring network. The text showed how this problem is analogous to the traveling salesman problem in the operations research discipline and summarized some high-level heuristic solution approaches.

▰▰ ▰▰ References

[1]   G. Ash, *Dynamic Routing in Telecommunication Networks,* McGraw-Hill, 1997.

[2]   R. Mina, *Introduction to Teletraffic Engineering,* Telephony Publishing Corporation, 1974.

[3]   D. Bear, *Principles of Telecommunication Traffic Engineering,* Peregrinus, 1976.

[4]   A. Odlyzko, "Data Networks are Lightly Utilized, and Will Stay That Way," October 7, 1998, http://www.research.att.com/~amo/doc/networks.html.

[5]   C. Villamizer, "MPLS - OMP," First International Workshop on Multi-protocol Label Switching (IW-MPLS'98), November 13, 1998, http://engr.ans.net/omp/.

[6]   R. Cahn, *Wide Area Network Design — Concepts and Tools for Optimzation,* Morgan-Kaufmann, 1998.

[7]   G. Chartrand, *Introductory Graph Theory,* Dover, 1977.

[8]   T. Cormen, C. Leiserson, R. Rivest, *Introduction to Algorithms,* McGraw-Hill, 1990.

21

Where to Go from Here

"Errors using inadequate data are much less than those using no data at all."

— Charles Babbage

This chapter provides some pointers for the reader interested in continuing the study of traffic engineering in greater depth. It begins by describing the underlying principles of event-based simulation tools. The discussion includes enough information to develop simple simulations using a spreadsheet. The text also discusses some simple statistical methods involved in interpreting simulation results. We then introduce the important topic of traffic parameter estimation. Since the degree of self-similarity has a profound impact on system performance, the text summarizes some methods to analyze traffic measurements to detect signatures of self-similarity.

The chapter concludes by reviewing the state of our knowledge in performance analysis, congestion control, and network design. Although we understand much about optimizing traffic engineering of modern communication networks, some important questions remain unanswered. Finally, we conclude with some speculations about the possible future of QoS and traffic management in IP and ATM networks.

Principles of Event-Based Simulation Tools

This section summarizes some important concepts and techniques used by the computer programs in simulation tools.

Foundations of Event-Driven Simulation

Although analysis is the best approach if feasible, the complexity of real-world devices and networks often prohibits precise analytical solution. Therefore, a commonly employed technique is that of simulating a mathematical model of a switch or router, or a network of interconnected devices [2]. Most simulation models utilize a discrete event-based technique [2, 5]. The foundation of the method requires description of the system or network under study in terms of a state variable, which frequently can be an arbitrary database defining the state of each element in the simulated device or network.

We illustrate the event-based simulation approach with reference to the simple two-node window-based flow control protocol model shown in Figure 21.1. Packet arrivals occur to a queue in the source node according to a stochastic process defined by a set of parameters $\underline{a}$. One state of interest in the system is the number of packets currently waiting for, or receiving, service designated by the variable q. The network services packets in queue according to a service process defined by a set of parameters $\underline{s}$. At the destination node, the number of unacknowledged packets k is the state variable of interest. Acknowledgements occur according to a feedback process characterized by a set of parameters $\underline{f}$. Thus, we can characterize the entire system by the simple state vector $<q,k>$.

The memoryless property of Poisson traffic described in Chapter 8 fundamentally simplifies the operation of event-driven simulation

Figure 21.1
Event-based simulation model for a simple window-based flow control protocol.

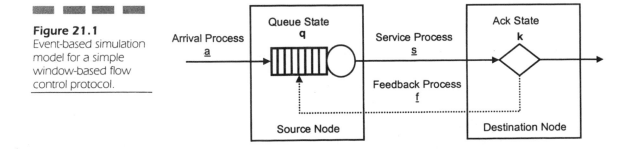

models. Indeed, this technique enables implementation of a relatively straightforward simulation of any system describable via an event graph [6]. When the transition processes are Markovian, an event graph is equivalent to the State transition rate diagram (STRD) studied in Chapter 11. Thus, simulation is quite useful if the subject STRD does not have a closed-form analytical solution. Recall that such a diagram has a set of states, with transitions occurring at a specific rate between states. The solution to the set of differential equations for an STRD involves negative exponentially distributed lifetimes in a particular state. The event-driven simulation implication of the memoryless property and negative exponentially distributed state lifetimes is as follows. Given a particular current state, the simulation need only generate a negative exponentially distributed random variable for each possible transition out of this state. Next, the simulation selects the random variable with the lowest value, since this corresponds to the transition event that occurs first. Finally, the simulation sets the current state to the target of this transition event and repeats the above process anew.

Figure 21.2 illustrates the use of this technique for the simple window flow control system when the arrival, service, and feedback processes are all Markovian. The arrival process occurs at a rate of λ packets per second (pps), the service process operates at a rate of μ pps, and the feedback process operates at a rate of ϕ pps. Arrivals increase the state variable q corresponding to the number of packets in queue, while feedback events decrease the unacknowledged window size state

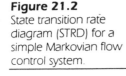

Figure 21.2
State transition rate diagram (STRD) for a simple Markovian flow control system.

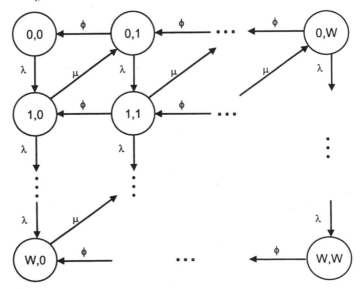

variable k, as shown in the figure. Service events simultaneously decrease the number in queue and increase the number of unacknowledged packets.

If the processes in the model are not all Markovian, then the simulation must keep an ordered list of when future events should occur. That is, the simulation must keep the memory of past event history, for example, events delayed by propagation delay, in order to determine the next event. The speed and efficiency with which the simulation tool manipulates this future events tree can have a significant impact on the amount of computer time required. Since general simulations require a much more sophisticated database than simple state variables, spreadsheets are a cumbersome tool. A number of off-the-shelf simulation tools implement the event-based paradigm [2]. Of course, you can write your own simulation using a high-level programming language.

Generating Random Variables

A closed-form analytical inversion from a uniform random variable u exists for some probability distributions [5, 7]. The general inversion procedure for a random variable $\mathbf{x}$ with cumulative distribution function $F_x(x) \equiv Pr[\mathbf{x} \leq x]$ involves solving the equation $F_x(x) = u$. For example, this technique determines that a negative exponential random variable $\mathbf{x}$ with mean α^{-1} has the following generator function based upon a random variable $\mathbf{u}$ uniformly distributed in the interval (0,1):

$$\mathbf{x} = \frac{-\ln(\mathbf{u})}{\alpha} \tag{21-1}$$

The Microsoft Excel RAND() function generates a pseudo-random number between 0 and 1. In the end, the accuracy of simulated results depends upon understanding that these numbers are not truly random [2, 3], but are instead just a series of numbers, which repeats after a point. As studied later in this chapter, statistical significance results from running many independent simulations with different "random" sequences of numbers.

In general, the above inversion procedure works for discrete-valued random variables as well. Unfortunately, many continuous distributions do not have a closed-form inversion solution, and hence we must turn to other means.

We now use the above function for a negative exponential random variable in a simple example. Figure 21.3 shows a few rows of a

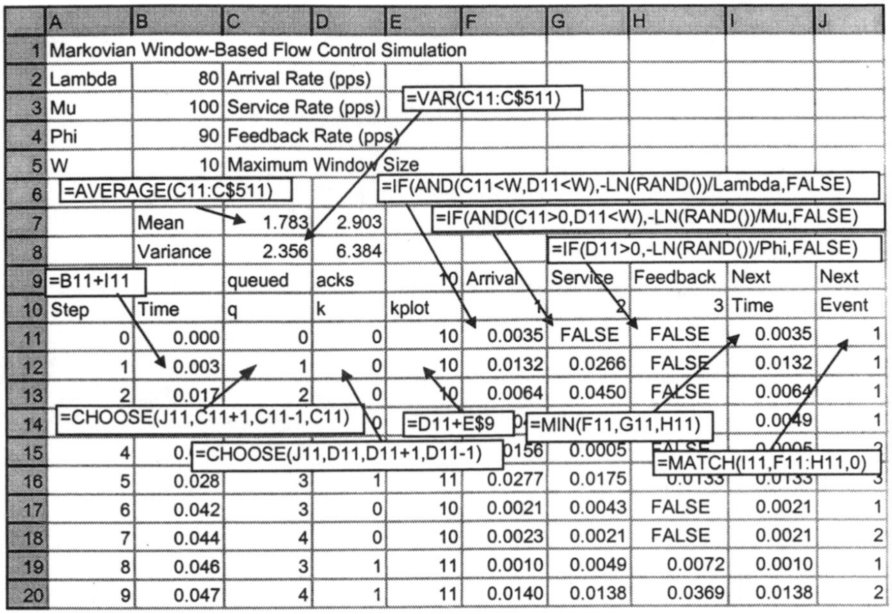

Figure 21.3
Spreadsheet for the
Markovian flow control
system of Figure 21.1.

	A	B	C	D	E	F	G	H	I	J
1	Markovian Window-Based Flow Control Simulation									
2	Lambda	80	Arrival Rate (pps)							
3	Mu	100	Service Rate (pps)	=VAR(C11:C$511)						
4	Phi	90	Feedback Rate (pps)							
5	W	10	Maximum Window Size							
6	=AVERAGE(C11:C$511)				=IF(AND(C11<W,D11<W),-LN(RAND())/Lambda,FALSE)					
7		Mean	1.783	2.903	=IF(AND(C11>0,D11<W),-LN(RAND())/Mu,FALSE)					
8		Variance	2.356	6.384	=IF(D11>0,-LN(RAND())/Phi,FALSE)					
9	=B11+I11		queued	acks	10	Arrival	Service	Feedback	Next	Next
10	Step	Time	q	k	kplot			3	Time	Event
11	0	0.000	0	0	10	0.0035	FALSE	FALSE	0.0035	1
12	1	0.003	1	0	10	0.0132	0.0266	FALSE	0.0132	1
13	2	0.017	2	0	10	0.0064	0.0450	FALSE	0.0064	1
14	=CHOOSE(J11,C11+1,C11-1,C11)			0	=D11+E$9	=MIN(F11,G11,H11)			0.0049	1
15	4	0.	=CHOOSE(J11,D11,D11+1,D11-1)		0156	0.0005	FALSE		0.0005	3
16	5	0.028	3	1	11	0.0277	0.0175	=MATCH(I11,F11:H11,0)	0.0133	3
17	6	0.042	3	0	10	0.0021	0.0043	FALSE	0.0021	1
18	7	0.044	4	0	10	0.0023	0.0021	FALSE	0.0021	2
19	8	0.046	3	1	11	0.0010	0.0049	0.0072	0.0010	1
20	9	0.047	4	1	11	0.0140	0.0138	0.0369	0.0138	2

spreadsheet that implements the simple Markovian window flow control system described in the previous section. The example shows the formulas for row 11. True to the Markovian nature of the simulation, every formula is a function of either the row above it (i.e., the previous state) or else items to the left of the current cell (i.e., the current state). Cells B11:D11 contain the initial conditions for the system, namely q=0 and k=0 at t=0. Columns F through H contain the negative exponential random variables corresponding to the arrival, service, or feedback events if valid for the current state. As described in the preceding section, cell I11 selects the next event time as the minimum value using the MIN function, which the cell in the next column uses to determine the next event type using the MATCH function. Now, the state evolution formulas in columns C and D in the next row use the next event from column J in the previous row to CHOOSE the manner in which the state variable changes, as defined in the state-transition-rate diagram of Figure 21.2.

One advantage of implementing simple simulations in a spreadsheet is that generating a sample trace of the state variables involved in the time history of the simulation is straightforward. Figure 21.4 illustrates such a plot of the state variable q for the queue depth and unacknowledged packets k. In order to plot the time traces of these two variables on the same plot, a useful trick is to add a constant greater than the maximum value to the plotted series as shown in column E of the above spreadsheet. All of the plots of simulated random

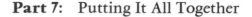

Figure 21.4
Example evolution of
system state for the
Markovian flow control
system of Figure 21.1.

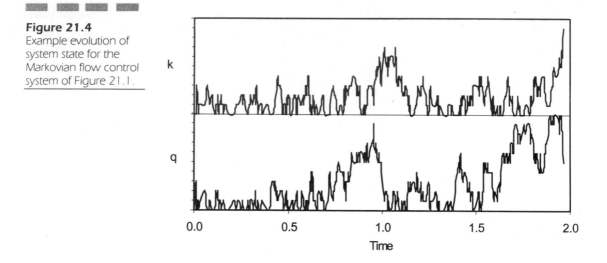

variables or traffic system performance throughout this book employed a technique similar to that described above.

Erlangian Method of Stages

Other techniques for generating random variables derive directly from basic tenets in probability theory. For example, the law of large numbers described in Chapter 8 states that the sum of a set of independent random variables tends toward a normal distribution. What is important here is to ensure that the sample mean and variance of this sum matches the desired mean and variance of the normal distribution. Indeed, as shown in Chapter 18, the sum of only a few random variables possessing a negative exponential density tends toward a normal distribution. The distribution of this sum is in fact the Erlang distribution, which we explore further in this section.

Erlang's method of stages demonstrates the concept of a miniature event-driven simulation using the state-rate transition diagram depicted in Figure 21.5.

The n-stage Erlang distribution normalized to have a constant mean

Figure 21.5
State-rate transition
diagram for n-stage
Erlang system.

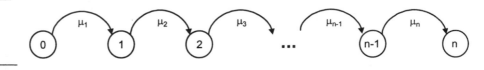

μ^{-1} independent of n is:

$$f_x(x) = \frac{n\mu(n\mu x)^{n-1}}{(n-1)!} e^{-n\mu x} \tag{21-2}$$

Figure 21.6 plots an n-stage Erlang density defined in the above formula for $\mu=1$ for various values of n. Notice how the density tends toward a bell shape as n increases above a value of 5. The variance of the above distribution is $Var[x]=(n\mu)^{-1}$. Thus, an n-stage Erlang distribution for relatively large n is an approximate generator of the normal distribution.

A generator for a random variable x with an n-stage Erlang distribution is determined from a set of independently generated uniform random variables u_k, $1 \leq k \leq n$, each with identical mean $\mu_k = \mu$ as follows [5]:

$$x = \sum_{k=1}^{n} \left(-\frac{\ln u_k}{n\mu} \right) = \frac{\ln \prod_{k=1}^{n} u_k}{n\mu} \tag{21-3}$$

Note that the coefficient of variation for an Erlangian distribution is always less than one. A number of other distributions are relatively easy to generate. See Reference 2 for a detailed treatment of this subject. Microsoft Excel's Analysis Tool Pack contains a utility that generates random variables for a number of different distributions.

Figure 21.6
An n-stage Erlang distribution with mean $\mu=1$ for various values of n.

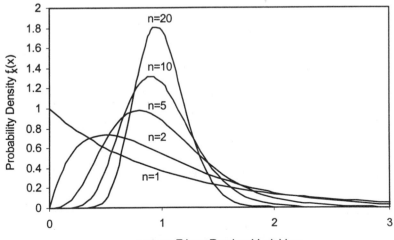

n-stage Erlang Random Variable x

Simulating Self-Similar Processes

The development of techniques to generate traffic patterns that exhibit self-similar properties is fairly recent. This section summarizes two techniques that appear promising [9, 1]. The first technique involves modeling a number of on-off sources to create a random variable corresponding to the number of active sources. The distribution of the times between on and off transitions use a heavy-tailed distribution, like the Pareto distribution studied in Chapter 9, instead of the negative exponential distribution. The second technique involves simulating an M/G/∞ queue. Here, the arrivals are Markovian, but the general service time distribution is not. The state variable in this case is the number of users in the M/G/∞ queue itself. The study of effective means to generate self-similar traffic is an active area of research. See Reference 11 for more information on leading-edge theoretical research on self-similar mathematical models.

Sample Mean and Confidence Intervals

A fundamental difference between an analytical method and a simulation is that we need only perform the computation for an analysis once, while we must perform a number of independent simulation runs to obtain a statistically significant result [2, 5]. Therefore, understanding statistical significance is of paramount importance to the traffic engineer who must employ simulation techniques. We model the result of simulation run i as a random variable x_i, which might represent a QoS measure like loss, delay variation, or availability. One important measure for N simulation runs is the sample mean X, defined as follows:

$$X \equiv \frac{1}{N} \sum_{i=1}^{N} x_i \qquad (21\text{-}4)$$

Note that the sample mean X is itself a random variable. If the x_i are independent random variables, and $\theta = E[x]$ is the true expected value of the underlying random process, then the expected value of the sample mean X is the parameter θ. In fact, the sample mean is the maximum likelihood estimator for the mean of a random process [5].

The variability of simulation results from the randomness of X. Hence, we are interested in understanding how accurate an estimate the sample mean X is of the true parameter θ. The discipline of statistics defines two related terms to measure the quality of the estimate:

the confidence interval and the confidence probability [7, 8]. The following equation relates the confidence interval $(\theta_{-1}, \theta_{+1})$ and the confidence probability Θ for the sample mean random variable X:

$$\Theta \equiv \Pr[\theta_{-1} < X < \theta_{+1}] \qquad (21\text{-}5)$$

As discussed above, the expected value of X is the parameter θ. If the x_i are normally distributed with mean θ and standard deviation σ, then the sample mean has a standard deviation of $\sigma/\sqrt{N}$. A particularly simple expression results for the case where the confidence interval is symmetric about the mean, that is, $|\theta_{-1}\text{-}\theta| = |\theta_{+1}\text{-}\theta|$. If the x_i are not normally distributed, then the following results are approximate for large values of N because of the Central Limit Theorem studied in Chapter 8. Since we know the properties of normal variables quite well, the confidence probability Θ has the following closed-form solution:

$$\begin{aligned}\Theta &= \Pr[X > \theta_{-1}] - \Pr[X > \theta_{+1}] \\ &= Q\left(\frac{\theta_{-1}-\theta}{\sigma/\sqrt{N}}\right) - Q\left(\frac{\theta_{+1}-\theta}{\sigma/\sqrt{N}}\right) \\ &= 1 - 2Q(\delta)\end{aligned} \qquad (21\text{-}6)$$

where $Q(\alpha) \equiv \dfrac{1}{\sqrt{2\pi}} \displaystyle\int_\alpha^\infty e^{-x^2/2}\ dx$ as defined in Chapter 8.

Hence, we can solve for the symmetric confidence interval terms $\theta_{\pm1}$ from the above equations by setting the variable δ equal to the value in the Q function with the following result:

$$\theta_{\pm1} = \theta \pm \delta\sigma/\sqrt{N} \qquad (21\text{-}7)$$

Figure 21.7 illustrates the distribution of the sample mean X, the confidence interval $(\theta_{-1}, \theta_{+1})$ and the confidence probability Θ.

If we don't know the variance of the samples, which is frequently the case, then the procedure becomes more complex [5, 7, 8]. First, we must form the sample variance s_X^2:

$$s_X^2 = \frac{1}{N-1} \sum_{i=1}^N (x_i - X)^2 \qquad (21\text{-}8)$$

This estimate tends toward the true variance σ^2 as $N\to\infty$. In a manner similar to the sample mean, an estimate of the confidence prob-

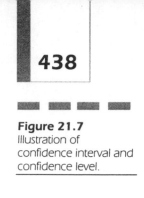

Figure 21.7
Illustration of
confidence interval and
confidence level.

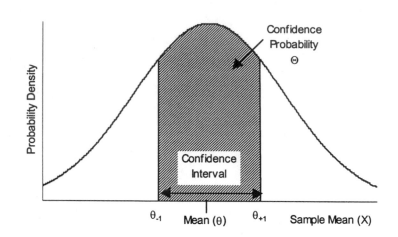

ability $\Theta \equiv \Pr[\phi_{-1} < X < \phi_{+1}]$ follows from the assumption that the x_i are normally distributed. The fundamental result is the confidence probability for a specific interval using the sample mean X and the sample standard deviation s_X:

$$\Theta = \Pr\left[-t\left(\frac{\Theta+1}{2}, N-1\right) < \frac{X-\theta}{s_X\sqrt{N}} < t\left(\frac{\Theta+1}{2}, N-1\right)\right] \qquad (21\text{-}9)$$

where $t(\alpha, n)$ is the Student-t distribution with n degrees of freedom for the probability α that the value is within a symmetric interval about the mean [7, 8]. A number of books tabulate the Student-t distribution; however, Microsoft Excel implements the function $t(\alpha, n)$ as

Figure 21.8
Values of the Student-t
distribution versus the
probability α.

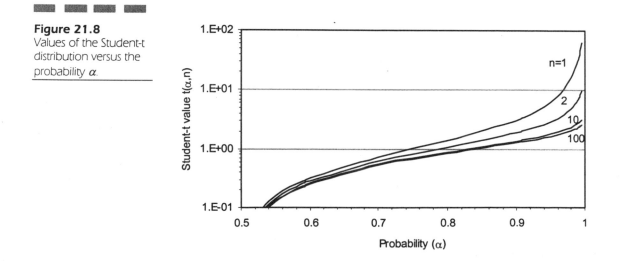

TINV(2(1-α),n). Figure 21.8 plots values of the Student-t distribution t(α,n) versus the probability α. For small values of n, the normalized confidence interval will be quite large, as defined in Equation (21-9). Since for n>30, the normal distribution is a good approximation to the Student-t distribution, the simpler expression for the confidence interval given in Equation (21-7) is a good practical substitute.

Required Number of Simulation Runs to Achieve a Specified Confidence

What does all this mean to analysis of simulation results? The confidence interval and probability determine the minimum number of independent simulation runs required. To better understand this relationship, this section considers a simple case for Poisson variables where $\theta=\sigma^2$ [7]. Therefore, from Equations (21-6) and (21-7), the confidence probability for Poisson random variables becomes:

$$\Theta = 1 - 2Q(\delta) = 1 - 2Q\left(\frac{|X - \theta|}{\sqrt{\theta/N}}\right) \qquad (21\text{-}10)$$

Thus, for a specified confidence probability Θ, we can solve for the number of independent simulation run observations N_{req} required to achieve a desired fractional confidence interval $\Delta \equiv |X-\theta|/\theta$ with the following result:

$$N_{req} \geq \left(\frac{\delta}{\Delta}\right)^2 \frac{1}{\theta} \qquad (21\text{-}11)$$

The above formula captures an important rule of thumb for analyzing simulation results. If your simulation attempts to model a system that has a mean value θ that is very small, then the required number of independent simulation results can be quite large. For example, simulations are not used to estimate QoS parameters like Cell Loss Ratio (CLR) for CBR services which have a mean value $\theta \approx 10^{-9}$, since hundreds of billions of independent observations would be required.

In fact, the required number is inversely proportional to the mean value times a constant, as shown by Equation (21-11). The constant $(\delta/\Delta)^2$ depends upon the confidence probability Θ and the fractional confidence interval Δ as defined above. As an example, for a confidence probability $\Theta=0.95$, $\delta \approx 2$, and a fractional confidence interval

$\Delta=0.05$, we have $(\delta/\Delta)^2=100$. In words, this means that a simulation with Poisson statistics must generate at least $N_{req}=100$ independent events to have a 95% confidence Θ that the measured average value X is within 5% of the true value θ. Equations (21-6) and (21-7) define the basic relationships necessary to determine the number of required independent simulation results for probability densities where the mean does not equal the variance.

Another practical matter involved in formulating simulation runs and analyzing the results is ensuring that the observations are indeed independent [5]. The basic approach involves running the simulation with different sequences of pseudo-random numbers to yield independent observations. Most simulation tools allow the user to specify a random-number generator seed for this purpose. Another consideration in collecting simulation results is allocating sufficient warm-up period to reach the steady-state condition. A related problem is determining when to stop the simulation after it has been in the steady state for a sufficiently long period to approximate an infinite time interval. Usually, some experimentation and iterations are necessary to determine the steady-state value, the warmup period, and the simulation duration. Since simulation runs can consume significant amounts of computer time, selecting the smallest warmup period and simulation duration that yield valid results is an important practical consideration.

Formulating Traffic Models

This section introduces some of the important methods involved in developing a traffic model for use in a simulation or analysis.

Determining Event Distributions

As studied in Parts 4 and 5, a fundamental part of a traffic model is the probability distribution for interarrival, service time, and other events. Although the Poisson model yields tractable analytical results and makes simulation easier, it is not a good model for many real-world traffic processes. Failure to select a good model for the distribution can lead to invalid conclusions. Indeed, the Poisson model typically is a good model only for human-initiated events like telephone calls or the aspects of computer communication sessions that involve human activity, like the initiation of a terminal or file transfer session [1]. The duration of Web or file transfer sessions and the amount of packets and data transferred are often not well modeled by Poisson processes at all.

One technique illustrated in this section to select an appropriate distribution is to collect a set of traffic measurements and visually compare the histogram of the distribution against several candidate theoretical distributions. The human brain has remarkably good pattern recognition capabilities. Other statistical techniques provide a goodness-of-fit test against a set of hypothesized candidate distributions [2, 7]. Another technique is to compute the sample mean and variance as described earlier and plug these into a distribution that is easy to simulate.

It is important to keep in mind the fact that we are dealing with random variables. Don't expect a perfect fit to the theoretical distribution, even if the underlying process truly matches the theoretical model. Figure 21.9 illustrates this point via showing a histogram of 1,000 random numbers generated according to Equation (21-1) versus the theoretical distribution. Note how the histogram for the generated random numbers matches the general shape of the theoretical distribution, but does exhibit deviations. The Microsoft Excel FREQUENCY function employed in this example is also a useful tool for generating histograms like this in the analysis of collections of traffic measurements.

Estimating Parameters

Of course, estimating the correct parameters for any distribution is of paramount importance to achieve relevant conclusions. Central to this is the notion of ergodicity and correlation. Let's consider a simple example. If we attempt to determine whether a type of die is fair, we

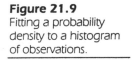

Figure 21.9
Fitting a probability
density to a histogram
of observations.

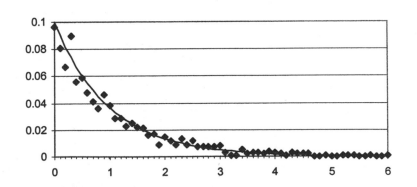

can perform two types of experiments. The first involves assembling a large number of people and have each person roll his or her die and record the results. This is the *ensemble average*. The second approach involves only a single die. However, we roll this single die a large number of times. This is therefore a *time average*. Formally, a random process is ergodic if the ensemble average equals the time average. That is, a random process $x(t)$ is ergodic for the kth order moment if the following equality is true:

$$\lim_{T \to \infty} \frac{1}{T} \int_0^T x^k(t)dt = E[x^k] \tag{21-12}$$

Frequently, the only traffic measurements available are a single time sequence $x(t)$. Hence, the assumption that the underlying process is ergodic is essential when applying analytical or simulation techniques. You might ask, why don't we just use an actual measurement of the process $x(t)$ in a simulation? If such a measurement is available, then this can be the most accurate approach. However, this approach is valid only if the measurement reflects source activity independent of any network congestion or flow control responses. For example, a measurement trace based simulation approach is not valid when simulating Internet traffic, which is largely composed of TCP sessions that employ the congestion control techniques described in Part 5 [4].

Detecting Self-Similarity and Estimating the Hurst Parameter

As studied in Part 4, the distribution and correlation properties of traffic arrivals have a significant impact on the likelihood of congestion occurring and the buffer size required to meet specific QoS objectives. After we know the mean and variance of the process, we must also determine its correlation properties. A technique commonly employed to determine the degree to which a traffic measurement exhibits self-similar characteristics is the variance-time plot [1, 9]. As described in Chapter 9, the normalized time series aggregated over m samples $x_k^{(m)}$ of the original measurements x_i is self-similar if the following tendency occurs:

$$Var[x^{(m)}] \approx \frac{Var[x]}{m^\beta} \tag{21-13}$$

where $\beta \equiv 2(1-H)$, with $0.5 \leq H < 1$ defined as the Hurst parameter.

Taking the logarithm of each side of the above equation yields the following result:

$$\log\left[\text{Var}\left[\mathbf{x}^{(m)}\right]\right] \approx \log[\text{Var}[\mathbf{x}]] - \beta \log[m] \qquad (21\text{-}14)$$

Recall that a Poisson process has H=0.5, or β=0, and therefore the variance of the time aggregated series is equal to that of the original series itself. When plotted on a graph of the variance versus the aggregation time m, a Poisson process has a straight line with slope equal to -1/m, as shown in Figure 21.10. The time averaging involved in constructing the process $\mathbf{x}_k^{(m)}$ from the original samples effectively determines the degree of smoothing achievable. The figure also plots the logarithm of Var[x^{(m)}] versus the logarithm of the aggregation interval m for the samples from the Poisson and self-similar traffic traces shown at the end of Chapter 7. As expected, the aggregated variance of the Poisson samples lines up nicely with the theoretical result. On the other hand, the self-similar traffic samples have a different slope that is approximately linear on the log-log scale of this plot. The shallower slope of the time aggregated variance Var[x^{(m)}] means that a self-similar process does indeed smooth out with averaging; it just does so more slowly than a Poisson process. Graphically estimating the slope for the self-similar samples from this plot yields β≈0.5, which implies that H≈0.75. As described in Chapter 9, the actual value of H used to generate these samples was H=0.8. More-accurate means exist to estimate the Hurst parameter. See References 9 and 10 for further details.

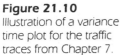

Figure 21.10
Illustration of a variance time plot for the traffic traces from Chapter 7.

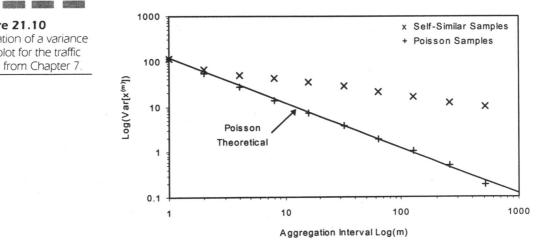

The Future of QoS and Traffic Management

This last section examines the prospects for QoS and traffic management in IP, ATM, and other networks in our rapidly evolving technological future.

Summary of Ongoing Research

As technically and mathematically intense as this book may seem, it is only an introduction to the depth and complexity of the techniques applied by experts. A number of fields relate to the study of QoS and traffic management. These include probability theory, queuing theory, control system theory, traffic engineering, hardware/software design, operations research, and distributed computing.

The subjects of QoS, traffic management, and constraint-based routing are all active areas of research. For a good survey see Reference 12. The reader interested in keeping track of developments, applications, and new approaches should consult the technical literature produced by the IEEE and various conferences dedicated to these subjects. Internet drafts are also a good source of references to theoretical works applied to real-world network problems. Experimental networks are also a good way to identify design alternatives for future networks.

What We Know— And What We Don't

Although this is a thick book, which references many other thick books and huge stacks of journal and conference articles, we know the answer to but a handful of questions with certainty. This section recaps the problems that have a known optimal solution and the range of networking problems that they address.

Part 3 showed how the Markov model for traffic-driven queuing systems is the simplest to analyze. However, it fails to model some important real-world traffic phenomena, for example, self-similar traffic. Parts 5 and 6 summarized how the Weighted Fair Queuing (WFQ) model yields the optimal tradeoff between QoS and capacity for a known traffic level. However, many applications don't know the required capacity precisely, which diminishes the utility of WFQ. Related results also determine bounds on router or switch buffer size to meet these bounds. Part 6 demonstrated how the Dijkstra algorithm yields optimal routing for a single metric. Unfortunately, this elegant, simple algorithm fails in the design of networks that must satisfy a traffic-constrained QoS metric.

Will We Really Need QoS in the Future?

A book on QoS would not be complete without representing the dissenting opinions that advances in technology and a different economic environment will obviate the need for QoS and traffic management in future networks. This section attempts to summarize the position of these arguments, referencing papers or publications that the reader can research and form his or her own opinion. The presentation then offers the author's counterpoint as to why these predictions may not come to pass, or identification of flaws that exist in the reasoning of the arguments against the need for QoS and traffic management.

One argument is that the cost of transmission capacity will become so low that there will be more than ample capacity for every application, and hence there will be no need to manage traffic in order to provide differentiated QoS [13]. While the argument that over provisioning of capacity may be valid in highly concentrated parts of access and backbone networks, there will always be the potential for bottlenecks. Repeatedly, history has shown that creative application developers invalidate claims of limitless bandwidth. Furthermore, even with ample capacity, there is always the potential for a bottleneck. Finally, the bursty and unpredictable nature of traffic can create congestion even in lightly loaded systems.

Another study presents the thesis that declining prices do not produce unlimited demand [13]. As an example, it cites the constant level of approximately 40 minutes usage of local telephone service on a daily basis as an example of how applications limit growth. Certain validity exists in this type of reasoning, since people can spend but only a certain amount of time on any activity and the number of people in the world grow at a limited rate. However, this type of reasoning also ignores the cross elasticity of demand. While it is true that usage of wired local telephone service may have stabilized, it is also true that the usage of wireless services for local calling also increased markedly. Another flaw in this reasoning is that not all communication will be person-to-person, or person-to-machine. The traffic growth of machine-to-machine communication may indeed be a tremendous factor in the future.

History has shown that new applications generate discontinuities in telecommunications growth trends. Therefore, using the past as a vehicle to predict the future is inherently flawed [4]. For example, the introduction of computers in the 1960s created an entirely new market for private lines that did not exist previously. The deployment of cable television offered a much greater variety of programming and the number of hours that people spent watching television grew commensurately. Similarly, the innovation of the Web browser made accessing remote databases and services via the Internet user-friendly, from which a great deal of the current growth rate derives.

Another line of thinking is that applications should all become resilient to variable capacity and quality delivered by the network in a manner similar to the way that TCP works today [14]. As discussed in Chapter 4, there is some support for such techniques for video signals. This approach holds some promise to make applications more resilient to varying quality and capacity delivered by the network. However, much of the utility of common applications declines rapidly once quality falls below a certain threshold. Hence, these adaptive schemes fail to provide a complete solution. Thus, the requirement for traffic engineering networks and preferentially service applications requiring minimum levels of capacity and quality will likely remain.

Trends for Traffic Patterns of the Future

High-speed networks enable fundamentally different service architectures. For example, a gigabit-per-second switch or router port is capable of serving tens of millions of voice connections. The service rate for large numbers of packet flows with rates so small compared with the link rate creates a huge statistically relevant population. Faced with the relatively small capacity requirements for such flows, high-speed networks introduce the additional capability to send tremendously complex messages in real-time. This distinction enables separation of control and signaling from the flow of information-bearing data. For example, a high-speed, high-capacity network enables transfer of an entire database to a user for high-speed local searching, versus the current paradigm of productivity robbing long-delay query-response applications like many Web pages do today. Applications that transfer large amounts of data to the user, or those that push information, will likely also increase overall traffic volumes.

Review

This chapter introduced the important tool of computer simulation and illustrated its use via a simple example. This included a description of statistical methods necessary to interpret simulation results. The text then summarized commonly employed means to identify distributions and estimate parameters from traffic measurements for use in analysis and simulation. The text then described some avenues that the interested reader can follow to perform further exploration in the area of traffic management. Finally, the chapter concluded by summarizing some possible future directions for QoS and traffic management in IP and ATM networks.

References

[1]   V. Paxson, S. Floyd, "Wide Area Traffic: The Failure of Poisson Modeling," IEEE/ACM Transactions on Networking, June 1995.

[2]   A. Law, W. Kelton, *Simulation Modeling & Analysis*, McGraw-Hill, 1991.

[3]   I. Ekeland, *The Broken Dice and Other Mathematical Tales of Chance*, The University of Chicago Press, 1993.

[4]   V. Paxson, S. Floyd, "Why We Don't Know How to Simulate the Internet," Proceedings of the 1997 Winter Simulation Conference, 1997.

[5]   D. Gross, C. Harris, *Fundamentals of Queuing Theory*, Wiley, 1998.

[6]   G. Higginbottom, *Performance Evaluation of Communication Networks*, Artech, 1998.

[7]   A. Papoulis, *Probability, Random Variables and Stochastic Processes, Third Edition*, McGraw-Hill, 1991.

[8]   E. Suhir, *Applied Probability for Engineers and Scientists*, McGraw-Hill, 1997.

[9]   W. Leland, M. Taqqu, W. Willinger, D. Wilson, "On the Self-Similar Nature of Ethernet Traffic (extended version)," IEEE/ACM Transactions on Networking, February 1994.

[10]   W. Stallings, *High-Speed Networks — TCP/IP and ATM Design Principles*, Prentice-Hall, 1998.

[11]   B. Mandelbrot, *Multifractals and 1/f Noise*, Springer, 1998.

[12]   H. Michiel, K. Laevens, "Teletraffic Engineering in a Broad-Band Era," Proceedings of the IEEE, December 1997.

[13]   A. Odlyzko, "The Economics of the Internet: Utility, Utilization, Pricing, and Quality of Service," July 7, 1998, http://www.research.att.com/~amo/doc/networks.html.

[14]   V. Antonov, "ATM: Another Technological Mirage," Pluris Inc., http://www.pluris.com/ip_vs_atm/, 1996.

About the Author

Dr. David Edward McDysan is a Fellow at MCI WorldCom and has been working in the data communications industry since 1976. He has held a number of architectural, design, development, testing, and operational positions in support of private and service provider networks. He was a board member and traffic management committee chairman of the ATM Forum. He is currently technical committee chairman of the Multiservice Switching Forum.